TURTLE CONSERVATION

Turtle Conservation

Edited by Michael W. Klemens

SMITHSONIAN INSTITUTION PRESS
Washington and London

Copy editor: Eva M. Silverfine
Production editor: Deborah L. Sanders
Designer: Janice Wheeler

Library of Congress Cataloging-in-Publication Data

Turtle conservation / edited by Michael W. Klemens.
    p.   cm.
   Includes bibliographical references (p.   ).
   ISBN 1-56098-372-8 (alk. paper)
   1. Turtles.   2. Wildlife conservation.   I. Klemens, Michael W.
  QL666.C5 T82 2000
  333.95′79216—dc21   00-030115

British Library Cataloguing-in-Publication Data available

Manufactured in the United States of America
07 06 05 04 03 02 01 00   5 4 3 2 1

♾ The paper used in this publication meets the minimum requirements of the American National Standard for Information Sciences—Permanence of Paper for Printed Library Materials ANSI Z39.48-1984.

For Nicole, Daniel, and Robert

CONTENTS

CONTRIBUTORS

GEORGE D. AMATO
Wildlife Conservation Society
Science Resource Center
2300 Southern Boulevard
Bronx, New York 10460

DORENE BOLZE
Wildlife Conservation Society
International Programs
2300 Southern Boulevard
Bronx, New York 10460

VINCENT J. BURKE
Smithsonian Institution Press
470 L'Enfant Plaza, Suite 7100
Washington, D.C. 20560-0950

C. KENNETH DODD, JR.
U.S. Geological Survey
Biological Resources Division
7920 NW 71st Street
Gainesville, Florida 32653

DAVID EHRENFELD
Department of Ecology, Evolution, and
    Natural Resources
Cook College, Rutgers University
P.O. Box 231
New Brunswick, New Jersey 08903

JOSEPH FLANAGAN
Houston Zoo
1513 North MacGregor
Houston, Texas 77030

NAT B. FRAZER
Department of Wildlife Ecology and
    Conservation
University of Florida
303 Newins-Ziegler Hall
P.O. Box 110430
Gainesville, Florida 32611-0430

J. WHITFIELD GIBBONS
Savannah River Ecology Laboratory
University of Georgia
Drawer E
Aiken, South Carolina 29802

JAMES P. GIBBS
State University of New York
College of Environmental Science and
    Forestry
1 Forestry Drive
Syracuse, New York 13210

MICHAEL W. KLEMENS
Wildlife Conservation Society
International Programs
2300 Southern Boulevard
Bronx, New York 10460

CYNTHIA J. LAGUEUX
Wildlife Conservation Society
International Programs
2300 Southern Boulevard
Bronx, New York 10460

JEFFREY E. LOVICH
U.S. Geological Survey
Canyon Crest Field Station
c/o Department of Biology
University of California at Riverside
Riverside, California 95251-0427

JAMES McDOUGAL
Wildlife Conservation Society
International Programs
2300 Southern Boulevard
Bronx, New York 10460

ANNE B. MEYLAN
Department of Environmental Protection
Florida Marine Research Institute
100 Eighth Avenue SE
St. Petersburg, Florida 33701

JOSEPH C. MITCHELL
Department of Biology
University of Richmond
Richmond, Virginia 23173

DON MOLL
Department of Biology
Southwest Missouri State University
Springfield, Missouri 65804

EDWARD O. MOLL
Department of Zoology
Eastern Illinois University
Charleston, Illinois 61920

RICHARD A. SEIGEL
Department of Biological Sciences
Southeastern Louisiana University
Hammond, Louisiana 70402-0736

JOHN THORBJARNARSON
Wildlife Conservation Society
International Programs
2300 Southern Boulevard
Bronx, New York 10460

FOREWORD

Because they are still living, turtles are commonplace objects to us; were they entirely extinct, their shells—the most remarkable defensive armor ever assumed by a tetrapod—would be a cause for wonder.
Alfred Sherwood Romer

Since they first arose in Permian wetlands some 200 million years ago, turtles have been extremely successful—not only expanding their domain to include standing and flowing freshwater habitats but also colonizing both the marine and terrestrial environments. As Romer (1966) pointed out to us early in the twentieth century, their "remarkable defensive armor" no doubt played a large part in their effectively surviving "all the vicissitudes which have swamped most of the reptilian groups"—including, we now believe, the giant asteroid that wiped out the great dinosaurs.

But now, after a rich heritage extending far longer than almost any other vertebrate group, turtles are in trouble. The combination of habitat destruction or severe deterioration, due to the expansion of human activities, and heavy exploitation, either intentionally or incidental to the harvest of other species in the same habitat, has adversely affected at least two-thirds of the turtle species. Although still common in many places, as a group turtles are no longer safe, whether they inhabit terrestrial, freshwater, or marine ecosystems.

Most people seem to like turtles. Given that many of us, as children, became fascinated by these "commonplace objects" because of the very same "remarkable defensive armor" that fascinated Romer, how is it that we have allowed turtles to come to such a precarious existence at our own hands? I think it is due to three things.

First, there is a deep ignorance on the part of the general public. Think back to the very first thing you probably learned about turtles: "The turtle carries his house on his back wherever he goes." The image of a nomadic being who is safe in his fascinating armored house wherever he goes is reinforced in the public's mind by images from cartoons to insurance company advertisements. The depth of ignorance regarding turtles is revealed by questions I have been asked by upper-level college biology students who were surprised to learn that turtles could not leave their shells at will to roam around at faster speeds "like they do in some cartoons." Surely, a public that thinks turtles are carrying their comfortable homes around with them wherever they may go (if and when turtles are ever thought of at all) will not be concerned that we could possibly deprive turtles of suitable habitats in which to live. It's difficult to imagine how any animal that carries its home with it should have specific habitat requirements when seeking a new place to settle down.

Second, there is a lack of understanding as to the consequences of the life histories of turtles. Over the past 200 million years, most turtles have evolved a suite of life history traits that includes high but fluctuating rates of egg and young juvenile mortality balanced by low rates of adult mortality and iteroparity (repeated reproductive episodes). The highly evolved state of turtles anticipates highly challenging, though fluctuating, environmental selective pressures on their young. For the most part, however, their life history also anticipates a low level of fairly stable or predictable threats to adult survival. Unfortunately for turtles, we have reversed this selective regime in many places, continuously depleting the eggs and young while increasing the mortality rates of adult turtles through habitat destruction and exploitation.

For example, because we see marine turtles producing hundreds of eggs again and again, we are lulled into thinking that we can constantly and continuously exploit their eggs. But the turtles' strategy banks on the now-no-longer-true situation that once in a while exploitation will ease off or that they will be able to swamp their egg predators, at least in some years. Also, because we see the prolific production of eggs and young turtles each year, we may assume that we can take adults, whether in directed fisheries or incidental to the take of other species, and these adults will easily be replaced by their high fecundity. It seems obvious now that if we take both adults and eggs, the turtles will eventually disappear.

What is not so obvious, even to many turtle scientists, is that life history patterns are just as much a part of what an organism is as are its anatomy, physiology, and morphology. The fundamental lack of understanding of life history patterns may lead even some of us scientists to make unwise decisions when attempting to "save" turtle species. We may rely on conservation programs that protect eggs and young while continuing to allow the take (intentional or incidental) of adults.

Third, there is a lack of awareness as to the consequences of our actions. As management guru Stephen Covey (1989) has pointed out, "The way we *see* the problem *is* the problem." Too often, we see the problem simply in terms of the number of turtles. Charles Darwin reminded us that "rarity is the precursor to extinction." When we see turtle populations dwindling, we are tempted to do anything we can to provide more turtles. On the one hand, this does nothing to fix the problem of why the numbers of turtles are decreasing in the first place. On the other hand, how we go about increasing the number of turtles is vitally important. If we provide more turtles by lowering mortality on the young while allowing continued high rates of death among the adults, we will have exactly reversed 200 million years of evolutionary forces that produced the turtle species we know today. How long can we continue to do this before we will have drastically changed the basic life history pattern of the very organisms we set out to conserve? At what point will turtles no longer be turtles?

There are many practical and philosophical issues related to turtle conservation. If we are to have a world that is habitable by both humans and turtles, we need a much better understanding of the threats to turtles as well as a deeper understanding of turtle biology. Given the nature of turtle life histories, advances in both of these areas will depend on the continuation of long-term studies and the dedication of scientists who are willing to devote their entire professional careers to advancing this understanding.

For this important book, Michael Klemens has assembled a formidable array of the world's foremost turtle scientists and conservationists. Each of them has devoted decades of his or her life to the study of turtles. In this volume, they provide the fruits of their understanding to give you the current state of our knowledge as to why turtles are threatened and what we can and should do about it. After an introductory chapter, in which Klemens sets the stage and outlines the overall problem in general, the first few chapters provide a deeper look into the problems and threats faced by turtles due to human activities. These chapters review the two major threats faced by any modern species—habitat destruction (Mitchell and Klemens, Chapter 1) and exploitation (Thorbjarnarson et al., Chapter 2)—and how humans have exacerbated the challenges turtles face due to disease (Flanagan, Chapter 3). The chapters that follow will introduce you to the peculiarities of the many types of turtles based on the habitats in which they live—the sea (Meylan and Ehrenfeld, Chapter 4), rivers (E. O. Moll and Moll, Chapter 5), semiaquatic and nonriverine freshwater environments (V. J. Burke et al., Chapter 6), and deserts and other terrestrial environments (McDougal, Chapter 7). Each of these habitat-specific chapters includes a discussion of the unique problems that turtles face in that habitat. In Chapter 8, Gibbs and Amato explore how our recent understanding of genetics and demography provides insights into both the problems turtles face and how we might attempt to help them. A critical assessment of some of the past and present efforts to protect turtles through manipulating their populations is then provided (Seigel and Dodd, Chapter 9). Klemens (Chapter 10) closes the book by addressing our prospects—what needs to be done in order to ensure that the planet remains habitable by both turtles and humans and the likelihood that we will succeed.

At the close of the twentieth century, turtles are still a common sight in many places. During a 100-km road trip one rainy Saturday morning in South Carolina, my wife and I stopped three times to rescue turtles crossing the highway. These three fascinating individuals represented three different species in two different families of hard-shelled freshwater turtles. But for none of them would their "remarkable defensive armor" have been any match for the tires of a speeding automobile. I sincerely hope that turtles remain "commonplace objects" for those of you who might read these words in the late twenty-first century. For those of you who read the book sooner, I'm sure you will be convinced that turtles certainly need not become extinct in order to "be a cause for wonder."

NAT B. FRAZER

REFERENCES

Covey, S. R. 1989. The Seven Habits of Highly Effective People. Simon and Schuster, New York.

Romer, A. S. 1966. Vertebrate Paleontology. 3rd edn. University of Chicago Press, Chicago.

ACKNOWLEDGMENTS

This book has benefited greatly from the input of many people. Jim McDougal played a major role by helping me to organize the book and attend to the myriad of details required to move it from concept to reality. I would especially like to recognize the contributing authors: their collective efforts have resulted in a book that should have a major impact on the practice of turtle conservation. The downside of a team effort tends to be that there are a few participants who do not meet the deadlines. For those who kept to the writing and production timetables and then patiently waited for the others to catch up, I am especially grateful.

All the contributions to this book were peer reviewed. Many contributors arranged for independent reviews before submitting their manuscripts. They have acknowledged such reviewers in their respective chapters. Once contributions were received, they were sent to one or more of the following people for additional review: Ernst Baard, Vincent J. Burke, R. Bruce Bury, Marydele Donnelly, Nat Frazer, John Iverson, Dale Jackson, Jeffrey E. Lovich, James McDougal, Anne Meylan, Joseph C. Mitchell, Don Moll, Christopher J. Raithel, Basil Tangredi, John B. Thorbjarnarson, and Joseph Ventura. Erik Kiviat and Thomas Rohan supplied photographs. The Wildlife Conservation Society provided both financial and technical support, and I appreciate the efforts of John Robinson, Nancy Granchelli, Susan Stenquist, Kristi MacDonald, Diane Murphy, and Gail Tarkan. The skillful editing of Eva Silverfine is also greatly appreciated. Last but by no means least, I am grateful to my wife, Nicole, and my two sons, Daniel and Robert, who support my endeavors on behalf of turtles and other creatures in so many ways.

TURTLE CONSERVATION

MICHAEL W. KLEMENS

INTRODUCTION

The threats to turtle populations are well defined and are addressed comprehensively and in specific detail in the ensuing chapters. Loss and alteration of habitat are still the major causes of turtle decline around the world. Habitat fragmentation is an increasing problem because many species have complex habitat requirements and use a variety of different habitats. For example, spotted and Blanding's turtles *(Clemmys guttata* and *Emydoidea blandingii)* often use a series of small wetlands over an annual activity cycle. After hibernating in a marsh, in early spring they move to vernal pools, which are warmer and contain abundant food resources in the form of tadpoles and salamander larvae. With the advent of summer, the vernal pools begin to dry up, and the turtles move into wooded swamps. As cooler weather approaches, they may move back into the marsh prior to hibernation. Spotted turtles may even move onto land and burrow into leaves for several days or even weeks. These complex habitat requirements necessitate the protection of habitat blocks, a mosaic of different wetland types with intact upland habitat joining them—a landscape condition that is not factored into most conservation plans.

Historically, turtles and tortoises often have been exploited by local inhabitants for food, traditional medicines, oil, and other products. Increasingly, they are being exported to urban centers. In the last decade of the twentieth century, the exploitation of wild turtles in Southeast Asia has brought many species to the brink of extinction. Some previously undescribed species have been discovered and described not from specimens found in the field but from purchases in the food and pet markets of Southeast Asia. Increasingly, the wildlife trade is a contributing (and in some instances primary) factor in the decline of tortoises and many species of freshwater turtles. Although the concept of sustainable management of turtles continues to be promoted by some, there are many, myself included, who question whether such long-lived animals can be widely and effectively managed on a commercially viable, sustained-yield basis. Subsistence exploitation may be a viable option in areas where turtle populations are large and human populations are small; however, subsistence exploitation almost invariably will evolve into larger-scale, unsustainable, commercial activities.

Threats to turtles usually work in tandem, creating a downward spiral that results in the depletion and loss of turtle populations. Habitat destruction is often followed by increased human populations, resulting in further destruction of the habitat infrastructure (i.e., fragmentation) followed by introduced species, subsidized predators (see Mitchell and Klemens, Chapter 1), and commercialization for food and the wildlife trade. Disease is now a major issue in managing wild populations of turtles and tortoises. Outbreaks of disease in wild turtle populations are increasing, and some outbreaks have been attributed to animals that have been infected in captivity and released into the wild where they rapidly infect free-ranging tortoises (see Flanagan, Chapter 3). Tumors on sea turtles may be caused by depressed immune systems resulting from chemical and heavy metal pollution of marine habitats. Increasingly, health and genetic issues are major components of management programs of wild turtles and tortoises, as well as components of any program that responsibly releases, repatriates, or relocates chelonians.

To understand and then propose integrated solutions to these synergistic threats requires an empirical approach to collecting the information needed for conservation action. Therefore, turtle conservation programs must be firmly rooted in good science, but we must also recognize that science alone is insufficient to conserve turtles and tortoises. To fashion and then implement solutions that are both empirically based and sustainable requires that science be integrated into conservation, which, in turn, is integrated into management and policy. Managers of protected and multiple-use areas, entrusted with the stewardship of turtle populations and their habitats, must be able to access the most up-to-date information to develop management and recovery strategies. In addition to knowledge about the organism and its habitat, risk assessment is an integral part of conservation planning and implementation. One must often pose the question, when data are not sufficiently conclusive to support an intervention on behalf of turtles, what are the risks of acting with incomplete data versus the risks of inaction?

This last point should be tempered with a recognition that there continues to be an overemphasis on interventionist management, including captive breeding, translocations, and headstarting (see "Conservation Measures," Meylan and Ehrenfeld, Chapter 4; Seigel and Dodd, Chapter 9). Headstarting is useful only if used in tandem with a strategy that will reduce the loss of adults. Clearly, if turtles have become scarce because of overharvesting, releasing more hatchlings and subadults into the rivers and seas, without alleviating the loss of adults, will not meet with success. Yet, it is exactly these type of measures that have been—and are still being—used to "conserve" turtles. These measures have an intrinsic appeal to many: they require visible infrastructure, such as hatcheries, that serve as tangible proof that managers are "doing conservation." Wildlife managers gain the hands-on control over nature that seems to be so deeply embedded in the human psyche. Hatcheries produce fairly predictable, consistent results—eggs are gathered and incubated and hatchlings are released, often as part of a media opportunity.

In contrast, addressing the loss of adult turtles requires making hard, often politically unpopular choices that have the potential to pit turtles against the perceived economic interests of the local communities. These choices can include conducting evaluations of impacts of proposed economic activities, such as the construction of buildings, roads, and dams, or regulating the exploitation of turtle populations. However, although conserving turtles does require society to make some hard decisions about the importance of protecting wilderness and biodiversity, it doesn't have to result in controversy. A great deal of grassroots conservation can be accomplished at the local level. State, provincial, and national governments can provide the enabling framework (such as identifying species that are endangered or threatened and providing technical assistance) to allow local communities to become engaged in conservation. Increasingly, some of the most effective conservation programs are being created at the local, community level.

The major advantage of these bottom-up conservation strategies, as opposed to more traditional top down approaches, is that they originate and are supported locally and are not imposed by federal, provincial, state, or even county governments. For turtles to become beneficiaries of such community-based conservation enterprises will require

- building conservation partnerships to conserve turtles by integrating efforts into larger multidisciplinary initiatives;

- linking conservation and public policy agendas—especially in the spheres of regional land use planning, watershed management, landscape preservation, and the promotion of legislation that enhances sound land use planning at the local, regional, national, and international levels;

- developing education programs that foster national and regional pride in natural resources and conservation awareness in both developed and developing countries;

- developing ecotourism and other economically driven systems that value wildlife resources in situ and reflect the long-term economic costs of resource depletion; and

- forming coalitions to conserve turtles that will maximize human capital—linking scientists, conservationists, turtle fanciers, zoos, museums, educational institutions, and concerned individuals with the local communities that share their land with turtles.

The turtle conservation crisis is likely more widespread than the well-publicized amphibian decline phenomenon, yet, because of the long generation time of turtles, it has not engendered the same level of concern. It is indeed difficult to convince decision makers that many of the turtles they see today are members of "living-dead" populations. These populations are increasingly composed of aged adults with limited reproductive capability, the result of increased mortality of breeding adults, as well as of eggs and young, due to human activities. Without the benefit of recruitment of young turtles into these populations, either through reproduction or immigration (when possible), over the next decades these populations will continue to decline. Turtles will become increasingly rare and even disappear in many areas where they are now considered secure.

Despite a tremendous amount of effort to conserve turtles, we continue to lose more ground than we gain. The goal of this book is twofold: first, to help all of us become more informed, effective, and interactive in designing and implementing turtle conservation programs that have the potential for higher rates of success and, second, to heighten public awareness and concern for the plight of this ancient order. How tragic it would be for 200 million years of turtle evolution to all but disappear by the close of the twenty-first century. It is my hope that this book will play a small but important role in deflecting this trajectory toward extinction.

JOSEPH C. MITCHELL AND
MICHAEL W. KLEMENS

1

PRIMARY AND SECONDARY EFFECTS OF HABITAT ALTERATION

Among the principle factors responsible for the accelerating decline of the world's biodiversity are loss, degradation, and fragmentation of habitats. Such alterations result in impoverished and dysfunctional ecosystems (Ehrlich and Ehrlich 1981; Wilcox and Murphy 1985; Wilson 1985, 1992; Soulé 1991; Mittermeier et al. 1992; Primack 1993; Hunter 1996). In the past, species extinctions stemmed from catastrophic events or overharvesting by humans. Today, habitat destruction is the primary cause of extinctions (Diamond 1984). Anthropogenically altered landscapes are subject to a host of secondary problems, including elevated levels of nutrient inputs, pollution, introduced species, and subsidized predators (Klemens 1989; see "Subsidized Predators," this chapter).

Habitat loss is alteration that results in the virtual elimination of the original natural system. Familiar examples include urbanization, conversion to agricultural use, and the inundation of valleys that follows construction of flood control and hydropower dams. The result is that original ecosystems are altered to the degree that they no longer support much of their original biota. **Habitat degradation** is the alteration of the physical properties of natural systems that does not lead to the elimination of these systems. Examples include oil spills, discharge of untreated sewage into aquatic systems, and elevated nutrient levels from fertilizers, as well as contamination from pesticide, heavy metal, and herbicide residues. **Fragmentation** is a direct consequence of habitat loss and degradation and results in increasingly isolated patches of original habitat. Such landscape alteration, coupled with the frequently decreasing size of patches, can lead to increased mortality and reduced fecundity of the residual fauna and flora. Alone, or in synergy, these habitat modifications can compromise ecosystems to the extent that they can no longer support self-sustaining populations of turtles.

Many widespread domestic species, including dogs *(Canis domestica)* and cats *(Felis catus)*, are not native to many parts of their current range. They pose threats to a myriad of wildlife species, including turtles and other reptiles, when they are allowed to roam freely or become feral. Introduced species, either as a primary cause or secondary effect of habitat change, have a long history of detrimental impacts on turtle populations. Feral domestic pigs *(Sus scrofa)*, rats *(Rattus* spp.), goats *(Capra* spp.), and other species have caused significant mortality of tortoises that inhabit oceanic islands, even contributing to extinctions of entire species (Honegger 1981; Swingland and Klemens 1989; Baillie and Groombridge 1996). Turtles occupying mainland habitats have been affected by introduced plants that change the structure of natural ecosystems and by a growing list of animal species implicated in elevated predation rates or habitat alteration (e.g., Klemens 1993a). Eradication and control of invasive species has proved problematic because the very characteristics that made such species successful invaders render them difficult to eliminate (Ehrlich 1989).

Human activities may subsidize (i.e., enhance) populations of native turtle predators by providing shelter and food sources to these predators and by assisting in their dispersal. Although there are only a few well-documented cases of the effects of subsidized predators on turtles and tortoises, there is much anecdotal information. If these anecdotal accounts reflect reality, many areas have not only severe problems but problems that may be approaching a level at which subsidized predators have contributed to the decline and extirpation of turtle populations.

Here we provide an overview of the complex and interrelated management challenges posed by habitat loss, degradation, and fragmentation and species introduction and subsidization. A comprehensive accounting of the habitat-related causes of decline of the world's turtles is not possible because many species have not yet been investigated in sufficient detail. However, recognition of the scope and breadth of these problems is essential because most conservation actions remain focused at the single-species level whereas conservation issues almost invariably exist at habitat, ecosystem, and landscape levels (Harris 1984; Noss and Harris 1986; Klemens, Chapter 10). We cannot overemphasize that in order to halt the global decline of turtles, we must expand our efforts to include the conservation of ecosystems on which the turtles depend in addition to conservation efforts on behalf of individual species and isolated patches of habitat. Only intact, functional, dynamic ecosystems are able to support the full range of naturally occurring processes that turtle populations require for their long-term survival. This is, indeed, a daunting task for conservationists, given the demands of an ever-expanding human population.

Differentiating among the terms habitat, ecosystem, and landscape is fundamental to our review. **Habitat** is the physical and biological environment used by a population of turtles. For example, a portion of the Mojave Desert used by a population of desert tortoises *(Gopherus agassizii)* in southern California constitutes only one type of habitat used by this tortoise in its geographic range. The common mud turtle *(Kinosternon subrubrum)* uses both aquatic and terrestrial habitats during its annual activity cycle in the southern mixed hardwood forest of South Carolina (Frazer et al. 1991; V. J. Burke and Gibbons 1995). Finer-scale habitat distinctions based on seasonal or behavioral activities (e.g., overwintering habitat and nesting habitat) may also be made. An ecosystem, such as the Amazon rainforest or Sonoran Desert, usually encompasses more habitat types than are used by a population of turtles. Thus, a habitat is a subcomponent of an ecosystem. Our use of the term **landscape** will be restricted to geographically defined areas, such as a watershed or other topographically delineated unit. An ecosystem may encompass numerous landscape units.

An **introduced species** is one that has been introduced by humans into an ecosystem or habitat in which it did not evolve. Well-known examples include the eastern cottontail *(Sylvilagus floridanus)*, the English sparrow *(Passer domesticus)*, and the fire ant *(Solenopsis invicta)*. **Subsidized predators** are native species whose populations in some parts of their range are able to survive and, in some cases, expand in part due to resources provided by humans. The Virginia opossum *(Didelphis virginiana)* in eastern North America and crows and ravens *(Corvus* spp.) on several continents serve as examples.

HABITAT LOSS

We define habitat loss as the elimination of natural vegetation and alteration of the land surface to such an extent that it no longer is able to support its indigenous biota. Habitat loss results from urbanization, agriculture, road construction, forestry operations, mineral exploration and extraction, military and industrial development, and inundation of low-lying areas following dam construction. Habitat loss has been cited as one of the primary causes of population declines in land and freshwater turtles (Table 1.1). For marine turtles, habitat loss occurs when nesting beaches are destroyed (Table 1.1). Deterioration and pollution of marine habitats, particularly in the shallow coastal zone, is a growing problem (Morreale and Burke 1997).

Freshwater wetlands around the world are among the most endangered of ecosystems. In the United States, freshwater wetlands have been drained and filled since European colonization in the 1600s. Approximately 53% of 159 million

Table 1.1

Threats to turtle habitats of selected species

Ecosystem and species	Region	Threats	Source(s)
Marine species			
Caretta caretta	USA	Seawalls, beachfront development	Frazer (1994); Lutcavage et al. (1997)
Chelonia mydas	Kenya	Beachfront development, beach erosion, seawalls, ocean pollution (plastics and garbage)	Wamukoya and Haller (1995)
Eretmochelys imbricata	Kenya	Beachfront development, beach erosion, seawalls, ocean pollution (plastics and garbage)	Wamukoya and Haller (1995)
Riverine species			
Chitra chitra	Thailand	Dams, water pollution (reduced oxygen and chemical and sewage inputs), sand mining	van Dijk and Thirakhupt (1995)
Rafetus euphraticus	Turkey	Dams, water pollution (thermal alteration), sand mining	Taskavak and Atatür (1995)
Nonriverine freshwater species			
Clemmys muhlenbergii	USA	Wetland loss and alteration, road construction, water pollution (nutrient loading), impoundments, urban development	Klemens (1993a)
Geoemyda silvatica	India	Conversion of evergreen forest to plantations, bush fires	Das (1991)
Heosemys spinosa	Malaysia	Timber harvesting	IUCN (1989)
Pseudemydura umbrina	Australia	Lowered water table, road construction, urban development, agricultural expansion, bush fires	Burbridge et al. (1990); Kuchling (1995a)
Pyxidea mouhotii	India	Timber harvesting, slash and burn agriculture	Das (1991)
Terrapene coahuila	Mexico	Wetland alteration, irrigation projects	IUCN (1989)

Terrestrial species

Species	Location	Threats	Reference
Chersina angulata	South Africa	Road construction, urban development, high-intensity fires caused by fuel load of invasive, nonnative plant species	Branch (1989a)
Geochelone chilensis	Argentina	Livestock grazing, agricultural expansion	Waller and Micucci (1997)
Geochelone elegans	Sri Lanka	Agricultural expansion, bush fires, road mortality	A. De Silva (1995)
Geochelone radiata	Madagascar	Livestock grazing, land-clearing fires, timber harvesting	Durrell et al. (1989b)
Gopherus flavomarginatus	Mexico	Livestock grazing, agricultural expansion, irrigation	Morafka et al. (1989)
Gopherus polyphemus	USA	Road construction, urban development, fire suppression, tree plantations with mechanized reforestation	Diemer (1989)
Indotestudo forstenii	India	Conversion of evergreen forest to plantations, impoundment for hydropower	Das (1991)
Testudo graeca	Morocco	Livestock grazing, timber harvesting, conversion to mechanized agriculture	Highfield and Bayley (1995)
Testudo hermanni	France	Road construction, urban development, agricultural expansion, increased frequency of fires in human-altered habitats	Stubbs (1989a)
Testudo horsfieldii	Turkmenistan	Livestock grazing, agricultural expansion, irrigation	Makeyev et al. (1997)

hectares of wetlands in the conterminous United States have been lost (Dahl 1990); 87% of this loss was due to agricultural practices (Nelson 1989). Freshwater turtles have presumably declined in abundance because of these losses. However, there are few quantitative studies of such a relationship. Most of the literature on this subject is qualitative and is based on reconstructions using presence versus absence data or on examinations of age–size–recruitment profiles of populations (Klemens 1989).

Habitat loss has severely affected all four species of the genus *Clemmys*, semi-aquatic North American turtles that depend on freshwater wetlands as well as terrestrial habitats to complete their life cycles. Spotted turtles *(C. guttata)* are found in an unusually wide variety of shallow wetland types in eastern North America (Klemens 1990, 1993a). Wetland loss has directly caused the decline of this species in many parts of its range (Lovich 1989; Harding and Holman 1990; Klemens 1993a; Ernst et al. 1994; Mitchell 1994; Graham 1995). Wood turtles *(C. insculpta)* occupy streams, rivers and their adjacent floodplains, and upland terrestrial habitats. Channelization, dam construction, agriculture, and urban development have reduced natural habitat throughout its range (Harding and Bloomer 1979; Ernst and McBreen 1991; Klemens 1993a). The number of known localities for the stream-dwelling western pond turtle *(C. marmorata)* in southern California declined from 87 in 1960 to 20 in 1987 (Brattstrom 1988; Brattstrom and Messer 1988). During this period, wetland losses were significant, stemming from dam construction, channelization, sand and gravel operations, and diversion of water for agricultural and urban uses. Although the western pond turtle was previously considered to be a primarily aquatic species, recent work by Reese and Welsh (1997) demonstrated significant terrestrial habitat use along riparian corridors inhabited by this species. Bog turtles *(C. muhlenbergii)* occupy shallow wetlands from southern New England to the southern Appalachian Mountains. They have declined dramatically in the northern portion of their range due to draining and alteration of these wetlands in agricultural and urban areas (Figure 1.1; Bury 1979a; Klemens and Warner 1983; Collins 1990; Klemens 1993a; USFWS 1997).

Other freshwater turtles have also experienced habitat loss due to destruction of wetlands. Drainage of ponds and floodplain wetlands in west-central Illinois contributed to the decline of the Illinois mud turtle *(Kinosternon flavescens spooneri)* (L. E. Brown and Moll 1979; D. Moll 1980). Loss of seasonally wet swamps in western Australia due to draining and drawing down of the water table has caused the severe decline of the western swamp turtle *(Pseudemydura umbrina)* (Burbridge et al. 1990; Georges 1993; Kuchling 1995a, 1997a). The Coahuilan box turtle *(Terrapene coahuila),* along with two other endemic subspecies, the Cuatro Ciénegas slider *(Trachemys scripta taylori)* and black spiny softshell *(Apalone spinifera ater),* are restricted to small, spring-fed pools in the Cuatro Ciénegas basin of northern Mexico (W. S. Brown 1974). Past irrigation projects in the region drained many of the marshes and reduced turtle population sizes. In 1964 the original surface area of one marsh–pool complex was reduced from about 10 km^2 to 0.2 km^2 (Cole and Minckley 1966). D. Moll (1986) reported that dynamite used to collect Central American river turtles *(Dermatemys mawii)* in Belize destroyed wetland habitat. Forest clearing to create pasture has altered the small ponds and brooks inhabited by Dahl's toad-headed turtle *(Phrynops dahli)* in Colombia (IUCN 1989). The wetlands occupied by Hoge's side-necked turtle *(Phrynops hogei)* in Brazil and Zulia toad-headed turtle *(Phrynops zuliae)* in Venezuela have declined in size due to a variety of human activities (IUCN 1989). Dam construction, sand mining, and drawdown for irrigation have caused the decline of aquatic habitats used by the Euphrates soft-shelled turtle *(Rafetus euphraticus)* in the Middle East (Taskavak and Atatür 1995).

The entire habitat of an area does not have to be destroyed to cause turtle populations to decline. Reducing reproductive success by eliminating nesting habitat can quickly reduce population sizes and alter demographic structures. Destruction of sea turtle and river turtle nesting beaches are the best examples of this threat. In southern Asia, commercial sand mining from the banks of the Kedah River in Malaysia has destroyed beaches used by nesting river terrapin *(Batagur baska)*, and riverine sand mining threatens nesting beaches used by the painted terrapin *(Callagur borneoensis)*, narrow-headed softshell turtle *(Chitra indica)*, Asian giant softshell turtle *(Pelochelys bibroni)*, and various species of roofed turtles *(Kachuga* spp.) (E. O. Moll 1997).

Human interference with natural erosion and deposition processes along coastlines often results in increased erosion and lack of sand replenishment. Beachfront development includes seawalls, rock revetments, sandbag installations, groins, and jetties (National Research Council 1990; Lutcavage et al. 1997). Coastal beaches used for nesting by sea turtles have been destroyed by sand mining in Sabah, in the eastern Mediterranean region, and on islands in the Gulf of Kutch in northwestern India; by beach development for tourist and industrial complexes on the west coast of Malaysia; and by construction of seawalls in Kerala State in India (Bjorndal 1995 and references therein). Protective seawalls and coastal development for resort facilities destroyed a loggerhead turtle *(Caretta caretta)* nesting beach on St. Simons Island, Georgia (Frazer 1994).

Established by some states in the United States, **wetland buffer zones,** a width of protected terrestrial habitat surrounding a wetland, are designed to maintain water quality. In most instances these zones do little to conserve the terrestrial habitat required by wetland species. In Massachusetts, state law requires a buffer zone of 30.5 m (Klein and Freed 1989). Yet, the upland requirements of many of the turtles and amphibians using such wetlands often extends 275 m or more from the water's edge (Congdon et al. 1983; V. J. Burke and Gibbons 1995). Recorded distances of nests from water for various United States turtles follow: spiny soft-

a

b

c

d

e   f

Figure 1.1. Poorly planned development (Sussex County, New Jersey). Sussex County contains some of the best remaining bog turtle populations in the northeastern United States. Although this species receives regulatory protection at both the federal (threatened species) and state (endangered species) level, poor land management decisions and practices at the local government level pose a major threat to its survival. These photographs were all taken in wetland complexes inhabited by bog turtles and illustrate typical threats to shallow-water wetlands. Shallow-water wetlands, including wooded swamps, ephemeral wetlands, and wet meadows, are critical for the survival of many turtle species around the world. (Photographs by Michael W. Klemens.) (**a**) Seasonal wetlands such as vernal pools are especially vulnerable to activities such as the disposal and dumping of garbage, debris, and chemicals. (**b**) Shallow wetlands are easily filled for construction of homes, roads, and factories. Here a headwater, spring-fed wetland, a primary source of water to an adjacent wet meadow and wooded swamp, is being filled. (**c**) The pipe in the center of the photograph drains storm water runoff from roads and roofs of a newly constructed housing development directly into this wetland. Such runoff is frequently polluted with oil and salt from the road surface as well as fertilizers and pesticides from lawns. (**d**) Roadways constructed along the edge of wetlands create barriers to movements of small, wetland-dependent species (mice, shrews, snakes, turtles, salamanders, and frogs) and significantly increase mortality. Here small animals disperse from the wooded hillside (behind the houses) into the wooded swamp (to the left of the road). Lawns along a road bordering a swamp result in additional runoff of fertilizers and pesticides directly into the wetland. (**e**) Curbs and retaining walls create barriers to the movement and dispersal of small animals. (**f**) High curbs also serve as a drift fence, catching turtles, salamanders, and snakes that attempt to cross roads. These animals move along the base of the curb until they fall into one of the storm water catch basins (in the center of the photograph) and perish.

shell *(Apalone spinifera)*, up to 100 m (Wisconsin, Vogt 1981a); painted turtle *(Chrysemys picta)*, typically less that 200 m but up to 600 m (Idaho, Lindeman 1992); western pond turtle, up to 500 m (California, Reese and Welsh 1997); chicken turtle *(Deirochelys reticularia)*, an average of 70 m (South Carolina, K. A. Buhlmann, personal communication); Blanding's turtle *(Emydoidea blandingii)*, 650 to 900 m (Illinois), an average of 135 m (Michigan), and an average of 168 m (Wisconsin) (Ernst et al. 1994); false map turtle *(Graptemys pseudogeographica)*, 5 to 150 m (Wisconsin, Vogt 1981a); common mud turtle, an average of 49 m (South Carolina, V. J. Burke et al. 1994; V. J. Burke and Gibbons 1995); common musk turtle *(Sternotherus odoratus)*, an average of 14 m (South Carolina, K. A. Buhlmann, personal communication); and smooth softshell *(Apalone mutica)*, 4 to 90 m (Kansas, Fitch and Plummer 1975). Conversion of terrestrial habitat around wetlands for agricultural and urban purposes occurs worldwide. Maintenance of viable freshwater turtle populations clearly requires the protection of terrestrial habitat as well as the wetlands themselves (V. J. Burke and Gibbons 1995).

The estimated loss and alteration of terrestrial habitats are also cause for alarm. Approximately 76% of the world's primary forest was destroyed by the late 1980s, including 50% of the tropical rainforest and 55% of the coastal temperate rainforest (Postel and Ryan 1991; Noss et al. 1995). In addition, 65% of the habitat in sub-Saharan Africa has been lost, as well as 67% in Asia (Noss et al. 1995). Prairie, savanna, and desert grassland habitats continue to be converted into farmland and pasture and are increasingly lost through urbanization and associated land uses, including roads, power lines, and other infrastructural improvements instituted for an ever-expanding human population.

Loss of original ecosystem vegetation affects all wildlife, including turtles. In North America, which contains approximately 20% of the world's turtle species, at least 95 to 98% of the virgin forests has been lost, including 99% of the turtle-rich eastern deciduous forest biome (Postel and Ryan 1991; Whitney 1994). In Southeast Asia, loss of primary evergreen forest is directly attributable to the endangerment of species such as the Travancore tortoise *(Indotestudo forstenii)* Cochin forest cane turtle *(Geoemyda silvatica)*, and keeled box turtle *(Pyxidea mouhotii)* (Das 1991), as well as the spiny turtle *(Heosemys spinosa)* (IUCN 1989). Conversion of vast areas of evergreen forests to tea, cardamom, rubber, and opium plantations, logging, slash and burn agriculture, and the construction of hydropower facilities have all contributed to the loss of forested habitat.

Over 90% of the tall-grass prairie of the midwestern United States was converted to agriculture and grazing land during the 1880s. The remaining prairie exists only in small fragments (Madson 1990; Whitney 1994). The loss of prairie and grassland has caused the terrestrial ornate box turtle *(Terrapene ornata)* to decline, although its ability to adapt to human-altered landscapes (e.g., grazing lands and open areas without extensive tilling) and inhabit desert grassland (Legler 1960) has allowed it to remain common in some areas. Loss of grassland to agriculture and grazing in Argentina has severely affected the Chaco tortoise *(Geochelone chilensis)* (Waller and Micucci 1997). In the Turkmen Republic, irrigation of semidesert steppe has adversely affected the Central Asian tortoise *(Testudo horsfieldii)* (Makeyev et al. 1997).

Loss of terrestrial habitat has been especially detrimental to tortoises. Of the approximately 40 known tortoise species, at least 60% are threatened by habitat loss in all or a portion of their range (Swingland and Klemens 1989). Extreme examples of tortoise habitat loss are on the island of Madagascar, where four species have evolved in isolation: the angonoka *(Geochelone yniphora)*, radiated tortoise *(Geochelone radiata)*, common spider tortoise *(Pyxis arachnoides)*, and flat-tailed spider tortoise *(Pyxis planicauda)*. Destruction of the xerophytic forests of Madagascar by burning, cattle grazing, and exploitation for building supplies and fuel has significantly reduced the range of the radiated tortoise and the common spider tortoise (Durrell et al. 1989b, d). Decline of the angonoka is attributed to the expansion of savanna–grassland at the expense of the original dry deciduous tropical forest in northwestern Madagascar. This expansion has been caused by deliberate burning to generate fresh forage growth for cattle and has resulted in a severe range contraction for the angonoka, which now inhabits an area of less than 25 km by 60 km of secondary bamboo and scrub forest (Juvik et al. 1981; Curl et al. 1985; Curl 1986; Durrell et al. 1989c). The flat-tailed spider tortoise is restricted to ecologically intact, dry lowland deciduous forest along the west coast (Kuchling and Bloxam 1988). Agricultural development of this area, largely for maize, and deforestation for fuel and commercial purposes have reduced the flat-tailed spider tortoise's range to two isolated patches of original forest totaling about 15,000 ha (Durrell et al. 1989a).

In contrast, three species of North American tortoises occupy large geographic ranges (Stebbins 1985; R. Conant and Collins 1991; Iverson 1992a). Still, they are subjected to a suite of processes that destroy their habitats. The xeric habitat supporting desert tortoise populations in the Southwest has been degraded and destroyed by urban and agricultural development, road construction, military and industrial development, mineral exploitation and development, and disposal of toxic and radioactive wastes (Berry 1989; Corn 1994). The Texas tortoise *(Gopherus berlandieri)* occurs in semidesert scrub habitat in southern Texas and northeastern Mexico. Over 90% of this habitat has been eliminated in the Rio Grande Valley since the 1930s (Ramirez 1986). Extensive agriculture is the primary cause of habitat loss. Tortoises in Texas are less threatened by habitat loss than other *Gopherus* species because populations remain healthy in areas where cattle grazing is managed (F. L. Rose and Judd 1989). Gopher tortoises *(Gopherus polyphemus)* occupy habitats with sandy or well-drained soils in the southeastern United States. Loss of habitat is the most significant threat to this species and results from housing projects, industrial centers, broad-scale agriculture (including cattle farms and citrus plantations), conversion of natural habitat to pine plantations, military activities, phosphate mining, and sand extraction (Auffenberg and Franz 1982; Diemer 1986, 1989, 1992).

HABITAT DEGRADATION

Habitat degradation is the process by which habitats are diminished in their ability to support populations of native wildlife. Habitat degradation is brought about by many means, including agricultural activities, timber harvesting, mining, pollution, alteration of fire regimes, alteration through introduction of nonnative plants, and direct impacts from human activities.

The earliest recorded forms of habitat degradation by human activities were agriculture and deforestation, both beginning about 5,000 years ago (Perlin 1989). Agriculture and deforestation have undoubtedly eliminated and degraded large portions of turtle habitat. Unfortunately, it is not possible to provide quantitative estimates of the effects of these two forces. At best, we can infer historical turtle distributions from present ranges, archaeological evidence, subfossil remains, and knowledge of previous vegetative cover.

Degradation of terrestrial habitats as a result of agricultural activities is considered a threat to at least 26 of the world's tortoises (Swingland and Klemens 1989). The use of fire to eliminate and control undesirable vegetation and to promote new growth for cattle forage degrades large areas of tortoise habitat and causes substantial mortality. Examples include the angonoka (Curl et al. 1985; Curl 1986; Durrell et al. 1989c); Chaco tortoise (P. Walker 1989a); Hermann's tortoise *(Testudo hermanni)* (Stubbs et al. 1985; Stubbs 1989a); Natal hinge-back tortoise *(Kinixys natalensis)* (Broadley 1989a); South African bowsprit tortoise *(Chersina angulata)* (Branch 1989a); Karroo cape tortoise *(Homopus femoralis)* (Branch 1989b); and geometric tortoise *(Psammobates geometricus)* (Baard 1989a, b). Conversely, fire suppression (usually to protect houses and other structures) also adversely affects habitats that are dependent upon regular fires to regenerate trees and maintain a sparse understory. Regular fires are required to maintain open canopies and ground-level vegetation required by gopher tortoises in the pine–scrub oak habitats of the southeastern United States (Diemer 1989).

Livestock grazing in terrestrial habitats has occurred for centuries. Cattle and sheep (*Ovis* spp.) compete with tortoises for many of the same forage plant species. Livestock can reduce plant productivity, decrease the perennials and forbs preferred by desert tortoises, and trample soil and vegetation, sometimes killing young tortoises in their burrows (Luckenbach 1982; Avery and Neibergs 1997). Tortoises must contend with habitat degraded by livestock in various parts of their range (see Swingland and Klemens 1989). Grazing by free-ranging goats, cattle, and sheep has altered much of the semixerophilic forests and desert shrublands inhabited by the Chaco tortoise in Argentina (Waller and Micucci 1997). Livestock outcompete Chaco tortoises for ephemeral spring plants and summer fruits, trample burrows, and compact soil, forcing tortoises into marginal habitats. A similar situation exists for the Mediterranean spur-thighed tortoise *(Testudo graeca graeca)* in Morocco, where overgrazing by camels *(Camelus dromedarius)* and goats is degrading tortoise habitat (Bayley and Highfield 1996).

Off-road vehicle use is increasing throughout the world, and it has become prevalent in the deserts of the American Southwest, especially southern California. Thousands of dune buggies, motorcycles, minibikes, and all-terrain and four-wheel-drive vehicles have had significant effects on desert tortoises and their habitat (Bury et al. 1977; Luckenbach, 1982). These effects include direct mortality of adults and juveniles, collapsed burrows, compaction of desert soils, destruction of native vegetation, and alteration of ecosystem productivity (Jennings 1997a).

Human recreation in areas that support turtles can result in population declines even in the absence of significant habitat degradation. Garber and Burger (1995) reported that two populations of wood turtles in Connecticut were stable until these areas were opened for large-scale passive recreation (i.e., hiking and fishing). Both populations became extirpated within a decade of recreational access. The authors suggested that extirpation resulted from collection, road kills, and disturbance of individual turtles by humans and dogs. Elevated predation levels may have also been caused by an increased number of predators drawn to the site by garbage left by recreationists. In Costa Rica, the presence and behavior of tourists on beaches during the nesting season of the common green turtle *(Chelonia mydas)* resulted in the disturbance of nesting females (S. K. Jacobson and Lopez 1994).

Channel and shoreline modification, agricultural and urban runoff, and industrial discharges have degraded rivers, streams, lakes, and oceans around the world. Many turtle species have been negatively affected by these activities. Populations of the smooth softshell in the Illinois River declined after erosion from the surrounding landscape silted over nesting beaches (D. Moll 1980). Rising water levels from lock and dam construction on the Illinois River in the 1930s degraded large areas of floodplain marsh and caused a decline in Blanding's turtles (D. Moll 1980). The riverine habitat of the yellow-blotched map turtle *(Graptemys flavimaculata)* in the Pascagoula River, Mississippi, has been diminished by removal of logs and snags, which are essential for basking, as well as by increased sedimentation and turbidity from mining activities and channelization (USFWS 1993a). Populations of the flattened musk turtle *(Sternotherus depressus)* have been severely affected by siltation, pollution by organic and inorganic chemicals, changes in water level and streamflow regimes due to mining activities, extirpation and reduction of prey resources, and physical alteration of habitats used by the turtles for cover (Dodd et al. 1988; USFWS 1990a). Habitat alteration and pollution of rivers have caused population declines in the ringed sawback turtle *(Graptemys oculifera)* in Mississippi and Louisiana, the Madagascan big-headed turtle *(Erymnochelys madagascariensis)*, and Hoge's side-necked turtle in southeastern Brazil (IUCN 1989).

Pollution can affect turtles directly. Uptake of heavy metals and pesticides by snapping turtles in North America is well documented (Stone et al. 1980; Helwig and Hora 1983; Bryan et al. 1987), but long-term effects are unknown. Declines in wood turtle populations in New Jersey were noted by Harding and Bloomer (1979) following spraying of pesticides in the 1950s and 1960s for the introduced gypsy moth *(Lymantria dispar)*, even where habitats remained otherwise unchanged. Use of pesticides has contributed to the decline of the European pond turtle *(Emys orbicularis)* in northeastern Spain (Mascort 1997).

Some freshwater turtles that occupy aquatic systems nutritionally enhanced by sewage discharge grow larger and faster than turtles in nearby unpolluted ecosystems (Gibbons 1967; Ernst and McDonald 1989). Enhanced growth also occurs in thermally polluted systems (Gibbons 1970a; Gibbons et al. 1981; Thornhill 1982). Snapping turtles *(Chelydra serpentina)* and yellow-bellied sliders *(Trachemys scripta scripta)*, among others, have derived benefits from enriched, thermally altered habitats (Gibbons 1990a).

Degradation of marshes and other shallow freshwater habitats occupied by semiaquatic turtles occurs from alteration of the hydrology through ditching and overgrazing by cattle. Ditching of wetlands can eliminate marsh habitat, but more often it lowers water levels to favor less moisture-tolerant plants. These plants are often invasive and nonnative species. Excessive trampling of wetland vegetation and compaction of the mud substrate can occur when too many cattle are grazed too frequently in a small area (J. C. Mitchell and M. W. Klemens, personal observations). Overgrazing can alter hydrologic patterns, including surface runoff, and lead to increased nutrient levels, which in turn accelerate the growth of invasive plants (Herman 1994). Conversely, low-intensity grazing can be a valuable management tool, preventing the growth of woody vegetation that leads to canopy closure. Succession has been documented for numerous wetlands supporting bog turtles and spotted turtles; closing of the canopy and changes in hydrology caused by woody plants diminish the suitability of the habitat (Tryon 1990; Mitchell et al. 1991; Klemens 1993a; Herman 1994; Graham 1995; Herman and Tryon 1997).

Coastal ecosystems are also especially vulnerable to degradation by human activities. Beaches are often "stabilized" with rock revetments, sandbags, groins, and jetties or "nourished" by replacing sand (National Research Council 1990; Lutcavage et al. 1997). Unnatural structures can interfere directly with turtle nesting or cause abnormal movement of sand, resulting in beach accretion or erosion. New sand can interfere with nesting behavior and hatchling success. A growing problem for sea turtles on nesting beaches is beachfront illumination from buildings, street lights, and vehicles as a result of urban development and a thriving global tourist industry (K. L. Eckert 1995). Hatchling sea turtles orient to the sea by visually responding to brightness on the horizon and horizon silhouette, shapes associated with the horizon, or both (Salmon et al. 1992; Witherington 1995). Artificial lighting from land-based sources causes disorientation; hatchlings move inland only to be caught in vegetation or debris or killed on roads or in parking lots (Verheijen 1985; Lutcavage et al. 1997). Adult female sea turtles will avoid brightly lit nesting beaches (Mortimer 1982). Vehicular traffic on beaches, tar balls from oil spills, and waste disposal are also documented causes of beach degradation (Witham 1982; K. L. Eckert 1995). Shoreline development, destruction of salt marshes from bridge and seawall construction, pollution, and urban and recreational development on nesting habitat has significantly reduced populations of diamondback terrapin *(Malaclemys terrapin)* in estuarine and coastal ecosystems throughout its range (Seigel and Gibbons 1995; R. C. Wood and Herlands 1995).

Pollution of the ocean by oil spills, debris from human sources, and sewage from ships and cities as well as damage to coral reefs and sea grass beds from human waste appear to degrade turtle habitat (Lutcavage et al. 1997). W. H. Allen (1992) described damage to coral and sea grass beds from ships' anchors as well as erosion and sedimentation from coastal and upland development that reduced light for photosynthesis and smothered benthic marine organisms. Ingestion of plastic debris and tar has caused mortality of juvenile and adult sea turtles (Balazs 1985; Carr 1987a). Abandoned and active fishing nets and lines are hazards to sea turtles. Long-line drift nets and hooks used in the open sea for fishing may kill numerous individual turtles (Morreale and Burke 1997). Although the cumulative impacts of these habitat alterations are unknown, hundreds to thousands of turtles are killed annually from these sources (National Research Council 1990; Bolten and Balazs 1995).

HABITAT FRAGMENTATION

Many of the factors discussed under habitat loss also contribute to habitat fragmentation. Meffe and Carroll (1997) consider fragmentation to be one of the greatest threats to regional and global biodiversity. Fragmentation of turtle populations occurs when habitat destruction creates a landscape of patches of suitable habitat isolated from one another by barriers such as roads or other tracts of inhospitable, degraded habitat. The remaining patches of habitat (habitat fragments) become de facto islands (Harris 1984). These islands are smaller and able to support fewer individual turtles than the original expanse of habitat (Wilcox 1980; Wilcox and Murphy 1985; Wilcove et al. 1986). Typically, habitat fragmentation begins with the dissection of the original ecosystem by roads or logging, followed by the conversion of natural habitat to agricultural lands or single-species tree farms. As more and more of the ecosystem is converted to agriculture or silviculture, these disturbed patches expand and join together, increasing the isolation of original habitat. As more people move into the area, increased development occurs. Attrition of the ecosystem occurs when the patches of remaining natural habitat become smaller and farther apart (Hunter 1996).

Terrestrial turtles are especially vulnerable to fragmentation because many individuals have limited abilities to migrate effectively between isolated patches; therefore, the potential of individuals to "rescue" dwindling populations from extinction is limited (J. H. Brown and Kodric-Brown 1977). Adult common box turtles *(Terrapene carolina),* for example, frequently occupy the same patch of habitat for many years and do not move long distances, although rare individuals (mostly males) are transients and may move several kilometers (Kiester et al. 1982). Mobile individuals face higher risks of mortality when they cross inhospitable terrain between patches of suitable habitat. One male studied by E. R. Schwartz et al. (1984) in Missouri crossed five highways and a river. Turtle populations may also be vulnerable to high mortality rates and potential extinction because the increased length of edge habitat around isolated patches allows greater penetration by predators (Meffe and Carroll 1997).

Small populations experience many problems when the number of reproductively active individuals is reduced. This may result in inbreeding, outbreeding, changes in demographic structure, and increased vulnerability to predation, disease, and natural disasters (Gilpin and Soulé 1986; M. L. Shaffer 1990). On Long Island, New York, Zweifel (1989) conducted an 18-year study of a small, isolated population of painted turtles that varied in size from 21 to 57 animals. Survival of single individuals and cohorts of hatchlings from single nests had dramatic effects on the structure of that population.

In eastern North America, many common box turtle populations exist in isolated fragments of forested habitat, many of which are located in urban and suburban areas (Figure 1.2). The demographic structure of these populations is often limited to aged adults; successful reproduction and recruitment is minimal or nonexistent (Klemens 1989). The sizes of these small, isolated populations are whittled down by roadkills, subsidized predators like raccoons *(Procyon lotor)* that flourish in disturbed areas (Hall 1981), and collection of turtles for pets. In Wisconsin, Do-

Figure 1.2. Suburban sprawl (Long Island, New York). Roads and development have fragmented both the upland (top right) and wetland (lower left) habitats of this landscape. This type of urban–suburban land use pattern is rapidly increasing around the world, with dire consequences for turtles and many other forms of wildlife. At this site, common box turtles, spotted turtles, and tiger salamanders *(Ambystoma tigrinum)* have become increasingly scarce. (Courtesy of AeroGraphics Corp.)

roff and Keith (1990) found that the accidental loss of even one adult box turtle every year could not be sustained by the population. Ornate box turtle populations in savanna and prairie habitats isolated by fragmentation have shorter active seasons, larger home ranges, and longer incubation periods, which lead to lower recruitment and higher adult mortality (Curtin 1997).

Although expanding human populations, which convert natural ecosystems into human-dominated ecosystems, are the primary cause of habitat fragmentation (Hunter 1996), particular factors contribute significantly to the fragmentation of turtle populations. Roads, especially multilane expressways and railroads, kill turtles and isolate habitat patches. Road construction causes direct habitat loss, whereas curbs and silt-retention fencing limit terrestrial movements of turtles and increase mortality on roads (J. C. Mitchell and M. W. Klemens, personal observations; see Figure 1.1e, f). Catch basins, culverts, and other drainage and safety structures trap turtles that ultimately die (J. C. Mitchell and M. W. Klemens, personal observations). Vehicular traffic creates a kill zone along the road, over time effectively depleting the road corridor of turtles. Turtle populations are therefore split into fragments, with reduced probabilities for successful movement of individuals (and therefore gene flow) among fragments. Dodd et al. (1989) recorded 160 turtles on a series of state roads traveled in north-central Alabama in 1985; 74.4% of the turtles were roadkills. Most of these (85%) were common box turtles. In coastal New Jersey, roadkills of diamondback terrapin along one road crossing a marsh numbered 4,020 during 1989 to 1995 (R. C. Wood and Herlands 1995). Vehicular traffic on roads in southern California has caused significant mortality and decimated desert tortoise populations within 1 km of the road (Nicholson 1978; Luckenbach 1982; Berry and Medica 1995; Boarman et al. 1997). High levels of mortality due to vehicular traffic on roads have been noted for many other species, including the ornate box turtle (Legler 1960), the gopher tortoise (Diemer 1986), and the radiated tortoise (Goodman et al. 1994). Roads also result in corridors of disturbed habitat that facilitate the dispersal of invasive weedy plants and subsidized predators, both of which further degrade natural habitat in the corridor and adjacent habitat. Disturbed corridors amplify the barrier that separates the road-created fragments. Placing fencing along roadsides may be an effective means of reducing tortoise mortality (Boarman et al. 1997), but it increases the fragmentation effect.

Fragmentation of habitat that supports tortoise populations has been reported as a problem for many species. In southern Africa, geometric tortoises survive in 13 isolated fragments of natural habitat varying in size from less than 10 ha to 30 ha (Baard 1989a, b). On Madagascar, the angonoka survives in only three forest fragments, and the flat-tailed spider tortoise survives in only two (Durrell et al. 1989a, c; Juvik et al. 1997). Stubbs (1989b) predicted a marked decline in marginated tortoise *(Testudo marginata)* populations in Greece due to habitat loss and fragmentation. The habitat of the widespread Hermann's tortoise is being fragmented by agriculture and tourist-related development around the Mediterranean (Stubbs 1989a). Fragmentation of Amazonian rainforest by logging, agriculture, and oil exploration is isolating populations of the South American yellow-footed tortoise *(Geochelone denticulata)* (P. Walker 1989b). Much of the aquatic habitat formerly used by the flattened musk turtle in the Warrior River basin in northern Alabama has been lost or degraded (Dodd et al. 1988; USFWS 1990a). Extant populations are now fragmented and apparently isolated (Dodd 1990). E. O. Moll (1984) reported that construction of dams in Malaysia prevented movement along rivers and effectively fragmented populations of the river terrapin. Klemens (1993b) cited isolation of bog turtle populations from one another by development-related landscape changes as one of the major causes of its decline, necessitating its listing (USFWS 1997) under the U.S. Endangered Species Act (16 U.S.C. §§ 1531 to 1544).

INTRODUCED SPECIES

Many habitats around the world now support species that were introduced by intentional or inadvertent human actions. Island floras and faunas are particularly vulnerable to introduced species. Many exotic species dominate human-modified habitats or alter habitat themselves. Introduced vertebrates and plants are the best documented cases, but there is a growing body of literature on the effects of introduced invertebrates (Wolff and Seal 1993; E. R. Jacobson et al. 1995). There is little information on the effects of introduced invertebrates or parasites on turtles. Indeed, one of the problems of evaluating this literature is the difficulty of determining whether the organism is native or has been introduced into the population or region.

The list of introduced vertebrates that prey upon different age groups of turtle populations demonstrates how widespread this problem has become. A review of the North American species of turtles described in Ernst et al. (1994) and tortoises worldwide discussed in Swingland and Klemens (1989) reveals that 23% of the tortoise species, 23% of the freshwater turtle species, and most sea turtle species are negatively affected somewhere in their range by an introduced vertebrate.

The most intensively studied chelonian from the standpoint of introduced species is the Galápagos tortoise *(Geochelone nigra)*. Eggs, hatchlings, and young tortoises are preyed upon by five introduced species: domestic pigs, dogs, cats, black rats *(Rattus rattus),* and Norway rats *(Rattus norvegicus).* Four feral domestic animals (goats, cattle, sheep, and donkeys *[Equus asinus]*) degrade native habitat and compete with Galápagos tortoises for forage. Pigs destroy the majority of nests and kill large numbers of young (up to 35 mm curved carapace length), whereas dogs kill Galápagos tortoises up to about 55 mm curved carapace length and depredate nests (Swingland 1989a). Cats kill hatchlings, yearlings, and 2-year-old Galápagos tortoises. Black rats have killed almost all the hatchlings on Isla Pinzon for over a century, leaving a population of only aged adults (M. H. Jackson 1993). Goats devastate the vegetation on all or part of six islands and leave little for young Galápagos tortoises to eat (Swingland 1989a). Other grazing animals vary in number and influence. Control of pigs, which can number as high as 3,000 animals (Isla Santiago, Coblentz and Baber 1987), and goats, which number as high as 30,000 on Isla Santiago (M. H. Jackson 1993) and are introduced or reintroduced by fishermen (Swingland 1989a), is difficult.

The exotic species most often cited as a predator of turtles is the domestic pig, which has been introduced into many island and mainland habitats worldwide. Feral and domestic populations of pigs are known to seek out nests by olfaction and destroy eggs and hatchlings of at least three species of tortoises, five species of freshwater turtles, and three sea turtles. The species most commonly involved is the domestic pig, although the bush pig *(Potamochoerus larvatus)* is a problem in Madagascar (Juvik et al. 1981; Durrell et al. 1989c).

Cats and dogs are well-known introduced predators of the eggs, hatchlings, and juveniles of sea turtles worldwide (Stancyk 1982). Domestic and feral cats depredate hatchlings of at least five species of turtles. Cats were introduced between 1890 and 1920 on Aldabra Atoll to control black rats (Seabrook 1989). Although they eat rats, cats also kill and eat large numbers of hatchlings of the green turtle. Seabrook (1989) found that cats cue on adult turtle nesting activity and that 90.4% of the scats examined contained turtle hatchling remains. Introduced domestic and feral dogs have been reported to kill hatchlings of at least 13 species of turtles. Dogs were the primary predators of green turtle nests at Tortuguero, Costa Rica, destroying 63 of 182 nests surveyed in a 5-month period in 1977 (Fowler 1979). Dogs were responsible for the loss of 16% of all recorded nests of sea turtles on a beach in southwestern Costa Rica (Drake 1996). Causey and Cude (1978) observed a pack of feral dogs dig out and attempt to kill an adult gopher tortoise.

Other introduced vertebrates have had varying effects on turtle populations. Mongooses are a threat to geometric tortoises in southern Africa (Baard 1989b) and green turtles, leatherback turtles *(Dermochelys coriacea),* and hawksbill turtles *(Eretmochelys imbricata)* in various parts of the world (Stancyk 1982; Ernst et al. 1994). In Australia, feral water buffalo *(Bubalus bubalis)* trample nesting banks used by the pig-nosed turtle *(Carettochelys insculpta),* destroy riparian vegetation upon which this turtle feeds in the dry season, and cause increases in turbidity that affect aquatic flora and fauna (Georges and Kennett 1989; Georges 1993; Georges and Rose 1993). Red fox *(Vulpes vulpes)* introduced from North America prey on eggs of the western swamp turtle and the Murray River turtle *(Emydura macquarrii)* in Australia (M. B. Thompson 1983, 1993). Bullfrogs *(Rana catesbeiana)* introduced into western North America from eastern North America eat young Sonoran mud turtles *(Kinosternon sonoriense)* (Ernst et al. 1994).

Very few observations of the effects of introduced invertebrates on turtles have been published. Fire ants introduced into the United States between 1933 and 1945 in Mobile, Alabama, have spread rapidly throughout the Southeast and have caused the decline of many populations of native species of vertebrates and invertebrates (Vinson and Greenberg 1986; Dodd 1995). Three species of turtles are known to have been killed by this species: gopher tortoises (Landers et al. 1980), common mud turtles (V. J. Burke, personal communication), and chicken turtles

(K. A. Buhlmann, personal communication). We suspect that individuals of numerous other species have been killed by fire ants, but such events have not been observed or reported in the scientific literature. In North American waters, the spread of the zebra mussel *(Dreissena polymorpha)*, introduced from the Black Sea in the late 1980s, has been dramatic (Benson and Boydstun 1995). This bivalve may occur in densities of greater than 800 per square meter and eliminates native mussels. Populations of mollusk-eating turtles (e.g., map turtles [*Graptemys* spp.] and musk turtles [*Sternotherus* spp.]) could be affected indirectly if zebra mussels cause the extinction of native mussels, snails, and even the ubiquitous introduced Asian clam *(Corbicula manilensis)*, on which some of these turtles feed (D. Moll 1980). Reports of turtles feeding on zebra mussels have not been published; therefore, it is unknown whether turtles will be able to use this exotic species as a food source.

Invasive plants can have direct and indirect impacts on turtle populations by changing the physical structure of the habitat and by altering food resources of turtle populations (Figure 1.3). Numerous species of plants have been introduced into turtle habitats around the world.

Exotic plants of Mediterranean origin now constitute a substantial proportion of the biomass of the vegetation in the western Mojave Desert (Jennings 1997b). These species restrict native plants used by desert tortoises to isolated patches in the landscape and present a different type of fire hazard because they burn hotter and longer. Australian *Acacia* has been introduced into Africa where it threatens South African bowsprit tortoises and geometric tortoises by canopy closure and by fueling frequent and intense fires (Baard 1989a, b; Branch 1989a).

A wetland-invading plant from Europe, purple loosestrife *(Lythrum salicaria)*, has greatly altered the structure and function of freshwater wetlands in northeastern North America (Malecki et al. 1993; Malecki 1995). This species often becomes established in wetlands once they are drained or when the hydrology or water quality is altered. After taking root in disturbed microhabitats, purple loosestrife spreads quickly into adjacent wetlands, replacing the natural vegetative community with a dense monoculture unsuitable for bog turtles and other chelonians that inhabit shallow fens and marshes (Bury 1979a; Klemens 1993a, b). Many bog turtle sites in the northeastern United States have been degraded severely or destroyed by these alien plants. Other invasive plants reported in bog turtle habitats include multiflora rose *(Rosa multiflora)*, reed canary grass *(Phalaris arundinacea)*, and giant reed *(Phragmites australis)*. The giant reed, long considered to be an introduced species (Klemens 1993a), is actually a native species (Marks et al. 1994) that under conditions of degraded water quality may have a competitive edge over other native wetland species such as cattails *(Typha* spp.). It could be considered, therefore, an example of a subsidized plant species (see "Subsidized Predators," this chapter). There is also speculation that some populations of giant reed in the

Figure 1.3. Invasive plants (Putnam County, New York). Giant reed *(Phragmites australis)* and purple loosestrife *(Lythrum salicaria)* have invaded bog turtle nesting habitat. The hummocks in the foreground (dominated by *Carex stricta,* a small, native sedge) are suitable for bog turtle nesting. The hummocks in the rear have been overgrown and shaded by invasive plants and are unsuitable nest sites. (Courtesy of Erik Kiviat, Hudsonia Ltd.)

United States are composed of a more vigorous, introduced Old World genotype of giant reed (Metzler and Rozsa 1987 *in* Marks et al. 1994).

SUBSIDIZED PREDATORS

In disturbed areas populations of predatory vertebrates can exist at unnaturally high levels because of subsidies provided by humans. These subsidies include food sources provided by agriculture and garbage, elimination of major predators, and inadvertent provision of water and shelter. Subsidized predators can reach high densities and inflict heavy mortality on turtle populations (Carr 1973; Boarman 1993). Mammalian predators, such as raccoons, red foxes, gray foxes *(Urocyon cinereoargenteus)*, striped skunks *(Mephitis mephitis)*, eastern spotted skunks *(Spilogale putorius)*, and crows and ravens abound in human-dominated landscapes and exert high predation pressure on ground-nesting animals in fragmented landscapes (Harris and Silva-Lopez 1992). Subsidies increase survival of such predators when natural resources are low and facilitate greater reproductive success during the breeding and postbreeding seasons (Boarman 1997). Ravens and raccoons are the only subsidized species studied from this perspective to date.

Ravens are diurnal scavengers with a broad diet. They frequently feed on road-killed vertebrates and human refuse and forage on grain, fruits, and other plant matter. They will also kill and eat a variety of animals, including beetles, frogs, lizards, snakes, turtles, lambs, and rodents (Boarman and Berry 1995). Over a 24-year period, ravens have increased from 10-fold to 74-fold in some areas of southern California, especially in the heavily urbanized coastal areas and in the Central Valley (Boarman and Berry 1995). Densities are highest along power lines, intermediate along highways, and lowest in open desert areas (see references in Boarman and Berry 1995). Berry (1985) reported high levels of predation on young desert tortoises in areas of high raven density. In Israel, populations of brown-necked raven *(Corvus ruficollis)* have increased dramatically due to increased numbers of garbage dumps and the greater availability of other food resources in expanding agricultural and urban areas (Geffen and Mendelssohn 1997). These authors observed this corvid kill and eat juvenile and adult spur-thighed tortoises *(Testudo graeca)* and Egyptian tortoises *(Testudo kleinmanni)*. Along Russia's Black Sea coast, the endemic subspecies of spur-thighed tortoise *(Testudo graeca nikolskii)* is preyed upon by two species of corvids, the numbers of which are increasing due to tourist development along the coastline. However, these corvids significantly reduce populations of this spur-thighed tortoise subspecies only in areas where fire, associated with development activities, has eliminated much of the dense, native chaparral-like vegetation that covers this subspecies' very restricted range (O. Leontyeva, personal communication). This is an excellent example of habitat disturbance subsidizing an increase in the number of predators. An avian predator recently discovered to eat turtle eggs is the wild turkey *(Meleagris gallopavo)*, a species whose numbers increased threefold in the United States during 1959 to 1990 due to effective wildlife management (Dickson 1995).

The raccoon is a highly generalized, nocturnal predator found in the eastern half of North America (Chapman and Feldhamer 1982). It has been mentioned as a predator of eggs, hatchlings, adults, or some combination for at least 58% of all

Table 1.2

Estimates of hatching success where raccoons were predators

Species and location	Percent survivorship[a]	Source
Caretta caretta		
Florida	29	G. E. Davis and Whiting 1977
South Carolina	3–90	Talbert et al. 1980
South Carolina	67–73	Stancyk et al. 1980
Chelydra serpentina		
Michigan	0–64	Congdon et al. 1994
New Jersey	0	Wilhoft et al. 1979
New York	6	Petokas and Alexander 1980
Quebec	13	C. Robinson and Bider 1988
Chrysemys picta		
Michigan	80	Tinkle et al. 1981
Michigan	59	Snow 1982
Clemmys guttata		
Pennsylvania	58	Ernst 1970
Emydoidea blandingii		
Michigan	22	Congdon et al. 1983
Wisconsin	0	D. A. Ross and Anderson 1990
Graptemys pulchra		
Alabama	5	Shealy 1976
Malaclemys terrapin		
New Jersey	23	Burger 1977

[a]Percent survivorship of nests is given; values are rounded to whole percents.

native North American turtles (Stancyk 1982; Ernst et al. 1994) and is considered by turtle biologists to be the single-most important predator of turtles in North America. Raccoon densities are often high in urban, suburban, and agricultural areas (Chapman and Feldhamer 1982). Rates of predation on turtles can reach extreme proportions. Reported egg and hatching mortality rates attributed primarily to raccoon predation range from 0 to 100% for freshwater turtles and 10 to 97% for loggerhead turtles, the species that nests most frequently on eastern beaches (Table 1.2). The large variation in mortality rates is probably attributable to variation in raccoon densities, although mammal density studies have not been done in conjunction with turtle studies.

Raccoon removal and protection of turtle nests are known to increase turtle survival. Removal of raccoons from a study area in Iowa resulted in substantially increased egg and hatchling success for seven species of turtles (Christiansen and Gallaway 1984). Egg and hatchling mortality increased when raccoons returned to the study area 2 years later. L. L. Smith (1997) found that 43% of hatchling gopher tortoises within protected enclosures survived raccoon predation over a 40-week period in north-central Florida, whereas only 20% of the hatchlings survived predation when unprotected. Removal of generalist predators, such as raccoons, can have unforeseen consequences and is not without controversy, however. The role of native predators in ecosystems and the ecological consequences of their removal should be evaluated before lethal removal methods are employed (Goodrich and Buskirk 1995; Ratnaswamy 1995).

Other species native to North America that have the potential to become subsidized predators and are known to kill and consume turtles or eat their eggs include fish crow *(Corvus ossifragus)*, American crow *(Corvus brachyrhynchos)*, black vulture *(Coragyps atractus)*, bald eagle *(Haliaeetus leucocephalus)*, nine-banded armadillo *(Dasypus novemcinctus)*, red fox, gray fox, eastern spotted skunk, striped skunk, coatimundi *(Nasua narica)*, and Virginia opossum. Most of the information on these species is anecdotal (Ernst et al. 1994). W. S. Clark (1982) reported shells of eight species of freshwater turtles in the nests of bald eagles in eastern North America. This bird is a protected species in the United States that has benefited substantially from years of conservation effort (Fuller et al. 1995). Historical and recent population level effects of predation by bald eagles and other subsidized predators on turtles are unknown.

We hope our overview will stimulate additional evaluations of and reports on these and other potential subsidized turtle predators. Almost all reports and studies of subsidized predation on turtles are from areas that have had a history of development and profound habitat alteration (i.e., North America and the Mediterranean basin). Because many parts of the globe are now undergoing unprecedented development and habitat loss, we anticipate that subsidized predation will become a substantial chelonian conservation issue on a global scale.

DISCUSSION AND CONCLUSIONS

Habitat loss has been documented for many species of turtles, and this single threat continues to be a primary cause of turtle population decline and loss. The related threats of habitat fragmentation and degradation contribute to population declines and extirpation. Most of the available reports, unfortunately, are anecdotal, and few provide a full accounting of the magnitude of the loss. Information on the effects of habitat loss, degradation, and fragmentation on survivorship of juveniles and adults, population age structure, reproductive parameters (clutch size and frequency), and growth seldom appears in the scientific literature. Detailed documentation of these threats is needed so that conservation biologists can evaluate ways to minimize their effects.

Habitat-related problems seldom operate alone; they tend to be synergistic. A descriptive example of these forces acting on a single species is the Mediterranean spur-thighed tortoise. Much of its original habitat has been destroyed and fragmented by agriculture and urban development. The altered habitats in which it survives are isolated and becoming smaller due to changing agricultural practices and overgrazing by camels, cattle, and goats, which degrade and destroy the vegetation needed by this tortoise for food (Lambert 1983, 1984; Highfield and Bayley 1995; Bayley and Highfield 1996). Conservation of this declining species will require, on an international scale, an integrated evaluation of agricultural practices, urban development, economic pressures, human population size and growth, collection for the pet trade, and direct impacts of habitat alteration.

Two aspects of habitat alteration, introduced and subsidized predators, are not usually thought of as habitat-related issues. Introduced species are especially problematic on islands and in certain mainland habitats. Subsidized species have become a problem in the last few decades and promise to affect many turtle populations severely. Both problems are occurring because of the changes the growing human population has made on the landscape. Many introduced species are generalists and become a problem in habitats degraded by human activities. Introduced species often cause habitat alteration through competition and predation, and for some species of turtles introduced species are increasingly the cause of habitat and population decline.

We advocate the control and, wherever possible, extermination of introduced species that harm native habitats and disrupt ecosystems. These organisms have been released into areas in which they did not evolve. Ecosystems with such harmful species will never be completely functional unless these organisms are removed. This view is championed by countries such as Australia, where realization of the magnitude of the problem of introduced species has placed a high societal value on the removal and control of nonnative species. We recognize, of course, that eradication of some introduced species is difficult and near impractical, but we emphasize that every effort should be made to achieve this management goal wherever and whenever possible. Removal of introduced species will be an enormous task in some areas, like the United States and Europe, where concerns for animal rights often outweigh the rights of native plants and animals. We urge chelonian conservationists to take every opportunity to educate the general public, as well as the appropriate decision makers, managers, and government officials, of the severity of the problems caused by introduced species.

Subsidized predators is a relatively new term and not in general use by conservation biologists other than those who work with turtles. We have made a clear distinction in this chapter between introduced and subsidized predators because they present different challenges to turtle conservationists. Control of subsidized predators, such as ravens and raccoons, is complex not only because of the nature of the subsidies (e.g., power lines, landfills and urban garbage, suburban landscape structure, and lack of natural predators), but because these animals are also part of the native fauna. Conservation efforts involving these animals must deal effectively with communicating the issues of human subsidy and its effects upon the ecosystem. Human attitudes can change, as evidenced by the way in which white-tailed deer *(Odocoileus virginianus)* and Canada geese *(Branta canadensis)* are now viewed as pests in much of the urban–suburban eastern United States. Public sentiment toward popular mammals such as raccoons will always present a challenge to control programs. However, removal of raccoons can have a dramatic but essentially untested effect on turtle survival (Christiansen and Gallaway 1984). Eradication efforts such as those used for the removal of introduced species will not be appropriate for subsidized predators because they are usually native species and in some cases have legal protection. Control of these animals in many cases will involve working with local citizens to find ways of lowering the carrying capacity. Such work could include keeping landfills out of particularly vulnerable areas, modifying areas where homeowners temporarily store their garbage, minimizing artificial cover and retreat locations, and providing contraceptive drugs in a safe form to reduce fecundity. Ultimately, controlling subsidized predators is also a complex problem because it involves a myriad of conservation activities in areas not directly supporting turtle populations. We urge chelonian conservation biologists to broaden their horizons when looking at the causes of, and solutions to, problems involving subsidized predators.

Intelligent conservation and management of many turtle populations require an approach that attempts to understand a turtle's use of its habitat, its short-term and long-term activity and movement patterns, and demographic responses to perturbations. A holistic approach to turtle conservation also requires knowledge of the regional distribution of turtle populations and the distribution of their habitats. Effective conservation of turtles will not be achieved by simply knowing where turtles occur. A comprehensive approach must consider the structure of the turtle population (the relative proportion of the various life history stages), the range of threats to turtle populations and their habitats, the spatial arrangement of appropriate habitats, and the relationship of these habitats to the landscape. This approach was adopted by the U.S. Fish and Wildlife Service (USFWS 1997) based on Klemens (1993b), which demonstrated that despite a large increase in sightings of individual bog turtles over a 20-year period, the health and viability of bog turtle populations throughout much of their range had plummeted over this same period (see "Consider Ecological and Population Issues across a Broad Range of Geographical Scales," Klemens, Chapter 10). In the most curious of ironies, a system that was supposed to inform conservation decision making actually worked against conservation, obscuring a rangewide population crash of an endangered species.

Truly effective programs to conserve chelonians require integration of activities and data at several scales, including data on the activities of local human populations. Protection and conservation of turtle populations and species must involve creative biologists who know the animals and their habitats and who are willing to work with local citizens and governments.

There is a strong need for more good science in turtle conservation. We are convinced that conservation efforts on behalf of turtle populations must be conducted by viewing turtles as components of larger systems and with a greater knowledge of the variables in these systems that affect turtle populations. Frazer (1992) pointed out very well that the headstarting of sea turtles, without concurrent efforts to guarantee the health of the marine environment into which they were released, constituted "halfway technology." In a similar fashion, protection of single populations or isolated habitats without consideration of the ecosystems in which they are embedded is just another form of halfway technology that may ultimately doom many turtle species to extinction.

ACKNOWLEDGMENTS
This chapter benefited from comments and critical review by a number of individuals, including Vincent J. Burke, Christopher J. Raithel, and James McDougal. JCM acknowledges Betty B. Tobias and Melanie M. Hillner of the University of Richmond (Virginia) Science Library for help in obtaining references. MWK acknowledges financial support from the Geoffrey Hughes Foundation and the Sweetwater Trust.

2

JOHN THORBJARNARSON,
CYNTHIA J. LAGUEUX, DORENE BOLZE,
MICHAEL W. KLEMENS, AND
ANNE B. MEYLAN

HUMAN USE OF TURTLES

A Worldwide Perspective

Because they are an easily captured and conveniently stored source of protein, turtles have been an important human food item for millennia. To varying degrees, rural people throughout the world depend on turtles and their products to meet subsistence needs; now more and more people are catching turtles to trade or sell them. As the paragons of long-lived animals, many cultures have imbued turtles with special medicinal or religious qualities that have promoted, or in some cases prohibited, their consumption. The collection of turtles to keep or sell as pets is also a significant threat for certain species. Throughout the world increasing pressure is being placed on wild populations of turtles to meet a variety of demands from growing human communities. The effects of human exploitation on wild turtle populations have not been well quantified, but it is clear that in many cases human use is the principal cause of turtle population declines and, in some cases, extinction (Klemens and Thorbjarnarson 1995). Understanding patterns in the human use of turtles is vital for developing rational conservation and management plans for chelonians.

Certainly foremost among the human uses of turtles is their use as food. Harrisson (1962a, b, 1967) reported the discovery of what appeared to be green turtle *(Chelonia mydas)* bones found in excavations in the Niah Caves of Borneo, providing evidence that sea turtles may have been an important food source for early humans. Levels of prehistoric use of turtles are hard to gauge, but there is evidence that exploitation by human populations could have played a role in the extinction of turtles on some islands and in some mainland habitats (Moodie and Van Devender 1979). Relatively recent human colonization of the Mascarene Islands, off

Madagascar, almost certainly caused the extinction of six species of tortoises (Arnold 1980) and local extinction of sea turtles (Frazier 1982a; Hughes 1982).

Of the endangered chelonian taxa listed in the International Union for Conservation of Nature and Natural Resources' *IUCN Amphibia–Reptilia Red Data Book* (Groombridge and Wright 1982), human consumption for food is the principal factor contributing to population declines in 46% of the taxa, and it is a cofactor in an additional 20% (Klemens and Thorbjarnarson 1995). Patterns of human use are frequently seasonal and depend to a large extent on the biology of the targeted species. Some species, such as large river turtles (South American river turtles [*Podocnemis* spp.], the Central American river turtle [*Dermatemys mawii;* Central America and Mexico], the Madagascan big-headed turtle [*Erymnochelys madagascariensis*], the pig-nosed turtle [*Carettochelys insculpta;* New Guinea], and the Indo-Malaysian river terrapin *[Batagur baska],* painted terrapin *[Callagur borneoensis],* Malaysian giant turtle *[Orlita borneensis],* painted roofed turtle *[Kachuga kachuga],* and Burmese roofed turtle *[Kachuga trivittata]*), softshell turtles, and the green turtle, are threatened principally by excessive exploitation for food. Because of their ability to survive extended intervals with minimal care, turtles can be kept for long periods before they are consumed, an attribute of considerable importance where refrigeration is not available. The eggs and adult females of colonial-nesting species are particularly vulnerable to human exploitation, and this vulnerability has been well documented in marine and river turtles worldwide.

Turtles have been, and continue to be, used for many purposes besides food. The commercial trade in highly valued commodities such as tortoiseshell from hawksbill turtles *(Eretmochelys imbricata)* and leather from olive ridley turtles *(Lepidochelys olivacea)* has fueled worldwide hunting of these species. In certain cultures demand for turtles has been associated with medicinal or religious uses. The carapaces of large species have been used for a variety of purposes, including wash basins, roofing material, canoe paddles, and shields.

For centuries, land turtles have been kept as pets around the world, but the pet market exploded after World War II in Europe, the United States, and Japan (HSUS 1994). The bulk of this expanding market was for hatchling aquatic turtles (especially red-eared sliders *[Trachemys scripta elegans]*), with turtle **ranches** (open-cycle operations in which adults, hatchlings, and eggs may be taken from wild populations to augment the captive breeding population) in the United States producing millions of hatchlings annually in the 1960s (Warwick 1986). There has also been an increased demand for a variety of other turtle species for pets, primarily pond turtles and tortoises. Hundreds of thousands of tortoises of several species (spur-thighed tortoise *[Testudo gracea],* Central Asian tortoise *[T. horsfieldii],* and Hermann's tortoise *[T. hermanni]*) were imported into Europe to meet this demand, in addition to smaller numbers of a wide variety of other species (Fitzgerald 1989; Smart and Bride 1993). This trade has caused population declines for widespread species (e.g., the spur-thighed tortoise in Morocco and common box turtle [*Terrapene carolina*] in the United States) as well as local extirpations, such as that suffered by the Egyptian tortoise *(Testudo kleinmanni)* in Egypt (Baha el Din 1994). Concern over the exploding demand for turtles as pets led to the first international controls over the trade in turtles in the 1970s (Fitzgerald 1989), but significant trade continues, in many cases simply shifting from protected to unprotected species.

In this chapter we will summarize information on use of turtles by humans on a regional basis according to two major themes: use for food, medicines, and other products and use as pets. The first section is subdivided into coverage of tortoises and freshwater turtles and then of marine turtles. With few exceptions, most notably marine turtles, little quantitative information is available on levels of exploitation and the effects of exploitation on turtle populations. Also, as the use of turtles by humans is so widespread, it is beyond the scope of this chapter to provide a comprehensive review (see, however, additional discussions in chapters 4 through 7 of this volume). Instead, we concentrate on regional overviews of representative cases. To provide a more detailed account of the human use of certain species, we present a number of case studies. We close by examining some of the biological and cultural factors that affect the exploitation of turtle populations and the implications for management programs based on sustainable use.

USE OF TURTLES FOR FOOD, MEDICINES, AND OTHER PRODUCTS

Tortoises and Freshwater Turtles

EUROPE AND NORTHERN ASIA

The use of turtles as a food resource in Europe and northern Asia is relatively minor. In most areas turtle populations are small, and there is a lack of a cultural tradition for the use of chelonians as food. However, in Bulgaria both the Asia Minor subspecies of the spur-thighed tortoise *(Testudo graeca ibera)* and Hermann's tortoise are consumed, particularly in areas where tortoises are relatively abundant. Before World War I, the collection of tortoises was mostly restricted to an area near Plovdiv. During World War II, the sale of tortoises became more common, and many were sent to Germany or to restaurants in the interior of the country (Sofia, Varna, and Burgas). Some estimates suggest that up to 90% of some local tortoise populations were collected at this time. Today, approximately 35 to 40% of Bulgarians have consumed tortoise. Over the past two decades, blood, meat, eggs, and other products have been used as "cures" for cancer and leukemia (Beshkov 1993).

NORTH AMERICA

Although the consumption of turtles is frequently associated with tropical, developing countries, it is still common in parts of the rural United States. In the early twentieth century, the consumption of diamondback terrapin *(Malaclemys terrapin)* contributed to the species' precipitous decline. In the mid-Atlantic states of Maryland, Virginia, Pennsylvania, and New Jersey the use of snapping turtle *(Chelydra serpentina)* in the preparation of soup is still widespread (Babcock 1919; King 1978; Klemens 1993a). In the southeastern United States the alligator snapping turtle *(Macroclemys temminckii)* is currently threatened by collection for food (Pritchard 1989; Sloan and Lovich 1995). In the 1960s and 1970s, commercial trapping of this species was intense in Mississippi, Georgia, Louisiana, Alabama, and Texas, and the meat was used domestically in a commercially produced turtle soup. Reports indicate that populations in Louisiana have been reduced to a level at which commercial trapping is no longer a viable activity (USFWS 1996a).

A significant trade in red-eared sliders for food exists in the southern United States. Commercial trade in wild-caught specimens for pets began around 1950 and later led to the establishment of commercial ranches (Warwick 1986). Most individuals exported from the United States go to the Far East, but the breakdown between animals being used as food versus sold as pets is unclear. Even small red-eared sliders are reportedly used for stews or fried. In the late 1980s, one turtle ranch estimated that during the collecting season 25,000 to 30,000 wild-caught turtles were sold every 1 to 2 weeks, almost all for human consumption. Most were shipped to California to supply the large Chinese population there. Warwick and Steedman (1988) reported that large numbers of adult turtles are shipped overseas from San Francisco. Shipments included North American softshell turtles *(Apalone* spp.), map turtles *(Graptemys* spp.), and, most commonly, species of sliders *(Trachemys)* and cooters *(Pseudemys)*. Up until about 1980, many turtle ranches purchased adult turtles for resale as food. Thereafter, buyers purchased turtles directly from professional hunters and dealers (Warwick and Steedman 1988). North American softshell turtles are consumed locally in the southern and central United States. Small, live animals and the meat from larger ones are sold to Chinese-American markets or exported, mostly to Japan, Hong Kong, and China. In 1993, 8,107 kg of North American softshell turtle meat were exported from the United States, and in 1994, 34,467 live North American softshell turtles were exported (USFWS 1996b).

In the southeastern United States the use of the gopher tortoise *(Gopherus polyphemus)* as food has a history that stretches back more than 4,000 years. More recently, it was an important food source during the Great Depression of the 1930s (Diemer 1989). Use of this species for food continues (Moler 1992).

SOUTH AND CENTRAL AMERICA AND THE CARIBBEAN

Throughout Central America turtles are frequently used as food. E. O. Moll and Legler (1971) found that in Panama subsistence hunters would harpoon common sliders *(Trachemys scripta)* at night, as they slept at edges of floating grass mats, and collect adult females as they emerged to nest. Mora and Ugalde (1991) reported that eggs and adults of common sliders were hunted by Guatuzo Indians and settlers in the Caño Negro Reserve in northern Costa Rica. Pritchard (1993) reported that a ranching program had been initiated at this site; eggs are collected and incubated, and the hatchlings are sold as pets in San José. Local egg collectors receive 50% of the proceeds. In northern South America the eggs and adults of common sliders are widely sought as food (Pritchard and Trebbau 1984; Rodríguez and Rojas-Suárez 1995). In Haiti the Hispaniolan slider *(Trachemys decorata)* is collected for food and sold in local markets. Consumption of turtle meat by children is believed to keep supernatural beings *(lutgaru)* from drinking the blood of the children (J. Thorbjarnarson, personal observation).

Along the Caribbean coast of Mexico, Belize, and Guatemala, the large Central American river turtle is much sought after as a food item (Alvarez del Toro et al. 1979). In Belize these turtles are collected using a variety of techniques, including harpooning, free diving, and netting, and are principally sold in local markets. Population size and structure and capture rates were used to assess the effects of exploitation on wild populations; data suggested that in the principal harvest areas exploitation levels were not sustainable (Polisar and Horwich 1994; Polisar 1995).

Throughout the Amazon and Orinoco river basins, river turtles (family Pelomedusidae) are preferred food items in riverine communities (Brito and Ferreira 1978). Historic use by indigenous groups throughout the Amazon and Orinoco river basins centered on the largest species, the giant South American river turtle *(Podocnemis expansa)* (N. J. H. Smith 1979; see "Giant South American River Turtle: Change in a Traditional Exploitation System," this chapter). With the depletion of populations of this species, human use has shifted to smaller species, particularly the yellow-spotted Amazon River turtle *(Podocnemis unifilis)*, the red-headed Amazon River turtle *(Podocnemis erythrocephala)*, the six-tubercled Amazon River turtle *(Podocnemis sextuberculata)*, and the big-headed Amazon River turtle *(Peltocephalus dumeriliana)* (Mittermeier 1975; Alho 1985; Ojasti 1995; Thorbjarnarson et al. 1997). In recent years the influx of large numbers of miners to the upper Orinoco region has resulted in considerable impact on local populations of the big-headed Amazon River turtle and other turtles in Venezuela (E. Seplaki, personal communication) as well as the red-headed Amazon River turtle in Colombia (O. Castaño-Mora, personal communication). Turtles continue to be highly valued as food and are widely hunted (Pritchard and Trebbau 1984; O. Castaño-Mora, personal communication; R. Vogt, personal communication).

All four species of South American giant tortoises (*Geochelone* spp.) have a long history of use by humans. Tortoises were an important source of protein in pre-Columbian times and continue to be widely consumed by many indigenous groups (Werner 1978; Mittermeier 1991; Vickers 1991). The widespread presence of *Geochelone* spp. throughout the Lesser Antilles has been attributed in part to dispersal by Amerindians who used them for food (A. Schwartz and Henderson 1991). In addition to their importance as food, tortoises were used ritualistically in some societies, as among the Ka'apor of northeastern Brazil: tortoise meat was traditionally eaten by girls at puberty and by menstruating women (Balée 1985). Since the European colonization of South America, the use of tortoises as food has become extremely seasonal, limited largely to the Holy Week prior to Easter. During this time the Catholic Church prohibits the consumption of meat but conveniently classifies tortoises as fish (Pritchard and Trebbau 1984; Rodríguez and Rojas-Suárez 1995). The collection of tortoises for food can be a particular problem for the red-footed tortoise *(Geochelone carbonaria)* because it frequently uses mixed woodland–savanna habitats, where it can be easily found and collected. The tragic history of the exploitation of the Galápagos tortoise *(Geochelone nigra)* is presented in more detail below as a case study.

AFRICA

Compared with Central and South America, the use of turtles for food is relatively minor in Africa. Pritchard (1979) noted that the large African softshell turtle *(Trionyx triunguis)* is widely used for food, but little is known about this use. Two species of *Cycloderma* and two species of *Cyclanorbis*, all African flapshell turtles, can attain large sizes, but little is known about levels of human exploitation. Pritchard (1979) reported that both species of *Cyclanorbis* were eaten by Bari tribesmen.

The largest African tortoise, the African spurred tortoise *(Geochelone sulcata)*, is not consumed widely because it is found principally in Moslem areas where religious taboos prohibit eating turtle flesh (Broadley 1989b). However, Lambert (1993) reported that in Mali this species was collected for food and for shipment overseas. Small, easily transportable specimens are usually taken within 10 km of villages for consumption. The Yoruba people of southwestern Nigeria use hingeback tortoises (*Kinixys* spp.) for food and medicinal purposes (J. A. Butler and Shitu 1985). The head and intestines are prized as medicine and used to treat cholera and burns and to prevent the death of children due to supernatural causes. Klemens (1992) reported that the pancake tortoise *(Malacochersus tornieri)* is consumed by the Hadza people in the Kidero Mountains of Tanzania. The leopard tortoise

(Geochelone pardalis) of sub-Saharan Africa is commonly used as food (Broadley 1989c; M. W. Klemens, personal observation). In Madagascar consumption of radiated tortoises *(Geochelone radiata)* is prohibited by tribal taboos in some regions, but it is considered a delicacy in urban markets (Juvik 1975; Durrell et al. 1989b).

Large river turtles, which can be an important food source for people in South America and parts of Asia, are not found in most parts of Africa (Iverson 1992a). In Madagascar the Madagascan big-headed turtle is regularly caught in fishing nets set in lakes, and local populations can be rapidly extirpated by fishers (Kuchling and Mittermeier 1993). A major factor contributing to overexploitation is the structure of the habitat: small, shallow, open lakes that are easily fished. Populations appear to be more depleted in areas where seine nets are used as opposed to hoop nets or lines. Subsistence hunting by local communities does not appear to be a problem in the areas surveyed by Kuchling and Mittermeier. Commercial hunting is closely associated with fishing, however, and turtle populations seem more depleted in areas near roads where fish can be marketed fresh as opposed to more remote areas, where fish are salted. Populations of the Madagascan big-headed turtle are reported to be declining as hunting pressure increases due to a growing human population and expanding inland fisheries.

INDIAN SUBCONTINENT

Choudhury and Bhupathy (1993) reported that in India 22 of 26 species of turtles were exploited either commercially or on a subsistence level. Turtles were sold in 12 of 61 markets surveyed, with the principal species offered being softshells: Indian flapshell turtle *(Lissemys punctata),* Indian softshell turtle *(Aspideretes gangeticus),* and Indian peacock softshell turtle *(Aspideretes hurum).* The preference for softshell turtles as food can be related in part to taste, in part to the large size of some species, and in part to the ease of butchering them (E. O. Moll 1990a). The larger softshell species, weighing up to 20 kg (e.g., Indian softshell), are preferred and bring a high price. Other species, such as the crowned river turtle *(Hardella thurjii)* and the three-striped roofed turtle *(Kachuga dhongoka),* are occasionally seen in markets. E. O. Moll (1990a) reported that human consumption of turtles in India is greatest in West Bengal. Howrah (Calcutta) is the major marketing center for turtles from the Ganges and Mahanadi river basins. At this one market, a survey in 1981 and 1982 estimated the annual trade was 50,000 to 75,000 small trionychids (Indian flapshell turtle), 7,000 to 8,000 large trionychids (Indian softshell, Indian peacock softshell, and narrow-headed softshell turtle *[Chitra indica]*), and 1,000 to 1,500 emydids (Vijaya and Manna *in* E. O. Moll 1990a). Softshells were present in 32 of 35 markets or villages where E. O. Moll (1990a) found turtles for sale. The sale of turtles and tortoises is reported to be considerable in the Himalayan foothills of Nepal (Shrestha 1997).

Turtle shells are widely used for medicinal purposes throughout India, usually as a by-product of eating the meat. In Uttar Pradesh turtle shells are sold for approximately US$0.15 each to manufacturers of combs and brushes. (Within this chapter, all monetary amounts are given in U.S. dollars.) Ground turtle shell, particularly that of softshells, is used for the treatment of eye allergies and the meat to relieve the symptoms of tuberculosis (Hanfee 1995). In Assam and West Bengal the consumption of turtle meat is believed to have medicinal value.

In Bangladesh, although the consumption of turtle meat is prohibited under Islamic law, the export of turtles is not (Das 1990). Since the late 1970s, a large export market has developed for two species of large softshell turtles, the Indian softshell and Indian peacock softshell, which are shipped to Hong Kong, Malaysia, South Korea, and Japan (Das 1990). The smaller Indian flapshell turtle is exported to India. Large numbers of animals are kept in holding facilities in Dhaka prior to shipment; the trade peaks during the winter months. Most turtles are exported alive, but meat, eggs, cartilage, and turtle oil are also exported. Das (1990) indicated that in many areas turtle populations still appear to be viable; however, continued, uncontrolled exploitation will threaten the resource. Sarker and Hossain (1997) reported that the value of turtles exported from Bangladesh is in excess of $600,000 annually and wild populations are in rapid decline.

SOUTHERN ASIA

Southern Asia represents the largest regional market for freshwater turtles and tortoises in the world. In part this is due to cultural beliefs regarding the health benefits of eating turtle meat and the use of turtles as medicines. What was once a domestic trade has now become a large-scale business, mostly with mainland China (Jenkins 1995). In some countries (e.g., Thailand and Vietnam) turtle populations appear to have been significantly affected, although a lack of data on the status of turtle populations in these areas hampers detailed analysis. Increased trade with China appears to be related to recent changes in currency convertibility, the rapid economic growth of southern China, and the increased demand for traditional Chinese foods and medicines (Li Wenjun et al. 1996). Softshell turtles are the most widely used group; however, trade in tortoises and emydid turtles is also important. Certain species, particularly the large river turtles, the river and painted terrapins, have been significantly affected by exploitation, traditionally for eggs but increasingly for meat.

Throughout Southeast Asia, high human population densities and habitat loss have severely affected turtle populations. In many areas habitat loss has historically been compounded by exploitation of turtles for subsistence purposes. Over time subsistence use shifted to the commercialization of turtles in local markets. Today, the import and export of turtles for food and medicinal purposes is becoming increasingly important, and a large and complex trade in turtles has emerged. This trade deserves special mention due to the significant impacts it is presumably having on wild populations.

Jenkins (1995) noted that patterns of trade in turtles in Southeast Asia have changed dramatically in recent years, primarily due to increased commercial demand by mainland China. Large numbers of turtles from throughout Indochina are shipped through Vietnam to supply that demand. Within China turtles are used for a wide variety of medicinal purposes and for food. The level of trade is hard to quantify because much of it is illegal, but anecdotal evidence suggests that in many areas turtle populations are severely affected. Softshell turtles are the most sought-after food species, and evidence suggests that this trade is a huge regional business and growing. There are a large number of farms for the Chinese softshell turtle *(Pelodiscus sinensis)* in eastern China, but most turtles sold in restaurants are wild caught because these are larger and less expensive than are farm-reared animals (Cen Jianqiang, personal communication). Most softshell turtles originate from outside China and are sold in markets in southern China (e.g., Yunnan and Guangxi). Aside from the softshells, many other turtle and tortoise species are traded for their shells, which are used for medicinal purposes. Some of the larger river turtles (especially the river and painted terrapins) are widely consumed and vulnerable to overexploitation.

A large regional export market exists in Indochina. In Thailand all native species of softshells have been intensively exploited, and evidence suggests that populations have declined as a result (Jenkins 1995). Thirakhupt and van Dijk (1997) concluded that subsistence use of turtles has severely depleted the populations of most species in unprotected areas of western Thailand. Most collecting now is opportunistic because it is no longer economically viable to hunt specifically for turtles. Within Thailand, however, trade still exists, and the Asiatic softshell turtle *(Amyda cartilaginea)* is the most important species in economic terms. Throughout the country the small-scale trade of turtles for local consumption or to supply restaurants and turtle breeding farms is common. Breeding farms in this region appear to concentrate on the exotic Chinese softshell turtle. In Thailand the trade in other turtle species appears to be much less important than is the trade in softshells. In Myanmar, even though trade in turtles is illegal, they are viewed as an essential part of the diet and are consumed locally or traded over the border in Thailand and China, where native populations are more depleted (Jenkins 1995).

A large and expanding illegal trade in softshells has resulted in turtles being shipped from Laos to Vietnam (Jenkins 1995), with the final destination for many of these turtles being China. Jenkins (1995) reports that in some areas the commercial sale of turtles began as late as 1994. Previously, turtles had been consumed locally. Some of the turtles traded in Vietnam reportedly originate in Cambodia, which has a widespread system of collecting tortoises (particularly the elongated tortoise [Indotestudo elongata]). An estimated 2 to 4 metric tons of turtles are exported daily from Phnom Penh, principally to Vietnam (E. B. Martin and Phipps 1996).

Within Vietnam a highly organized turtle trade exists, involving at least 17 of the 21 known native species. Regional turtle collection points exist throughout the country. Also, changes in the country's economic system have opened Vietnam to foreign markets. Within Vietnam trade passes through Ho Chi Minh City or Hanoi, and an estimated 90% of the turtles go to China. Total trade of all turtle species in Vietnam has been estimated at 200,000 individuals annually but may be much higher (Le Dien Duc and Broad 1995).

In Sumatra softshell turtles are commonly eaten, particularly by ethnic Chinese. Many turtles are also exported. In 1988, 66,500 kg of the Asiatic softshell and 37,000 kg of the Malayan box turtle (Cuora amboinensis) were exported from Sumatra (P. van de Bunt, unpublished). Other freshwater turtles and tortoises are consumed to a much lesser degree (P. van de Bunt, unpublished). Recent reports suggest that the trade of turtles for food is growing and spreading throughout Indonesia (Jenkins 1995).

In Peninsular Malaysia the Asiatic softshell and Malayan box turtle appear to be the most heavily exploited species. Softshell turtle eggs are also eaten when found (Jenkins 1995). Historically, a large industry sprang up around the colonial-nesting sites of river terrapin along the Perak River (E. O. Moll 1987 in Jenkins 1995; E. O. Moll 1989a; see "Habitat Alteration," E. O. Moll and Moll, Chapter 5). Traditional egg harvest rights were owned by the Sultan of Perak, who had guards protect beaches during the nesting season, collected all the eggs from the first two nesting events, and left eggs from the last nesting to hatch naturally. A somewhat similar system was reported for the Sungei Muda and Sungei Kedah Rivers in Kedah State, Malaysia. The population of river terrapin in the Perak apparently did not begin to decline until World War II, when adult river terrapin were killed for food during the Japanese occupation (Siow and Moll 1982). After World War II the system controlling the harvest of eggs changed when permits were sold to egg collectors with the stipulation that one-third of the eggs go to the Sultan and one-third be reburied (E. O. Moll 1987 in Jenkins 1995). However, few eggs were reburied, and by the 1960s annual egg harvests were 20,000 to 30,000 (Siow and Moll 1982), down from a pre–World War II level of 375,000 to 525,000 eggs. Licenses are still issued for collecting, the eggs sold either to the government hatchery (for release) or on the open market (Jenkins 1995). A similar system is in effect for the collection of eggs of painted terrapin from ocean beaches along the east coast of Peninsular Malaysia. In recent times the consumption of river terrapin meat in Peninsular Malaysia has varied along cultural lines. Indigenous groups and

Chinese and Indian ethnic groups eat the meat, whereas the Islamic Malaysians do not (E. O. Moll 1976).

Throughout southern Asia tortoises are also consumed. Das (1986, citing Blyth 1863) reports the Burmese star tortoise *(Geochelone platynota)* was very highly sought after as a food item. Other species, including the Travancore tortoise *(Indotestudo forstenii)*, elongated tortoise, and Asian brown tortoise *(Manouria emys)*, are also important food resources.

AUSTRALIA AND OCEANIA

In Australia the exploitation of turtle populations for food is not considered to be a significant problem, although the pig-nosed turtle is eaten by Aborigines. In New Guinea, however, the greater availability of boats with outboard motors has resulted in increased exploitation of pig-nosed turtle populations for meat and eggs (Georges and Rose 1993). Here, female pig-nosed turtles are collected on nesting beaches, and eggs are located by probing the sand beaches with sticks or spears. In some cases pitfall traps are used to capture adults (Groombridge and Wright 1982). During the non-nesting season, this species is captured by hand, on baited lines, or in basket traps. Harvesting of adults and eggs was considered the principal threat to this species in southern New Guinea, and populations were reported to have declined significantly between 1960 and 1980 (Groombridge and Wright 1982).

In Papua New Guinea the Asian giant softshell turtle *(Pelochelys bibroni)* is consumed on a subsistence basis and sold in local markets. Due to its large size this species is an important dietary item. This species is also highly sought for its carapace, which is used for decorative purposes, including ceremonial masks (Rhodin et al. 1993).

Marine Turtles

A considerable volume of information exists, both historical and recent, on human exploitation of sea turtles. Although there is a substantial body of evidence reflecting the human use of sea turtles, these reports offer only brief snapshots of patterns of exploitation over time. Coverage is most complete since the 1960s.

ATLANTIC OCEAN

Probably the first mention by Europeans of sea turtles as a food source was during the discovery of the Cape Verde Islands in 1456 (Cadamosto 1937 *in* Parsons 1962). In the late 1400s and early 1500s, the French and Portuguese sent those afflicted with leprosy and syphilis to the Cape Verde Islands to be cured by eating fresh turtle meat. In addition, those afflicted with leprosy would rub affected areas of their skin with turtle blood (Simmonds 1885, Fontoura da Costa 1939, and Villiers 1958 cited *in* Parsons 1962). More recently in the Cape Verde Islands, hawks-bills have been exploited for their shells, and stuffed specimens have been sold to tourists (Maigret 1977 *in* Brongersma 1982). In addition, D. Graff (unpublished) reported that eggs of all four species found in the region (olive ridley, green turtle, hawksbill, and leatherback turtle *[Dermochelys coriacea]*) were harvested.

Due to its geographic location between Europe and the West Indies, and its once-large assemblage of nesting and foraging green turtles, Parsons (1962) suggested Bermuda as the site where commercial turtling began. By 1620, however, only 8 years after permanent English settlement, there was so much concern over the extirpation of green turtles that the Bermuda Assembly passed legislation for their protection (Garman 1884 *in* Carr 1952). In spite of this legislation, within 150 years green turtle populations around Bermuda were so depleted that boats sailed to the Bahamas and Ascension Island in search of turtles (Parsons 1962). Carr (1954) suggested that Bermuda was the first-documented green turtle rookery to be extirpated.

In 1671, Bahamian officials prepared legislation that would protect green turtles against high exploitation levels; however, no action was taken (Great Britain Public Record Office 1889, 1893, 1898). By the 1700s, green turtle populations were severely depleted in the region, and boats traveled north to Florida to harvest turtles (Carr 1954).

In the 1660s, the Cayman Islands were settled by English from Jamaica. These fishermen were renowned for their turtling skills, possibly learned from the Miskitu Indians of Nicaragua during previous contact (Parsons 1962). By 1688, 40 boats were engaged in transporting green turtles from the Cayman Islands and south cays of Cuba to Jamaica (Sloane *in* Lewis 1940). Trade between the West Indies and London began in the mid-1700s (Parsons 1962). By 1802, green turtle populations around the Cayman Islands had become so depleted that the islanders took turtles from Cuban waters. When these waters were depleted, Cayman Islanders moved on to the Gulf of Honduras and then to the Miskito Cays of Nicaragua (Lewis 1940; Carr 1954; Parsons 1962). Today, green turtles no longer nest on the Cayman Islands and are rarely found in the surrounding waters.

The documented exploitation of green turtles throughout the Caribbean spans over 400 years. Carr (1954) credited the combined characteristics of the green turtle as making it the single most important resource that opened up exploration into the Caribbean and supported colonization, buccaneering, and naval operations in the region. He describes the species as big, abundant, available, herbivorous, savory, tenacious of life, air breathing, and easy to catch with simple equipment in shallow water or, easier still, on the nesting beaches. The green turtle provided the colonists with a continuous source of readily available meat.

In the eastern United States sea turtle fisheries developed in Florida, Georgia,

Louisiana, Mississippi, North Carolina, Texas, and Virginia (Ingle and Smith 1949; Rebel 1974; Cato et al. 1978). In Florida, Georgia, and the Carolinas turtle eggs, almost exclusively loggerhead turtle *(Caretta caretta)* eggs, were in demand because of their excellent qualities for baking (Caldwell and Carr 1957; Cato et al. 1978). Carr and Ingle (1959) speculated that prior to the arrival of Seminole Indians and Europeans, Florida was the site of large assemblages of nesting green turtles. In the Dry Tortugas, the green turtle rookery was extirpated within 100 years of the initiation of commercial exploitation (King 1982).

Ingle and Smith (1949) reviewed the annual take of turtles from a number of southern states at the onset of the twentieth century. In general, from Texas to North Carolina, the turtle fishery was in decline. In Florida the turtle fishery consisted of the green turtle, Kemp's ridley turtle *(Lepidochelys kempii)*, and loggerhead turtle; the green turtle was the most valuable as a food resource (Caldwell and Carr 1957). By the late 1950s, the Florida sea turtle fishery was confined to the Gulf Coast, and by then only small, immature green turtles were captured, almost entirely for local markets (Caldwell and Carr 1957; Caldwell 1960).

As early as 1519, in the area of the Bay of Campeche along the Atlantic coast of Mexico, Spaniards encountered Indians carrying turtle shell shields (Díaz del Castillo 1908). In 1554, sea turtles were used as a form of payment to the Spaniards (Archivo General de la Nación 1952 *in* Parsons 1962). In recent times Mexico has had one of the largest sea turtle fisheries in the world. Target species were the green turtle and olive ridley on the Pacific coast and the loggerhead and green turtle on the east coast (Cato et al. 1978). The Kemp's ridley is the most endangered of the seven species of sea turtles; one of the principal contributing factors has been the overharvest of eggs (Pritchard and Márquez M. 1973; Ross et al. 1989; Márquez M. 1994).

Along the Atlantic coast of Central America sea turtle eggs are eaten and turtles are hunted for their meat. In the early 1960s, sections of the 35-km nesting beach at Tortuguero, Costa Rica, were leased for egg collection (Parsons 1962). The 1970s decline in nesting females at Tortuguero was attributed to this harvest (Carr 1984).

Miskitu Indians on the Caribbean coast of Nicaragua have long been known for their turtle hunting skills (Parsons 1962). Nietschmann (1973, 1979a) studied patterns of resource use by a Miskitu–Creole community in the late 1960s and early 1970s, documenting changes in Miskitu society as it moved from a subsistence to a cash-based economy. As the international demand for green turtle products increased, turtle hunters sold more of their harvest and returned home with fewer animals to share among family and community members. In one coastal community Nietschmann (1973) documented a 228% increase in the annual turtle harvest and a 1500% increase in the sale of turtles to outside markets, whereas the amount of turtle meat consumed in the community decreased by 14%. From 1969 to 1976, up to 10,000 green turtles were exported annually. During this period the average amount of time it took to capture one turtle increased from two person-days in 1971 to six person-days in 1975 (Nietschmann 1979b, 1982). Although green turtle products are no longer exported from Nicaragua, Miskitu Indians continue to harvest turtles to meet their dietary and monetary needs. From 1985 to 1990, J. Montenegro Jiménez (unpublished) recorded the sale of 16,700 green turtles in the Puerto Cabezas, Nicaragua, market.

Today, a very active Miskitu and Rama Indian and Creole marine turtle fishery continues off the Caribbean coast of Nicaragua (Lagueux 1991, 1998). Green turtles are the focus of the fishery, and the majority of those harvested are large juvenile females. The current annual harvest rate, a minimum of 10,000 green turtles, has probably remained fairly constant since 1991. Hawksbills are taken occasionally, and loggerheads and, rarely, leatherbacks are captured incidentally in nets set for green turtles. Loggerheads and leatherbacks are discarded unconscious or dead when they are captured; loggerheads are sometimes used for lobster or shark bait. Although loggerheads and leatherbacks are sometimes released alive, most turtlers club them unconscious to facilitate their removal from the nets.

INDIAN OCEAN

Less is known about the historical and current human use patterns of sea turtles from the coasts and nearshore areas of continental Africa than about those from any other geographic region. There is, however, evidence of a long history of exploitation of these species.

The decline in the number of green and hawksbill turtles on the Kenyan and Somalian coasts is due to 2,000 years of exploitation and, more recently, coastal development and pollution (Parsons 1962; Frazier 1982b). In Tanzania, Frazier (1982b) reports that sea turtle populations have probably been reduced since prehistory.

Hughes (1973, 1975, 1982) reported that in Madagascar the green turtle, loggerhead, olive ridley, and leatherback are exploited for domestic consumption; only the hawksbill is exploited commercially. From as early as 1613 until the early 1970s, tortoiseshell has been an important export for Madagascar (Decary 1950). Parsons (1972) cited the Red Sea as the source of the tortoiseshell of antiquity. The tortoiseshell trade in the Indian Ocean was well established by the first century (Freeman-Grenville 1962). Frazier (1975) cited overharvest and habitat destruction by humans as the two main causes of the decline of both green and hawksbill turtles in the western Indian Ocean. For example, he estimated that in the early 1970s there were fewer than 5,500 nesting green turtles in the western Indian Ocean. Only 38 years earlier, 12,000 animals were harvested in 1 year from the vicinity of

Aldabra Atoll alone. Sea turtles no longer nest on Mauritius due to human exploitation (Frazier 1982a; Hughes 1982).

Hawksbill and green turtles have been important resources for the inhabitants of the Republic of Seychelles since those islands' discovery in 1609 (Frazier 1982b; Mortimer 1984; Stoddart 1984). As early as the eighteenth century, there was concern expressed over the exploitation of both species (Frazier 1974; Mortimer 1984). Until July 1994, the Turtle Act of 1925 was the basis for management of the turtle harvest in the Seychelles. The focus of the Turtle Act was not protection of turtles but rather establishing ownership rights and compilation of catch statistics. Many changes have been made to the Turtle Act over the years, including the setting of minimum size limits, protection of female turtles and their eggs, seasonal harvest restrictions, and the regulation of local and international trade (Mortimer 1984). In 1994, complete legal protection for all sea turtles and their eggs was imposed under the Wild Animals and Bird Protection Act. In the same year the government began a program to purchase the available stock of hawksbill shell and to assist hawksbill shell artisans in securing alternative forms of employment through compensation and job training (Collie 1995). No legal export of sea turtle products now occurs, although illegal trade may be occurring with Asian markets (J. Mortimer, personal communication).

The general decline in the annual number of hawksbills captured in the Seychelles between 1894 and 1959 reflects a population decline caused by overharvest (Mortimer 1984). For green turtles the most drastic decline began in the early twentieth century with the organized exploitation of the species for **calipee** (the cartilaginous material located between bones of the plastron). Indications that the harvest negatively affected the population were (1) a decrease in numbers harvested, (2) a decline in the size of turtles, (3) a change in the distribution of green turtles throughout the islands (Hornell 1927), and (4) a decline in the number of nesting animals encountered (Hornell 1927; Hirth and Carr 1970; Frazier 1975, 1979; Mortimer 1984, 1985).

Based on a study conducted from 1981 to 1984, Mortimer (1984, 1985, 1988a) concluded that the estimates of green turtle nesting density on Aldabra were more than twice as high as those made by investigators in the 1960s and early 1970s. She attributed the apparent increase to a reduction of human-induced mortality on the nesting grounds, periodic historical decreases in exploitation, and a 6-month-long closed season imposed each year from 1948 to 1962.

There are sea turtle populations in the northwestern Indian Ocean that have not been significantly reduced by exploitation. This could be due, in part, to the large Muslim population in the region. Islamic law prohibits the consumption of turtle meat (but not turtle eggs). There are, however, several areas in the region where this religious prohibition no longer is followed, and some turtle meat is consumed locally (J. P. Ross and Barwani 1982). Throughout the Persian Gulf it is a common practice to render oil from leatherbacks for use in treating wooden boats (J. P. Ross and Barwani 1982). In Iran green turtle eggs are harvested (J. P. Ross and Barwani 1982). From both the Persian Gulf and Red Sea coasts of Saudia Arabia, sea turtles and their eggs are harvested for subsistence use and sale at local markets (J. D. Miller 1989). On the Red Sea coast the turtle penis is considered an aphrodisiac, and thus turtlers select males (J. D. Miller 1989).

In India sea turtles are captured at sea or on the nesting beaches, and their eggs are collected (Kar and Bhaskar 1982). In addition to the use of sea turtles for protein and as a source of income, sea turtle oil is used to caulk boats and to protect wood against boring insects, and salted flipper skin is sometimes used to make shoes (Kar and Bhaskar 1982). The state of Orissa has the largest known concentration of nesting olive ridleys in the world (Mohanty-Hejmadi and Sahoo 1994). In 1975, the Bhitar Kanika Wildlife Sanctuary was established, in part to protect the nesting turtles and their eggs. Prior to 1975, the government sold rights to collect approximately 2 million eggs per year, which were sold locally and regionally (Bustard 1980; Kar and Bhaskar 1982). People along the southeast coast use sea turtle meat and blood to treat certain ailments (Silas and Rajagopalan 1984), and for several decades a green turtle fishery has existed in this area, both for subsistence use and export to Sri Lanka (Silas and Rajagopalan 1984).

In Sri Lanka, historically only green turtles were eaten; other species of sea turtle were released if caught accidentally in fishing nets. However, Frazier (1982a) reported that now all species are eaten, and there is tremendous pressure on nesting turtles. Salm (1975 in Frazier 1982a) estimated that 50,000 people in Sri Lanka were dependent on the turtle fishery. Hawksbills have been extirpated from the waters of the southern part of the country (Frazier 1982a).

PACIFIC OCEAN

In Thailand green, hawksbill, olive ridley, loggerhead, and leatherback turtles have been exploited for their eggs. From 1963 to 1973, there was a 70% decrease in the number of eggs collected annually at one site (Polunin 1975; Settle 1995). Today, the loggerhead is believed to be extirpated, and the other four species are seriously depleted (Polunin 1975; Mortimer 1988b, Settle 1995). Due to Islamic influence, sea turtles have not been harvested in Malaysia for the past 500 years (Hendrickson 1958; Polunin 1975). However, local customs do not prohibit eating sea turtle eggs, which are considered delicacies with aphrodisiac properties (Hendrickson 1958; Siow and Moll 1982). Egg collecting has had particularly drastic consequences on the Rantau Abang leatherback rookery in the state of Terengganu, where Mortimer (1990a) and Chan and Liew (1995) have documented a 98% decrease in nesting. Egg collecting has also been a significant factor in the decline of green turtle and hawksbill nesting on Pulau Redang Island (Mortimer 1991; Limpus 1994).

As early as 1839, it was reported in Sarawak that between 5,000 and 6,000 green turtle eggs were collected daily from Talang Talang Kechil (one of three Sarawak islands known for green turtle nesting); however, the duration of this harvest rate was not reported (Hendrickson 1958; Harrisson 1962a). By the mid-nineteenth century, systematic collection of green turtle eggs began. Sections of beach were leased by the government, and nearly 100% of the eggs were collected (Harrisson 1951, 1962b; Hendrickson 1958). Prior to the nesting season an elaborate ceremony was held so that turtles would return to lay their eggs (Harrisson 1951, 1954–59). In 1941, management of the egg harvest fell under the jurisdiction of a Turtle Board of Management, specifically created to oversee egg collection, a hatchery program, the management of funds produced from the sale of the eggs, and disbursement of the proceeds to Malaysian mosques and charities (Hendrickson 1958; Harrisson 1962b). In spite of a controlled egg harvest, and the implementation of an egg hatchery program, there has been more than a 90% decline in egg production on the three turtle islands of Sarawak since 1927 (Harrisson 1962a, 1962c, 1966, 1967; Chin 1968, 1969, 1970, 1975; G. S. de Silva 1982; Limpus 1994).

In Sabah, hawksbill and green turtle nesting occurs on three main island groups off the coast. Exploitation of turtle eggs began over 50 years ago (G. S. de Silva 1982). From the mid-1950s to the mid-1970s there was a 50% decline in green turtle egg yields (Harrisson 1964, 1966, 1967; G. S. de Silva 1982; Limpus 1994).

Aside from the overharvest of eggs in both Sabah and Sarawak, much of the decline in sea turtle populations has been attributed to exploitation by the Japanese for meat and for turtle soup (Harrisson 1964). In Sabah factors that have resulted in the continued decline of sea turtle populations are (1) the presence of brightly illuminated fishing vessels near the nesting beaches, (2) illegal hunting of turtles, (3) increased powerboat activity off the nesting beaches, (4) dynamiting of fish near turtle rookeries, and (5) the uncontrolled harvesting of large numbers of turtles outside Sabah waters by Filipino and Japanese fishing vessels (G. S. de Silva 1982).

In Indonesia large numbers of adult and juvenile sea turtles are killed for their meat and shell, and thousands of eggs are collected annually from nesting beaches. These activities appear to have had a significant impact on the wild populations (e.g., a more than 80% reduction in the number of green turtle eggs laid from 1934 to 1984; Schulz 1984). Barr (1992) estimated that 7 to 9 million sea turtle eggs are collected annually in Indonesia, essentially 100% of all eggs laid. Most are consumed locally, but an export trade has been reported (Chin 1968).

One of the world's largest green turtle fisheries occurs in southern Bali (Barr 1992; Limpus 1994). Turtles are killed mainly for their meat and are used in religious ceremonies and feasts. Barr (1992) reported that at the peak of the trade over

30,000 sea turtles were brought into Bali every year. By 1950, local sea turtle populations were seriously depleted (Sumertha Nuitja 1974 in Polunin and Sumertha Nuitja 1982). With the depletion of the Bali populations, sea turtles have been taken from a wider area. Limpus (1994) reported an annual harvest of 25,000 animals, mostly large green turtles taken from throughout Indonesia. In addition to being sold for meat, skin, eggs, and bones, green turtles are exploited for their shells, which are used in Jakarta as a furniture veneer and possibly in Chinese medicine (Barr 1992).

In 1953, over 1 million eggs were harvested from the Philippine turtle islands (Parsons 1962). Kajihara (1974 in Polunin 1975) reported that between 1961 and 1972, 5,000 adult hawksbills and 50,000 green turtles were captured annually in the Sulu Sea, and tortoiseshell from approximately 45,000 hawksbills was exported to Japan. From 1951 to 1984 there has been a greater than 75% decline in green turtle egg production from the Philippine turtle islands (Domantay 1953). The population decline is attributed to overharvesting of eggs from 1951 to 1993 (Domantay 1953; Ramirez-de Veyra 1994). Hawksbill populations have also been severely depleted due to overharvest of eggs and the large international demand for tortoiseshell (Ramirez-de Veyra 1994).

For 40 years prior to 1954, green turtles were hunted on Capricorn Reef, Australia, transported to Brisbane, and shipped to England (F. McNeill 1955). A turtle-processing plant located on the west coast of Australia processed meat until 1951. Today, marine turtles are protected in Australia; however, indigenous people in Queensland and Western Australia are allowed to take turtles for their own use (Limpus 1982). It is estimated that 10,000 green turtles are harvested annually from the Torres Straits. Of these, approximately 4,000 are harvested by the Torres Strait Islanders and used locally; the remainder are harvested by Papua New Guineans and sold in their coastal markets (Limpus 1982; Daly 1990). In areas where indigenous communities are located near nesting beaches, nearly 100% of the eggs laid are collected (Limpus 1982).

In Papua New Guinea, marine turtles are second to fish as a source of protein (Spring 1982a). Traditionally, marine turtles were important for feasts, celebrations, and ceremonies, for example, repayment for a bride, funerals, building of a canoe or house, and the birth of a first child. Today, turtle meat plays a role in nontraditional celebrations regarding business, political, and religious activities, with up to 60 turtles used for a feast. Adult female green turtles are preferred over juveniles and males because of their higher fat content (Spring 1982a). Because of overharvesting, turtles are no longer found feeding in offshore areas or nesting on beaches in proximity to villages (Spring 1982b). However, in villages where the residents have become Seventh-Day Adventists (who do not eat turtle meat), an increase has been noticed in turtle populations over 30 to 50 years (Spring 1982a, b). Spring (1982a) attributed the decline of marine turtle populations to the break-down of traditional restraints on catching turtles, the introduction of modern fish-ing methods, the increase in human population, and the change to a cash-based economy in the villages.

Hawksbills are consumed in Papua New Guinea, and the shell is used to make jewelry, combs, and, in some places, bride-price items. In the past, the scutes were used to make everyday household items (Spring 1982a). Entire hawksbill shells are also kept as wall decorations or sold to tourists. Leatherback meat and eggs are usually consumed locally (Spring 1982b).

In the eastern Pacific a large industry developed after 1960 based on hunting sea turtles for their skins. The amount of skin available on a sea turtle is small (it is only removed from the front flippers and underside of the neck), and sea turtle skin is thinner than cowhide and not as durable (Pritchard 1979). Mexico and Ecuador have been the leading exporters of turtle skins and leather, the majority of which was imported by Japan followed by France, Spain, Italy, and the United States (Pritchard 1978; Mack et al. 1982; Milliken and Tokunaga 1987a). Both the olive ridley and the green turtle were hunted for their skin, but the olive ridley's habit of congregating in large aggregations to nest made it an especially easy target.

Along the Pacific coast of Mexico, the commercial exploitation of olive ridleys began in 1961 (Márquez M. et al. 1976; Cato et al. 1978). The government's strategy was to conserve sea turtles through controlled exploitation of the adults and total protection of eggs on the nesting beaches (Pritchard 1978, 1979). How-ever, according to Cato et al. (1978), the marine turtle industry developed in re-sponse to the high prices paid for turtle skin and the discovery of large aggrega-tions of nesting turtles. During the 1960s and 1970s, new markets had developed for sea turtle skin and leather because of the decrease in availability of crocodil-ian skins (Mack 1983; Alvarado et al. 1990). Eggs of all species of sea turtle con-tinued to be collected illegally.

Extremely high levels of exploitation of olive ridleys were reported by Márquez M. et al. (1976), and during the peak period of exploitation, between 1965 and 1969, over 30,000 metric tons of olive ridleys, representing over 775,000 individu-als, were slaughtered. Exploitation was so great that at Piedra de Tlacoyunque, one of only four principal nesting beaches on the Pacific coast of Mexico, the nest-ing aggregation of turtles had been reduced from 30,000 to only a few hundred between 1968 and 1969 (Carr 1972; Pritchard 1979). By the early 1970s, three of the four nesting aggregations of olive ridleys had been destroyed (Carr 1967, 1979; Frazier 1981), and the remaining site, at Playa Escobilla, Oaxaca, was being heavily exploited.

By 1969, Mexican law allowed the exploitation of sea turtles only by those com-panies that used the entire animal (Cahill 1978; Cliffton et al. 1982). Illegal hunting, and legal harvesting with reduced quotas, continued through the 1970s and the 1980s. In 1976, a ban on taking turtles during the nesting season was lifted (Cahill 1978; Cliffton et al. 1982). In 1977, there were between seven and nine fishing cooperatives licensed by the government to harvest up to 1,500 turtles per month. All of the cooperatives sold their catch to one company, Pesquera Industria de Oaxaca (PIOSA) (Cahill 1978). Based on what was legally allowed, Cahill (1978) estimated 40,000 animals were slaughtered between July and September 1977. However, Cliffton et al. (1982) estimated that PIOSA had processed 70,000 animals in 1977, almost twice as many as the legal limit. An estimated 90% of them had been gravid (Cahill 1978; Pritchard 1978; Frazier 1981; Cliffton et al. 1982). During this time olive ridley meat was also smuggled into the United States as Tabasco river turtle. In October 1977 no *arribada* (mass nesting) occurred. In May 1990, Mexico declared a permanent ban on all harvest and trade in sea turtles and their products, and in 1991 Mexico became a signatory to the Convention on International Trade in Endangered Species of Wild Fauna and Flora (CITES 1973; Aridjis 1990; D. A. Rose 1993).

In Mexico green turtles have a long history of exploitation. Nineteenth-century whaling vessels replenished their meat stores with green turtles captured along the Pacific coast of Baja California (Caldwell 1963; Felger and Cliffton 1977), and by the turn of the twentieth century there was an active turtle fishery. Green turtle meat was canned in Baja California and exported to England, and live turtles were shipped to San Francisco. Though the cannery was closed 15 years later, shipments of live turtles to San Francisco continued (E. W. Nelson 1921). By the 1930s, the market for fresh turtle meat in the United States had declined; however, the demand grew in the border towns and cities of Baja California and Sonora. According to Felger and Cliffton (1977), green turtles once nested along the coasts of Nayarit, Sinaloa, southern Sonora, and Baja California. Today only the olive ridley nests in these areas. The increase in human population and subsequent exploitation of nesting females were responsible for the disappearance of these northern Pacific Mexico populations.

Green turtles once nested widely along the southern Pacific coast of Mexico, but today only one major nesting site remains at Colola-Maruata Bay, Michoacán. Here Nahuatl Indian informants reported to Cliffton et al. (1982) that there were 10 to 20 times more nesting green turtles in 1970 than in 1979. Apparently prior to the 1970s, these people disapproved of the wholesale slaughter of green turtles at turtle rookeries because they viewed such slaughter as a threat to their own commercial interests. However, by the early 1970s, they began to sell large numbers of sea turtle eggs.

In 1978, PIOSA began processing green turtles legally harvested by the fishers (Cliffton et al. 1982). At about the same time, a coastal highway was completed that passed adjacent to the two nesting beaches. The highway provided the means to increase the commerce in sea turtle products between the nesting beaches and other states within Mexico. Although in 1979 the Mexican government declared a closed season for the nesting beaches in an attempt to gain control of the green turtle fishery, approximately 3,000 green turtles were illegally taken (Cliffton et al. 1982). In 1980, the government decided to allow a legal take of 250 male green turtles per month between September and December. Cliffton et al. (1982) reported that the attitude of the local fishers toward the green turtle recovery program changed when they were allowed to harvest turtles legally. The local people now participate in protecting the nesting females and respect the established harvest quota.

In Ecuador, olive ridleys were harvested during the 1970s and early 1980s, primarily for their skin but also for their meat. In the 1970s, at least six companies were involved in exporting frozen sea turtle meat for human consumption and salted skin for the leather trade. (Green and Ortiz-Crespo 1982). Some reports state that turtles were often skinned on board ship and the meat discarded (Hurtado G. 1982).

From 1965 to 1987 in Peru the estimated annual harvest (based on an average weight per individual) ranged from less than 100 to more than 22,000 animals (Aranda and Chandler 1989). The harvest most likely represented a combination of green turtles, olive ridleys, and leatherbacks. Aranda and Chandler (1989) reported an increase in the consumption of turtle meat in larger cities, more out of economic necessity than for any particular desire to consume it. Turtle meat is sold in local markets and restaurants, and varnished shells are sold to tourists. Vargas et al. (1994) reported that the marine turtle fishery in Peru was still active. Apparently, the mesh size of nets used to trap turtles has decreased from a 59-cm bar used in 1979 to a 25-cm bar used in the early 1990s (Hays Brown and Brown 1982; Vargas et al. 1994), which may indicate that the animals have decreased in size due to overharvesting.

It is clear that turtles have a long history of exploitation for their meat, eggs, and a variety of by-products. Apart from the well-known cases of the giant tortoises (*Geochelone* spp.) of the Galápagos and islands of the Indian Ocean, and some of the larger river turtles (e.g., the giant South American river turtle and the river terrapin), relatively little is known of the extent or levels of use of most tortoise and freshwater turtle species, either historically or at present. In contrast, there is a great deal of information regarding the exploitation of marine turtle populations. This is undoubtedly due to the exceptional value of marine turtles as both a food source and an item of commerce throughout recent human history. Both historic and recent records document the extraordinary level of take from marine turtle populations around the world. In some regions (e.g., the Caribbean) these intensive levels of exploitation began earlier than in others, corresponding with the beginning of intensive European explorations and colonizations and the resulting expansion of trade activity in these regions. In other parts of the world the use of marine turtles and their eggs remained of a subsistence nature, and only relatively recently (i.e., during the twentieth century) have levels of exploitation increased significantly in some of these areas. During the twentieth century the exploitation of marine turtle populations has increased to unprecedented levels. Experience has shown that the unregulated take of both adult turtles as well as their eggs, whether intentional or otherwise, results ultimately in greatly diminished populations levels.

USE OF TURTLES IN THE PET TRADE

EUROPE AND NORTHERN ASIA

Europe is a major market for both native and exotic species of turtles as pets. Information is most complete for this region and provides us with a picture of the dynamics of the turtle pet trade. Also, concerns about the overexploitation of turtle populations for international pet markets originated in Europe and initiated some of the first controls on the trade. Most detailed information on the European market is limited to the United Kingdom, and these data are mostly limited to CITES statistics (Smart and Bride 1993). Because many countries do not accurately track imports and exports, and do not report illegal activities, CITES information represents the minimum level of trade in these species. Data on the international trade in species not listed under CITES and domestic turtle trade are rarely available.

In the early 1980s, chelonians were a major segment of the reptile trade in the United Kingdom, especially tortoises of the genus *Testudo,* North American box turtles (*Terrapene* spp.), and hatchling red-eared sliders. From 1980 to 1983, imports of tortoises were dominated by just two species: the spur-thighed tortoise (84%, or 131,640) and Hermann's tortoise (14.4%, or 22,500). Since 1984, the European Union has prohibited the importation of these two species as well as the marginated tortoise *(Testudo marginata)* (Fitzgerald 1989; Smart and Bride 1993). The Testudinidae (tortoises) represented almost 70% of all imports of species listed under CITES into the United Kingdom from 1980 to 1989 (Smart and Bride 1993).

Tens of thousands of other, nonlisted species of turtles were also imported into the United Kingdom during the late 1980s. Over 43,000 turtles not listed under CITES were imported from 1986 to 1989, almost one-quarter being common box turtles from the United States (Smart and Bride 1993). The next three most prevalent species were imported in numbers half that of the common box turtle. Emydids dominated nonlisted species imports, though 5,300 kinosternids (three species), 4,000 chelydrids (two species), and almost 3,000 trionychids (two species) were imported as well. In addition, red-eared slider hatchlings were a dominant component of the pet turtle market. Although exact import figures are unknown, some reports suggested as many as 200,000 per year were imported prior to a consumer campaign to discourage their purchase (Rowe 1993).

According to Smart and Bride (1993), a change in the market appears to have occurred during the 1980s, when turtles no longer formed a dominant segment of reptiles listed under CITES that were imported into the United Kingdom. By the early 1990s, only about 10% of the reptile species on dealer lists (in the United Kingdom) were turtles. This change may be attributed partly to the import ban on the main species of turtles traded in the early 1980s. As discussed below, it appears from the limited information on nonlisted species that other turtles, primarily North American box turtle species, were imported in ever-increasing numbers to replace the banned species of *Testudo*.

Two tortoise species, the spur-thighed and Central Asian tortoises, bore the brunt of most of the collecting prior to the 1980s. Populations of the widespread spur-thighed tortoise were greatly affected by the trade, and Lambert (*in* Smart and Bride 1993) found that adult survivorship of spur-thighed tortoises was reduced by 20% in areas with high collection pressure. During the 1970s, Morocco was the main supplier of this species to Europe, and populations of the spur-thighed tortoise were estimated to have been reduced by up to 90%. Morocco banned exports in 1978 when it ratified CITES. From 1980 to 1985, Turkey became the main supplier, exporting at least 263,000 tortoises to Europe. With the European import ban, Turkish exports plummeted. In 1996, Turkey finally set an export quota of zero, after pressure from the CITES Significant Trade Review recommended that all signatories to CITES suspend imports of the species from Turkey until the CITES Secretariat assessed the status of the species and effect of the harvest (USFWS 1996c).

Large numbers of the Central Asian tortoise were exported to Europe in the 1970s and 1980s. In 1967, 43,000 Central Asian tortoises were reported to have been collected in Kazakhstan; this number climbed to over 110,000 per year through the 1970s and was about 150,000 per year in the 1980s (Brushko and Kubykin 1982 *in* Inskipp and Corrigan 1992). Such high collection levels have led to the complete extirpation of the species from large areas. Although in 1984 the former Soviet Union imposed restrictions on the trade of the Central Asian tortoise, in 1989, 52,000 were reported in international trade statistics, mostly from the Soviet Union (Inskipp and Corrigan 1992). The Soviet Union reported exporting 20,000 Central Asian tortoises to France in 1989, a year after the European Union imposed a ban on importation of the species (Inskipp and Corrigan 1992). From 1989 to 1994, the Central Asian tortoise was the species most commonly imported into the United States, predominantly from the Soviet Union (HSUS 1994).

Once the European import bans on species of *Testudo* were in place, trade in turtles switched to other genera. Importations of hinge-back tortoises increased until 1992, when the European Union prohibited imports of this genus (Smart and Bride 1993). However, according to the United Kingdom and United States statistics, imports probably switched more to nonlisted species under CITES, predominantly to North American box turtles (Smart and Bride 1993). The United States began to track nonlisted species in international trade in the late 1980s and reported that from 1990 to 1994 over 100,000 common box turtles were exported, mostly to Europe (Bright 1994 *in* HSUS 1994). This volume of trade is not much lower than the imports of spur-thighed and Central Asian tortoises into Europe in the first four years of the 1980s, indicating that within several years of the *Testudo* ban, trade had shifted to other species and could have reached the same levels by the early 1990s.

NORTH AMERICA

Surveys by the pet industry and veterinary associations have estimated that between 1.5 and 3.2% of the general public in the United States owns a pet turtle. Because many people own more than one turtle, there might be 2.5 million to 15 million pet turtles in the United States alone (HSUS 1994). These surveys also have found that 35% of the owners obtained their turtle(s) from the wild, whereas 50% purchased them from a pet store. Species native to the United States are also collected in large numbers for export to overseas pet markets, predominantly in Europe and the Far East. Analysis of the domestic market is difficult because there are no requirements for the U.S. government to track domestic sales, and it has been only since 1989 that systematic records of turtle imports and exports have been kept.

The United States imports at least 30,000 turtles a year, primarily for sale as pets, and almost all of these are wild caught according to the Humane Society of the United States (1994). According to U.S. statistics, from 1989 to mid-1994 all but one of the most common genera imported were covered by CITES (HSUS 1994). The one exception was the genus *Cuora* (Asian box turtles), with approximately 33,000 imported over the 5-year period. The highest level of trade was found for the Central Asian tortoise, reportedly at over 22,000 animals. The total import volume for the 5-year period was a minimum of 124,000 turtles.

Recently, the United States has imposed import prohibitions on six species based on CITES recommendations: since late 1994 a ban on pancake tortoises and since mid-1995 a ban on leopard tortoises from Tanzania; since mid-1995 bans on three species of hinge-back tortoises from Ghana; and a ban for the first half of 1996 on spur-thighed tortoises from Turkey (USFWS 1994a, 1995a, 1996d). The ban on the spur-thighed tortoise was lifted once Turkey set an export quota of zero, thus making exports illegal (USFWS 1996c).

The sale of captive-hatched red-eared sliders was an economically important business in the southern United States during its peak years in the 1960s (Warwick 1986). Approximately 150 turtle ranches, all stocked from the wild, were supplying the U.S. market with 10 million animals every year. In 1975, the U.S. Food and Drug Administration linked the turtles to the transmission of *Salmonella* bacteria to humans, and the sale of turtles with a carapace less than 10 cm in length was banned (Warwick 1986). In the mid-1980s, some 50 ranches remained in business, supplying approximately 4 to 5 million hatchlings annually to overseas markets, for pets and food. Adults were also sold for food both domestically and internationally, though to a much lesser degree (Warwick 1986; Warwick and Steedman 1988). Just over half of this production went to Europe, with the remainder going to Asian markets. In 1993, South Korea was the single largest importer (over 1.38 million), Italy second, and Japan third (HSUS 1994). Red-eared slider ranches rely on large numbers of wild-caught, gravid females for stocking their facilities. For four ranches Warwick (1986) estimated 9,400 adults were collected annually, which could mean about 100,000 adults removed each year by the entire industry. Warwick and Steedman (1988) referred to anecdotal reports of tenfold decreases in the catch of adults in harvested areas. These operations appear to have caused a decline in local red-eared slider populations.

In the late 1980s and early 1990s, the United States also exported large numbers of other turtles, almost all wild caught. Federal statistics reported about 800,000, whereas a compilation of exporter declaration reports for 2 years during the same period totaled an additional 140,000 for just four of the commonly exported species. Turtles from six different genera constituted the most common exports. With the exception of one genus (*Clemmys,* with approximately 5,000 exported), more than 10,000 individuals of each genus were exported, and several genera had over 100,000 individuals exported (HSUS 1994). At over 300,000, painted turtles *(Chrysemys picta)* topped the export list, and North American box turtles and map turtles averaged around 100,000 each. Over 60,000 North American softshell turtles were exported, followed by 10,000 to nearly 30,000 mud (*Kinosternon* spp.), musk (*Sternotherus* spp.), snapping, and alligator snapping turtles. Export prices of around $5 per turtle indicate that these are not for the high-end pet market, though underreporting the value of exports is a common practice. Only the export price of alligator snapping turtles reached nearly $20 per turtle (HSUS 1996).

There is growing cause for concern that high export levels are negatively affecting wild populations of many of these commonly exported species. The effects of overcollection of North American box turtles for the pet trade, both domestic and international, are exemplary. Once ubiquitous throughout the eastern third of the United States, the common box turtle has declined in the wild due to habitat loss and fragmentation and collection for the pet trade. The U.S. government began tracking exports in the late 1980s. Though it is unknown how many common box turtles are collected for the domestic pet trade, international trade rose dramatically from only 1,000 turtles in 1989 to an average 25,000 annually from 1992 to 1994 (USFWS 1994b). Combined with tens of thousands of ornate box turtles *(Terrapene ornata)*, at least 100,000 North American box turtles of both species were exported in the first half of the 1990s (Bright 1994 *in* HSUS 1994; USFWS 1994b). Following the European ban on imports of species of *Testudo,* these exports were predominantly to Europe. Though both species of North American box turtles were protected in 50% of the political jurisdictions where they occur, many states report extensive illegal trade activity.

Based on a 10-year study of a disjunct population of the ornate box turtle, Doroff and Keith (1990) concluded that the population could not withstand the loss of just one adult per year. Such results suggest that collecting can be a serious threat to wild populations. This study, in conjunction with the rapid increase in exports and the lack of controls on collection, motivated the U.S. federal government to list the genus *Terrapene* on CITES Appendix II in 1994 (USFWS 1994b). Listing on Appendix II requires that all trade be conducted in a manner that will not jeopardize the wild source populations. Although the CITES listing required an assessment that exports would not be detrimental to wild populations, in 1995 the United States approved an export quota of nearly 10,000 North American box turtles based on prior export levels from Louisiana, the only state approved to export this species. Upon reevaluation, and pressure from experts and conservation groups, the 1996 export quota was set to zero; thus, no exports of North American box turtles from the United States are currently allowed (USFWS 1996e).

Demand by collectors, both in the United States and overseas, drives the exploitation, legal and otherwise, of rare species. In 1992, the bog turtle *(Clemmys muhlenbergii)* was transferred from CITES Appendix II to I, thereby prohibiting international trade (USFWS 1992a). This small species has very specific habitat requirements and is found in isolated populations throughout its range. Already suffering from severe habitat loss, collection for the pet trade can easily eradicate entire populations or drastically reduce reproductive potential. In 1992, the wood turtle *(Clemmys insculpta)* was also listed on Appendix II of CITES because of trade that took advantage of the varying levels of protection afforded the species by different states within its range (USFWS 1992b).

SOUTH AND CENTRAL AMERICA AND THE CARIBBEAN

There is only limited information regarding Central and South American turtle species in the international pet trade. Several species of *Geochelone* are exported, primarily to the United States. Three species appear in U.S. import statistics for 1989 to 1994, with two having been imported in the thousands—the South American red-footed tortoise and yellow-footed tortoise *(G. denticulata)*. A CITES review in 1988 highlighted the trade in the Chaco tortoise *(G. chilensis)*. Though this review reported that there was insufficient information to assess whether collection of this species for international trade was a threat, it found that populations in central and northern Argentina suffered marked declines due to this trade in the early 1980s. Tens of thousands were collected annually for both domestic sale and international markets, principally the United States (see Waller 1997).

A CITES review of international trade in the red-footed tortoise reported high trade levels from Guyana (Inskipp and Corrigan 1992). About 8,500 were exported from Guyana between 1983 and 1988, though volumes were erratic (as high as 3,600 one year and less than 200 in another). In 1991, the country set an export quota of 1,000 per year and then instituted a ban on exports before establishing new quotas in 1996. Export quotas that CITES signatory countries must honor are 500 each of red-footed and yellow-footed tortoises. For Suriname, a quota of 630 and 692 was established for each species, respectively (CITES Secretariat 1996). These quotas are about the same as the recent annual imports into the United States alone (HSUS 1994).

AFRICA

The Egyptian tortoise and pancake tortoise (see "Pancake Tortoise: Exploitation for the Pet Trade," this chapter) are prime examples of species for which the demand for pets has driven overexploitation and caused severe population declines. The rarity of other African species, and those endemic to Madagascar, makes individuals worth thousands of dollars in the wildlife trade.

Collection for the pet trade is responsible for the near extirpation of the Egyptian tortoise from Egypt (Baha el Din 1994); only a few small, probably nonviable, populations remain. In the 1970s, Egypt was the main source of this species for Europe (Baha el Din 1994; Egypt 1994). Exports in the mid-1980s were relatively low, probably around 200 annually. In 1990, trade increased due to smuggling of Egyptian tortoises from Libya. Based on visits to Cairo's main wildlife market, Baha el Din (1994) estimated that over 8,000 Egyptian tortoises, almost all from Libya, were sold from 1990 to 1994, 80% domestically and the remainder for export. In 1994, the resurgence in exports, collection pressure, and illegal activity prompted the transfer of the species from Appendix II to I of CITES to buttress the domestic prohibitions with an international ban (Egypt 1994).

Tanzania's lack of control over exports and illegal trade was also a concern in regard to the leopard tortoise and hinge-backed tortoises. A 1992 CITES review concluded that international trade was probably threatening these species in Tanzania (Inskipp and Corrigan 1992). From 1989 to 1994 more than 10,000 leopard tortoises and about 30,000 hinge-back tortoises were imported to one major U.S. market (HSUS 1994).

INDIAN SUBCONTINENT

The Indian pet trade in turtles targets only a few species. Two, the Indian black turtle *(Melanochelys trijuga)* and the Indian roofed turtle *(Kachuga tecta)*, appear to have entered the markets recently but are not commercially exploited on a large scale (Choudhury and Bhupathy 1993). The Indian star tortoise *(Geochelone elegans)* is the most important Indian species in both the domestic and export pet trade. Export markets include Europe, the United States, and major Southeast Asian cities (Choudhury and Bhupathy 1993; HSUS 1994; Jenkins 1995). The annual trade volume in the 1990s was estimated to be around 10,000, but there are no accurate figures because this trade is illegal under Indian law. Animal dealers in many Indian cities reported selling hundreds, and from 1991 to 1992 over 1,500 were seized by authorities in cities in India and in European markets such as Amsterdam.

In Bangladesh the nature of the turtle pet trade is unclear. Das (1990) reported that in the 1980s there was no pet trade in native turtles. However, Jenkins (1995) reported the export of over 1 million kilograms of elongated tortoises from 1991 to 1993. Though this species is commonly exported to the United States and Japan from Southeast Asian countries for the pet market, it is entirely possible that this huge increase in exports from Bangladesh represents animals destined for human consumption, especially if the turtles were exported to China.

SOUTHERN ASIA

There are both local and regional pet markets for turtles in Southeast Asia, and in recent years there has been a rapid growth in the international trade in turtles originating from this region. This expansion has been driven largely by the Chinese markets for turtles, primarily for food and medicine, and it is difficult to determine to what extent the pet trade is involved. In general, hatchlings are sold as pets for export to Europe and the United States. Export of live turtles to China are presumed to be used mostly for food, although a recent market study indicates that demand for pet turtles is growing in southern China and Hong Kong (F. Holland 1996).

The sale of turtles for pets regionally, especially hatchlings, is common. Interestingly, the most popular turtle species sold in pet stores in the larger cities, such as Bangkok and Kuala Lumpur, is the red-eared slider, imported from the United

States (Jenkins 1995). Also popular in the pet trade in these cities is the Indian star tortoise, mostly illegally imported (Jenkins 1995). Pet stores in Peninsular Malaysia commonly sold two native species, the Malayan box turtle and Asiatic softshell turtle (Jenkins 1995). However, it is unclear to what degree these sales are for pets versus human consumption because pet shops in this area sell turtles for both purposes.

Local markets for turtles as pets have also been reported in Vietnam. There is a seasonal business in Tam Dao hill resort in Vinh Phu Province, about 85 km north of Hanoi, where juvenile black-breasted leaf turtles *(Geoemyda spengleri)* are sold to tourists for around $0.05 (Le Dien Duc and Broad 1995). A second native species, the Malayan snail-eating turtle *(Malayemys subtrijuga)*, is extensively traded in Vietnam and commonly sold as pets. It was the most common turtle species recorded in the main wildlife market, Cau Mong, in Ho Chi Minh City (Le Dien Duc and Broad 1995). The juveniles are sold for pets, and the adults are a major export to China, presumably for food and medicine.

Southeast Asian turtles are exploited for the international wildlife trade although they do not appear to be a major component of that market. Reported export statistics of species listed under CITES are not as high as the numbers reported from other regions. This difference could be a reflection of the lack of access to species from this region, which may be changing, as the rising Vietnamese export market indicates. Also, in many cases, it is not clear if turtle exports are for pets or human consumption because they are used for both purposes. In evaluating the existing information, unless specified it was assumed that exports to Western markets were to supply the pet trade and exports to China were for food. In some cases the prices paid for these turtles imply that they are destined for the higher-end pet market in Western or Far Eastern markets.

Several species of Asian box turtles are commonly exported from the region, especially the Malayan box turtle but also the Indochinese box turtle *(Cuora galbinifrons)* and the Chinese three-striped box turtle *(Cuora trifasciata)* in lesser quantities. Because this genus is not listed by CITES, there are few international trade statistics, and those that do exist are rarely species specific. From 1989 to 1994, this genus was the most common import into the United States with almost 33,000 specimens reported (HSUS 1994). The main exporting countries, in descending order, were Indonesia, Malaysia, Thailand, Hong Kong, Philippines, and China, though some of these countries are reexporting nations (based on U.S. federal import statistics supplied by the Humane Society of the United States). Indonesia apparently exported hundreds of thousands of Malayan box turtles annually in the late 1980s, though not all for the pet trade. This export level far exceeds the domestic harvest quota of 10,000 a year set in 1991 (Jenkins 1995).

A variety of Southeast Asian tortoises are also targeted for the pet trade. Indonesia and Malaysia are the primary exporting countries, and the main importing nations are the United States and Japan. The main species exported are the Asian brown tortoise, impressed tortoise *(Manouria impressa),* elongated tortoise, and Travancore tortoise. From 1988 to 1993, Indonesia exported 450 Asian brown tortoises (75% to the United States) and over 1,700 Travancore tortoises (>50% to the United States) (Jenkins 1995). From 1990 to 1993, Malaysia exported 5,400 elongated tortoises, 1,200 Asian brown tortoises, and 800 impressed tortoises, in all cases with approximately two-thirds going to Japan and the remainder to the United States (Jenkins 1995). Most of these animals are for the high-end pet market, with few seen in local markets in Malaysia. Prices of $150–180 for an impressed tortoise and around $100 for an Asian brown tortoise appear to reflect the degree of difficulty in obtaining these species.

A CITES review in 1992 indicated that international trade in the Asian brown tortoise and elongated tortoise from Malaysia was a problem and recommended that Malaysia justify the biological basis of its export levels and undertake a field assessment of both species (Inskipp and Corrigan 1992). Malaysia set 1996 exports at 300 and 1,000, respectively. These numbers were similar to the average annual exports of these species from 1990 to 1993 (CITES Secretariat 1996). These export levels, of animals primarily for the pet trade, are tiny compared with the 1 million kilograms of elongated tortoises exported from Bangladesh during the same period (Jenkins 1995).

Other Southeast Asian turtle species, usually rare ones, are in demand by the pet market as well. This demand is not high but can constitute a major threat to rare or dwindling wild populations. Though Myanmar is not a member of CITES, statistics from CITES signatory countries indicate a pet trade in the endemic Burmese star tortoise. Japan reported importing over 1,000 specimens from 1990 to 1992, even though this species is apparently quite rare in the wild due to local consumption (Jenkins 1995). The narrow-headed softshell is severely depleted in its range in Thailand from habitat loss, pollution, and hunting, and Japanese collectors have put added pressure on the species. Large adults are taken alive and sold for hundreds of U.S. dollars (Jenkins 1995). In Malaysia large river turtles, such as the river terrapin, painted terrapin, and Malaysian giant turtle, are also exported for pets, with adults bringing high prices (Jenkins 1995). International trade in river terrapin has been prohibited by CITES since 1975.

CASE STUDIES

Giant Tortoises: The Overharvesting of Vulnerable Populations

Human-related factors have caused the decline, and in some cases the extinction, of giant tortoises on islands in the Indian and Pacific Oceans. These factors include

high levels of exploitation for food (both commercial and subsistence), the introduction of feral animals that act as predators of eggs and young or competitors
for scarce vegetation, and the modification of habitat associated with growing
human populations. On Madagascar, two species of giant tortoises became extinct
at approximately the same time the island was being settled by humans (Van Denburgh 1914). The Malagasy species *Geochelone grandidieri* is known from subfossil
remains and was also found on many of the oceanic islands that surround Madagascar, such as Réunion, Mauritius, and Rodrigues (Van Denburgh 1914; Pritchard
1979). The world's most critically endangered tortoise, the angonoka *(Geochelone
yniphora),* a Madagascar endemic, was intensively exploited by Arab traders from
the seventeenth to the nineteenth centuries. A small population remains in the
Baly Bay region of northwest Madagascar, where indigenous peoples have a taboo
against eating it (Juvik et al. 1981).

Historically, tortoises on the Seychelles and Mascarene Islands were reported to
be extremely abundant, but populations on most islands were extirpated prior to
1800, and the subgenus *Cylindraspis* was driven to extinction on the Mascarenes
(Stoddart and Peake 1979; Arnold 1980). Reports by early visitors to these islands
comment on the high quality of the turtle meat and oil, which was used as butter (Stoddart and Peake 1979). One account of six voyages to the Mascarenes reports the taking of almost 21,000 tortoises from the islands (Milne Edwards 1874).
The survival of the only remaining population, on Aldabra Atoll, has been attributed to its distance from traditional shipping lanes and the inhospitality of the atoll
for human habitation (Pritchard 1979).

When humans first arrived on the Galápagos Islands, the Galápagos tortoise
was abundant throughout the archipelago. The first recorded visit to the islands
was in 1535 by Fray Tomas de Berlanga, a Spaniard so impressed by the quantity
of tortoises *(galápagos)* that he named the archipelago after them (Van Denburgh
1914). Over the next 350 years, the islands became a convenient stopping point for
all types of ocean travelers in need of replenishing their supplies of water and food.
Van Denburgh (1914) provided a fascinating account of the succession of buccaneers, whalers, fur sealers, and others who left written records of their visits to the
islands. Galápagos tortoises made excellent repast. They were easy to catch, tasty,
and an ideal protein-rich food source easy to store in oceangoing vessels. Animals
were collected alive and would frequently live for months (some reports state tortoises were stored alive in the ship's hold for over 1 year) without food or water.
Tortoise meat was a welcome change from the usual sailors' fare, and oil rendered
from the fat was saved in jars and used instead of butter or shortening (Van Denburgh 1914; Townsend 1925). Even the water in the bladder and pericardium was
consumed (Darwin 1845). Visitors to the archipelago would make short visits, usually to outlying islands, for the purpose of collecting tortoises. Boats arriving from

the north would typically stop at Isla Pinta, and those approaching from the south would frequent Isla Española or Santa María (Pritchard 1979). Hundreds of Galápagos tortoises could be collected at a time. Some reports suggested that medium-sized tortoises (23 to 34 kg) were preferred because they were more easy to carry long distances to the landing beaches yet provided appreciable quantities of meat (Townsend 1925). This preference may have led to a bias in the sex of the animals taken, as tortoises of this size were mostly females. Large tortoises were sometimes killed and their meat taken for immediate consumption (Townsend 1925). Only the extremely rough terrain, the predilection of Galápagos tortoises to inhabit mountainous parts of the islands, and their large size prevented the harvest from having an even more dire effect on tortoise populations.

Few records are available regarding the harvest of Galápagos tortoises by early explorers, buccaneers, seal hunters, and military vessels. British whalers began hunting sperm whales *(Physeter macrocephalus)* in the eastern Pacific in the early 1790s, and the Americans followed within a decade (Creighton 1995). Based on the logs of 79 whaling vessels that made 189 visits to the Galápagos, Townsend (1925) calculated a minimum take of 13,013 tortoises from the islands between 1831 and 1868. He stated that this represented only a small fraction of the overall take; there were in excess of 700 whaling vessels in the North American fleet at one time, and most of these made repeated visits to the Pacific. Based on these figures he estimated (as of the time of his writing) that following 1830 the total harvest by the North American whaling fleet was at least 100,000 Galápagos tortoises.

The first permanent settlement on the Galápagos, composed principally of political prisoners from Ecuador, was established in 1832 on Isla Santa María and was later moved to Isla San Cristóbal. These inhabitants survived principally on tortoise meat (Darwin 1845). The introduction of domestic animals to the Galápagos Islands also adversely affected Galápagos tortoise populations, and by 1838 the number of feral dogs, pigs, goats, and cattle had increased to such a number on Santa María that no Galápagos tortoises were found by a visiting vessel, which had to buy them at six shillings each on Isla San Cristóbal. By 1875, Galápagos tortoises were reported to be extirpated on Santa María, and numbers on three other islands (Española, San Salvador, and Santa Cruz) were reported to be so reduced that hunting had stopped (Van Denburgh 1914). Only on two of the larger islands (Isabela and Pinta) were tortoises still relatively common. Van Denburgh (1914) confirmed the extirpation of Galápagos tortoises on Santa María and Isla Santa Fé in 1905 and reported that many were killed on Isabela for meat and oil.

Galápagos tortoises were also used for the commercial production of oil. A group of hunters killing turtles for oil were reported on Isla San Salvador as early as 1835 (Van Denburgh 1914). Beck (1903) noted that hunting on the south end of Isabela was leading to the rapid decline of one of the last remaining populations. Oil hunters would camp near water holes during the dry season, kill the tortoises, and cut out their fat before moving on to a new site. When sufficient fat was collected it was "tried out" by cooking it in metal pots. Hunters concentrated on large tortoises, which yielded more oil (4 to 11 l each). At one site Beck (1903) reported finding 4.5 kl of oil.

The exploitation of tortoises for food and oil continued through much of the twentieth century. With the growth of the local fishing industry, Galápagos tortoises from many parts of the archipelago were taken for food. The island of Santa Cruz was settled during the 1920s, and in the following decade at least 1,000 to 2,000 tortoises were taken by oil hunters. Tortoises were also hunted for oil by workers at a salt mine on San Salvador. What was reported to be an almost untouched population of Galápagos tortoises on the southern volcanoes of Isabela were almost wiped out by oil-hunting occupants of a prison colony who operated until 1959 (MacFarland et al. 1974). Since 1959 most of the archipelago has been declared a national park, and although human consumption of tortoises has declined, it still continues in some areas (MacFarland et al. 1974; Swingland 1989a).

Giant South American River Turtle: Change in a Traditional Exploitation System

Throughout the Amazon and Orinoco river basins, river turtles (family Pelomedusidae) have long been a preferred food item of riverine communities (Brito and Ferreira 1978; Klemens and Thorbjarnarson 1995). Historic use by indigenous groups throughout the Amazon and Orinoco river basins centered on the largest species, the giant South American river turtle, and its eggs (N. J. H. Smith 1979). Prior to contact with Europeans, peoples living along the Amazon included river turtles as one of their dietary staples. Father Gaspar de Carvajal, who accompanied Francisco de Orellana on his fabled trip across the Andes and down the Amazon in 1541 to 1542, made reference to a large number of villages along the Amazon, and turtles were listed as the most common food item (Medina 1988). It was stated that in one village more than 1,000 turtles were found in enclosures and pools. Throughout the period of European colonization of the Amazon basin, turtles were noted to be an important dietary component of indigenous groups and colonists (Ferreira 1786; La Condamine 1992).

A well-regulated system of exploitation of turtles and their eggs was established on the major nesting beaches of the Amazon. N. J. H. Smith (1979) summarized several historical accounts of turtle exploitation in the vicinity of Itacoaitiara, Brazil. In the late eighteenth century, the giant South American river turtle was reported to be particularly abundant in the area and remained common through at least the 1850s. N. J. H. Smith (1979) estimated that at this time some 48 million eggs were harvested annually along the Amazon in the Río Negro–Río Madeira region. Oil extracted from the eggs was in much demand for use in cooking and as fuel for lamps. At the same time an estimated 2 million turtles were taken annually for food in the state of Amazonas.

The vivid accounts of Bates (1863) indicate that at that time the Brazilian upper Amazon supported large populations of South American river turtles. The giant South American river turtle was intensively exploited at all life stages. Although turtles were captured almost exclusively during the low-water dry season, in the mid-1800s residents of the town of Tefé lived almost year-round on turtle meat because every house in the village was reported to have a pen for holding turtles. Turtles were caught using a variety of techniques (e.g., seine nets and bow and arrow) from inland lakes or along the rivers during the dry season. Bates reported that the smaller yellow-spotted Amazon River turtle was used to a lesser degree at this time, not only because of its smaller size but also because it apparently did not live as long in captivity as did the giant South American river turtle and did not use the forest lagoons as readily as did its larger congener. Little mention was made of the consumption of the smallest of the region's species of *Podocnemis*, the six-tubercled Amazon River turtle, at the time.

In addition to the meat, turtle eggs were a valuable resource. Giant South American river turtles nest colonially during the dry season on elevated sand beaches. In perhaps one of the first attempts to manage the exploitation of a species, the excavation of giant South American river turtle eggs was controlled by Amazonian municipal councils based on a system established by the Portuguese governors more than a century before it was reported by Bates (ca. 1855). Each year the council of Tefé would appoint a commandante to supervise the excavation of eggs at each of four *praia reales* located within 240 km of the village. Sentries were posted at each beach to monitor the nesting of the turtles and protect the beaches from unauthorized egg harvesters. When the turtles had finished nesting, an announcement was made of the date for initiating the excavation of eggs at the nesting beaches. The commandante would record the names of the heads of households and collect a tax from each (the money was used to pay the beach sentinels). On a signal, all participants (Bates reported 400 at one beach) were permitted to begin digging up the eggs, which were tossed into canoes, mashed, and then placed in the sun to allow the oil to rise to the surface. This oil was then skimmed off, purified in copper kettles, and stored in jars. The oil was used for a variety of purposes, the most important being fuel for lamps. Bates estimated that 48 million eggs were destroyed annually in this fashion on the upper Amazon alone. This represents the reproductive output of approximately 400,000 nesting females.

Even during the period that Bates lived in the Brazilian Amazon (1848–1859) he reported that turtles were becoming scarcer and more expensive to purchase. Since that time continued exploitation has reduced populations of both the giant South American river turtle and yellow-spotted Amazon River turtle near Tefé to small numbers of animals of little commercial importance. The third species, the relatively small six-tubercled Amazon River turtle, is the only one still regularly captured in large numbers. These turtles are captured principally using long nets, *malhadeiras*, in bays along the rivers.

A similar chronology of exploitation occurred in the Orinoco River basin (Gumilla 1741; Humboldt 1859; Carvajal 1956; Castro 1986). Prior to the arrival of Europeans, a large indigenous population depended heavily on turtles, particularly the giant South American river turtle. According to accounts by early missionaries, Otomaca Indians organized the exploitation of turtles on the nesting beaches, assigning guards to minimize the disturbance to nesting females. After egg laying was finished, groups of Indians would congregate, some from considerable distances, to harvest the eggs. Aside from organizing the collection of turtles and eggs, this annual event had considerable economic and social importance for it facilitated trade and interaction among groups.

Although eggs, hatchlings, and adult turtles were eaten, the primary harvest was eggs. Throughout the Orinoco, indigenous groups anointed themselves with oil, usually at least twice daily for utilitarian (protection against insects) and social reasons (Gumilla 1741). Painting with dyes that used a turtle oil base was an extremely important part of the lives of all the indigenous groups along the Orinoco. The oil from turtle eggs was also used for cooking and as a hair cream. Enormous quantities of eggs were harvested, and the oil was prepared using methods very similar to those reported for the Brazilian Amazon. During the colonial period, two of the four principal Jesuit missions were established (in the 1740s) adjacent to turtle nesting beaches, and the missionaries took charge of the egg harvest (Castro 1986). According to Humboldt (1859), the Jesuits measured the size of the nesting area and set aside a part not to be harvested. Following the expulsion of the Jesuits in 1767, the Capuchin and Franciscan monks did not employ such an enlightened system, and the entire nesting beach was excavated.

The Europeans brought their own demand for turtle oil, principally as a fuel for lamps. The Capuchin monks reserved a section of the beach for the commons, the oil from which was used by their missionaries throughout southern Venezuela (Castro 1986). The monks, as well as local merchants, also purchased oil from the Indians. The traditional annual festival of Indian groups was soon changed into a seasonal market with buyers coming from all over Venezuela and even Trinidad to buy turtle oil and trade a wide variety of items. In the early 1800s, the Spanish Crown began demanding a tribute from the Indians in the form of oil, which was used for lighting in Angostura, the provincial capital. Following the war of independence, the new republic began poorly organized attempts to tax the production of oil. Rights to collect the oil tax were auctioned off to members of the commercially important families in the nearby town of Caicara. The winner of the auction would use their position for personal financial gain.

Although a decline in the production of eggs in the early 1800s had been noted by Humboldt (1859), enormous quantities of eggs were still taken throughout the nineteenth century. Control of exploitation during this period was spotty and was principally in the form of beach judges nominated by state authorities. Even this limited control seems to have completely broken down during the 1890s, with the large-scale capture and sale of adult females on the nesting beaches. Beginning at this time alternative fuel sources for lamps became available, and the principal objective of the exploitation shifted to the adult females, which were sold for meat. During the twentieth century, the traditional fair and market associated with the annual egg harvest disappeared, and people living along the Orinoco lost the opportunity to earn money from the harvest. However, the dwindling number of turtles was still exploited intensively, focusing almost entirely on nesting females. By 1945, the estimated number of turtles on the two principal nesting beaches was approximately 124,000. Despite attempts to regulate the harvest by the national government, by 1956 this number had been reduced to just over 24,000 animals (Ojasti 1973). In 1962, the sale of the giant South American river turtle was outlawed in Venezuela, but this control measure was largely ineffectual, and in the early 1990s the number of nesting females was just over 1,000 (Licata 1992).

Turtles are still consumed throughout both the Amazon and Orinoco river basins, but instead of providing a basic food staple to riverine communities it is now an expensive, and illegal, delicacy (Alho 1985). In Brazil, a large-scale government-sponsored effort to protect nesting beaches has resulted in a 1200% increase in egg production over the last 13 years (Cantarelli 1997). A more recent small-scale effort has been undertaken in Venezuela but has yet to result in any significant recovery of the population (Licata 1992).

Olive Ridley: An Attempt at Conservation through Controlled Egg Harvest

The controlled harvest and commercialization of olive ridley eggs from the Ostional National Wildlife Refuge on the Nicoya Peninsula of Costa Rica's Pacific coast is an example of a project that is attempting to conserve a natural resource through local use and community participation (Campbell 1998). The beach is the location of one of several large, synchronous nesting emergences *(arribadas)* of the olive ridley worldwide. During the nesting season, *arribadas* tend to occur monthly over a 3- to 4-day period, and thousands of turtles emerge on the beach to lay their eggs (Richard and Hughes 1972).

The egg harvest program at Ostional is based on the premise that a harvest of a portion of the eggs during each *arribada* will not diminish current recruitment levels into the population. The probability that a female will find an area on the beach where another female has not already laid her eggs, and in which a subsequent nesting female will not dig her nest chamber, is density dependent. The more females in an *arribada* the greater the chance that a female will lose her clutch to intraspecific destruction of nests. Nest destruction is caused not only by intra-*arribada* competition for nest space but also by inter-*arribada* competition. The average incubation period for olive ridley eggs is 45 days; however, the monthly *arribadas* result in females from a subsequent *arribada* destroying eggs that have not yet hatched. In addition, a large percentage of egg clutches that survive to term do not hatch. Therefore, allowing the harvest of egg clutches at the beginning of an *arribada* will likely remove egg clutches that have a high probability of being destroyed by subsequent nesting females. Sea turtles and their eggs have been protected in Costa Rica since 1966 (Campbell 1997, 1998). Although sea turtles on the Pacific coast of Costa Rica are not killed for their meat, the demand for eggs of all species remains high.

The residents of Ostional and surrounding communities have harvested eggs for food and as a source of income from this nesting beach for decades (Cornelius 1982). According to Cornelius (1982), olive ridley eggs harvested from Playa Ostional have illegally supplied the Guanacaste Province and Central Highland markets of Costa Rica for years. Since 1971, the other Costa Rican *arribada* beach, Playa Nancite, has been protected through the establishment of Santa Rosa National Park. Nancite is geographically isolated, and as a result human exploitation of olive ridley eggs has probably been minimal (Cornelius et al. 1991).

Residents of Ostional have long advocated for a legalized subsistence and commercial harvest of turtle eggs (Cornelius et al. 1991). In 1977, a controlled harvest of eggs was proposed but subsequently denied (Cornelius 1982). In 1979, the Costa Rican rural guard began to patrol the beach at Ostional to protect the eggs, primarily against human and domestic animal predation (D. Robinson, personal communication *in* Cornelius 1982). In 1980, Cornelius and Robinson (1981, 1982, 1983, 1984, 1985) began a 5-year study to (1) evaluate nest survival and hatching success at both Nancite and Ostional, (2) examine the parameters that influence reproductive success at both sites, and (3) develop a management plan for Ostional. In late 1983, Ostional was declared a National Wildlife Refuge under a new wildlife conservation law. The new law included stricter fines and penalties for the illegal sale of wildlife products but, more importantly, allowed for exceptions to the prohibition on the sale of wildlife products under two conditions. These conditions were that human use would have to be justified through scientific study and a legal community-development association would have to be formed (Cornelius 1985; Cornelius and Robinson 1985; Campbell 1997, 1998).

Scientific support for the egg harvest program was based on a comparison of several parameters associated with egg hatching between Nancite, a rookery with little or no human predation of eggs, and Ostional, a rookery with a well-documented history of human predation. Cornelius et al. (1991) compared Nancite and Ostional and found that (1) Ostional had a significantly greater percentage of nests survive to term, (2) the average hatching rate of successful nests was significantly higher at Ostional, and (3) there was no difference between the percentage of nests that were at least partially successful. However, as Cornelius and Robinson (1985) and Cornelius et al. (1991) have pointed out, differences found between the parameters measured at the two sites could have been a result of other factors, such as variations in available nesting space and possible differences in the length of time during which *arribadas* have occurred at these two sites. Based on their findings, Cornelius and Robinson (Cornelius 1985) proposed an egg harvest program at Ostional as a solution to the then illegal and uncontrolled collection of eggs and the poor socioeconomic conditions of the area. Concerns were expressed that enforcement would be difficult and the legal egg harvest program at Ostional might provide an outlet for the illegal harvest of marine turtle eggs from other rookeries throughout the country. Proponents of the egg harvest program argued that the price of eggs from Ostional would be kept so low that the price of illegal eggs would be undersold. By law, the retail price of an olive ridley egg was not to exceed 50% more than the cost of a chicken egg (Araúz Almengor et al. 1993).

In 1984, Cornelius and Robinson (Cornelius 1985) recommended that (1) the egg harvest should occur during the first 24 hours from the onset of an *arribada* (>200 turtles on the nesting beach), (2) egg harvest for commercial purposes should occur only on the main nesting beach within the refuge, (3) the harvest of eggs from all species of marine turtles within the refuge but outside the main nesting beach should be prohibited, (4) Ostional residents should be allowed to harvest eggs for personal consumption but only from the main nesting beach, and (5) vehicles and horses should be allowed on the beach only during daylight hours. Eggs should be transported from Ostional in sealed (nonreusable) bags to bars and restaurants preapproved by the government for legal sale of eggs from Ostional (Cornelius 1985). All of these recommendations were incorporated into the harvest program.

By 1985, a community-development organization was established to operate the legal harvest of eggs. Since 1987, the organization has been known as the Asociación de Desarrollo Integral de Ostional (ADIO) (Cornelius 1985; Cambpell 1997). Only residents of Ostional are permitted to join the organization, although being a resident does not automatically entitle one to membership (Cornelius 1985). Campbell (1997) found membership requirements and regulations ambiguous.

By law, revenues from the sale of turtle eggs were to be divided between ADIO (80%) and the Costa Rican Departamento de Vida Silvestre (Department of Wildlife) (20%). The community association funds were to be used to pay egg collectors and to fund community-development projects. Government funds were to be used for constructing research facilities at Ostional, hiring biologists and guards, and implementing conservation programs (Cornelius 1985). However, there is no evidence that the government portion of the revenues was ever reinvested back into the egg harvest program or the community (Campbell 1997, 1998).

Since the original agreement, several changes have been made regarding the egg harvest, administration of the program, and distribution of revenues. According to Campbell (1997, 1998), the egg harvest period has increased from a 24-hour period to a 36-hour period from the onset of an *arribada,* and the 36-hour harvest period applies only during the wet-season months (May to December). There are no restrictions on egg collection during the dry-season *arribadas,* when neonate production is extremely low. The biologist at Ostional is now employed by ADIO, which now receives only 60% of the proceeds of the egg harvest. The government, represented by the Ministerio de Agricultura y Ganadera (Ministry of Agriculture and Livestock), now receives 40% of revenues.

According to Campbell (1997), the egg harvest is well organized. Eggs are packaged in plastic bags, sealed, and stamped to identify them as legally harvested from Playa Ostional. According to Araúz Almengor et al. (1993), the community initially distributed the eggs in the local market; however, because profits were low ADIO contracted a national distributor from 1989 at least through 1991. Campbell (1997) reported that eggs are now distributed by people from the community who are selected yearly to work a specified route. Theoretically, the selection of community sellers is based on economic need; however, there are complaints of favoritism. Drivers are also selected on a yearly basis, and theoretically the positions are rotated among community members. However, because drivers must own a vehicle or at least have access to one, the same people from year to year are selected. Conflicts often develop among the sellers because they earn their income based on the number of eggs sold. If illegally harvested eggs have met the market demand or the buyers on their route do not purchase as many eggs as usual, the sellers may encroach on other routes to sell their supply (Campbell 1997).

Capital improvements to the community through the sale of olive ridley eggs have been many, including (1) structural improvements to the school, (2) construction of a community center, (3) improvements to the soccer field, (4) construction of a basketball and volleyball court, (5) road improvements, and (6) electrification of the community. Many socioeconomic problems, however, still remain (Ordoñez et al. 1994; Ordoñez and Ballestero 1994; Campbell 1997, 1998; A. Chaves, personal communication).

The critical question that remains to be answered about the Ostional project is whether the egg harvest is sustainable. At present, this is unknown. Compared with the numerous socioeconomic reviews and evaluations, very little information has become available regarding the status of the nesting population since the studies of Cornelius and Robinson in the early 1980s. Only recently have methods been developed for even counting the number of females that nest during an *arribada* (Gates et al. 1996; Valverde and Gates 1999). Without an accurate record of the number of females nesting annually at Ostional over time (long enough for hatchlings that were produced since the harvest began to return to nest), recruitment rates, and thus sustainability, cannot be evaluated. Unfortunately, knowledge of the demography of olive ridley populations currently lags behind that of most other marine turtles. Similarly, the life history of olive ridleys is poorly understood, and thus rates of survival of the various life history stages remain unknown. A sustainable harvest will require a thorough understanding of all the mortality factors that affect the population both at the nesting beach and on distant foraging grounds (e.g., pelagic fisheries), and these factors are constantly changing.

Although sustainability is not known, it seems clear that the Ostional project confers better protection to the nesting population than would otherwise exist. Marine turtle eggs are being heavily exploited on the Pacific coast of Costa Rica, as they are elsewhere along the Pacific coast of Central America. What has not been evaluated—and what is of vital interest to marine turtle conservation on a broader scale—is the effect the legal Ostional egg trade has on the illegal trade of eggs of other olive ridleys and other marine turtles that nest in Costa Rica. The eggs of olive ridleys cannot be reliably distinguished from those of hawksbills and green turtles on the basis of size, and once the Ostional labels are removed, all appear the same. To enforce the regulations governing which eggs can be legally sold in the thousands of bars and street markets seems a daunting task. Illegal egg harvest has escalated on the Atlantic coast of Costa Rica in recent years, affecting both green turtles and leatherbacks. Whether the legal Ostional trade has stimulated trade in general or has reduced it by saturating at least a part of the booming market for eggs has never been evaluated.

The Ostional egg harvest represents an interesting and useful experiment in community participation in resource conservation, but its utility as a model for use with other marine turtle species is extremely limited. Only the Kemp's ridley and olive ridley nest in *arribadas,* and the Kemp's ridley is now restricted to one major breeding aggregation in the entire world. The other species almost never nest in the densities that occur in *arribadas,* and therefore the situation that exists at Ostional—in which eggs are harvested that would otherwise be destroyed—does not exist. For all other species, harvesting would remove viable nests and could only be presumed to decrease recruitment rates.

Pancake Tortoise: Exploitation for the Pet Trade

The pancake tortoise is distributed in patches of rocky savanna–woodland habitat from central, possibly even northern, Kenya south to central Tanzania. When the first specimens of this bizarre, flattened tortoise became known to science in the 1920s, experts speculated that the tortoises were deformed or injured individuals of one of the known species of East African tortoises. Subsequent studies have shown that the pancake tortoise is a highly specialized land tortoise for which the bony elements of the shell have become reduced as an adaptation to living in rock fissures. The species is small, usually no more than 15 to 18 cm long, 10 cm wide, and 2.5 cm or less in height. Apart from being flat, the shell is soft and flexible, offering little protection from birds of prey, ground hornbills, secretary birds (*Sagittarius serpentarius*), or small carnivores, particularly genets (*Genetta* spp.) and mongooses. The pancake tortoise depends totally upon its crevice retreat for protection from predation and desiccation in the hot sun.

When a pancake tortoise ventures outside its protective crevice to eat grasses and succulents, it remains ever vigilant, moving rapidly back into its retreat at the slightest hint of danger. When threatened in its crevice, the animal withdraws its legs tightly into its shell, causing the soft central part of the plastron to balloon out, increasing the animal's height and wedging it between the top and the bottom of the rock fissure. Availability of suitable crevices may be the single most important factor limiting the size of pancake tortoise populations. For example, within each habitat surveyed, the number of crevices of suitable depth and dimensions was only a small percentage of all the available natural crevices (Klemens and Moll 1995; D. Moll and Klemens 1996).

During the 1980s, pancake tortoises began to appear with increasing frequency in the wildlife trade, finding their way into pet shops across the United States, Europe, and Japan. Although the tortoises were initially quite expensive, over time, as the numbers of pancake tortoises in the trade increased into the thousands, prices began to drop dramatically from a high of perhaps $300 to as low as $30 per tortoise. And when the pancake tortoises became inexpensive, they were purchased as novelty items by people who lacked both the knowledge and the commitment to care for them properly.

Pancake tortoises have been listed on Appendix II of CITES since 1975. However, as there was little information on this species' geographic distribution, population size, life history, and ecology, the effects of trade could not be properly evaluated. In 1991, Dutch customs officers at Schiphol Airport intercepted a shipment of several hundred pancake tortoises bound for the United States (see more at "Repatriation, Relocation, and Release Programs," McDougal, Chapter 7). The crate was packed so tightly that many of the tortoises were crushed by the weight of other tortoises on top of them. This well-publicized seizure helped focus attention on the trade in tortoises and other reptile species originating from Tanzania. The CITES Animals Committee added the pancake tortoise to its list of significantly traded species that are listed on Appendix II and urged a complete assessment of the trade and its impact on wild pancake tortoise populations.

In 1992, a study was initiated to investigate the scope and impact of trade on Tanzania's wild populations of pancake tortoises (Klemens and Moll 1995) and to gather data on the ecology and life history of this rupicolous species (D. Moll and Klemens 1996). It was discovered that accessible areas in north Tanzania had been severely depleted. Pancake tortoises had become scarce, even eliminated, at sites where collectors had previously been active. Habitats lying within easy access of the road between Arusha and Dodoma had been heavily collected, and populations there were in serious jeopardy. Collectors had destroyed rock outcrops and crevices, using car jacks to pry the rocks apart to reach the reptiles. Collectors had even poached pancake tortoises by means of this technique within Tarangire National Park. Collectors readily admitted that pancake tortoises were becoming more difficult to find because they had taken so many. To compound this tragedy, the money that the collectors received for their efforts was minimal, often barely enough to buy a few soft drinks or cigarettes.

These disturbing findings were reported to the Tanzanian government. Officials were informed that in less than 10 years of intensive collection, the pancake tortoise had become severely threatened throughout much of its range in Tanzania. Three options for the management of this species were presented to the government: (1) continued uncontrolled trade, which would deplete as-yet-untapped pancake tortoise populations while reaping low economic returns, particularly at the local level, (2) strictly regulated trade coupled with a substantial export tariff, perhaps providing the capital and the incentive to manage and conserve the country's pancake tortoise populations, though possibly encouraging illegal trade, and (3) the option the Tanzania government decided to adopt, a moratorium on pancake tortoise trade exports. Because this moratorium must be enforced by the more than 100 countries that are signatories to CITES, controlling the trade became a joint effort, not solely the responsibility of Tanzania. The importing countries, primarily the United States, were now legally mandated to refuse entry of pancake tortoise shipments originating from Tanzania. The trade moratorium is now entering its fifth year, which is good news indeed for the pancake tortoise.

However, in 1997 new attempts were made to revive the pancake tortoise trade by means of exports destined for the United States "originating" from northern Zambia, far outside the range and natural habitat of this species. Apparently, pancake tortoises are now being smuggled across the southern border of Tanzania for reexport from adjoining countries. The "laundering" of Appendix II reptiles, through extralimital countries, presents new challenges to the enforcement of CITES and other laws that protect wildlife from exploitation.

DISCUSSION

It is abundantly clear that the human use of turtles is widespread and can have significant effects on the status of wild populations. The presence of large numbers of easily harvested turtles has probably played a significant role in the history of human enterprise and endeavor. Pre-Columbian and early European populations in the Amazon and Orinoco river basins subsisted to a large degree on turtle meat. Carr (1954) commented that the exploration and colonization of the Caribbean was, to a large degree, facilitated by protein availability in the form of sea turtles. Long ocean voyages were made possible by stocking giant tortoises from the Galápagos and islands in the western Indian Ocean. The use of turtles for medicinal purposes also has a long history, which has been exacerbated in recent decades by increased long-distance trade, a result of trends in the globalization of the world economy. An international market for turtles as pets is a relatively recent development, but for certain species this trade has had major impacts on wild populations.

The collection of both eggs and adult turtles has had drastic effects on turtle populations worldwide. In some areas the exploitation of turtles has resulted in the extirpation of local populations; in some cases, exploitation has resulted in extinction. Within historical times, populations of sea turtles in the Cayman Islands, Bermuda, the Dry Tortugas, and the Mascarenes have been extirpated. Tortoises in the Mascarenes were also extirpated soon after humans colonized the islands. Although not as significant globally as the exploitation of turtle populations for food or medicine, the pet trade is a major, if not the primary, threat to certain species (see the case study regarding the pancake tortoise). The effects of overcollection are amplified in rare species that have specialized habitats, like the pancake tortoise (Klemens and Moll 1995) and bog turtle (USFWS 1992a).

The exploitation of turtles has been well documented; however, the effects of human use on wild populations is difficult to evaluate in a quantitative fashion (see Doroff and Keith 1990). Much available information concerns colonial-nesting species such as sea turtles and certain freshwater species such as the giant South

American river turtle and river terrapin. For these species the number of nesting females can be used as an index of population size, and data for many of these species demonstrate precipitous population declines. It is also true that predictable patterns of nesting in time and space make these same species extremely vulnerable to human exploitation. Nevertheless, many biological and human factors play roles in determining which species are more likely to be exploited and how this exploitation will affect wild populations.

Biological Factors in Turtle Exploitation

Several features of the biology of turtles have facilitated their exploitation by humans. Like all reptiles, turtles have low metabolic rates and reduced energy requirements when compared with endotherms (Pough 1980). As a result, turtles have high production efficiencies and are often found at much higher biomass levels than are mammals or birds (Iverson 1982). The ecological consequences of reptilian metabolism play an important role in determining the number and rate at which turtles can be taken sustainedly. Another consequence of their physiology is that turtles are able to survive long periods without food and, in some cases, water. Before the advent of refrigeration, turtles were one of the few animals that could be collected during periods of seasonal abundance and kept alive for long periods with minimal care. In many rural areas this is still an important factor in the exploitation of turtles.

Although there is considerable variation within the group, turtles are characterized by a coevolved suite of life history characteristics that typically include slow, indeterminate growth, delayed sexual maturity, and a long reproductive life span (Gibbons 1987; Wilbur and Morin 1988; Congdon et al. 1993; see "Demographic Issues in Turtle Conservation," Gibbs and Amato, Chapter 8). These life history traits place biological constraints on the levels of harvest that turtle populations can sustain. Recent studies of a number of North American species have drawn attention to the consequences of longevity and delayed reproduction (Doroff and Keith 1990; Congdon et al. 1993). These analyses have demonstrated that turtle populations are very sensitive to increases in mortality of adults and large juveniles (Crouse et al. 1987; Congdon et al. 1993). Chronic reduction in the survivorship of adult turtles would require an increase in the survivorship of eggs or juveniles or density-dependent increases in fecundity (by increasing clutch size or clutch frequency or decreasing age at sexual maturity) to maintain a stable population size (Congdon et al. 1994). However, even significant increases in the survivorship of eggs and juveniles are unlikely to compensate for increases in mortality of adults (Heppell et al. 1996). Given the need for high rates of survivorship in large juvenile and adult life stages, these studies have questioned whether any level of turtle harvest can be sustainable.

Another general attribute of turtle life histories is high rates of egg and hatchling mortality (Wilbur and Morin 1988; Iverson 1991a). This suggests that harvesting systems based on the collection of eggs are less likely to have negative impacts on the population than those based on killing adults. In fact, many of the long-term, traditional turtle exploitation systems were based on harvesting eggs (e.g., see the case study regarding the giant South American river turtle). However, although some of these traditional systems existed over a period of centuries, there is little evidence that they were sustainable. In fact, in the case of the giant South American river turtle there are strong indications that egg collecting was so intense it significantly reduced populations of this species. Although this system was certainly less damaging than the large-scale collection of nesting females (which occurred later and devastated populations), some early accounts decried the shortsightedness of egg exploitation. What is clear is that the growth in demand for eggs associated with European colonization, the local shift to a cash-based economy, and the taking of nesting females doomed the traditional system.

Societal Factors in Turtle Exploitation

Religious beliefs and cultural factors play an important role in shaping the patterns of human exploitation of turtles. In some cases these factors have played a key role in limiting the consumption of turtles, whereas in others they have promoted it. For example, throughout Central and South America turtles are classified as fish by the Roman Catholic Church, creating a traditional seasonal increase in the consumption of chelonians during the week before Easter when eating meat is discouraged. In Papua New Guinea, villagers who have become Seventh Day Adventists have stopped eating turtles and report increases in nesting sea turtles. The unsubstantiated belief that turtle eggs act as an aphrodisiac has led to their widespread consumption in bars throughout Central America. Religious considerations prevent higher castes (e.g., Brahmins) from eating turtles in Nepal (Shrestha 1997). The prohibition on the consumption of turtle meat by Islam has certainly been an important factor in reducing the exploitation of turtles in parts of India and the Middle East, as well as in Bangladesh, Indonesia, and Malaysia. Despite intense human population pressures, freshwater turtles are still abundant in Bangladesh, a fact that Das (1990) attributes to 90% of the population being Muslim. Nevertheless, no religious restrictions are placed on eating turtle eggs or catching and selling turtles domestically or for export. In recent years exports have increased to meet changing regional patterns of the consumption of turtles for both food and medicine.

The widespread consumption of turtles in China and Southeast Asia is intimately tied to cultural beliefs (Jenkins 1995). In China turtles are classified as a "hot" food that strengthens the body during the winter. Eggs are believed to be aphrodisiacs, and turtle blood is thought to provide an energy boost. The shells of turtles are believed to have a wide variety of medicinal uses in Chinese cultures (Jenkins 1995). The carapace of softshell turtles is used to produce *bie jia*, which is used in a variety of forms including powders and jellies, to treat problems of the kidney, spleen, and liver (Jenkins 1995). The plastron of hard-shelled species is used to produce *gui ban* for treatment of the heart, liver, and kidneys. Recent changes in regional economic systems have also resulted in the increased ability of the Chinese to purchase imported turtles, and this expanded market has important implications for the conservation of chelonian biodiversity, particularly in southern Asia.

Aside from cultural influences, common patterns in the human use of natural resources have tended to result in overexploitation. As human populations have grown, turtle populations have decreased due to a variety of human-related factors, principally habitat destruction and overexploitation. With time, the general pattern of exploitation has been one of growing demand and dwindling supply of a resource that is typically considered to be open, or accessible, to all members of the community. The common ownership of a resource such as turtles makes managed use problematic, as perhaps has been best promulgated by Hardin's (1968) *The Tragedy of the Commons.* Hardin's basic thesis is that as a collectively owned resource begins to decline due to overexploitation, individuals will compete for a larger share of the dwindling supply, and the ultimate demise of the stock can be seen as a logical result. In the example of a community harvesting turtles from a lake, each person receives a direct benefit from each turtle captured and suffers delayed costs from the deterioration of the turtle population. As the number of turtles declines, each person is motivated to put more effort into capturing turtles because each one obtains a direct benefit from the turtles caught but bears only a portion of the cost of the declining population, which is shared among neighbors. Hardin (1968) summarized by stating, "Ruin is the destination towards which all men rush, each pursuing his own best interest in a society that believes in the freedom of the commons."

However, this argument ignores the presence of cultural values and social institutions and their role in regulating the use of common property (McGoodwin 1990; Gadgil et al. 1993). For turtles, there is some evidence of cultural controls in traditional harvest systems. The historic cases of green turtles in Sarawak and river terrapin in Malaysia, and the contemporary example of olive ridley eggs in Costa Rica, are instances in which attempts have been made to regulate harvests. Conversely, the case of regulated South American river turtle egg harvests in the Brazilian Amazon appears to have been specifically designed to maximize the number of eggs collected, with no regard whatsoever to the concept of sustainability.

Cultural and economic changes have resulted in the loss of traditional systems. Inhabitants throughout the central Pacific Ocean have harvested marine turtles for thousands of years, and green and hawksbill turtles supply the basic needs of these communities (Daly 1990). Turtle hunting helped to pass on traditional knowledge that has formed the basis of rituals, taboos, and ownership rights that regulated the levels of harvest in the past. The breakdown of traditional practices was a result of the introduction of cash-based economies, the decline of traditional authority, and the imposition of colonial laws and practices (Balazs 1982a; M. A. McCoy 1982), and marine turtle populations are reported to have declined within historical times (Balazs 1982a). M. A. McCoy (1982) cited an increase in human populations and the preference for modern boats and motors as other factors that have contributed to the decline in marine turtle populations, and he emphasized the need for a conservation system to replace the traditional taboos and social restrictions. Another example is the Kiwai people of Papua New Guinea, who hunt green turtles for ceremonial uses and for trade. Prior to the transformation to a cash-based economy, the Kiwai people viewed green turtle meat as a resource to be shared among family and kin relations and to establish reciprocal obligations. With a cash-based economy, green turtles are now viewed as individual property and consideration of cultural obligations are ignored (Eley 1989).

Options for Management of Turtles

With increasing pressures being brought to bear on turtle populations, and the loss of traditional systems that may have regulated harvest levels in the past, new ways must be found to manage turtle populations. Solutions to the overharvest of common resources are usually framed in two major contexts, these being governmental regulation of exploitation or privatization (Ostrom 1990; Hardin 1994). Both approaches can offer substantial pitfalls, including the failure to take local social institutions into consideration when designing management programs and the assumption that privatization will lead to sustainable management.

Instances of governmental regulation of turtle exploitation are usually limited to total prohibitions, which in many cases are unenforceable. Bermuda is an example of what was perhaps the first-ever protective legislation for a turtle (in 1620), as well as the first case of a green turtle rookery to be extirpated. In most instances, restrictions can reduce large-scale commercial harvests, but subsistence consumption and small-scale commercial sales continue. Virtually all documented attempts to regulate a managed harvest have been related to the collection of eggs on traditional nesting beaches. However, due to the demographic importance of adults, protective measures or managed collection schemes involving eggs can be ineffective if high rates of human-related adult mortality are not addressed (Crouse et al. 1987; Heppell et al. 1996). Attempts by the Mexican government to regulate the commercial harvest of olive ridleys by permitting the harvest of adults while protecting nesting beaches were a dismal failure. In some cases, exploitation is permitted for subsistence purposes by certain cultural groups. In Australia, a national ban on killing sea turtles is in place with the proviso that aboriginal groups can still legally harvest them for subsistence. If harvest levels are low enough, offtake may be sustainable, but there are no cases known for which enough information is available on the population ecology of the turtles and exploitation levels to allow the evaluation of the sustainability of the harvest. At the international level, CITES and national trade restrictions on turtles in the pet trade have shifted market demand from one species to another, where similarly unsustainable levels of exploitation occur.

For some, privatization is a means of eliminating some of the perceived problems with common property resources. However, the managed harvest must have enough built-in controls to ensure that harvest levels are sustainable and that the benefits of the harvest accrue to a wide segment of society. In the case of the giant South American river turtle in Venezuela (see the case study above), control of the resource was managed by the upper socioeconomic strata of one town, principally for their own financial gain (Castro 1986). This led to a situation described by May (1992) as the "tragedy of the non-commons," where "resources have been privatized so as to curtail benefits obtained through common management, and those excluded are denied compensation due to lack of either bargaining power or of legal legitimization of property rights." The program developed to manage the giant South American river turtle population in Venezuela in the eighteenth and nineteenth centuries was loosely based on the pre-Columbian system but was controlled by individuals removed from the resource. This resulted in the economic marginalization of the local communities, which had traditionally managed the turtle beaches. Nonetheless, approaches like the one at Ostional (see the case study above) offer hope that at least under certain circumstances community institutions, governmental organizations, and scientists can work together to discuss the need to limit harvest levels. Although the case of harvesting eggs from *arribadas* of ridley turtles is perhaps the most extreme example of this, it can provide useful lessons as to how, and how not, to implement community-based egg collection programs. It is clear, however, that the situations most amenable to the development of managed-use programs are those involving egg collection at mass-nesting events. Whether programs can be developed for the sustainable use of eggs of solitary nesters, the collection of live animals for pets, or the harvesting of adults for meat has not yet been addressed.

The sustainable use of wildlife has been widely promoted as a practical means of promoting conservation (McNeely et al. 1990). Conservation efforts have focused to a large degree on the declaration of protected areas in tracts of sufficient size to protect natural resources from human use and habitat alterations. However, this approach often has neglected the needs of the human communities that live in the area, and communities surrounding protected area often have found that their customary areas for resource exploitation have been incorporated into the protected area without their consent or consideration, at times leading to volatile situations between protected area managers and local inhabitants.

In recent years, several authors have argued to include local communities in natural resource management and to allow local inhabitants continued, controlled access to the resource (Bodmer 1994; J. G. Robinson and Redford 1994). It is believed that conservation efforts will have a much better chance of succeeding if local people are included in initial planning discussions, as well as in the implementation and management of the protected area. In these cases the local population must be allowed to benefit directly or indirectly from the resource. If communities choose to be involved, they not only must be allowed to participate in the conservation of local resources but should be expected to share in the responsibility of maintaining local biodiversity.

The challenge of creating sustainable-use management programs for turtles is daunting. There is very little biological or economic foundation upon which sustainable-use programs for turtles can be based, and virtually no case studies have evaluated harvest programs. The past history of turtle exploitation has clearly been one based on short-term economic gain. Although the rapid overexploitation of a resource such as a turtle population may seem extremely shortsighted, it can also be viewed in economic terms as a rational course of action. The key is understanding the effect of discount rates on the present value of future earnings from a renewable resource. As shown by C. W. Clark (1976), the best economic and biological strategies of harvesting are the same only when the exploited population's growth rate is high. Capital "expands" at an annual rate of approximately 10% (Caughley and Gunn 1996; C. W. Clark [1976] suggested a lower rate of 2 to 4%). Therefore, harvesting wild animals sustainedly pays only when a population's growth rate following harvest exceeds 10% per year. Otherwise, a purely economic analysis of the situation would recommend a large "capital reduction" (overharvest) and investment of the earnings in another enterprise with a higher rate of return. The almost universal status of turtles as a common-property resource, and the relatively low economic return of a sustained yield from turtle populations, creates problems for the concept of commercial-use management of these animals. As long as the return on investing profits from present overharvesting exceeds the expected return on future (sustainable) harvests, and as long as profits accrue to the individual and costs are spread among society, the overexploitation of turtle populations is inevitable.

It is clear that before we can evaluate the potential of sustainable-use management of turtles as a conservation tool, we need three things: (1) a better understanding of the population biology of those species harvested, (2) more information on the resource economics of sustained-yield harvesting, and (3) case studies that evaluate trial sustained-yield harvest programs.

The development of management efforts based on sustainable use is relatively new, and most efforts have suffered from a long series of technical, political, and institutional impediments (Ojasti 1995). As we have seen, a wide variety of biological and human factors play significant roles in exploitation and how it affects turtle populations. Sustainable-use programs involve a complex milieu of biological, economic, sociological, and political factors that need to be addressed for each individual case (see also Seigel and Dodd, Chapter 9). Implementation of such a program requires a multidisciplinary effort rarely found in most conservation initiatives. For instance, programs must be able to evaluate the potential levels of harvest in terms of economic benefits for the various program stakeholders. Aside from generating economic incentives for local communities to protect turtles and turtle habitat, the program should, ideally, generate revenues (through taxes and user fees) to the governmental entity responsible for program oversight. These fees would be used to support the enforcement of program regulations as well as monitoring of the program to measure the effects of harvest on the turtle population.

From a theoretical standpoint, sustainable-harvest programs of wild populations, and ranching programs that invest in rearing individuals but still rely on wild stock to maintain the operation, can give direct economic justifications to maintaining wild populations. A ranching effort, for example, can involve selling hatchlings as pets, and this is the basis of an egg collection program for the Nicaraguan slider (*Trachemys scripta emolii*) in Caño Negro Nature Reserve in Costa Rica (Pritchard 1993). Eggs collected from the wild are incubated, and the hatchlings are sold as pets in San José. The local egg collectors receive 50% of the sale, thus providing local communities with direct economic benefits from the wild population and incentive to protect this resource. For such a program to avoid overexploitation of the population, collection levels have to be below natural replacement levels.

Farming of turtles has been suggested as a means to produce food and to remove hunting pressure on wild turtles. However, a completely closed-cycle farming program (captive adults produce all future generations) does not need any wild stock and, therefore, does not offer the economic incentives to conserve wild populations or habitat that are inherent in programs based on the sustainable use of wild populations. Nonetheless, the conservation benefit of closed-cycle farming, or captive breeding, is that it is possible to reduce, and even replace, the need to use wild-caught specimens. This reduction has been seen in other wildlife utilization programs, such as the large market for two of the most common pet birds, budgerigars *(Melopsittacus undulatus)* and canaries *(Serinus canarius),* which are completely supplied by breeding operations (Bolze 1992). Captive breeding may have the potential to meet the demand of the market for rarer turtle species, and captive-breeding efforts have increased in recent years to supply this market as the wild-caught supply has declined due to trade controls or reduced population levels. Trade controls and reduced wild populations have driven up prices, making investments in captive breeding economically attractive (Smart and Bride 1993; HSUS 1994). Commercial farming or breeding programs for rare and threatened species could be required to contribute a portion of their economic proceeds toward conservation efforts as a mechanism for these programs to benefit wild populations.

Whitaker (1997) has proposed a village pond-rearing system for the Indian flap-shell turtle as a means of producing meat for sale and removing hunting pressure on wild populations in India. In Thailand, Jenkins (1995) reported that approximately 15 turtle farms were commercially breeding and rearing Chinese softshell turtles, though he does not specify if these farms are really closed-cycle operations. This small species of softshell appears to be particularly well adapted to captive farming, and total production is estimated at 3 to 6 million hatchlings per year ($3 to 6 million annually). The industry is expanding quickly, and Jenkins (1995) cited one source as saying there could be 100 farms by 1996. Attempts to breed native softshells have met with little success, and as softshells native to Thailand become more scarce, the captive-bred species is more common in markets. Chinese softshell turtles are also being commercially farmed in Malaysia (Jenkins 1995). In Shanghai, China, there are reported to be over 100 farms rearing Chinese softshell turtles for the domestic pet trade and sale to medicinal companies (Cen Jianqiang, personal communication).

In Brazil, the sale of meat from farm-reared giant South American river turtles and yellow-spotted Amazon River turtles has been authorized by the government. Farms obtain hatchlings from a government-run program that protects nesting beaches and annually releases millions of hatchling turtles (IBAMA 1989). However, it is unclear what, if any, direct conservation benefits will accrue to the wild turtle populations from the sale of captive-reared individuals for food.

Farming operations may not be generally applicable to a wide range of turtle species or market uses. Although they may be economically viable for some uses (e.g., red-eared slider hatchlings as pets), turtles tend to grow slowly, and their meat usually has a relatively low market value. Also, given the difficulties of rearing captive animals, the capture of wild individuals may be hard to discourage. The experience in Thailand suggests that the husbandry of many species is difficult on a large-scale commercial basis. Jenkins (1995) doubted that captive breeding would remove much hunting pressure on wild stocks while viable populations remained. Alho (1985) proposed a system for the giant South American river turtle, combining annual releases of headstarted animals (see "Headstarting," E. O. Moll and Moll, Chapter 5) and the harvest of captive-reared turtles after 8 years, but trial programs have suggested that this scheme is not economically viable. For sea turtles, Dodd (1982a; see also Seigel and Dodd, Chapter 9) concluded that farming programs would detract overall from conservation goals. Although breeding of certain species that do well in captivity is an option for supplying turtle meat markets, the risk of introducing exotic species from farming operations becomes an additional concern.

The value of sustained-use programs as a conservation tool for turtle populations is difficult to evaluate at this time. Very little biological information is available for most species, and in very few cases is there any type of quantitative information on levels of harvest and the effects of harvest on wild populations. Nevertheless, turtles are, and will continue to be, widely used for food, medicinal purposes, and as pets around the world. In most cases these uses will have negative effects on wild populations. It is clear that one of the greatest challenges that faces turtle conservationists is to understand these patterns of use, the effects they have on wild populations, and how the use and intrinsic value of turtles can be used as a tool for their conservation.

ACKNOWLEDGMENTS

DB would like to thank the Humane Society of the United States for providing import and export statistics on turtles that it obtained through its request under the Freedom of Information Act to the U.S. Department of Interior. CJL would like to acknowledge Jeanne Mortimer for her review of the Malaysian, Indonesian, and Seychelles country overviews and Cathi Campbell for her review and comments on the sea turtle portions of this chapter. She also thanks Lisa Campbell, Anny Chaves, and Claudette Mo for providing unpublished reports and theses on the egg harvest program at Ostional.

3
DISEASE AND HEALTH CONSIDERATIONS

Chelonians are increasingly threatened throughout the world by habitat loss and fragmentation, the introduction of exotic species, and exploitation by humans for food, medicine, and the pet trade. In free-living animals, disease is considered to be an important factor in natural selection (Bush et al. 1993). It is a factor that has likely always played a role in turtle population dynamics but which has only recently become a threat to the survival of species. Whereas historically, infectious disease may have played a role in the demise of localized populations of chelonians, a rebound of those populations could occur through the increased survivorship of progeny from surviving individuals or the migration of individuals from adjacent populations or geographic areas that may have been unaffected by the specific disease process. Currently, many populations are so small or so isolated that recovery after a disease outbreak is not likely. Adjacent populations may have been eliminated due to habitat fragmentation or other factors, resulting in little or no potential for migration from a previously contiguous range. Surviving individuals within a population may be unable to reproduce the population due to factors such as predation, limited nesting or feeding habitat, lack of access to migration corridors, and stochastic demographic, genetic, or environmental processes.

Increasing human activity in chelonian habitats is resulting in new impacts of disease on wild populations. In the Galápagos Islands the introduction and establishment of populations of exotic mammal species has dramatically influenced vegetational structure and interfered with the ecology and behavior of native tortoise populations (Swingland 1989a). These changes can lead to nutritional disease processes or increase an animal's susceptibility to disease-causing organisms. The suspected release of ill tortoises in the southwestern United States may have resulted in the introduction of a new bacterial organism, which resulted in high mortality of native desert tortoises *(Gopherus agassizii)* (E. R. Jacobson et al. 1995). Widespread production and use of chemicals has resulted in residues showing up in at least one species of wild chelonian. Tissues of loggerhead turtles *(Caretta caretta)* in the western Mediterranean have shown residues of organochlorine compounds such as DDD, DDT, DDE, and PCBs (Martinez-Silvestre 1995).

The effects of certain chemical compounds in populations of wild birds are well known. Similar effects may well be present in chelonian populations and may be increasingly important factors in reproductive processes, possibly resulting in nesting failure or reduced survivorship of hatchlings. Thorough observation and ongoing monitoring of wild populations are necessary to determine the impacts of these substances on chelonian species. The impacts of altered habitats, infectious diseases, and contaminants can only be determined by knowing the baseline health status of a population prior to these changes. These factors become increasingly significant when efforts are made to restore populations through habitat restoration, translocations, or reintroduction of a species to its historic range. A general lack of data on the incidence, distribution, and risks of disease in wild and captive populations, on effective quarantine requirements, and on the detection and monitoring of disease has resulted in the lack of a working database for informed risk assessment (Wolff and Seal 1992).

DISEASE PROCESSES

Chelonians have both benefited and suffered from their popularity with humans. They are commonly kept as pets and display animals by individuals and institutions. In captivity they are afflicted with a number of disease problems rarely observed in wild animals (E. R. Jacobson et al. 1994a). Their popularity has resulted in a significant body of knowledge concerning husbandry, nutrition, and disease, as well as significant activity in the study of wild populations. Until relatively recently, however, disease processes have not been a focus of field studies. Today, the line distinguishing captive and wild states continues to blur as human activity increasingly affects wildlife and habitat. Nest protection, captive breeding for release, **headstarting** (rearing juveniles to a certain size before release to reduce the impact of predation), and rehabilitation of wild individuals, as well as the confining conditions of smaller and smaller preserve areas, all require the consideration of disease and the overall health status of the population of concern as well as other species in the environment that may potentially be affected.

Disease problems can be broken down into infectious and noninfectious processes. **Infectious diseases** include those known or suspected to be caused by viral, bacterial, fungal, or parasitic organisms. It is important to note that infectious organisms may be present in an animal without concurrent signs of disease. This can occur when the animal has only recently encountered the disease organism and that disease organism is still in an incubation period; when the animal has mounted an effective immune response but still harbors the organism; or when the disease organism requires some precipitating factor (e.g., nutritional, environmental, or social stressors) to induce disease. **Noninfectious diseases** are brought about by nutritional, traumatic, toxic, neoplastic (cancerous), and genetic factors, among others.

Chelonians have a dynamic relationship with their environment. They have seasonal activity patterns and may migrate great distances in one or more of their life phases to reproduce or locate adequate food resources. In spite of—or perhaps because of—this, however, they may not be able to cope with changing conditions in the environment by modifying their behavior. Site fidelity for nesting, feeding, and migration activities can have adverse short- and long-term effects on individuals and populations when these required habitats are modified, for example, through the introduction of exotic species; the alteration of temperature or moisture regimes of nesting areas or salinity levels, turbidity, or temperature of aquatic habitats; or harvest of part of the chelonian population or harvest of its food source(s) (Lutcavage et al. 1997). Chelonians may therefore demonstrate compound diseases that result from a mixture of infectious and noninfectious causes. Susceptibility to infectious organisms is increased when animals are stressed by poor nutrition, crowding due to drought, captivity, or human manipulation. Determining the exact cause of morbidity or mortality may be difficult, if not impossible, under certain circumstances. Those studying such events should be careful to record all findings and interpret only results that are unequivocal. Cooper (1989:53) identified potentially conflicting interpretations of the same event of avian mortality based on the professional training of the researchers:

It can be particularly difficult to evaluate disease in "threatened" birds. Such populations are already under pressure—often because of habitat destruction or toxic chemicals or a combination of other factors. If deaths occur and a disease is diagnosed it may not be possible to say whether this was per se responsible for death, one of a number of factors contributing to death, or of no significance at all. The picture that emerges may even depend upon who is investigating the problem: thus, a veterinarian may implicate disease and underestimate the importance of (for example) the bird's poor condition and damaged plumage, while an ecologist might focus on the latter, attributing death to starvation, and ignore (or perhaps be unaware of) the presence of lesions such as abscesses in the bird's lungs or excessive urates in the kidneys.

It is important to report findings accurately without drawing conclusions based on limited data or observations.

INFECTIOUS DISEASES

Infectious diseases in chelonians are increasingly recognized as having significant effects on the population dynamics of certain species. Diseases such as upper respiratory tract disease of desert tortoises and green turtle fibropapillomatosis of sea turtles can have devastating effects on populations and complicate recovery efforts to preserve these species. Potentially **zoonotic organisms** (disease-causing organisms that can spread from animals to humans) such as *Salmonella* spp. may cause problems opportunistically in animals suffering other stresses but are unlikely to depress populations by causing high mortality under natural circumstances. Other infectious disease organisms have been associated with disease or mortality in isolated circumstances. Their effects on wild populations and even the natural occurrence and distribution of these infectious organisms are unknown or rarely documented (Obendorf et al. 1987; Rideout et al. 1987; Gordon et al. 1993; E. R. Jacobson et al. 1994b; Snipes et al. 1995; Pettan-Brewer et al. 1996; Westhouse et al. 1996).

Susceptibility of a host to infectious organisms is dependent upon the strain of organism involved and its specific pathogenicity in that host species, the number of organisms to which the host is exposed, and the immune status of the host. For example, chelonians can often harbor various strains of *Salmonella* without showing signs of illness and thus could be considered inapparent hosts of *Salmonella*. These same individuals, however, can become affected by such an organism when they undergo periods of stress (such as hibernation, nutrient deficiencies, or reproductive or environmental stresses) and ultimately show signs of illness that can be attributed to these organisms.

As mentioned earlier, infectious diseases have played a role in natural selection. Human activities, however, have altered the distribution and facilitated the spread of disease organisms. Likewise, human efforts to control disease processes, both naturally occurring and introduced, can alter the selective processes on a population. Humans have also altered habitats, which may result in increased susceptibility of hosts to pathogenic organisms.

Infectious agents are commonly found in wild chelonians. However, relatively few organisms are associated with naturally occurring outbreaks that cause significant morbidity or mortality of hosts. Diseased individuals in wild populations may have little opportunity to transmit infection to their healthy cohorts under normal behavioral and environmental conditions. Transmission of infection is facilitated when animals aggregate during breeding or nesting or when they are concentrated due to natural phenomena, such as drought. Morbidity and mortality due to infectious diseases are more commonly reported from captive chelonians (E. R. Jacobson 1994a). In captivity, the spread of infectious organisms is facilitated when animals are housed in close contact with one another, when a common water source is provided for a number of animals, when poor hygiene permits the buildup of abnormally high numbers of normally nonpathogenic organisms, and when other suboptimal environmental conditions predispose animals to infection by disease-causing organisms.

DISEASE AND POPULATION MANAGEMENT

The detection of disease in an animal population does not necessarily warrant intervention or the initiation of preventative medical programs. Most disease organisms live in balance with their hosts. Host population densities are moderated by the presence of infectious organisms as well as by the availability of resources, dispersal, predation, and other factors (Thrushfield 1995). However, human activity can influence disease processes, causing the disease organisms to become out of balance and threaten isolated (or entire) populations of host animals. It is in these circumstances that mitigation of human impact and an attempt to return to the original equilibrium should be attempted.

Disease can be identified as the cause of decline in some chelonian populations, such as the desert tortoise (E. R. Jacobson et al. 1991, 1995). Upper respiratory tract disease is caused by *Mycoplasma agassizii* and has been associated with **epizootics** (an outbreak of disease in an animal population) resulting in high mortality of desert tortoises in certain populations in the western United States. The decline of these populations resulted in the U.S. Fish and Wildlife Service listing these populations as threatened under the U.S. Endangered Species Act (16 U.S.C. §§ 1531 to 1544). It is thought that the causative organism was released into the wild in multiple locations through the release of infected pet tortoises. Spread of the organism is facilitated by the ease with which tortoises can be collected, later to be released in different locations (E. R. Jacobson et al. 1991).

Upper respiratory tract disease has far-reaching implications in the management and recovery of affected populations. Attempts to enhance populations through captive propagation, repatriations, and relocations (see "Repatriation, Relocation, and Release Programs," McDougal, Chapter 7; Seigel and Dodd, Chapter 9) must take into account the prevalence and pathogenicity of this as well as other potential disease-causing organisms. The disease can be manifested as an intense upper respiratory infection causing the affected animal to be listless and anorectic and ultimately to succumb to dehydration and systemic disease (E. R. Jacobson et al. 1991). Upper respiratory tract disease can also be present in a subclinical state. Desert tortoises showing no clinical signs have been shown both to have had a history of exposure to the disease based on serology and to culture positive for *My-*

coplasma in the absence of serological evidence. It is for this reason that the movement of animals from one population to another should not occur without a full medical evaluation using the latest available technology to detect infectious disease organisms. Medical evaluations should be done on not only the animals to be moved but also the source population (whether captive or wild) and the population into which the animals are to be introduced. As a general rule, if evidence of disease is present in both populations at relatively similar incidences the project can proceed. If any identifiable disease is absent from or more prevalent in one population, no transfers should occur. Placing unexposed animals into a population affected by an infectious agent places them at increased risk. Moving animals infected with pathogenic organisms into a naive population can result in an epizootic in the previously unexposed population (E. R. Jacobson et al. 1995).

Although upper respiratory tract disease has emerged as one of the most significant infectious diseases of wild tortoises, other potential disease-causing organisms should also be monitored to prevent similar catastrophic effects in other species or populations. For example, ticks *(Amblyomma marmoreum)* are commonly found on tortoises and other reptiles in southern Africa. Immature ticks can feed on different birds and wild mammals before they attach to a reptile. Tick species are recognized vectors of disease in humans and domestic animals, but the role of *Amblyomma marmoreum* in the transmission of disease in wildlife is unknown (Ghirotti and Mwanaumo 1989). Transport of tick-infested wildlife into or out of a region could result in transmission of previously unrecognized syndromes.

Syndromes such as shell disease, seen in turtles from Lake Blackshear, Georgia (Lovich et al. 1996), and cutaneous dyskeratosis in desert tortoises in southern California (E. R. Jacobson et al. 1994b) appear to be of limited natural distribution, though occurring in a relatively high percentage of animals in these localized populations. The etiologies (causes) of these conditions are unknown, but it is suspected that toxins or nutritional factors may be involved. Although there is no evidence of infectiousness, it would be unwise to move animals from or to these locations until the etiology is determined.

Cutaneous fibropapillomatosis, an infectious disease affecting sea turtles, is being observed more frequently in those areas where turtles occur in proximity to large human populations. Also known as green turtle fibropapillomatosis, this disease has been seen most commonly in green turtles *(Chelonia mydas)*, loggerheads, olive ridley turtles *(Lepidochelys olivacea)*, hawksbill turtles *(Eretmochelys imbricata)*, and flatback sea turtles *(Natator depressa)*. The disease is characterized by fibrous growths on the skin, commonly around the conjunctiva, chin, neck, flippers, and the base of the tail and limbs. These growths are characterized as cutaneous papillomas, fibromas, and fibropapillomas, all of which are typically irregular growths from the surface of the skin that are supported by proliferative connective tissue.

Lesions can also occur internally, involving the lungs, liver, gastrointestinal tract, kidneys, or some combination (R. H. George 1997).

Green turtle fibropapillomatosis was first described in green turtles from Florida waters in 1938 (G. M. Smith and Coates 1938) and has since been seen in this species throughout the Caribbean, in Hawaii, and, with increasing frequency, throughout the world (R. H. George 1997). The disease is infectious and is believed to be caused by a herpesvirus, although the causative agent has not yet been isolated (Herbst et al. 1995). It is more frequently seen in animals inhabiting areas adjacent to large human populations and areas with low water turnover; it is less often seen in animals from more remote or deeper waters. The disease is more often seen in juvenile turtles in the 40 to 90 cm carapace length sizes and is rare in nesting adults (R. H. George 1997).

Cutaneous fibropapillomatosis is disfiguring and debilitating to affected animals. It is progressive, and affected animals often die, although spontaneous recovery has been reported. Although the disease has been demonstrated to be infectious, the mechanism of transmission and factors that predispose an animal to infection have not been determined (R. H. George 1997). Attempts to rehabilitate affected animals and strategies to enhance populations of threatened or endangered sea turtles must consider the impact of this disease on turtle populations. In some cases, rehabilitation of affected animals may be attempted if adequate precautions are taken to prevent the release of contaminated materials (including wastewater) into the range of unaffected individuals. Rehabilitated animals that recover should be returned to the area or population from which they originated during the same season at which they were first encountered. Doing so will minimize the risk associated with exposure to other animals or populations due to migratory behavior of the recovered animal. If possible, these animals should be monitored for the reoccurrence of disease to elucidate further the pathologic process. Turtles that recover from this disease may have important genetic material to add to wild populations, potentially allowing future generations to survive in the presence of this agent.

Population enhancement efforts such as headstarting and egg translocation have the potential to increase the risk of infection by cutaneous fibropapillomatosis as well as other diseases as compared with in situ nest protection. The concentration of individuals into one location can potentially facilitate the spread of pathogenic organisms. When these aggressive management strategies must be utilized to protect or enhance populations, careful attention to health concerns should be made. Eggs and animals should not be moved from one location to another across the naturally occurring boundaries that separate populations of the same or similar species.

For example, the captive rearing and reintroduction of Kemp's ridley turtle (*Lepidochelys kempii*) involved translocating eggs from the population's main nesting beach in Rancho Nuevo, Tamaulipas, Mexico, to Padre Island National Seashore near Corpus Christi, Texas. After hatching and making their way to the water, hatchlings were transported to Galveston, Texas, to be raised to approximately 1 year of age (Caillouet et al. 1995a). This program involved moving eggs or animals within the normal geographic range of the species. Animals were raised in isolation from animals from other geographic areas. The health of each individual was monitored, and infectious diseases were not identified as a problem. Mycotic pneumonia, attributed to exposure of juvenile turtles to low ambient temperatures, resulted in high mortality during the early years of the program. It is believed that immunosuppression caused by the low temperatures resulted in increased susceptibility to environmental organisms. The problem did not appear to be infectious although many animals subjected to the same conditions were affected. The problem did not recur in subsequent years (J. Flanagan, personal observation).

In contrast, transfer of Kemp's ridleys to the Cayman Islands for rearing and maturation removed the individuals from their natural range (Caillouet et al. 1995b) and could have potentially exposed them to infectious agents not present in the wild population. These individuals should not be considered for return to the wild population without thorough health screening.

HEALTH CONSIDERATIONS FOR CAPTIVE HUSBANDRY

Diseases of chelonians that are associated with captivity generally involve poor husbandry practices. Inadequate nutrition, improper environmental conditions, poor hygiene, crowding, and other failures to consider the species' biological requirements contribute to the development of diseases. In a captive environment, disease problems can be amplified by the relatively high density of animals being maintained, which permits ready transmission of infectious organisms. A proactive health care program and sound planning can reduce or eliminate disease problems.

Captive-rearing facilities, if needed, should be constructed within or immediately adjacent to the natural range of the population in order to take advantage of natural environmental conditions and potentially to use natural foodstuffs in the diet of captives. Planning should consider requirements for maintaining adults for captive breeding (e.g., the need for space, social interaction, seasonal variation of temperature or food resources, and so on), harvesting and incubating eggs from wild or captive adults, and rearing hatchlings, as well as criteria for release of progeny.

Maintenance requirements for adult chelonians are highly species dependent. Efforts to maintain adult animals for reproduction should start with a review of pertinent literature on their natural history and ecology as well as on successes and failures of previous husbandry attempts. Complete records should be maintained as to the identity of breeding individuals, the foods provided to and quantity consumed by individuals, the environmental conditions maintained throughout the year, and the production and fertility of individuals. Regular health monitoring and infectious disease screening of the captive group should be standard. There should be a regular review of data to identify trends and to fine-tune practices for maximum production.

Successful incubation of chelonian eggs depends on the maintenance of proper species-specific environmental conditions throughout the developmental period. Thorough research should be made into the conditions found in natural nests and those conditions that are reported to have been used successfully in other captive-breeding attempts with the same or similar species. Consideration should be given to proper temperature and moisture levels during incubation. The type and consistency of the substrate used for incubation will influence the microbial environment to which the eggs and hatchlings are exposed. Gas exchange is also critical to the development and hatching of eggs because the developing embryo uses oxygen and produces carbon dioxide. Impairment of gas exchange can result in death of the embryo due to anoxia. Eggs should be handled carefully. Turning or jostling eggs that have started to develop can result in the death of the embryo due to detachment of fetal membranes, which will compromise gas exchange. Eggs moved on the day they are deposited are less likely to suffer the effects of being handled than those handled later in the incubation process (Ewert 1979).

For those species with temperature-dependent sex determination, a decision to produce predominantly one sex, or to produce equal numbers of each sex, should be made recognizing the potential ramifications of either decision (Lovich 1996). In addition to sex determination, incubation temperature also influences the development time of the embryo.

Upon hatching, the young should be inspected for physical abnormalities. Unhatched eggs should be evaluated on a microbiological basis. The relative quantities of minerals and vitamins can be assayed. Deficiency of nutrients in the adult female can result in an egg with insufficient nutrients for full embryonic development. If abnormally high numbers of eggs fail to hatch, causes of failure could include improper handling, improper incubation parameters, poor nutrition in the adults, or infection before or after the egg is laid. Although genetics undoubtedly plays a role in egg viability, the determination of cause is difficult without controlling for other variables and performing repeated breeding trials with similar genetic pairings. Very little disease screening is indicated for hatchlings produced within natural nesting areas when they are released immediately upon hatching. A survey of unhatched eggs in the nest can give a perspective of the microbial contamination within the clutch. Healthy-appearing young should be released with timing and conditions as appropriate for the species.

The rearing or release of hatchlings should be done in a manner consistent with the biology of the species. Rearing hatchlings for any period of time increases the potential for problems caused by infectious disease. The required macro- and microenvironmental needs of each chelonian species can be difficult to meet in captivity. Requirements for diet composition, social grouping, temperature, moisture, and shelter should be considered. In order to reduce or prevent the transmission of infectious agents, hatchlings should not be reared in contact with adults or with other species.

The growth rate of chelonians can be accelerated in captivity because of the availability of food and the reduced need to forage. Nutritional diseases most commonly seen include metabolic bone disease (related to problems with calcium metabolism), vitamin A deficiency, and obesity. Careful attention to the nutritional composition of the diet of the wild counterparts of captive-reared individuals will permit the formulation of a captive diet with essential nutrients in appropriate quantities. Sexual maturity in captive turtles is determined primarily by the size of the individual (DeNardo 1996). Captive-reared individuals typically grow faster than do their wild counterparts and thus are able to breed at a younger age.

The justification for captive rearing is often to raise the young to a size at which they are less susceptible to predation, resulting in a higher survival rate for hatchlings. However, captive-reared young should be given the opportunity to perform species-typical behavior relative to recognizing and foraging for natural foodstuffs, avoiding predators, and using shelter or refugia. Dependence on human provisioning or protection from predators and environmental conditions should be avoided in animals destined for release.

Ongoing health monitoring should be performed during the period of captive rearing. Regular measurements of weight and length and assessments of behavior should be made. Routine screenings for parasites, hematology and serum chemistry levels, and infectious diseases should be performed. Only healthy and vigorous animals should be maintained for release. Animals that show evidence of illness or infirmity should be isolated from their healthy counterparts and treated appropriately. If there is no response to therapy, the animals should be euthanized and necropsied to attempt to understand the particular disease process and to prevent the spread of potentially infectious organisms.

Follow-up assessment of released individuals should be performed to identify causes of morbidity and mortality. Captive-reared animals can have trouble adapting to a natural environment. Causes of mortality should be investigated and captive-husbandry and release protocols modified to enhance survival. Information gained from the failures in one release may help reduce mortalities in future efforts.

CONCLUSION

With the current knowledge of disease processes in wild populations, researchers no longer have the luxury to disregard infectious diseases and their impact on population dynamics. Disease plays an important role in the evolution of species. However, alteration of habitats through human activities has resulted in the fragmentation of populations. These isolated subpopulations are more vulnerable to extinction due to environmental changes, the introduction of exotic species, and infectious diseases as well as other factors. Mitigation must use a holistic approach and address the causes for declines while not allowing the last individuals of a species to go extinct.

ANNE B. MEYLAN AND
DAVID EHRENFELD

4

CONSERVATION OF MARINE TURTLES

Cosmopolitan distributions, large size, striking appearance, and high resource value have made marine turtles one of the best-known groups of turtles. Together, the seven recognized species occupy every ocean basin, ranging from the Arctic Ocean to Tasman Sea. They range in size from the relatively small ridley turtles (*Lepidochelys* spp.), which average less than 45 kg as adults, to the enormous leatherback turtle *(Dermochelys coriacea),* which attains more than 900 kg. Their relatively large body size makes marine turtles a valuable resource for humans; for centuries, they have been sought after for meat, calipee (cartilage), eggs, oil, skin, and shell (see Thorbjarnarson et al., Chapter 2). Use of the brilliantly patterned shell of the hawksbill turtle *(Eretmochelys imbricata)* can be traced back as far as the fifteenth century before the common era (Parsons 1972). Still valued in modern times, tortoiseshell has been traded in international commerce at prices exceeding those of ivory (Mack et al. 1979). The availability of fresh meat of the green turtle *(Chelonia mydas)* was a major factor in the exploration of the New World in the sixteenth through eighteenth centuries (Carr 1954; Parsons 1962; Thorbjarnarson et al., Chapter 2).

Marine turtles pique the curiosity of humans, and this, too, has given them great visibility. Their brief departures from the sea to lay eggs on sandy beaches bring them into direct contact with people, and few who view their dramatic nesting behaviors are not awed by the spectacle. Their long migrations across seemingly trackless oceans are the fabric of legend, stirring the imaginations of laypersons and scientists alike.

Despite considerable scientific and public attention devoted to marine turtles during the last quarter of the twentieth century, their long-term survival remains in jeopardy. Major threats that were identified in 1979 at the World Conference on Sea Turtle Conservation (Bjorndal 1982)—overexploitation, habitat destruction, and accidental drowning in fishing gear—have not abated. Massive harvests of green turtles, including eggs and nesting females, continue in the Australasian area (Limpus 1994, 1995). Destruction and degradation of nesting beaches and foraging habitats continue elsewhere (Raymond 1984; Balazs 1985; Carr 1987b; Groombridge 1990; National Research Council 1990; Wilkinson 1993; Meylan et al. 1995; NMFS and USFWS 1995). Use of turtle excluder devices (TEDs) in shrimp trawls remains limited outside U.S. waters. Efforts to manage populations at the regional level—a necessity for this migratory group of animals—have been initiated and show great promise, but few regional plans have been implemented.

In this chapter, we review (1) the current status designations of marine turtle species, (2) key biological characteristics relevant to their conservation, (3) threats to their survival, and (4) management options to promote conservation.

STATUS OF MARINE TURTLE POPULATIONS

Knowledge of the status of sea turtle populations has improved markedly since the 1970s. Global status reviews of marine turtles are provided by Bjorndal (1982, 1995), Groombridge and Wright (1982), Groombridge and Luxmoore (1989), and Limpus (1995). Regional status reviews are available for the western Atlantic (Bacon et al. 1984; Ogren et al. 1989), the South Pacific (South Pacific Commission 1980), the North Pacific (K. L. Eckert 1993), the Mediterranean (Groombridge 1990), and the western Indian Ocean (Humphrey and Salm 1996). Status reviews of marine turtle species listed under the U.S. Endangered Species Act (16 U.S.C. §§ 1531 to 1544) were recently conducted by the National Marine Fisheries Service and the U.S. Fish and Wildlife Service (NMFS and USFWS 1995).

A few conservation successes can be claimed for recent years: an increase in the number of Kemp's ridleys (Lepidochelys kempii) nesting at Rancho Nuevo, Mexico, since the mid-1980s (Márquez M. et al. 1996); an increase in nesting green turtles in Florida (Meylan et al. 1995); increases of the South African loggerhead turtle (Caretta caretta) nesting populations since the early 1960s (Hughes 1989); increased usage of TEDs on shrimp trawls in U.S. waters (NMFS and USFWS 1991a) and corresponding declines in turtle strandings in some areas (Crowder et al. 1995); reduction of international trade in sea turtles due to the implementation of the Convention on International Trade in Endangered Species of Wild Fauna and Flora (CITES 1973); and since January 1993 a moratorium on the importation of tortoiseshell into Japan, the world's largest trader in this commodity.

There have been many more conservation failures than successes, resulting in large population declines. These declines include leatherback populations in Sri Lanka, Malaysia, Indonesia, Thailand, and Pacific Mexico (Limpus 1994, 1995; Sarto et al. 1996; Spotila et al. 1996); green turtle populations in Indonesia, Malaysia, the Philippines, Japan, and French Polynesia (Limpus 1994, 1995); eastern Pacific green turtle populations in Mexico (NMFS and USFWS 1995); loggerhead populations in eastern Australia and the United States (National Research Council 1990; Limpus and Riemer 1994; NMFS and USFWS 1995); hawksbill populations in the Caribbean, Madagascar, Seychelles, and Indonesia (Schulz 1984; Groombridge and Luxmoore 1989; Mortimer 1990b; Bjorndal et al. 1993; Meylan 1999; Meylan and Donnelly 1999); and olive ridley *(Lepidochelys olivacea)* populations in Malaysia, Thailand, Costa Rica, and Suriname (Reichart 1993; Limpus 1995; NMFS and USFWS 1995). These declines must be added to the historical declines of sea turtles chronicled by Parsons (1962), Groombridge and Wright (1982), King (1982), J. P. Ross (1982), Bacon et al. (1984), Groombridge and Luxmoore (1989), and Ogren et al. (1989).

The most widely used status designations for marine turtles are those published by the Species Survival Commission of the International Union for Conservation of Nature and Natural Resources (IUCN 1996). These "Red List" categories reflect the global status of whole taxa and are based on criteria such as population level (numbers), population trend, extent of occurrence, and probability of extinction in the wild. After major revisions of the category definitions in 1994, the status of each species of marine turtle was reconsidered; all are now listed (that is, the six species mentioned above plus the flatback *[Natator depressa]*) as critically endangered, endangered, or vulnerable. Category definitions (IUCN 1996) are as follows:

> critically endangered—facing an extremely high risk of extinction in the wild in the near future;
>
> endangered—facing a very high risk of extinction in the wild in the near future; and
>
> vulnerable—facing a high risk of extinction in the medium-term future.

All marine turtle species remain on Appendix I of CITES (USFWS 1995b); international trade in products derived from species listed on Appendix I is tightly regulated.

Individual countries may maintain their own status listings for endangered animals and plants, and the criteria on which these status listings are based may differ from those of the IUCN's Red List. Designations by the U.S. government, for example, are either threatened or endangered and are in accordance with the U.S. Endangered Species Act of 1973. In the United States, the designations usually trigger different levels of response on the part of management authorities. For example, activities that require permits, such as dredging, may be allowed higher levels of incidental take for a species listed as threatened than for one listed as endangered. Habitat acquisition priorities may also be guided by the status designations of species present in the habitat.

BIOLOGICAL CHARACTERISTICS RELEVANT TO CONSERVATION

Sea turtles exhibit several biological characteristics that have important implications for their conservation. Traits such as delayed maturity and great longevity are shared among other turtles, whereas other traits are unique to sea turtles.

Migratory Behavior

All sea turtle species undertake long-distance travel. Migrations of adults between feeding and nesting habitats are the best-known examples, but long-distance travel by juvenile and subadult turtles (developmental migrations) and by adults in search of prey is also common (Carr 1982). The scale of these movements can be monumental: according to genetic evidence, immature loggerheads in the Pacific appear to traverse nearly one-third of the planet during their developmental migrations (B. W. Bowen et al. 1995). Tag returns of all species suggest that migrations of hundreds or thousands of kilometers are not uncommon (Meylan 1982; Limpus 1992). An important consequence of these migrations is that sea turtles frequently cross national boundaries or pass through international waters. Thus, migratory behavior makes sea turtle conservation an international issue requiring regional management.

Complex Life Histories

There is abundant evidence that sea turtle life histories are complex. Carr et al. (1978) proposed a general life history model of seasonal and ontogenetic changes in the occupation of habitats (Figure 4.1). The first stage of the model is the lost year—the first year or years of a sea turtle's life during which it remains largely unseen by humans. For most species the lost year is spent at the surface in the open ocean. The model also recognizes developmental habitats for juveniles and subadults, adult feeding grounds (which may be shared with subadults), nesting beaches, and internesting habitats. In many cases, these various habitats are known

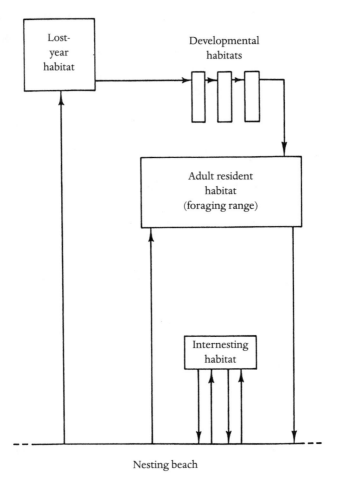

Figure 4.1. Seasonal and ontogenetic changes in the ecological geography and habitat of the green turtle (adapted from Carr et al. 1978).

to be widely separated geographically. The model was developed principally from data on the green turtle; other species depart from it in varying degrees. For example, the locations of feeding habitats of both leatherbacks and olive ridleys are not fixed, as they are for the green turtle. Despite departures from the model, however, the concept of a turtle occupying multiple, spatially separated habitats during its lifetime seems to apply well to most marine turtle species. From a conservation perspective, it is important to know that these distinct life history stages exist. It is also important to know the actual physical location where each population spends each life history stage. Only when this "ecological geography" is known can all threats be identified and addressed.

Natal Homing

Another biological trait believed to be common, possibly universal, among marine turtles is the tendency of nesting females to return to the beach where they were born (Carr 1967; Meylan et al. 1990; B. W. Bowen and Avise 1996). Thus, nesting populations may be demographically independent in time scales relevant to management. Depletion of one population will not be compensated by recruitment from other nesting populations. For example, the green turtle nesting colonies destroyed by early explorers in the Caribbean were never replenished. Thus, nesting populations must be treated as independent management units.

Slow Growth, Delayed Maturity, and Extended Longevity

Estimates of age to maturity for sea turtles in the wild range up to 50 years or more (Balazs 1982b). These estimates, combined with the knowledge that some adults remain reproductively active for more than two decades (Carr et al. 1978; Fitzsimmons et al. 1995), suggest that lifetimes of 50 to 75 years or more are possible. The consequences of these traits are profound (Congdon et al. 1993, 1994; Crouse and Frazer 1995). We discuss this issue further in "Headstarting," below (see also Seigel and Dodd, Chapter 9).

Delayed maturity confounds efforts to assess the status of populations and to judge the long-term success of conservation efforts. Turtles nesting this year may have hatched some 20 to 50 years ago, when circumstances at the nesting beach or on distant foraging grounds were far different. One of us (DE) once compared looking at green turtle population data with looking at the light from a star 25 light-years away. Although the star may appear to be shining now, we are in fact looking at the way it was 25 years ago, and there is no way of telling whether that star has increased in brightness or has gone out altogether in the intervening years (in Bacon et al. 1984). Similarly, adult turtles we see now hatched and matured decades ago, when conditions affecting their survival may have been very different from what they are today. Mortimer (1995a) illustrated this phenomenon with an example of the overharvest of sea turtle eggs (Figure 4.2). The figure shows the hypothetical case in which 100% of the eggs at a beach are harvested. Adult females continue to show up to nest at the beach for 50 years, giving the impression to management authorities that this level of harvest is supportable. But during this period, the pipeline becomes progressively depleted of hatchling, juvenile, and

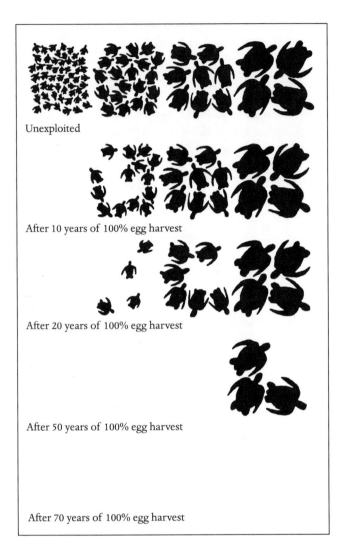

Unexploited

After 10 years of 100% egg harvest

After 20 years of 100% egg harvest

After 50 years of 100% egg harvest

After 70 years of 100% egg harvest

Figure 4.2. This figure (source, Mortimer 1995a) represents the destruction of a green turtle nesting population through overharvest of eggs. For this model, females are assumed to take 20 to 50 years to reach adulthood (National Research Council 1990) and then to remain reproductively active for about 20 years (Carr et al. 1978). In the unexploited green turtle population, four life stages are indicated: hatchlings, juveniles, subadults, and breeding adults. After 10 years of 100% egg harvest, no hatchling turtles will remain in the population, and the number of juvenile turtles will be reduced. However, the numbers of subadults and breeding adults will be the same as in the unexploited population. After 20 years of 100% egg harvest, there will be no hatchlings

subadult turtles. The decline is not obvious to the general public for 50 years! After 70 years, this population of sea turtles becomes extinct.

Vulnerability during Reproduction

Other than for basking, which is rare, almost the only time sea turtles leave the water is when females crawl onto beaches to nest. During these short terrestrial excursions, they are particularly vulnerable to human-related disturbances such as direct harvest, disruption of the nesting process, and artificial lighting, which causes disorientation. Eggs and hatchlings are also subject to intense pressures on the nesting beach. Vulnerability extends to reproductive adults, which aggregate to mate in the waters off the nesting beach and along the migratory corridor. Mating pairs often float at the surface and fail to flee when threatened by humans attempting to capture or harpoon them.

Site Fidelity

Carr and Carr (1972) noted that reproductive female turtles often returned to nest near previous nesting sites, both during and between nesting seasons. This faithfulness was later discovered to extend to other habitats as well, such as feeding grounds and courtship areas for some species (Carr 1982; Limpus 1993). This predictability of behavior is likely to attract predators to both the nesting beach and the foraging grounds, and human exploitation is facilitated by such site fidelity.

It is not clear what happens when natal nesting sites become unavailable, as in the case of catastrophic hurricanes, or highly degraded due to artificial lighting, beachfront development, or **armoring** (placement of rigid structures such as seawalls and revetments on the beach to control erosion). However, it is doubtful that turtles can achieve their full reproductive potential under these circumstances, especially if adjacent sites are also unavailable or degraded.

---

and fewer juveniles and subadults than were in the population 10 years after 100% egg harvest. However, the number of breeding adults will remain the same as in the unexploited population. After 50 years of 100% egg harvest, there will be no hatchlings, no juveniles, and no subadults remaining in the population. The number of breeding adults that come to the nesting beach will have begun to decline. Only at this point will it be apparent to the general public that the population is in decline. By now, however, the population is on the verge of extinction. All the females remaining in the population are at least 50 years old. After 70 years of 100% egg harvest, the turtle population will be extinct by the 71st year. (Courtesy of Jeanne A. Mortimer.)

Temperature-Dependent Sex Determination

As for many other reptiles, the sex of sea turtles is determined by the temperature regime in the nest during incubation (Standora and Spotila 1985). This trait is important for practical conservation purposes because of the potential effect management techniques (e.g., nest relocation and artificial incubation) and habitat alterations (e.g., beach nourishment and exotic vegetation) can have on sex ratios (Mrosovsky and Yntema 1980; Shaver et al. 1988; NMFS and USFWS 1991a; Crain et al. 1995).

THREATS TO SURVIVAL

Threats to marine turtles have been described extensively in the literature (Groombridge and Wright 1982; Groombridge and Luxmoore 1989; National Research Council 1990; K. L. Eckert 1995; Lutcavage et al. 1997). The vast majority of threats are human-related (Appendix 4.1, found at end of chapter). Direct harvest, drowning in fisheries gear (particularly shrimp nets), and habitat loss were identified as cardinal threats in 1979 at the World Conference on Sea Turtle Conservation (Bjorndal 1982), and these continue to be the principal threats to marine turtles today.

Direct Harvest

Direct harvest remains legal in many countries where marine turtles occur. Where protective legislation exists, implementation and enforcement are often lacking. Exploitation spans a continuum from pure subsistence use to highly organized international trade (see Thorbjarnarson et al., Chapter 2). More than 600,000 hawksbills were required to produce the volume of tortoiseshell imported by Japan during 1970 to 1986 (Milliken and Tokunaga 1987a). Tortoiseshell trade is considered to be the foremost cause of the hawksbill's critical endangerment. As of 1995, approximately 100,000 green turtles were harvested annually in Australasia alone, threatening the stability of Australian and other regional stocks (Limpus 1995). Worldwide, the green turtle is the species most widely hunted for its meat and the hawksbill for its shell, but all marine species are exploited to some degree.

Incidental Capture

Drowning in fisheries gear of various types is a widespread and very significant cause of mortality for marine turtles. An independent study of the causes of turtle mortality in the United States (National Research Council 1990) concluded that incidental capture in shrimp trawls was the most important source of mortality for juvenile, subadult, and breeding turtles and accounts for more deaths than all other human-related causes combined. Shrimp trawling is conducted in numerous countries—in most cases without efforts to mitigate effects on turtles. The impact of this fishery on sea turtles worldwide has not been estimated. In addition to its role in depleting loggerhead and Kemp's ridley populations in the United States, shrimp trawling is implicated in declines of loggerheads in Australia and olive ridleys in Suriname (Limpus and Riemer 1994; NMFS and USFWS 1995).

The scope of fisheries-related mortality in marine turtles has expanded during the last two decades. As traditional resources have become depleted, new species of fish and invertebrates are targeted and pursued in novel ways. For example, longline fisheries and high-seas drift-net fisheries are relatively new and have only recently been recognized as major sources of mortality for marine turtles. More than 20,000 loggerheads are estimated to be captured annually as a result of the Spanish longline fishery in the Mediterranean; 20 to 30% of these turtles are estimated to die (Aguilar et al. 1995). The high-seas drift-net fisheries in the North Pacific are estimated to have captured 6,100 turtles in 1990, incurring a minimum mortality of 1,700 turtles (Wetherall et al. 1993). Turtles are also inadvertently drowned in many other types of fishing gear, such as gill and trammel nets, pound nets, trap or buoy lines, and trawls used for species other than shrimp.

New problems for sea turtles from fisheries continue to appear. Florida commercial fishers, stymied by a statewide inshore net ban, are pursuing alternatives, such as trawling offshore for jellyfish to sell to Japanese markets. Existing legislation does not address this activity, although the co-occurrence at sea of leatherbacks and jellyfish (their primary prey) is likely to result in incidental take.

Habitat Loss and Degradation

There is a broad diversity of threats to the quality and integrity of the terrestrial and marine habitats on which marine turtles depend (Appendix 4.1). One of the most important is artificial light in the vicinity of the nesting beach. Lights can deter nesting females from emerging on the beach, disorient nesting females that do emerge, and disorient hatchlings when they emerge from nests and search for the sea (Witherington and Martin 1996). Disorientation increases exposure to predators and the elements, and death is often the result. Along highly developed coastlines, lighting problems can be the foremost threat to hatchlings on the nesting beach, forcing the caging of nests and supervision of hatchling releases or, in some cases, the relocation of nests to hatcheries.

Armoring, or hardening, of shorelines to prevent erosion is one of the most pernicious among the various causes of habitat degradation in the terrestrial environment. Armoring structures usurp the high ground of the beach where many nests would be placed and may exacerbate erosion problems. Nests placed seaward of armoring structures are more vulnerable to tidal inundation and destruction. Although the threat posed to nesting turtles by vertical cement walls on the beach is obvious and familiar, revetments, rockpiles, and buried sandbags also represent barriers that prevent turtles from nesting. As sea levels continue to rise, we predict that armoring of the coastline will increase in the future. By 1991, approximately 21% of Florida's, 10% of Georgia's, and 10% of South Carolina's beaches were armored (NMFS and USFWS 1991a). The placement of armoring structures is done piecemeal; each small, incremental change is argued to have minimal impact on turtle populations, but the cumulative result—a continuously armored shoreline— is disastrous.

Nourishment of eroded beaches with sand is often billed as a turtle-friendly alternative to armoring. The deceptively simple argument that some sand is better than no sand is usually proffered. Adverse effects of this restoration, such as sand compaction (preventing hatchling emergence), scarp formation (interfering with nesting), and altered microenvironments for incubating eggs, are currently given only limited consideration. Timing of nourishment projects is also a critical issue. Nourishment during the nesting season is highly disruptive; operations often involve 24-hour-per-day activity on the beach with heavy equipment and artificial lighting. Shore-parallel pipes conveying sand slurry are obstacles to nesting females, and nests can be buried with sand, which can be fatal to hatchlings. Most direct effects can be avoided by scheduling nourishment projects outside the nesting and hatching season. Unfortunately, this compromise does not appear politically acceptable in Florida, and large-scale nest relocation efforts in renourishment project areas have been favored despite known adverse impacts.

The suitability of replacement sand used in nourishment projects is also an important issue. Depletion of stores of offshore sand along the southeast coast of Florida has led to proposals to use nonnative sands such as aragonite. Pilot studies have demonstrated a 1.4 to 2.4°C lower temperature in loggerhead nests incubated in aragonite compared with Florida sand; hence, there is concern about possible effects on sex ratios of turtles hatched on beaches nourished with aragonite (Schulman et al. 1994). The cooler temperature of nests incubating in aragonite resulted in incubation times that were 3 to 10 days longer than those of nests in native sands. Concern about these and other as yet unknown effects on sea turtles is heightened by the recognition that aragonite sand may eventually replace native sands along a significant stretch of Florida's nesting beaches.

Habitat degradation in the marine environment threatens marine turtles on a global scale. Coral reefs provide important shelter and food for hawksbills, loggerheads, and green turtles, but it is believed that 10% of the world's coral reefs have already been extensively degraded; 30% are in a critical state such that they will be lost in the next 10 to 20 years; and another 30% will disappear in 20 to 40 years. Only 30% are considered stable at this time (Wilkinson 1993). Other marine ecosystems are also showing signs of collapse (M. J. Butler et al. 1995).

Open-water habitats of sea turtles are also becoming degraded. A wide variety of pollutants have been identified in the *Sargassum* rafts typically inhabited by juvenile Atlantic loggerheads during their first year (Carr 1987b). Thirty-four percent of neonate loggerheads captured at sea off the eastern coast of Florida had tar in their digestive tracts (Witherington 1994a). The extent to which persistent chemicals such as PCBs—with known effects on the reproductive biology of reptiles—threaten marine turtles at sea is unknown, but the occurrence of these substances in marine food webs is documented (Colborn et al. 1996).

There are significant mortality factors operating at each life history stage of marine turtles and in both the terrestrial and marine environments. Because these factors are additive and sometimes interactive, the result is that conservation of sea turtles is both urgently needed and complex.

CONSERVATION MEASURES

Without active intervention and management, sea turtle populations are expected to continue to decline to extinction (IUCN 1995). A global strategy for sea turtle conservation was developed by the IUCN Marine Turtle Specialist Group (IUCN 1995). The strategy promotes (1) research and monitoring, (2) integrated management of marine turtles and their habitats, (3) capacity for conservation, research, and management, (4) public awareness, information sharing, and education, (5) community participation in conservation, (6) regional and international cooperation, and (7) evaluation of the status of marine turtles. The document reflects our growing recognition of the global nature of many of the problems that threaten sea turtles and the need for regionally coordinated conservation efforts.

Regional sea turtle programs are already in place in many areas, including the Mediterranean, western Indian Ocean, northern Indian Ocean, South Pacific, and Caribbean. Cooperative tagging programs, conservation education campaigns, and exchange of technical information are common elements of many of these regional programs. Detailed action plans have been developed for individual countries within the Caribbean by participants of the Wider Caribbean Sea Turtle Conservation Network. Conservation efforts in the United States are guided largely by the recovery plans prepared for individual species of marine turtles by the National Marine Fisheries Service and the U.S. Fish and Wildlife Service.

Table 4.1

International and regional treaties affecting marine turtle conservation

Treaty or convention and date of adoption	Geographical region
Convention on Nature Protection and Wildlife Protection in the Western Hemisphere, 1940	Western Hemisphere
Convention on International Trade in Endangered Species of Wild Fauna and Flora, 1973	Global
Convention on the Conservation of Migratory Species of Wild Animals (Bonn), 1979	Global
ASEAN (Association of Southeast Asian Nations) Agreement on the Conservation of Nature and Natural Resources, 1985	Southeast Asia
Convention for the Protection of the Natural Resources and Environment of the South Pacific Region, 1986	South Pacific
Convention for the Protection and Development of the Marine Environment of the Wider Caribbean Region (Cartagena), 1990	Caribbean
Inter-American Convention for the Protection and Conservation of Sea Turtles, 1996	Western Hemisphere

International and regional treaties have provided important conservation benefits for marine turtles, and they hold great promise for the future. With its 146 signatory countries, CITES tightly restricts international trade in all sea turtles and sea turtle products. This convention has dramatically lowered trade and lessened hunting pressure on several species of sea turtles, most notably the hawksbill, from which tortoiseshell is derived. It has also curtailed international trade in turtle skins and in stuffed juvenile turtles for the curio trade. It does not address domestic trade. The Inter-American Convention for the Protection and Conservation of Sea Turtles addresses intentional harvesting, accidental drowning of sea turtles in fisheries gear, and habitat protection. Other international and regional agreements relevant to sea turtle conservation are listed in Table 4.1. Not listed are the various international agreements that deal with oil pollution of the sea, dumping of wastes at sea, and pollution from ships. All of these are of considerable importance to marine turtles and their habitats.

Low-Manipulation Strategies: Conservation at the Nesting Beach

The conservation strategy adopted in 1979 at the World Conference on Sea Turtle Conservation (Bjorndal 1982) remains a useful guiding document. Its hierarchical approach to management of habitats and populations was in many ways ahead of its time. It advocated the least-manipulative techniques in every situation, on the grounds that the biology of sea turtles is complex and our knowledge inadequate. The wisdom of this approach has been borne out countless times, as in the case of temperature-dependent sex determination: inappropriate temperature regimes in hatcheries inadvertently produced biased sex ratios among hatchlings (Shaver et al. 1988). Incubation environment is known to have a broad range of effects on the morphology and physiology of turtles that have flexible-shelled eggs, including nitrogen excretion (G. C. Packard et al. 1984), mobilization of calcium (M. J. Packard and Packard 1986), mobilization of yolk nutrients (G. C. Packard et al. 1985), hatchling size (G. C. Packard et al. 1981; McGehee 1990), energy reserves in the yolk at hatching (G. C. Packard et al. 1988), and locomotor ability of hatchlings (K. Miller et al. 1987).

An inherent problem of manipulative management techniques is that once intervention (e.g., relocation of a nest) has been chosen as a strategy, one is forced to make many decisions, such as where on the beach and how deep to place the nest, how to shape the egg chamber, how to arrange the eggs, how to pack the sand when covering the nest, how to camouflage the nest, and so forth. In most cases, the information needed for this decision making is inadequate. By our intervention, we risk negating benefits that have accrued to turtles from millions of years of natural selection. For example, because of temperature-determined sex selection the survival of a particular population of sea turtles is dependent on an extremely complex, evolved interaction between genes and maternal effects (Roosenberg 1996). We are capable of manipulating sex ratios by manipulating the temperature regimes of relocated nests, but we cannot possibly know the conservation consequences of our chosen sex ratio. Given this lack of knowledge, minimum alteration of the natural nest temperature regime—as with other nest parameters—is still the safest policy.

Another important contribution to the philosophy of sea turtle conservation was made by Frazer (1992), who urged managers and conservationists to address problems, not symptoms, in conservation efforts. He made the case that hatcheries, headstarting, and captive breeding were doomed to failure if the offspring were released into the same degraded environment in which their parents could not flourish. Frazer singled out TEDs and low-pressure sodium lights as examples of successful solutions that directly addressed problems—in these cases, accidental drowning in shrimp trawls and disorientation of adult females and hatchlings on the nesting beach.

This philosophy of addressing problems rather than symptoms can be applied broadly in nesting beach management. In Florida, the current goal of management is to leave nests and hatchlings alone and to make human activities on and near the nesting beach compatible with sea turtle nesting. This is diametrically opposed to previous policy, which responded to each threat by taking the eggs off the beach and incubating them in Styrofoam boxes or plastic buckets inside garages and offices. Today, to the extent possible, threats to individual nests posed by predators, artificial lighting, beach cleaning, and coastal construction activities are evaluated on a case-by-case basis; intervention, if required, is stepwise. If a nest must be moved, a site higher on the beach at the same location is chosen. The next level of intervention might be screening or enclosing an individual nest in a self-releasing cage. Relocation to a hatchery is seldom required in Florida, but if it is, a self-releasing design is used if possible. If not, hatchlings are released at night, in the dark, at dispersed sites along the beach; hatchlings are allowed to traverse the beach and enter the water on their own, to provide opportunity for the imprinting process that may occur at this time.

Depending on the nature of the threat, the minimal level of intervention required to protect nests may be greater than that described above. In some countries, every nest on a particular beach may be subject to poaching if not removed to a hatchery. In this event, hatchery practices should mimic nature in every way possible, including immediate release of hatchlings into the water after they have emerged from the nest to preserve the hatchling frenzy behavior. Conservation education and other efforts should work simultaneously toward removing the threat of poaching so that nests can be left on the beach at some time in the future.

Captive Rearing

Headstarting, ranching, and farming are terms that refer to captive rearing along a continuum of increasing intensity and duration of effort. **Headstarting** involves raising turtles in captivity from the egg or hatchling stage and releasing them at an age of 1 month to several years. **Ranching** involves rearing turtles to marketable size (which usually takes 3 to 4 years) and then slaughtering them; eggs, hatchlings, or breeding stock are taken from wild populations. **Farming** is similar to ranching, but no eggs or turtles are taken from the wild to restock the farm; the breeding females are themselves farm bred and raised.

Conservation benefits have been claimed for all three varieties of captive rearing, especially headstarting. The great allure of captive rearing for many people is not hard to understand. First, captive rearing requires the application of large amounts of ingenious, expensive technology. This makes it seem modern—state of the art: it appeals to a power- and technology-oriented culture. Second, unlike redwoods or desert tortoises *(Gopherus agassizii)*, sea turtles are hidden from us for more than 99% of their lives. Captive rearing prolongs our contact with these marine animals, reinforcing the sense of control that is for many people a necessary part of conservation. We now know that captive rearing of sea turtles can be done. Whether it should be done—that is, whether it helps to conserve these threatened species—is considered in the following sections. For a detailed history and analysis of headstarting, ranching, and farming of sea turtles, readers should consult the monograph by Donnelly (1994).

HEADSTARTING

Headstarting is a widely popular practice that has been applied most commonly to Kemp's ridleys (Byles 1993), green turtles (Huff 1989; F. Wood and Wood 1993), hawksbills (Milliken and Tokunaga 1987b; Suwelo 1990), and, less frequently, olive ridleys and loggerheads (Donnelly 1994). The conservation rationale for headstarting is based on four common assumptions: first, that only 1% or fewer of hatchling wild sea turtles survive to maturity, with the great majority of the loss occurring in the first year of life; second, that raising hatchlings in captivity during the vulnerable first year will let them escape most of the causes of mortality that would have threatened them had they remained in the wild; third, that after headstarted turtles are released, large numbers of them will grow to maturity and replenish their dwindling populations with viable eggs that produce viable hatchlings; and fourth, building on the other three assumptions, that headstarting is a good method of conserving sea turtles. The first of these assumptions is no more than an informed guess (Mortimer 1988c); there is no way to prove or disprove it. The other three assumptions, which are at the heart of headstarting, have been challenged by a series of problems, which are discussed below.

Removal of Eggs or Hatchlings from Wild Populations   All headstarting efforts have been or are now stocked primarily by eggs and hatchlings that have been removed directly from natural nesting beaches or by eggs acquired from captive adult breeders taken from the wild. This will continue for the foreseeable future. For example, over its 15 years, the world's premier headstarting project (a cooperative project of Mexico and the United States to release headstarted Kemp's ridleys) used 36,025 eggs taken from the natal beach in Mexico and raised those eggs in the U.S. National Marine Fisheries Service (NMFS) laboratory in Galveston, Texas (Caillouet 1995). This was 2.8% of the eggs laid during this period. The Galveston headstarting program complemented efforts to protect nests and release hatchlings at the nesting beach in Mexico.

At Cayman Turtle Farm (CTF), another headstarting operation, 10,573 yearling green turtles obtained from approximately 35,250 eggs were released between 1980 and 1991 (F. Wood and Wood 1993; Fosdick and Fosdick 1994). During this period, all of the eggs used by CTF came from its own captive breeders, which in 1994 comprised 163 wild-caught turtles, 52 **farm-reared** turtles hatched from wild-collected eggs, and 115 **farm-bred** turtles hatched from eggs conceived and laid in captivity. The female to male sex ratio of these turtles was approximately 3:1 (F.

Wood 1994). Because the farm-bred breeders were mostly immature during this period and because the eggs laid by farm-reared breeders had a very low hatch rate, nearly all of the headstarted turtles came from eggs laid by wild-caught breeders (J. Wood, personal communication). Assuming an annual average production of 200 eggs per female in the wild (half the captive breeders' rate), the 125 wild-caught females in the CTF herd—if they had all remained in the wild and survived during this 12-year period—would have laid 300,000 eggs. Given the large number of unknowables, it is impossible to calculate the actual reproductive impact of removing these breeding animals from their wild populations. We must assume, however, that a definite cost is associated with headstarting.

Other headstarting operations have existed and still exist; however, compared with the two operations mentioned above, nearly all of these take a higher percentage of eggs from local wild populations, have lower hatch rates, experience much higher mortality rates for their captive-reared animals, or exhibit some combination of these three variables (Milliken and Tokunaga 1987b; Donnelly 1994). In many of these cases, it is evident that the eggs used for headstarting would have been much better off left in place, except where egg mortality on the natal beach (from poaching and other causes) exceeds 85 to 90%. In the unusual cases of the Kemp's ridley project, which took only 2.8% of the eggs from the natal beach, and CTF, which no longer needs to take significant numbers of eggs or breeding adults from the wild, the impact on wild populations seems negligible. This is true even if we make a worst-case assumption that the headstarted turtles themselves have made no significant conservation contribution. But it should be noted that these two projects are exceptional: much of their quality is related to the very large sums of money that have been invested. Adequate diets, good seawater flow and sanitation, tank space to provide isolation for aggressive hatchlings, veterinary care, and the maintenance of adult breeding herds are all extremely expensive. In general, the lower the funding of any headstarting operation, the greater and less acceptable is the drain of eggs, hatchlings, and adult breeders from wild populations.

Genetic Mixing   Some headstarting projects mix turtles derived from different populations, making no effort to separate the genetic lineages or to release headstarted animals in the geographic area in which they evolved. Cayman Turtle Farm maintains in the same enclosures breeding adults from wild populations whose original nesting grounds are as widely separated as Ascension Island and Costa Rica and whose natural feeding grounds are, respectively, the coastal waters of Brazil and Nicaragua (Donnelly 1994). The headstarted progeny of these breeders are released at the Cayman Islands as part of the farm's tourist program. Furthermore, accidents can occur that compound the problem. For example, in 1989, a violent storm struck the island of Grand Cayman, washing hatchlings and yearlings from one tank to another and making it impossible to distinguish second-generation from first-generation farm-reared animals (Fosdick and Fosdick 1994). If, as is generally believed, the genetic variations that occur from one population to another within a species represent, in part, genetic adaptation to local conditions, then what is being done by interbreeding populations from regions A and B and releasing their offspring in region C? Will these offspring be as capable as they should be at evading predators, finding food and competing for that food with wild sea turtles, locating proper microhabitats and shelter, and using their remarkable powers of long-range navigation to locate appropriate nesting beaches? Again, there is no conclusive answer to these questions, but biological common sense cautions us that inappropriate genetic mixing of populations is likely to be a negative feature of any headstarting program.

Compounding the problem of genetic mixing is the likelihood that nongenetic maternal effects on eggs and hatchlings (such as hatchling sex ratio determination through nesting habitat selection by egg-laying females) may be rendered inappropriate if hatchlings are released in locations and habitats other than those selected by their mothers (Pennisi 1996).

Disease   There are three kinds of disease-related problems associated with headstarting: mortality during the period of captive rearing, transfer of infectious diseases from released captive-reared animals to wild populations, and vulnerability of released animals to infectious diseases already present in wild populations (see Flanagan, Chapter 3).

Diseases of hatchling and juvenile sea turtles in captivity have been well documented (Glazebrook and Campbell 1990a). Witham (1973) described necrotic, spreading skin lesions in headstarted green turtles and loggerheads reared in Florida. Witham and Futch (1977) noted both kyphosis (humpback) and lordosis (swayback) conditions among captive sea turtles. Leong et al. (1989) have divided the diseases they observed at the NMFS Galveston headstarting facility into 27 major categories. By our estimate, six of those categories involved infection caused by a variety of bacterial pathogens and seven categories involved fungal pathogens; the presence of viral pathogens was undetermined in most cases. Even in this advanced and carefully monitored facility, epizootics have occurred with disturbing frequency. For example, an outbreak of sudden hatchling death syndrome, believed to have been related to microbial contamination of the culture water, killed 40% of the entire population of captive loggerheads in a 4-week period. Leong et al. (1989) noted that isolation rearing and scrupulously clean seawater are cardinal requirements for maintaining the health of captive-reared turtles, but both of these requirements are very expensive.

At CTF, epizootics, including an outbreak of chlamydiosis that caused a die-off which cost the farm "hundreds of thousands of dollars," have also been observed (E. R. Jacobson 1996). Stress-induced viral diseases such as gray-patch disease, seen among hatchling green turtles at CTF, have been a serious problem (Lauckner 1985). It should also be noted that turtle farms which rely on a comparatively small number of breeders to produce their hatchlings will have a reduced genetic variation within their herd, which can result in inbreeding depression. Such inbreeding depression might be expressed as a lowering of the hatchlings' resistance to disease (Ballou 1993).

Not surprisingly, poorly supported operations—the great majority—are plagued with disease. In Palau, for example, the hawksbill headstarting project loses more than 50% of its hatchlings before release (Milliken and Tokunaga 1987b). The French headstarting facility for green turtles on Réunion Island in the Indian Ocean, notorious for its poor rearing conditions, has lost as many as 76.6% of its animals in 1 year (Donnelly 1994). Other operations, including cottage industry headstarting, also have high mortality rates (Glazebrook and Campbell 1990b). If a large percentage of headstarted turtles die during captive rearing, the conservation argument for headstarting breaks down.

The risk of captive-reared turtles spreading disease to wild populations is difficult to evaluate. In other taxa, unnaturally crowded populations (a common situation in the captive rearing of sea turtles) offer fertile ground for the breeding of new or modified infectious diseases. It is well known that pathogens have been widely spread by animals that have been captively reared for the pet trade—the retrovirus occurring among boas in the mid-1990s is an example. Whether such diseases have been spread by headstarted individuals to wild sea turtles is unknown. E. R. Jacobson (1993) has pointed out that upper respiratory tract disease (see Flanagan, Chapter 3) may have been "introduced into populations of tortoises [desert tortoises in the southwestern United States] . . . by release of ill, captive desert tortoises." No such case of introduction is known for sea turtles, where disease detection would be much harder. But we do know of one case in which an outbreak of fibropapillomatosis occurred among 26 headstarted green turtles at a holding facility in Florida; these turtles were eventually released. In recent decades, the incidence of fibropapillomatosis among wild sea turtle populations has increased dramatically, and this believed to be viral disease was reported to have been widespread at CTF in the early 1980s (Balazs 1986). Headstarted turtles with fibropapillomatosis have been captured in the wild, including one turtle from CTF and one from the Florida program mentioned above. However, the disease antedates CTF's and Florida's programs, and its worldwide incidence argues against the idea that captive rearing is the cause. More likely, the increasing pollution of shallow, coastal waters is in some way responsible for the epizootic. Yet we agree with E. R. Jacobson (personal communication) that because of the threat of disease and the cost and difficulty of screening headstarted turtles before release, "we cannot indiscriminately release captive-reared animals anymore."

It has also been suggested that captive-reared sea turtles will be especially vulnerable after release to diseases that they are exposed to in the wild (Woody 1990; E. R. Jacobson 1993). This vulnerability may be caused by a lack of immunity to specific pathogens or combinations of pathogens that captive turtles were not exposed to during a critical part of their life cycle or by a general immune system depression due to crowding and other stresses of captive rearing. Although increased vulnerability would be a difficult phenomenon to demonstrate, it is not unlikely that it occurs.

In summary, disease can be a formidable threat to the success of headstarting as a conservation measure. Again, disease control is directly related to the financial investment in a headstarting program, but there are some disease factors that cannot be controlled at any cost.

Behavior   It is well known that headstarted sea turtles can survive and grow in the wild, frequently for several years (F. Wood and Wood 1993; Caillouet et al. 1995a). Yet there is no doubt that at least some headstarted turtles behave abnormally in the wild, behaviors often exhibited long after their release from captivity. Aberrant behavior is to be expected of an animal that spends the developmentally important first year of its life not in the open ocean, with its myriad currents, waves, odor trails, magnetic fields, predators, symbionts, microhabitats, and food sources, but in a small tank or smaller bucket within a tank, being fed pelleted turtle chow at regular intervals and always in the presence of humans during the daylight hours. As Woody (1990), who coordinated the Kemp's ridley recovery effort for the Mexican and U.S. governments, has stated:

I've worked with enough species . . . to know that captive reared individuals don't cut it—be they trout, turtles, pheasant, wild turkey, or elk—unless they are intended for immediate human harvest by the gun or hook and line. These animals are not suitable for survival in the wild, they can't compete. This is not to say that 100% die; in some cases a few make it, but this is the exception and certainly not a rational use of the animal or our scarce resource dollars.

These differences in the behavior of captive-reared and wild individuals are more than anecdotal. In a review of the literature and description of laboratory studies, Olla et al. (1994) described numerous behavioral abnormalities among hatchery-reared Pacific salmon (*Oncorhynchus* spp.) and walleye pollock *(Theragra chalcogramma)* released into the wild. Hatchery-reared fish appear incapable of competing with wild fish for food; their tolerance of crowding inhibits their dispersal after release; they lack predator-avoidance behaviors; they consume fewer prey types than do wild fish; they seek out inappropriate microhabitats, adopting higher-than-normal positions above the substrate; and they show an inability to conserve energy by using pools and eddies where current flow is reduced.

Similarly, subadult headstarted ridleys have been found to consume more vegetation, mollusks, fish and shrimp (probably from shrimp and fish trawls), and other miscellaneous food items and consume many fewer species of crabs than do their wild relatives, even months after their release (Shaver 1991).

L. Ogren (1989; personal communication) has noted that headstarted Kemp's ridleys released at Panama City, Florida, showed none of the escape and avoidance response to humans shown by wild ridleys. They approached humans in shallow water and were easy to capture by hand. This abnormal behavior persisted 5 months after release. Ogren has also reported similar behavior in Florida of two tagged green turtles that had been headstarted at CTF 1 year earlier. Numerous cases in which headstarted green turtles, unafraid of humans, were easily hand captured have been documented in the files of the Florida Department of Environmental Protection. Headstarted loggerheads have shown similar behavioral abnormalities.

In May 1996, D. Shaver (1996; personal communication) reported the nesting on Padre Island, Texas, of two headstarted Kemp's ridley turtles that had been released on that beach. These turtles, of the 1983 and 1986 year-classes, deposited normal clutches of eggs that yielded a 96% and 33% hatch rate, respectively. In the 1997, 1998, and 1999 seasons an additional seven headstarted turtles (cumulative total) were found nesting on Padre Island and nearby Mustang Island (D. Shaver, personal communication). Thus olfactory detection (Manton et al. 1972), imprinting (Grassman et al. 1984), and mating and nesting behaviors (including orientation) may not be adversely affected by headstarting operations that include imprinting. In general, however, it is clear that the headstarting of sea turtles, as in captive rearing of other species, causes enough behavioral abnormalities to raise doubts about the ability of many, perhaps most, of the headstarted individuals to survive and reproduce in the wild. The bottom line is that after more than 30 years of releases of tens of thousands of headstarted turtles of at least four species in a variety of programs, from 1996 to 1999 only nine headstarted individuals have been documented to nest in the wild.

Demographic Concerns   Carr (1967:230) noted, "Protection of sea turtles is not a parochial problem. They cannot be saved in any one place, or by controlling any one phase of the life cycle." This basic truth is at the heart of one of the most serious and intractable problems of headstarting as a supposed conservation measure—demography. Conservationists are becoming increasingly aware that extremely long-lived and slowly maturing species require special strategies of protection that are directed at every age-class, not just at the juveniles (Crouse et al. 1987; Congdon et al. 1993). Heppell et al. (1996) have stated, "In general, the biological benefits of headstarting programs may be overestimated for turtles, and a careful examination of stage-specific mortality sources, demography, and life history can guide us toward more effective management strategies."

Headstarting does not eliminate the principal causes of excess mortality in most sea turtle populations: the loss of adults, subadults, and juveniles from drowning in shrimp nets and from overfishing. J. P. Ross, K. A. Bjorndal, and D. Crouse (unpublished) have claimed that the apparent recent increase in nesting adult Kemp's ridleys is more likely due to the use of TEDs in shrimp nets, which save about 40 adults a year, than to the release of thousands of headstarted hatchlings. Headstarting may seem to be working, but if many of the headstarted turtles are soon killed by shrimpers (Manzella et al. 1988) or by other kinds of human activity, headstarting is of little conservation value. Worse yet, it wastes precious time by creating a false sense of security and a false sense that events are under control when, in fact, they are not under control at all. Conservation energies and scarce conservation funds would be better spent if they were directed at the causes of the problems at various life stages, not at costly, hi-tech, showcase projects such as headstarting (Frazer 1992; Heppell and Crowder 1994; Heppell et al. 1996). When the Florida Department of Environmental Protection (then the Department of Natural Resources) terminated its 30-year headstarting program, it cited the need to pursue other strategies to ensure the future of its sea turtle populations (Huff 1989). Other strategies included promoting TED usage and protecting foraging and nesting habitats. As Mortimer (1988c) has stated, "When headstarting is advocated as a solution to the survival problems of turtles, the public can be lulled into believing that no other protective measures are needed."

Cost   Conservation funding is limited, and as we have seen, headstarting of acceptable quality is extremely costly. Proper enclosures, clean seawater, a high-protein diet, veterinary care, and the cash reserves to cope with unpredictable catastrophic events such as storms and epizootics make headstarting a "Cadillac" operation. If eggs come from a captive breeding herd, the price goes still higher.

According to Woody (1991), the U.S. and Mexico cooperative project for Kemp's ridley spent approximately US$0.65 per hatchling released directly from the protected natal beach in Mexico. On the other hand, the headstarting effort at the NMFS Galveston Laboratory spent, by conservative estimate, US$125 per turtle. Fosdick and Fosdick (1994) stated that CTF's cost of producing a hatchling Kemp's ridley (or green turtle) from the breeding herd was $10; a year of headstarting cost an additional $50 to $60. Of course, marginal headstarting operations are much less expensive. They are also much less successful. Woody (1991) noted, "I've seen far too many sick, lethargic, and dead hatchlings (olive ridley, hawksbill, logger-head, green turtle) resulting from headstarting efforts of well-intentioned people in other nations, many of whom are attempting this based solely on something they were told or read about the Kemp's ridley headstarting experiment in the U.S." Even minimal headstarting operations in less-developed countries can take away atten-tion and funding from more important conservation activities such as protecting nests and adult females at the nesting beach (Milliken and Tokunaga 1987b).

There is no shortage of supporters of headstarting (Manzella et al. 1988; W. H. Allen 1992; F. Wood and Wood 1993; Fosdick and Fosdick 1994) or of oppo-nents (Mortimer 1988c; Woody 1990; Frazer 1992; Taubes 1992; Heppell and Crowder 1994; Heppell et al. 1996). The strongest arguments in favor of head-starting are that (1) it has taught us a great deal about the biology and husbandry of captive sea turtles; (2) it has helped foster a public awareness of the plight of sea turtles and the need to protect them; and (3) some imprinted, headstarted sea turtles can survive in the wild and can reproduce at their "natal" beach. The strongest arguments against headstarting regard (1) detrimental genetic mixing of populations; (2) increased threat of disease; (3) abnormal behavior in the wild of headstarted hatchlings; (4) irrelevance to the principal causes of sea turtle mor-tality, especially to the causes of adult mortality; and (5) the high cost of doing it properly, with the result that more important kinds of conservation may go beg-ging. In poorly regulated operations (the majority), there is a sixth objection: head-starting can remove too many eggs and hatchlings from wild populations.

All of these arguments, pro and con, may be correct, so how can we decide what strategy is most appropriate? Ultimately, extinction is a biological matter, and the criteria for evaluating the success of headstarting must also be biological. The U.S. National Research Council's Committee on Sea Turtle Conservation (National Re-search Council 1990) lists the following four milestones for headstarting to be con-sidered a conservation practice:

1. Headstarted turtles must grow and survive after they are released into the wild.

2. Some headstarted turtles must nest on natural beaches.

3. A sufficient number of these turtles must nest to contribute to the main-tenance or recovery of a population.

4. It must be demonstrated that headstarted turtles are more likely to survive and reproduce than are turtles that have been released as hatchlings.

The first two milestones have been achieved at the time of this writing. The sec-ond two have not been achieved, nor in the opinion of the National Research

Council's committee are they likely to be. The formal governmental review of the Kemp's ridley headstarting program (S. A. Eckert et al. 1994) came to a similar conclusion. Headstarting can be considered successful (1) if headstarted turtles join wild populations, find their way to nesting beaches, and produce viable offspring and (2) if rates of survival to adulthood, and of fecundity for headstarted turtles, are as high as or higher than those for wild turtles. Again, the first has been demonstrated, but the second has not been shown, nor is it likely to be in the foreseeable future.

In the Blue-Ribbon Panel Review of the NMFS Kemp's ridley headstarting project, panel members, including staunch supporters of headstarting, stated (Wibbels et al. 1989):

Headstarting is an <u>experiment</u> and it should not be viewed as <u>the</u> means of saving the Kemp's ridley. Placing too much emphasis on the Headstart Program could jeopardize the primary element of the Kemp's ridley recovery plan (i.e., protection of Kemp's ridleys in their natural habitat).

A similar disclaimer was made by Charles Caillouet, Jr., of the NMFS Galveston Laboratory, regarding the two headstarted Kemp's ridleys that nested on Padre Island (*New York Times,* 16 July 1996, section C). Noting that the discovery of the two nesters does not prove that headstarting is a useful conservation technique, he said, "That's the kind of stretch we don't want people to make."

Thus, under the most favorable of conditions, headstarting must be judged an interesting experiment, not a conservation technique; it should never be used as an excuse to weaken protection for adult wild turtles or for the nests and juveniles of wild populations. When conditions are less than favorable, headstarting is not even an interesting experiment and may do serious harm to the conservation of sea turtles. As A. Carr has stated on a number of occasions (personal communication), headstarting is always a last resort for sea turtle conservation, to be relied on only when wild populations are nearly extinct and all else has failed.

RANCHING AND FARMING

There have been no fundamental changes in the arguments for and against the ranching and farming of sea turtles since the mid-1970s and early 1980s (Ehrenfeld 1974, 1980, 1982). Nevertheless, two decades' worth of additional experience with these forms of captive rearing has been accumulated. In this section, we are concerned only with conservation-related issues.

The principal conservation benefits claimed for ranching and farming are (1) the headstarting and release of a small percentage of the stock on hand for the purpose of augmenting wild populations and (2) the supposed reduction in demand for illegal (wild turtle) products because of the assured supply of high-quality products from captive-reared animals. Headstarting has already been discussed and rejected as a proven, or even likely, conservation technique. The issue of trade will be considered below. First, we examine briefly the question of the supply of eggs, hatchlings, and breeders taken from wild populations for turtle ranching.

At the outset, it should be noted that at none of the conferences of the parties to CITES have any sea turtle ranches or farms been approved because none of these has ever met CITES standards. A ranch, which takes either eggs or hatchlings from the wild, must provide a demonstrable conservation benefit to the local population of animals; farms are closed-cycle systems that can market only second-generation offspring (turtles themselves produced by farm-bred animals) to meet CITES criteria (Donnelly 1994). All existing operations either take eggs and hatchlings from the wild or, as in the case of CTF, rely principally on wild-caught, captive breeders. Because of the extremely low survival rates in most captive-rearing operations, large numbers of eggs are needed: it has been estimated that in some years as many as 80% of the green turtle eggs from natural beaches in Suriname were taken by the local ranching and headstarting program (Donnelly 1994). The eggs that were taken were often described as otherwise "doomed" by beach erosion or high tides. But the notion of doomed eggs seems self-serving; J. P. Ross, K. A. Bjorndal, and D. Crouse (unpublished) stated that "it is not possible to determine which particular egg might or might not survive to adulthood, except in a few trivial cases. The removal of eggs . . . should be recognized as an exploitative act and should not be justified only on the basis that the population as a whole will not suffer detriment as a result."

Cayman Turtle Farm, which has already produced some second-generation animals from its breeding stock, is the closest that any turtle farm has come to obtaining farm status under the CITES regulations. Nevertheless, hatch rates from the older group of captive-reared breeders, averaged over a 20-year period, are a very low 6% (Fosdick and Fosdick 1994), leading us to question whether something in the diet (perhaps soy estrogens) or another side effect of captivity reduces the viability of eggs from captive-bred animals. Even the wild-caught breeders at CTF produce eggs that have a hatch rate, averaged over 20 years, of only 30%, compared with typical 70 to 90% hatch rates for well-managed hatcheries at natural nesting beaches. We can speculate about the causes of this poor hatch rate or about the possibility that the abnormally high protein diet, fast maturation rate, and high rate of egg production will shorten the useful lives of these captive breeders, much as has happened with modern dairy cattle. Regardless of the reasons, however, the implications of the numbers are inescapable: CTF is very unlikely to become a true farm unless the CITES regulations are weakened to eliminate the requirement that only second-generation animals be marketed.

In 1993 J. P. Ross (1993) advocated international but restricted trade in ranched sea turtle products as an alternative to "the present uncontrolled and uncontrollable local slaughter." Similarly, J. P. Ross, K. A. Bjorndal, and D. Crouse (unpublished) advocated the careful regulation of trade in sea turtle products, provided—among many other requirements—that the source of each product (legal or illegal) is identifiable. In a more recent evaluation of ranches and farms, J. P. Ross (1999) admits that "[it] can be demonstrated . . . that [ranches and farms] are very expensive, require advanced technical knowledge, and are, to date, of unproved economic viability." He concludes that "the linkage of farms to direct conservation activities and strict trade control, through international cooperation, provides the potential that farms could contribute to the conservation of sea turtles, but this potential remains unrealized."

In 1994 at the Ninth Meeting of the Conference of the Parties to CITES (CITES Secretariat 1995), guidelines were adopted for the acceptable trade of ranched products, including unambiguous identification of ranched goods, quotas on ranch exports, monitoring and regulation of ranch operations, and approval of national and regional management plans for wild populations. These are the ideals. In practice, these admirable goals are unreachable for sea turtles for several clear and sufficient reasons.

Conservationists are frequently asked, if crocodile ranching helps reduce trade in wild crocodile products, why can't sea turtle ranching do the same for wild sea turtles? The answer is that major differences in the biology of crocodiles and sea turtles make the latter much less amenable to captive rearing. Sea turtles are migratory and nomadic; crocodiles are relatively sedentary. Crocodiles mature faster, their young are hardier, they are easier to feed, and they have a broader range of diets than do juvenile sea turtles. Nonbiological considerations include greater ease of tracking and regulating the trade in crocodile products. The fact that ranching works for some kinds of reptiles is no guarantee that it will work for others (see Table 4.2).

The high cost of ranched sea turtle products is an unavoidable obstacle to the idea that ranching can be used to inhibit illegal slaughter. For any responsible ranching operation, the cost of raising a sea turtle to marketable size is enormous. Although exact figures have not been published for the expense of raising a 4-year-old, 20- to 32-kg green turtle, we estimate the cost is well over $100 (Fosdick and Fosdick 1994). This cost is rising sharply because of increases in the prices of soy-based turtle diets and of fossil fuels. Cayman Turtle Farm lost money on every pound of turtle product it sold during its export years (J. Wood, personal communication); its annual profits are now entirely due to tourism (Fosdick and Fosdick 1994).

What this means is that ranched (and farmed) sea turtle products will always be

Table 4.2

Suitability of sea turtles and crocodiles for aquaculture

Aquacultural consideration	Nile crocodile			Green sea turtle		
	Suitable	Marginal or questionable	Unsuitable	Suitable	Marginal or questionable	Unsuitable
Growth rate	X					X
Ability to use inexpensive foods[a]			X			X
Tolerance to crowding[b]	X				X	
Hardiness	X					X
Easy access to supply of young		X				X
Husbandry requirements	X					X
Initial capital outlay costs			X			X
Water purification and waste product management costs[c]			X			X
Potential for conservation benefits to wild populations		X				X
Market demand[d]	X				X	
Price of products	X				X	

Note: Table adapted from Ehrenfeld (1982) and modified by Donnelly (1994); Nile crocodile *(Crocodylus niloticus)* information from Bolton (1989).

[a]Crocodiles are carnivorous, so almost any animal protein source will serve, and there is minimal pretreatment needed. Many crocodile ranches use manufactured high-protein feed for convenience. Sea turtles grow adequately on only artificial high-protein feed, which is not their natural diet, and will eat only in the water, which makes presentation more difficult.

[b]Both species appear to tolerate crowding well as long as food, nutrients, and water cleanliness are maintained, but young crocodiles seem to be naturally sociable, whereas sea turtles seem naturally solitary and will nip each other when crowded.

[c]Crocodiles produce soluble uric acid, which is very high in nitrates and difficult to purify. Sea turtle effluent probably contains less of a bacterial load. However, crocodile effluent is more easily cleansed by passage through freshwater wetland systems, whereas similar natural cleansing in marine systems is not known to exist at this time.

[d]Demand for sea turtle products (e.g., oil and meat) is essentially nonexistent in the United States at this time and would need to be re-created with intense marketing effort.

expensive, and this money-making potential will provide an incentive to poachers, whose costs are negligible and who will benefit from the diffuse, uncontrollable local demand stimulated by legal, ranched products. There is currently no inexpensive, portable, reliable method for distinguishing ranched from poached products. Even if there were, laundering of illegal products as ranch raised would be impossible to stop, at least at the local level. Free-trade blocs such as the European Economic Community have the potential to simplify some enforcement, but they have also opened new, wide loopholes for violations of CITES regulations (Donnelly 1992; J. Wood 1993).

In summary, with all of these biological, economic, and political considerations in mind, we cannot foresee any circumstances arising in which trade in ranched products could help the conservation of wild sea turtles.

CONCLUSIONS

The conservation strategies of the 1970s and 1980s have been criticized for being too beach oriented. To some extent, this is true. We now have good evidence from demographic models that protection of eggs and hatchlings, no matter how complete, will not compensate for heavy, unnatural losses of juveniles, subadults, and breeders. However, these same demographic models indicate that protection of marine turtles in all life history stages is needed. The high vulnerability of nesting females on the beach and the vulnerability of breeders of both sexes immediately off the nesting beach warrant high-level protection. Protection of turtles, eggs, hatchlings, and the nesting habitat itself is entirely feasible and involves well-established protocols, but it is the bare minimum of what should be done. Many of the other threats to marine turtles, including marine pollution and incidental catch in high-intensity fisheries, are far more intractable and require much more complex solutions.

Conservation strategies must constantly be reconciled with the latest research findings. We now know much more than we did in 1979 about the status of sea turtle populations around the world, about the genetic structures of their populations, about the complexities of their life histories, and about the magnitude of their migratory movements. We also have much more sophisticated and powerful population models that can help us predict the outcome of specific management actions without having to wait decades for results. To a greater extent than ever before, we can understand the biological constraints of sea turtles and take these into consideration in our conservation efforts. Nevertheless, what we know about sea turtles remains insignificant compared with what we do not know, and the wisest conservation measures will still involve the least manipulation of the turtles' life histories and environments.

ACKNOWLEDGMENTS

We thank Charles Caillouet, Jr., Marydele Donnelly, Allen Foley, Elliott Jacobsen, Larry Ogren, Barbara Schroeder, Donna Shaver, and Jim Wood for their advice and cooperation. Jeanne Mortimer kindly allowed us to use her figure (Figure 4.2). Tabitha Meyer, Karen Moody, and Andrea Mosier provided technical assistance. We thank Marydele Donnelly, Nat Frazer, Alan Huff, Judy Leiby, and Jim Quinn for their constructive comments on the manuscript.

Appendix 4.1
Natural and Human-Related Threats to Marine Turtles

Natural threats in the marine environment
• Predation by sharks, large fishes, and birds
• Habitat loss and degradation, such as hurricane damage to coral reefs
• Weather factors, such as sea level rise and cold stunning
• Diseases, such as fibropapillomatosis (possibly human related) and red tide poisoning

Human-related threats in the marine environment
• Direct harvest for meat, tortoiseshell, oil, and souvenirs for curio trade
• Incidental capture
  Commercial trawling, especially shrimp trawling, is a major source of mortality
  Other commercial fishing gears, including drift nets, longlines, gill nets, and pound nets,
    inadvertently drown turtles
  Recreational fishing is also a source of injury and mortality
• Habitat loss and degradation
  Pollution in the forms of oil and tar, toxins, persistent debris, and at-sea dumping may directly
    and indirectly affect turtle health and reproduction
  Siltation and eutrophication caused by terrestrial runoff of silt and nutrients damage coral reefs,
    cloud water, and shade sea grasses
  Increased human presence, in the forms of watercraft, swimmers, and scuba divers, disturbs
    turtles during feeding, mating, and nesting activities
  Oil and gas exploration, with associated explosions for platform removal, spills, and garbage,
    causes direct and indirect injury to turtles
  Dredging causes incidental take of turtles, damages benthic habitats, and causes sedimentation
  Reef dynamiting, a fishing technique, causes damage to feeding habitat
  Coral collection for aquaria eliminates feeding habitat
  Anchors and vessel groundings damage feeding habitats such as coral reefs and sea grass beds
  Construction activities, including those for marinas, ports, piers, and bridges, degrade habitat
• Disease by means of exposure to contaminants, which may compromise immune response in
    otherwise healthy turtles
• Accidental injury

Watercraft collisions cause direct injury and mortality

Entanglement, including in trap and pot lines, ghost nets, monofilament line, buoys, and garbage, causes drowning

Ingestion of marine debris, including plastic bags, tar balls, and Styrofoam, causes digestive tract impaction

Power plant entrapment at the cooling water intake causes direct injury and mortality

Natural threats in the terrestrial environment
• Predation by raccoons, coatis, monitor lizards, ghost crabs, birds, and other animals
• Habitat loss and degradation due to erosion, accretion, and accumulation of natural beach debris
• Weather factors, such as inundation from high tides and rain and accumulation of debris on beaches

Human-related threats in the terrestrial environment
• Direct harvest of eggs and adult female turtles (for meat, tortoiseshell, skin, and oil)
• Habitat loss and degradation

Armoring, which includes seawalls, revetments, geotextile tubes, retaining walls, and sand fences, eliminates habitat and interferes with nesting

Artificial lighting causes disorientation of hatchlings and nesting females and deters females from nesting

Beach nourishment increases sand compaction, creates escarpments, changes the microenvironment of nests, and can interfere with nesting activity

Beachfront development, such as construction, armoring, artificial lighting, and beach nourishment, and concomitant increased human presence and possibly increased predation, interferes with nesting activity and decreases hatching success

Beach cleaning increases sand compaction, disturbs nests, promotes wind erosion, and creates vehicular ruts that entrap emerging hatchlings

Pollution, which includes oil spills, tar balls, plastic, and other persistent debris, impedes or harms nesting females and hatchlings

Vehicular traffic on beach results in direct mortality of hatchlings and adults, increases sand compaction, degrades dunes, and creates vehicular ruts that entrap hatchlings

Sand mining of onshore sand, which is used for construction aggregate, and offshore sand reserves, which are used for beach nourishment, depletes sand or sand stores of nesting beaches

Increased human presence from recreation, ecotourism, or beach development may deter or disturb nesting females

Recreational beach equipment, such as beach chairs, sailboats, and paddleboats, entraps nesting females

Inundation from storm water runoff and drainage from beachfront swimming pools causes nest damage

Exotic vegetation creates unnatural shading, may alter or eliminate natural beach vegetation and habitat, and may prevent nesting because of plant roots

Livestock on beach disrupts nesting and nests and increases sand compaction
• Predation by unnaturally high densities of egg predators (e.g., raccoons) and introduced species (e.g., dogs, pigs, and mongooses) associated with human communities

Note: Species-specific information is provided in the most recent recovery plans jointly prepared by the U.S. Fish and Wildlife Service and the National Marine Fisheries Service (NMFS and USFWS 1991a, 1991b, 1992a, 1992b; USFWS and NMFS 1992).

5

CONSERVATION OF RIVER TURTLES

Turtles residing in riverine habitats are a taxonomically and ecologically diverse group. They are geographically widespread, ranging from the equator to relatively high latitudes of the temperate zones (to 60° N in Europe) and from sea level to altitudes of over 1,800 m in the mountains of tropical Asia. River turtles inhabit the lowland, multiple-order fluviatile sections of rivers that are often characterized by broad, deep channels and, at times, considerable current velocity. Such habitats also attract large concentrations of the turtle's primary exploiter, humans. Jeopardized by human predation and habitat degradation, many species of river turtles are now endangered. Here, we will provide an overview of the taxonomic and ecological characteristics of these species, describe the specific threats they face, and discuss methodologies that are appropriate for the management and restoration of their populations. Other freshwater turtles are discussed in Chapter 6.

BIOLOGICAL CHARACTERISTICS

The species discussed in this chapter are best defined by their predilection for riverine habitats. Reflecting this, diverse taxa of river turtles often share a number of independently evolved characteristics that contribute toward their successful existence in large, flowing bodies of water (Table 5.1). Although not all species possess every trait listed, most possess several, and collectively these traits characterize the group. Below we briefly summarize the relevance and relationship of these characteristics to the riverine niche and note species exemplifying these traits as well as some notable exceptions.

Table 5.1

Morphological and ecological characteristics of river turtles

---

- Optimum habitat: large, flowing bodies of water
- Locomotion: swimmers rather than bottom walkers (Zug 1971)
- Body size: medium to large species (25 cm to over 100 cm carapace length; *Graptemys* spp. and
    some *Kachuga* spp. are exceptions); most of the largest species are tropical
- Sexual dimorphism: females usually exceed males in size; at least three species seasonally sexually
    dichromatic
- Reproduction:
    type I reproduction (i.e., laying large numbers of relatively small eggs at ancestral nesting beaches
        during a discrete nesting season; E. O. Moll 1979)
    nesting on sandbanks
- Morphology:
    elongated snout or proboscis; sometimes elongated neck
    bony lung chambers, sometimes encased by large shell buttresses in diving species
    limbs flattened and oarlike; feet extensively webbed
    reduced shell lip (skin of neck attaches near leading edge of shell); other freshwater and terrestrial
        forms have a prominent shell lip
    streamlined body shape
    body more dense than water
    tendency for plica media of penis to have elaborate flaps (e.g., trionychids and *Batagur baska*)

Habitat

Unlike other turtles associated with riverine environments in the broadest context
(i.e., residents of streams, floodplain backwaters, swamps, sloughs, and even terrestrial habitats adjacent to the river), river turtles inhabit the higher-order, fluviatile sections of rivers that are often characterized by broad, deep channels and, at
times, considerable current velocity. Obst (1986) has categorized river turtles into
several distinct biotopes, and our emphasis conforms with his description of those
aquatic species of the open water that "are excellent swimmers and divers that can
cover extensive areas of great rivers and lakes."

Whereas many river turtles, such as the Central American river turtle *(Dermatemys mawii)* or the Asian giant softshell turtle *(Pelochelys bibroni)*, are completely
aquatic except for terrestrial oviposition, others, such as the riverine emydid genera *Callagur* (painted terrapin), *Kachuga* (roofed turtles), *Hardella* (crowned river
turtle), and *Graptemys* (map turtles) and the smaller trionychids (softshell turtles),
spend considerable time basking on snags, riverbanks, and sandbars. Some populations of river turtles thrive in large lakes, lagoons, and impoundments associated
with river systems (e.g., African softshell *[Trionyx triunguis]*, Central American river
turtle, and common map turtle *[Graptemys geographica]*). Some species that char-

acteristically inhabit large rivers regularly enter smaller tributaries or tidal creeks to forage (e.g., river terrapin *[Batagur baska]*; E. O. Moll 1980a). Finally, some species from groups more typically associated with other biotopes may occasionally fill river turtle niches where more characteristic riverine taxa are absent. Some of these species exhibit adaptations comparable to those associated with this niche (e.g., large size). Caribbean Costa Rican populations of common slider *(Trachemys scripta)* and black wood turtle *(Rhinoclemmys funerea)* are two examples of this phenomenon (Pritchard and Trebbau 1984; D. Moll 1994; D. Moll and Jansen 1995).

Several species are sufficiently powerful to inhabit the turbulent estuarine sections of major rivers (e.g., river terrapin and painted terrapin *[Callagur borneoensis]*; E. O. Moll 1980a, b). At least two softshells are sometimes found in marine habitats. One, the African softshell, has become established in the eastern Mediterranean Sea from Egypt northward along the Middle Eastern coastline to Turkey (Atatür 1979). Another, the Asian giant softshell turtle, is an estuarine inhabitant that also frequents coastal waters (Cantor 1847; de Rooij 1915; Smedley 1932; E. O. Moll and Vijaya 1986; Rhodin et al. 1993) and has been taken up to 5 km from shore (Nair and Badrudeen 1975).

Locomotion

Large river turtles tend to be swimmers rather than bottom walkers (sensu Zug 1971). The alligator snapping turtle *(Macroclemys temminckii),* a huge bottom walker inhabiting rivers of the southeastern and south-central United States, is one of the exceptions.

Body Size

Many river turtles are relatively to extremely large species. It is not unusual for riverine species to attain carapace lengths over 60 cm and weights exceeding 25 kg. The largest freshwater species are the giant softshells of the genera *Chitra* and *Pelochelys.* Constable (1982) recorded a Vietnamese specimen of the latter approximately 1.7 m in length and allegedly weighing 250 kg (see Rhodin et al. 1993 for other records). The largest of the hard-shelled river turtles are the giant South American river turtle *(Podocnemis expansa),* which reaches a carapace length of 107 cm (Ernst and Barbour 1989), and the Nearctic alligator snapping turtle, captive specimens of which have attained a carapace length of 80 cm and a weight of 114 kg (Pritchard 1989).

Large size is probably a selective response to multiple factors and may be advantageous in a riverine environment. The advantages that large size confers may include (1) strength and endurance to migrate and maneuver in the strong currents and turbulence associated with riverine habitats; (2) high fecundity, which is often associated with large body size; (3) large body mass for effective osmoregulation in estuarine and seagoing species; and (4) greater protection that large size and a heavy shell confer against predators such as crocodilians (Dunson and Moll 1980; E. O. Moll 1980a, b; Pritchard and Trebbau 1984; Dunson and Heatwole 1986; Dunson and Seidel 1986; D. Moll and Moll 1990; D. Moll 1994). Ernst and Barbour (1989) and Pritchard (1979, 1989) provided reviews of the sizes attained by the world's chelonian species. Pritchard (1980) provided record sizes attained for several riverine species from Florida and South America.

Smaller turtles, such as those in the genera *Apalone* (North American softshell turtles) and *Graptemys* and some species of *Kachuga,* also inhabit rivers. Many, but not all, of these species live in smaller rivers or in upstream or less-turbulent sections of larger rivers. Most Australian river turtles of the genera *Elseya* (Australian snapping turtles), *Elusor* (Mary River turtle), *Emydura* (Australian short-necked turtles), *Chelodina* (Australian snake-necked turtles), and *Rheodytes* (Fitzroy River turtle) also tend toward more modest proportions, as do the rivers they inhabit (see Cann and Legler 1994 for comparative size information).

Sexual Dimorphism

Most river turtle species are sexually dimorphic, with females attaining larger sizes than do males. This pattern is typical in highly aquatic, **nektonic** (free-swimming) species in which selection favors larger female size to increase fecundity (and perhaps secondarily as a defense against predation at nest sites) and smaller male size to enhance mobility and hasten reproductive contribution via early maturation (E. O. Moll 1979; J. F. Berry and Shine 1980; Gibbons and Lovich 1990). At least three large Asian species, river terrapin, painted terrapin, and painted roofed turtle *(Kachuga kachuga),* are seasonally and sexually dichromatic (E. O. Moll 1980a, b, 1986; E. O. Moll et al. 1981). The head, neck, and legs of male river terrapin turn jet black (from a dull olive gray), and the eye color changes to bright white (from yellowish) during the monsoon mating season. In painted terrapin males, the head changes from charcoal to white, and a red stripe develops between the black eyes. These color changes not only enhance sexual recognition but also may allow these often sympatric species to differentiate between one another in their turbid estuarine habitats. In the painted roofed turtle, the male's head and neck are brilliant red during the breeding season but fade thereafter. Male Burmese roofed turtles *(Kachuga trivittata)* have a reddish head and carapace striping that is absent in females (Theobald 1868). It is unknown if this dichromatism is seasonal, however.

Reproduction

TYPE I REPRODUCTION

Most river turtles reproduce in a **type I pattern** (E. O. Moll 1979), in which females lay relatively large clutches of relatively small eggs, produce multiple clutches during a well-defined nesting season, nest communally in well-defined ancestral nesting areas, and deposit eggs in carefully constructed pit nests that are sealed after oviposition. E. O. Moll (1979) considered this to be a primitive pattern in comparison to the **type II pattern,** which is characterized by small clutches of relatively large eggs (often brittle shelled with long incubation periods), acyclic or continuous reproduction, solitary laying in scattered locations, and poorly constructed nests or no nests. Type II patterns are typical of many nonriverine tropical species.

These two reproductive patterns represent the extremes of a continuum that can be observed in various taxa and geographic locations. Temperate-zone species, sea turtles, and river turtles (including tropical species) usually display several, if not all, of the type I reproductive characteristics. However, type II traits (particularly the relatively large brittle-shelled eggs laid in small clutches) are most characteristic of tropical species (E. O. Moll and Legler 1971; Legler 1985). Iverson et al. (1993) reported a significant inverse correlation between egg size and latitude and a positive correlation between clutch size and latitude among turtles generally.

Most riverine turtle species probably produce multiple clutches annually, but the natural history of some species is still too poorly known to state this categorically (E. O. Moll 1979). There is much variability in clutch size among the various riverine turtle taxa, with clutch sizes ranging up to 178 in *Chitra* spp. (Bhadauria et al. 1990) and 150 in the giant South American river turtle (Mittermeier 1978). Only a few large species have a clutch size of less than 20 eggs. Examples include the painted terrapin (E. O. Moll 1980b) and the Central American river turtle (Polisar 1992). Small clutches are typical in the smaller species (E. O. Moll 1979; Ernst and Barbour 1989). Large turtles produce heavier clutches and greater total annual clutch mass than do smaller turtles. However, if clutch mass is compared with body mass, then smaller species typically produce relatively heavier individual clutches and total annual clutch masses (Iverson 1992b).

It is uncertain whether most larger river turtle species nest annually or whether, like most sea turtles, they lay eggs at multiple-year intervals (E. O. Moll 1979). Many turtle species have temperature-dependent sex determination, in which lower nest temperatures typically produce male offspring and higher temperatures produce female offspring. Many species remain to be examined, however. At least some species of softshell turtles (Trionychidae) have genotypic sex determination, and nest temperatures are irrelevant in this regard (Bull and Vogt 1979; Bull 1980;

Vogt and Bull 1982, 1984; Alho et al. 1984, 1985; Vogt and Flores Villela 1986; Paukstis and Janzen 1990; Ewert and Nelson 1991; Janzen and Paukstis 1991; Vogt 1994).

NESTING SITES

Many riverine species require large, easily accessible, open expanses of well-
drained substrates for nesting, such as sandbars, islands, and beaches. These sites
are especially important in heavily forested regions where canopy cover, root systems, and waterlogged soils may preclude successful nesting in many areas. The
limited availability of suitable sites in some habitats undoubtedly influences the
timing (usually dry season in the tropics) and communal nature of nesting in many
riverine species. The Amazonian giant South American river turtle and Asian river
terrapin are examples of species that nest during the dry season; females migrate
to, and concentrate at, suitable nesting localities. Where suitable riverbank sites
are unavailable, several species, including painted terrapin (E. O. Moll 1980b),
Asian giant softshell turtle (Rhodin et al. 1993), pig-nosed turtle *(Carettochelys insculpta)* (Georges and Rose 1993), and Caribbean Costa Rican common slider (D.
Moll 1994), may utilize nearby sea beaches for nest sites.

Exceptions to this pattern (i.e., congregating on well-drained substrates) include
the Indian softshell turtle *(Aspideretes gangeticus),* the Northern Australian snake-
necked turtle *(Chelodina rugosa)* (Kennett et al. 1993), and the Central American
river turtle (Polisar 1992). These highly aquatic species nest on otherwise inaccessible mud banks when rivers are in flood. Their brittle-shelled eggs typically undergo embryonic diapause, allowing them to withstand considerable inundation
without damage. The yellow-spotted Amazon River turtle *(Podocnemis unifilis)* is
another riverine species that may not congregate at nesting sites and will nest on
a variety of substrates including mud (Ernst and Barbour 1989); embryonic diapause has not been reported.

Morphology

The remaining traits listed in Table 5.1 are presumably adaptations that increase
the efficiency of river turtles in their highly aquatic niche. For example, the elongated snouts characteristic of many riverine species (e.g., river terrapin, pig-nosed
turtle, and several softshell genera) allow them to obtain oxygen inconspicuously by
just breaking the water's surface, thereby avoiding attention from predators or prey.
The extremely long necks of some species, such as the Australian snake-necked
turtles *(Chelodina* spp.) and softshells (Trionychidae), accentuate this ability.

Some of the more accomplished diving species, such as river terrapin, painted
terrapin, crowned river turtle *(Hardella thurjii),* and some species of roofed turtles,

have bony lung chambers formed by the lateral walls of the carapace (Obst 1986). These may aid the lungs in withstanding the greater pressures encountered during deep dives. The heavy buttressing of the shell, particularly well developed in painted terrapin and river terrapin, probably also aids in deterring predation by crocodilians (E. O. Moll 1980a).

The extent of the development of pharyngeal, cutaneous, and cloacal respiration in the various riverine taxa is not well known but might be important adaptations for highly aquatic species. Both pharyngeal and cutaneous respiration are considered important respiratory mechanisms in the softshells (e.g., smooth softshell *[Apalone mutica]*, D. C. Jackson et al. 1976; spiny softshell *[Apalone spinifera]*, Dunson 1960; and African softshell, Girgis 1961). All Australian chelids can probably use cloacal respiration to some extent; the Fitzroy turtle *(Rheodytes leukops)* and the Northern Australian snapping turtle *(Elseya dentata)* are highly adapted in this regard (Legler 1993; Legler and Georges 1993; Cann and Legler 1994).

The extensive webbing and palmate shape of the feet (especially the hind limbs), streamlined body shape, and reduced shell lip (where the skin of the neck attaches near the leading edge of the carapace) all function to increase the hydrodynamic efficiency of river turtles. In the pig-nosed turtle the forelimbs have been modified into flipperlike structures similar to those of marine species.

Several river turtle taxa possess body densities greater than that of water, which allow them to sink quickly, as opposed to bottom walkers and tortoises, which tend to float (Zug 1971). Finally, there is a tendency for the plica media of the penis to display elaborate flaps in the trionychid and batagurid river dwellers (Zug 1966; E. O. Moll 1986). These flaps could be an adaptation to hold the penis in place during copulation in flowing water, but their function remains to be demonstrated.

THE ROLE OF TURTLES IN THE RIVERINE ECOSYSTEM

Turtles are valuable components of the riverine ecosystem. Until recently, however, they have received remarkably little recognition. While this neglect has likely been due to the perception that turtles are of limited economic value and of only minor importance in riverine ecosystems, there is a growing body of research on the subject that indicates quite the contrary is true.

Whereas the information presented below provides several perspectives on the value of river turtles to humankind, humans, who have an important stake in properly functioning rivers themselves, may also benefit indirectly from the roles river turtles play in the natural environment. Riverine species, although not attaining the level of diversity of fishes in most of the habitats that they share, still reach extremely high densities and contribute significantly to community biomass. Knowledge of river turtle densities and biomass is still rudimentary due to inherent difficulties in estimating aquatic turtle population sizes in open systems (compared with smaller **lentic,** or standing water, habitats) and the great variability of **lotic** (running water) habitats (and therefore turtle populations within them). Nevertheless, several studies suggest the potential importance of aquatic turtles in this regard (e.g., Chessman 1978; Iverson 1982; Congdon et al. 1986; Congdon and Gibbons 1989; D. Moll 1990; M. B. Thompson 1993; Vogt and Villareal 1993).

Odum (1957) included turtles in a study of the trophic structure and energy flow in a Florida riverine ecosystem. More recently, M. B. Thompson (1993) published an ambitious attempt to estimate the density, biomass, and contribution to energy flow of a river turtle community—consisting of Murray River turtle *(Emydura macquarii),* common snake-necked turtle *(Chelodina longicollis),* and giant snake-necked turtle *(Chelodina expansa)*—in Australia's Murray River. Based upon his own data and those of Chessman (1978), he estimated that densities of the first two species lie between 4 and 159 turtles per hectare and the third may be represented by only 1 per hectare. Given average body mass estimates, he projected that the three species combined may contribute between 3,050 and 230,000 metric tons to river biomass, with the best estimate falling between 10,000 and 100,000 metric tons. Furthermore, based upon the latter figures, he calculated the standard metabolic energy consumption of these turtles at between 13.5×10^7 and 13.5×10^9 kJ per day. Although more extensive fieldwork will be required to refine these very rough and wide-ranging estimates, they suggest the importance of turtles as components of riverine food webs and in energy flow and nutrient cycling throughout the system.

River turtle species are found at every level in riverine food webs (see Ernst and Barbour 1989 and Ernst et al. 1994 for general descriptions of diets), and they display many interesting ecological, behavioral, and morphological adaptations for catching and processing their food. Food preferences may change ontogenetically, seasonally, and between habitats as resource variability, competitive interactions, and other factors dictate (D. B. Clark and Gibbons 1969; D. Moll 1976, 1977, 1980, 1985, 1989, 1990; Parmenter 1980; Vogt 1980, 1981b; Parmenter and Avery 1990).

Many of the moderate to larger hard-shelled species are predominantly or totally herbivorous as adults. Although some species may be more carnivorous as juveniles, others such as river terrapin, some South American river turtles *(Podocnemis* spp.), the Central American river turtle, and some river cooter *(Pseudemys concinna)* populations are predominately herbivorous as juveniles also (E. O. Moll 1980a; D. Moll 1989; Davenport et al. 1992; Ernst et al. 1994). River terrapin, painted terrapin, Central American river turtle, giant South American river turtle, river cooter, and Northern Australian snapping turtle are examples of species that are generally strictly herbivorous as adults. A wide variety of aquatic vascular and nonvascular plants are eaten by various species in different habitats, in addition to inundated terrestrial vegetation and fruits, flowers, and leaves that fall into the water (Webb 1961; Legler 1976; D. Moll 1976, 1989; N. J. H. Smith 1979; Georges and Rose 1993; Fachin-Teran et al. 1995; D. Moll and Jansen 1995; Kennett and Tory 1996). River terrapin (Davenport et al. 1992) and Indian tent turtle *(Kachuga tentoria)* (Varghese and Tonapi 1986) readily feed upon water hyacinths *(Eichhornia crassipes)*, thereby helping to keep waterways from becoming clogged by this weedy pest.

Many river dwellers could probably best be described as opportunistic omnivores, with the proportions of animal versus plant material in diets varying greatly in response to the resources available in various habitats, the season, competitive interactions, and probably other yet poorly understood factors (J. F. Berry 1975; D. Moll 1976; Vogt 1981b; Georges 1982; White and Moll 1992; Legler and Georges 1993).

Some species seem to be largely carnivorous, although few species have been studied in enough detail to be certain. Examples of species that appear to be totally carnivorous are the Zambezi flapshell turtle *(Cycloderma frenatum)*, giant snake-necked turtle, several map turtles, and many trionychids. Carnivorous species may prey on many types of food items, from the smallest zooplankton, insects, and mollusks, to fishes, waterfowl, and other turtles. Among the carnivores, individual turtle populations or species may be very specialized or very generalized in the types of foods eaten. The shape of the jaws of carnivorous species are often quite specialized to process various types of prey efficiently (see Obst 1986). Turtles typically feed in a very simple manner, capturing prey with their jaws and swallowing it whole if small enough or using the forelimbs and jaws to dismember larger items.

Specialized feeding methods are used by some river turtle species, including **inertial feeding** (releasing jaws suddenly and using prey inertia to gain a new bite farther over the body [Gans 1961]); **neustophagia** (skimming zooplankton and other particulate matter from the surface film [Belkin and Gans 1968; Rhodin et al. 1981]); **benthic bulldozing** (eating large volumes of bottom detritus and benthic prey apparently indiscriminately, as observed in false map turtles [*Graptemys pseudogeographica*] and Ouachita map turtles [*Graptemys ouachitensis*] [D. Moll 1976, 1985]); **pharyngeal feeding,** also known as "gape and suck" feeding (creating a vacuum by opening the jaws, which literally sucks prey into the mouth, as observed in the matamata [*Chelus fimbriatus*] and the giant snake-necked turtle [Legler 1978; Pritchard and Trebbau 1984]); ambush feeding, as practiced by partially buried softshells (Pritchard 1984; Ernst et al. 1994); and angling or luring by the alligator snapping turtle (Pritchard 1989).

A particularly ubiquitous feeding strategy practiced by river turtles, with importance for both river ecosystems and human populations, is scavenging. Probably all river turtle species scavenge to some extent, and it may well be an important source of protein for many because few species are well adapted for capturing live fishes or other nektonic prey. M. B. Thompson (1993) conservatively estimated that the three species of Murray River chelid turtles he studied may scavenge at least 180,000 metric tons per year. This is only a rough estimate, but it suggests the magnitude of the role of river turtles in nutrient cycling. M. B. Thompson suggested that one result of declines in river turtle populations (as is occurring in the Murray River due to predation by introduced red fox [*Vulpes vulpes*]) may be increased problems related to eutrophication. In India, softshells (principally the Indian softshell and the Indian flapshell turtle [*Lissemys punctata*]) are recognized as playing major roles in scavenging detritus from rivers. The former has been propagated for release in the Ganges (where high levels of exploitation have reduced its numbers) to scavenge the numerous animal and partially cremated human corpses dumped into the river each day (E. O. Moll 1985b; Stackhouse 1992).

Finally, turtles themselves are important prey species in riverine food webs, especially in their early ontogenetic stages (see Ernst et al. 1994 for a review of predators of North American species). Eggs are often eaten by semiaquatic and terrestrial floodplain dwellers. Hatchlings, although perhaps not as helpless against predators as once thought (Semlitsch and Gibbons 1989; Britson and Gutzke 1993), fall prey to fishes, snakes, crocodilians, and birds. Skunks, foxes, raccoons *(Procyon lotor),* and other mammalian predators eat adult turtles on occasion (especially nesting females), and spiny softshells are known to be eaten by muskrats *(Ondatra zibethica)* (Parmalee 1989). Smaller turtle species, and juveniles of larger species, may be consumed by larger turtles such as alligator snapping turtles and Mexican giant musk turtles *(Staurotypus triporcatus)* (Pritchard 1989; D. Moll 1990) or taken by birds of prey. Larger adult river turtles, even those as formidable as the Asian giant softshell turtle, are eaten by crocodilians (Rhodin et al. 1993).

THREATS TO RIVERINE TURTLES

There is grave concern for the future of many of the world's river turtles. Although there are numerous criteria that may be used to set conservation priorities for threatened species (Georges 1993) and several rating systems have been established to rank the degree of threat that turtle species face (IUCN 1989, 1996), river turtles consistently have proportionately more species in the most threatened categories than any other nonmarine turtle group.

The reasons for the precipitous decline in so many riverine species are linked to human activity in almost every case. The problems may result directly from exploitation by humans, indirectly from habitat modification, or from a combination of both. Generally, however, the overexploitation of river turtles that has led to their demise is a consequence of their great value to humans. River turtles are in demand to provide a vast human population with a source of meat, eggs, medicines, and pets, and they are the subjects of extremely lucrative local, national, and international trade as a result. Probably no other vertebrate group of such benefit to humankind has received so little attention from scientists and conservationists and has been so poorly known by the general public. Of all reptiles, turtles are the most heavily exploited for human consumption (Klemens and Thorbjarnarson 1995). As with any limited resource whose use is not adequately regulated, overexploitation and resource degradation are inevitable, the classic tragedy of the commons (Hardin 1968). In the context of overexploitation of wildlife, there are three clear tragedies: the decline and possible extinction of a species; the degraded health of the ecosystem in which that species filled a vital niche; and the loss of a valuable resource to humans. Certainly the current trade in turtles for food, medicine, and other products in Bangladesh, India, Vietnam, and elsewhere and the U.S. turtle ranching export trade are unsustainable at current levels. These are not the only countries ruining their turtle stocks, but are countries for which relatively extensive data are available. Indications of similar exploitation of river turtle populations are also known from Mexico, Belize, Guatemala, China, Indonesia, Papua New Guinea, Brazil, Colombia, Venezuela, and Madagascar. Undoubtedly, there are problems in African countries and other locations as well from which no data are currently available. The overexploitation and resulting decline of the Madagascan big-headed turtle (Erymnochelys madagascariensis) (Kuchling 1988), Malaysia's river terrapin (E. O. Moll 1978a, 1984), and the giant South American river turtle (N. J. H. Smith 1975) are among the best-documented cases.

Besides the uses of turtles detailed below, other kinds of human activities may directly result in the decline of turtle populations. Automobiles kill untold numbers of river turtles annually as they cross roads separating rivers and nesting areas or as they disperse toward other aquatic habitats. In parts of the United States, irresponsible boaters still use basking turtles for target practice, and fishermen routinely kill turtles caught on hooks and in commercial nets.

Human Use of Turtles

River turtles are important to many human cultures, by which they may be used for food and other products as well as as an economic resource (see Thorbjarnarson et al., Chapter 2). River turtles have been an important source of protein for some human populations from prehistory to the present day. Aboriginal peoples were adept turtle hunters and egg harvesters, as attested to in the classic accounts of Humboldt (1861–62) and Bates (1863) concerning the use of Orinoco and Amazon Rivers' giant South American river turtles (see also accounts by Parsons 1962; Mittermeier 1975, 1978; N. J. H. Smith 1975, 1979; Klemens and Thorbjarnarson 1995; Thorbjarnarson et al., Chapter 2). Today, populations of river turtles are being used in much the same way (if not at such spectacular magnitude) by a variety of river-dwelling peoples, including some of the last remaining hunter–gatherer cultures.

With our ever-present need for freshwater, it is not surprising that civilizations have often developed and spread along rivers as their populations grew. Predictably, turtles and their eggs have continued to be used as a source of food by riverine peoples for the same reasons that aboriginal cultures used them. As turtles and eggs can often be harvested in large numbers, the surplus catch became natural fare for barter and sale. Today, river turtles and their eggs remain an important food resource for some cultures and are valuable market commodities around the world. With huge human populations to feed, and the development of effective, fast intra- and intercontinental transportation systems, the opportunity for more people to use river turtle products has expanded dramatically. As the strain on river turtle populations grows, their value as a human source of food and other products remains high.

The pressure on river turtle populations as a source of food is currently greater in the tropics than in the temperate zones, but this has not always been the case. The Mississippi River and its major tributaries supplied huge numbers of turtles for thriving local markets as well as markets in major cities of the Midwest and the eastern seaboard well into the 1950s (Townsend 1902; H. W. Clark and Southall 1920; Cahn 1937; D. Moll 1977, 1980; Bellrose et al. 1977). Today, commercial fisheries supplying turtles for food in the United States may be of moderate importance locally or regionally but have greatly declined overall. Legal and illegal commercial trade in alligator snapping turtles in some states of the lower Mississippi valley is still intense, however (Pritchard 1989; Sloan and Lovich 1995). The legal harvest of turtles in many states is now restricted to those species (usually snapping turtles [*Chelydra serpentina*] and North American softshell turtles) designated as game species and regulated by season, bag, and possession limits.

Currently, the magnitude of the river turtle trade in many tropical regions is huge by comparison. This is true not only in locations and cultures where river turtles are prized for food (e.g., northeastern India and China) but also in cultures where turtles are not an important food source but where money can be made from their collection and export (e.g., predominantly Islamic Bangladesh). The particulars, in terms of numbers and species traded and the monetary value involved, are poorly known in most cases because records are often incomplete, misleading (i.e., species are often misidentified), or unavailable (e.g., in those cases where the trade is illegal and conducted surreptitiously). Surveys of the turtle trade in Bangladesh (M. A. R. Khan 1982; Fugler 1984; Das 1990), India (E. O. Moll 1990a; Choudhury and Bhupathy 1993), Malaysia (Siow and Moll 1982; E. O. Moll 1985a), Thailand (Thirakhupt and van Dijk 1994), Vietnam (Le Dien Duc and Broad 1995), and Southeast Asia generally (Jenkins 1995) provide evidence of the importance and considerable financial value of the trade in these countries.

River turtles, their eggs, or both were formerly of significant commercial value in other tropical countries also (e.g., Brazil; Alho 1985), but the magnitude of the trade has declined substantially as stocks have dwindled. In Brazil, the eggs, hatchlings, and adults of the giant South American river turtle have traditionally been used as food (Mittermeier 1978). A large female can yield 4 to 7 kg of meat, which can provide a family with food for several days and is used in as many as 10 different dishes (Mittermeier 1978). In Mexico, Guatemala, and Belize, the Central American river turtle is relished for food, and in Belize it is considered the favored dish for festive occasions, such as Easter dinner (D. Moll 1986; Polisar 1992). In Malaysia, the collection of river terrapin eggs was formerly the prerogative of Sultans, and festive egg-collecting parties were organized annually by the royal family and their guests (E. O. Moll 1978a). Today, the eggs are harvested by licensed egg collectors who lease the remaining nesting areas from the government (E. O. Moll 1978a, b).

The majority of turtles traded in the countries mentioned above are probably used as a source of human food. Turtle meat and eggs are widely consumed, and even the cartilaginous flaps of softshell turtles may be used to make soup (Das 1990). Turtles are also highly valued throughout Asia as a component of local medicines and drugs to treat a wide range of illnesses. E. O. Moll (1982, 1990a), Choudhury and Bhupathy (1993), and Le Dien Duc and Broad (1995) provided numerous examples of how different turtle parts may be used in this capacity. In many cultures, turtle eggs and sometimes meat are considered aphrodisiacs and are frequently consumed for this purpose. Other turtle-based commodities, provided in part by riverine species, include oil from eggs for lamps and cooking; baskets, basins and bowls, stepping stones, household implements, fencing, and agricultural tools from shells; ash from burned shells (mixed with clay) for pottery; musical instruments from shell and skin; tobacco pouches and tambourines from neck skin; fat (mixed with resin) for caulking boats; and ground bone for poultry feed (Heriarte 1662; Ferreira 1786; N. J. H. Smith 1979; E. O. Moll 1984, 1990a; Pritchard 1989; Das 1990). Some species are also kept in water tanks and wells to consume algae and detritus (E. O. Moll 1985b).

Another commercial use of river turtles is in the pet trade, which may be supplied at local, national, and international levels. Choudhury and Bhupathy (1993) and Le Dien Duc and Broad (1995) noted the sale of juvenile river turtles and other chelonians as pets in India and Vietnam, respectively. We have personally observed numerous species, including river terrapin and painted terrapin, for sale in Malaysian pet markets. When the hatchling turtle trade was at its zenith in the United States in the 1960s and early 1970s, huge numbers of native species in the genera *Trachemys* (sliders), *Pseudemys* (cooters), and *Graptemys* were marketed. These were supplemented by imports of exotic species, including large numbers of yellow-spotted Amazon River turtles and giant South American river turtles (Weaver 1973; Mittermeier 1978). Although laws designed to stop infection by *Salmonella* bacteria have curbed the huge domestic trade in hatchlings in the United States, larger juveniles and adult river turtles are still sold in pet stores and are regularly available in the mail-order reptile trade. Remarkably, the southern Mississippi valley states still have thriving turtle ranches that annually export millions of turtles worth millions of dollars (mainly common slider but also North American softshell turtles and various species of map turtles) to overseas destinations, especially Asia (Warwick 1985a, b, 1986; Warwick et al. 1990; HSUS 1994). The fate of these turtles is unclear, in part because the sizes shipped out are usually not recorded. Presumably hatchlings will be sold as pets and larger animals used for food and medicines.

Finally, river turtles have value in many aboriginal and civilized cultures for their symbolism in religious rites and folklore. Turtles are of particular importance in this regard in Hindu, Buddhist, and Muslim beliefs. There is ritual feeding, ritual release (the stimulus for the purchase of many individuals in Asian pet markets), and protection in shrines and sanctuaries, all providing evidence of turtle veneration (M. A. Smith 1931; E. O. Moll 1976, 1985b; Choudhury and Bhupathy 1993; Le Dien Duc and Broad 1995). Pieces of turtle shell are hung from the neck of cows in Madhya Pradesh, India, to ward off spirits that will decrease the milk supply (E. O. Moll 1985b). The shells and other parts of some turtles may also be used ceremonially and have ritual significance in aboriginal cultures (Rhodin et al. 1993).

Habitat Alteration

Equally important to the decline of river turtle populations are factors that do not kill the animals outright but nevertheless reduce their chances of survival. Most of these factors involve alteration or contamination of habitat or both (see Mitchell and Klemens, Chapter 1). Habitat alteration does not necessarily affect species adversely, but river turtles are often habitat specialists that respond negatively to change. However, a diversity of chelonian generalists also inhabit rivers. These turtles typically do well in a variety of habitats and conditions and are less likely to be harmed by change.

A study of the Illinois River illustrates this well. Land clearing and wetlands draining for agriculture, pollution by sewage from the Chicago Sanitary District, and construction of locks and dams by the U.S. Army Corps of Engineers have seriously harmed or eliminated certain specialist species—for example, Blanding's turtle *(Emydoidea blandingii)*, Illinois mud turtle *(Kinosternon flavescens spooneri)*, and smooth softshell. However, generalist species, such as false map turtle, red-ear slider *(Trachemys scripta elegans)*, spiny softshell, and snapping turtle, have thrived in the altered environment (D. Moll 1980).

Chelonian generalists are extremely resilient vertebrates and are weedlike to the extent that they often do better in disturbed habitats than in undisturbed ones. In tropical Asia the Malayan box turtle *(Cuora amboinensis)* and the black marsh turtle *(Siebenrockiella crassicollis)* are more abundant in human-disturbed habitats than in pristine forests (E. O. Moll and Khan 1990). Painted turtles *(Chrysemys picta)* in polluted portions of the Kalamazoo River in Michigan exhibited more rapid growth rates than did populations inhabiting unpolluted areas in southwestern Michigan (Knight and Gibbons 1968). In Israel the Caspian turtle *(Mauremys caspica)* was the only vertebrate found in the most sewage-polluted water bodies studied by Gasith and Sidis (1984). Generalized species such as the Caspian turtle, red-eared slider, and snapping turtle are also highly tolerant of many chemical pollutants, such as pesticides, PCBs, and heavy metals (Yawetz et al. 1983; Meyers-Schöne and Walton 1994). Both the Asiatic softshell *(Amyda cartilaginea)* and the Malayan snail-eating turtle *(Malayemys subtrijuga)* appear to have benefited from the conversion of Thai wetlands into agricultural areas (Thirakhupt and van Dijk 1994). Due to this adaptability, generalized chelonians are typically of less concern to conservationists than are the specialist species. Herein we examine the negative effects of indirect factors on populations of riverine turtles, particularly the specialists.

The damaging effects of indirect factors are often less obvious than are those of direct factors. For example, land use changes and the extirpation of predators of raccoons have resulted in a population explosion of these extremely efficient nest predators in North America in recent decades. Removal or addition of shade plants on a beach could alter nest temperatures, thus adversely affecting hatchling sex ratios of species with temperature-dependent sex determination. Wibbels et al. (1991a) have warned that any environmental alterations affecting beach temperatures would be of particular concern for a species with limited distributions, such as Cagle's map turtle *(Graptemys caglei)*.

Even environmental alterations well outside the turtle's habitat can be consequential. For example, agriculture, deforestation, and mining are phenomena associated with terrestrial environments and might seem to have little impact on denizens of a river. However, each of these factors reduces plant cover and loosens soil so that nearby rivers may become deluged with runoff and silt. This, in turn, affects river turtles in a variety of ways.

Harmful effects of increased runoff and silt include additional flooding and damage to nesting beaches. Floods during the nesting season can destroy part or all of the annual reproductive output of a river turtle population because eggs of most species tolerate only short periods of submergence. Plummer (1976) found significant mortality in smooth softshell eggs submerged for 2 days and complete mortality in eggs submerged for 4 days. He also reported that smooth softshells in a Kansas river abandoned a popular sandbar nesting site when a short period of inundation covered it with a thick layer of silt. No hatchlings emerged from clutches laid prior to the flooding. Either the eggs did not develop or the hatchlings could not break through the hard silt crust.

Reproduction of the endangered river terrapin on Malaysia's Perak River also has been adversely affected by flooding and silt deposition. Factors contributing to these problems include large-scale deforestation and tin mining in upstream areas. Floods that destroy portions, or all, of this species' annual egg production are not unusual. M. K. M. Khan (1977) described an unseasonal flood in 1967 that destroyed some 2,000 river terrapin eggs on a major Perak nesting beach. Flooding destroyed part of the river terrapin reproductive output in each of three nesting seasons on the Perak River; one of these floods resulted from the release of water from an upstream dam for boat races (E. O. Moll, personal observation). In addition to the direct effects of these floods on eggs, each flood deposits layers of organic material over the sandbank nesting sites. This has promoted the growth of the tropical lalang grass *(Imperata cylindrica)*. Because river terrapins require sand to nest (E. O. Moll 1980a), these grass-covered banks have effectively destroyed most of the historic nest sites of the species. The only open sandbanks available today are those that are cleared annually by local egg collectors and the Malaysian Department of Wildlife and National Parks to attract nesting females. Ironically, the river terrapin of the Perak River are now almost totally dependent upon humans to provide nesting sites.

Direct alterations to rivers and their banks include channelization, damming, and sand and gravel mining. All can negatively affect river turtle populations. The deepening and straightening of streams and rivers reduces flooding and increases drainage (at least upstream), but it also simplifies habitats and reduces habitat diversity. Sandbars, pools, and riffles are eliminated. Aquatic productivity is reduced, as are the organisms depending on this productivity. Although most studies of the effects of channelization on vertebrates have concerned fishes, turtles are presumably affected as well. Christiansen (1981) and Christiansen and Bailey (1988) have attributed the decline of North American softshell turtle populations in Iowa to the straightening of rivers. Ironically, channel maintenance of the Apalachicola River in Florida has resulted in an increase of female-producing nest sites (higher incubation temperatures) for alligator snapping turtles as a result of dredge spoil being deposited on the floodplain (Ewert and Jackson 1994).

Damming a river harms river turtle species in a number of ways, including (1) the conversion of lotic habitats into lentic ones, with the subsequent loss of, or change in, available food organisms; (2) the prevention of migrations that may be part of the annual cycle; (3) the flooding of nesting beaches upstream; (4) the exacerbation of erosion of downstream sandbanks by irregular releases of water; (5) the alteration of flood cycles, which may be important in the timing of reproductive cycles; (6) the fragmentation of populations; (7) the prevention of sand transport within the channel to replace that lost by sand mining or erosion; and (8) changes in water quality due to decomposition of drowned forests, pollution produced by construction of the dam, or both.

The combination of several of these effects has nearly destroyed populations of river terrapin and painted terrapin on the Kedah River in Malaysia. Prior to 1960, populations of both species thrived in the river. Pantai Raja, one of the better nesting beaches controlled by the Sultan of Kedah, produced in excess of 20,000 eggs annually. As many as 700 river terrapin might nest on the beach in a single night. The decline of Kedah river terrapin populations occurred quickly. In the early 1960s, extensive construction work in the capital city created a demand for sand. The banks of the Kedah River provided much of this sand. Later in the decade two dams were built, one upriver and one downriver from the nesting sites. Within a decade suitable nesting sites were nonexistent. The upstream dam prevented new sand from moving downriver to replenish that which was continually being removed, whereas the downstream dam interfered with the annual migrations of the river terrapin between nesting sites and feeding areas near the coast. Today, natural reproduction by the turtles is virtually nonexistent.

Small breeding colonies of river and painted terrapins still exist on the river. At former nest sites, females annually leave the water looking for sand in which to nest. Finding none they return to the river or are captured by local egg collectors, who dig pitfall traps and trenches along the beach. Females caught in these traps are placed on sand substrate within bamboo enclosures where they remain until the eggs are laid. The Kedah Game Department purchases some of these eggs for a hatchery and headstarting program in an attempt to keep the turtles from becoming extirpated.

Sand mining in conjunction with dam construction is one of the most serious indirect threats to river turtle populations in developing countries. Sandbanks are required for nesting by a majority of the world's river turtles. Sand is continually in demand for construction purposes, and riverbanks offer a very accessible source. Until recently, most sand removal in Asian countries was done by hand loading small boats. With such primitive methods, it took a long time to do any appreciable damage, and in monsoon climates, floods from the heavy rains would annually deposit new loads of sand from upstream to replace that which had been lost. In recent decades, modern technology has taken over. With bulldozers and backhoes to remove the sand and trucks and tractors to haul it away, an extensive sandbank can be razed in days. If dams have been constructed upstream, none of this sand will be replaced. In a 1989 thru 1990 survey to assess the status of river terrapin in Bangladesh, India, Indonesia, Malaysia, and Thailand, E. O. Moll observed sand mining on every major river system visited (Table 5.2). Damage ranged from slight to almost complete removal of sand beaches, as on the Kedah, Muda, and Kelantan Rivers of Malaysia. These rivers all supported populations of river and painted terrapins that now, lacking adequate recruitment, dwindle toward extinction.

The Chambal River of India is a stronghold for a number of large sand-nesting, heavily exploited river turtles (e.g., narrow-headed softshell turtle [Chitra indica], three-striped roofed turtle [Kachuga dhongoka], and painted roofed turtle). Unfortunately, many of the best sites for nesting occur near the highway bridge between Rajasthan and Madhya Pradesh, making the sites easily accessible to exploitation. When the National Chambal River Gharial Sanctuary was established in 1978, the Indian government granted construction concerns the right to mine sand within a 3-km stretch from each side of the bridge. In recent years funds for enforcement of this edict have disappeared, and sand mining now occurs far outside the set limits. Turtle nests are being destroyed at an ever increasing rate. Fortunately, only some of the tributaries to the Chambal have been dammed, and during the annual monsoon floods new sand still replaces much of that removed.

Populations of the Euphrates soft-shelled turtle (Rafetus euphraticus) have suffered from damming and sand mining on the Euphrates River in Turkey. These activities have submerged former nesting grounds and generally altered the habitat (Taskavak and Atatür 1995). Van Dijk and Thirakhupt (1995) attributed the decline of the giant striped softshell turtle (Chitra chitra) to the damming of Thailand's Mae Klong River, the turtle's only confirmed habitat. They believed the dams blocked movements, fragmented the population, and reduced habitat quality.

Another potential indirect threat comes from the introduction of exotic species. The pet trade, and to a lesser extent the food and products trade, has led to the introduction of exotic species throughout the world. Such species may damage native turtle populations through competition or spread of disease.

Because of its generalized habits and aggressive nature, the common slider is one of the most likely species to cause problems as an exotic. Annually, millions

Table 5.2

Levels of sand mining on river turtle nesting beaches

Location[a]	Damage level[b]	Species affected[c]										
		Ac	Ah	Bb	Cb	Ci	Kd	Kk	Ks	Kt	Ob	Pb
Bangladesh												
Kali Ganga (Dhaka)	3	—	•	—	—	—	•	•	•	•	—	—
Padma (Dhaka)	3	—	•	—	—	—	•	•	•	•	—	—
India												
Chambal (Rajasthan and Madhya Pradesh)	3	—	—	—	—	—	•	•	•	—	•	—
Khrasrota (Orissa)	3	—	•	—	—	—	—	—	—	—	•	•
Indonesia												
Tulangbawang (Lampung-Sumatra)	1	—	—	•	•	—	—	—	—	—	•	—
Malaysia												
Kelantan (Kelantan)	4	•	—	•	•	—	—	—	—	—	—	—
Dungun (Terengganu)	2	•	—	•	•	—	—	—	—	—	—	•
Terennganu (Terengganu)	2	•	—	•	•	—	—	—	—	—	—	•
Pahang (Pahang)	2	•	—	•	•	—	—	—	—	—	—	•
Kedah (Kedah)	4	•	—	•	•	—	—	—	—	—	—	—
Mudah (Kedah)	4	•	—	•	•	—	—	—	—	—	—	—
Perak (Perak)	3	•	—	•	•	—	—	—	—	—	—	•
Muar (Johor)	3	•	—	—	•	—	—	—	—	—	•	—
Thailand												
La-ngu (Satun)	2	•	—	•	•	—	—	—	—	—	—	—
Pakpara (Satun)	2	•	—	•	•	—	—	—	—	—	—	—

Note: Data were collected during the course of a 1989 to 1990 status survey of Indo-Malayan rivers sponsored by the World Wide Fund for Nature.

[a]Location, by country, is given as the river and, in parentheses, the district.

[b]Damage levels reflect sand removal: (1) some local use; (2) moderate commercial usage; (3) heavy commercial exploitation; and (4) near total destruction of sandbanks.

[c]Affected species are abbreviated as follows: *Amyda cartilaginea* (Ac), *Aspideretes hurum* (Ah), *Batagur baska* (Bb), *Callagur borneoensis* (Cb), *Chitra indica* (Ci), *Kachuga dhongoka* (Kd), *Kachuga kachuga* (Kk), *Kachuga smithi* (Ks), *Kachuga tentoria* (Kt), *Orlitia borneensis* (Ob), and *Pelochelys bibroni* (Pb).

of turtles are exported from the United States into Europe, Asia, and other regions, where they are increasingly turning up in the wild (HSUS 1994). To date we are aware of no studies that have conclusively demonstrated that river turtle populations have declined due to introductions of exotic turtle species. However, some herpetologists have speculated that competition with the common slider for food has contributed to the decline of the European pond turtle *(Emys orbicularis)* (HSUS 1994). Another exotic species causing problems is the feral water buffalo *(Bubalus bubalis)* in northern Australia, which reportedly trample the nesting grounds of the pig-nosed turtle, crushing their eggs in the process (Georges and Rose 1993).

OVERVIEW OF CONSERVATION AND MANAGEMENT METHODS

A variety of methods have been used to conserve riverine turtles. Some methods require removal of the animal or its eggs from the natural habitat and are referred to as ex situ techniques. Other methods protect the animals and their habitat or improve the habitat and are referred to as in situ techniques. Hatcheries, headstarting, captive breeding, translocation, and reintroductions are examples of ex situ techniques, whereas protective laws, predator control, and protected areas are in situ techniques.

Few existing conservation programs have been operating sufficiently long, or have been monitored adequately, to make definitive conclusions about which combination of techniques is most effective. Among the problems of evaluating conservation techniques is the 10 to 30 years large river turtles may require to mature. Hence, a program must operate at least that long to see even preliminary results. Another difficulty in evaluating techniques is that conservation programs typically have limited funding and tend to concentrate expenditures on the conservation method rather than on its evaluation. The following discussion examines the use of various conservation and management techniques with river turtles and evaluates the benefits and drawbacks of each.

Ex Situ Techniques

Hatcheries, headstarting, and captive breeding are among the most popular ex situ strategies being used in turtle conservation programs. Much of the popularity of these programs is due to their high visibility. The large numbers of eggs, hatchlings, adults, or all three available at the project site impresses the public, the media, and visiting officials: conservation is indeed happening here. Such an impression, in turn, facilitates the fund-raising necessary to continue the work.

HATCHERIES
Hatcheries are the least controversial of the ex situ techniques. Hatchery techniques can be as simple as moving the eggs from the nest to a nearby protected

area of beach or as complex as rearing eggs in elaborate, environmentally controlled facilities. The technique reduces mortality at nesting sites where a high percentage of nests are annually destroyed. The mortality may be the result of egg collecting by humans, as in the case of the river terrapin (Maxwell 1911; E. O. Moll 1976, 1978a, 1984), predators, as in the case of roofed turtles (Rao 1986, 1991), or flooding, as in the case of the yellow-spotted Amazon River turtle (Paez and Bock 1993).

There are drawbacks to using hatcheries. Transferring eggs usually results in some lowering of viability. Data from sea turtles suggest that hatching success may be reduced from 20 to 70% (Mortimer 1988c). Obviously the technique is warranted only if the survival of transplanted eggs exceeds that of natural nests. If nest characteristics are not duplicated, incubation temperatures may be altered, resulting in skewed sex ratios in species with temperature-dependent sex determination. Although altering the sex ratio could be damaging, it might also be beneficial. Certain authors have discussed controlling incubation temperature in hatcheries to achieve a female-biased sex ratio as a method to increase reproduction (Mrosovsky 1981; Vogt 1994). However, the technique is not without risk, and an evaluation of such experimental methodology should be undertaken at the outset (Mrosovsky and Godfrey 1995; Lovich 1996).

HEADSTARTING

Headstarting (retaining young turtles for varying periods beyond hatching) may be used in conjunction with hatcheries, as in Malaysian programs with river and painted terrapins (E. O. Moll 1984) or the Indian softshell turtle on the Ganges River in India. Alternatively, hatchlings may be collected upon emergence from natural nests, as in South American river turtles (Mortimer 1987; Anonymous 1988). Usually the objective of this procedure is to grow hatchlings to a size at which they are less vulnerable to predators, which are presumed to take a high percentage of young turtles. In Malaysia the young turtles are kept in captivity for at least 1 year, and some cohorts have been kept for more than 10 years. In contrast, in Brazil, hatchling South American river turtles may be kept for only 2 weeks to 1 month or until the shell hardens and conditions are right for release (IBAMA 1989).

There has been little attempt to evaluate the success of the few programs that use headstarting for river turtles, and headstarting has yet to be proven an effective conservation tool. Much of the literature evaluating the procedure is based on sea turtle projects, where this technique has been used more commonly as a management tool (see Meylan and Ehrenfeld, Chapter 4). Even here, as of 1999 nine headstarted Kemp's ridleys *(Lepidochelys kempii)* that have nested at Padre Island, Texas, are the only turtles from any headstarting or hatchery program that have ever been identified as subsequently nesting (Frazer 1994; Shaver 1996; Meylan and Ehrenfeld, Chapter 4).

Proponents of headstarting techniques argue that the programs should be promoted because they increase the survival of juveniles and because the high visibility of headstarting programs enlists public concern and interest. Critics claim
that the benefits remain to be demonstrated, and many argue that the method may
be harmful to turtles. Biological questions that need to be addressed include (1)
will headstarted turtles be able to imprint properly to nesting sites if they are released 1 year or more beyond hatching? (2) will 1 year of confinement with unnatural foods and limited exercise affect their ability to survive in the wild? (3) will turtles
raised under crowded conditions spread diseases acquired in captivity to wild populations? and (4) how will the reduction in hatchlings affect natural ecosystems?

Frazer (1992) has eloquently made the case that headstarting exemplifies
"halfway technology," the equivalent of a medical doctor treating symptoms instead of the basic cause of a disease. It does not address the basic causes of turtle
mortality. Studies by Congdon et al. (1993, 1994) and Heppell et al. (1996) support
this view, suggesting that headstarting programs which are not coupled with reduction of adult mortality have little chance of success. Due to the expense and a
lack of evidence of the effectiveness of headstarting, E. O. Moll (1984, 1985a,
1989a, 1990a) recommended that river turtles from hatcheries be released at the
time of hatching, simulating natural conditions as closely as possible. The subject continues to provide lively debate in the literature. Recent reviews of headstarting can be found in Frazer (1994) and Mortimer (1995b).

CAPTIVE BREEDING
Captive breeding is another high-visibility approach being tried with river turtles.
Malaysia and Thailand currently keep captive populations of adult river terrapin
for breeding purposes. In 1990, the Malaysian captive population, composed of 62
females and 6 males, was kept at Bota Kanan on the Perak River in a 10 m² shel-
tered (roofed but open sided) pool that sloped to 0.6 m in depth. The pool adjoined
a fenced sand nesting area, 20 m by 10 m.

Productivity in this facility has been low. In 1986 to 1987 the captives made only
six nests, containing, in total, 186 eggs. In 1989 to 1990 that number had increased
to 13 nests containing 281 eggs. Although an improvement, this productivity for
62 females is low. Hatching success of eggs from captives is also low. According
to personnel at the hatchery only 20 to 25% of the eggs hatch, compared with a
hatch of 50% of the eggs taken from the nests of wild females. Possible reasons for
the low productivity are overcrowding, an inadequate diet, the low male-to-female
ratio, or the pool being too shallow for successful copulation (E. O. Moll 1990b).

Thailand maintains captive breeding stock of both river and painted terrapins,
along with a hatchery and headstarting facility in Satun Province. In 1990, the facility had 52 river terrapin (29 females and 23 males) and 47 painted terrapin (24

females and 23 males). Turtles were kept in a small, relatively shallow, crowded concrete pool (measurements not available) that had an adjoining artificial sand beach. According to facility records, 288 river terrapin eggs were laid in 1987 to 1988, 394 in 1988 to 1989, and 375 in 1989 to 1990. Hatching success was 63% in 1988 and 36% in 1989. Results from 1990 were not available.

Like headstarting, captive breeding is a halfway technology. It is also expensive, requiring large tracts of land, elaborate enclosures, and a permanent staff. The programs for river and painted terrapins discussed above exemplify the difficulties in successfully breeding large river turtles in captivity. The Tortoise and Freshwater Turtle Specialist Group of the Species Survival Commission of the International Union for Conservation of Nature and Natural Resources (IUCN 1989) regards captive breeding as an extreme approach for conservation purposes and one that should be used only after existing habitat has been destroyed or when the population becomes too small and scattered for natural reproduction to be effective.

Turtle **farming** (self-contained, or closed, captive-breeding operations) and **ranching** (operations that periodically incorporate eggs or breeders from the wild) extend the captive-breeding philosophy. Such ventures are sometimes touted as conservation methods, with claims that supplies of farm- and ranch-raised turtles will reduce the demand for wild individuals. Other than the red-eared slider ranches, which supply the pet trade, the most successful captive-rearing ventures have involved raising the Chinese softshell turtle (*Pelodiscus sinensis*) for food. Aquaculture projects with this turtle are scattered throughout eastern and southeastern Asia, and we know of at least one in Brazil. Such projects have regularly been suggested for large river turtles, but to date we are aware of no successful, large-scale projects that have continued for any length of time. The Tortoise and Freshwater Turtle Specialist Group refrained from adopting any opinion or judgement on commercial farms and ranches but felt that such operations offered little if any identifiable benefit to the conservation of freshwater turtles (IUCN 1989).

The giant South American river turtle and the yellow-spotted Amazon River turtle are among the species often recommended for such aquacultural projects. N. J. H. Smith (1975, 1979) felt that both species would be good choices for domestication. Although the giant South American river turtle requires 8 years to attain a marketable size (22.5 kg), N. J. H. Smith (1975) calculated that a well-managed turtle pond could provide some 24,700 kg of meat per hectare, compared with 56.25 kg per hectare for cattle on the Amazon's nutrient-poor pastures. Alho (1985) also provided calculations showing that if turtle farmers began with 5,000 hatchlings, in 8 years they could have 1,500 mature turtles for marketing. At the market prices of that time, he predicted that the farmer would make US$22,500 in gross income each cycle, or a net profit of $10,000 per cycle. More recently, in order to slow the exploitation of wild stock, the conservation arm of the Brazilian

government (Instituto Brasileiro do Meio Ambiente e dos Recursos Naturais Renováveis, IBAMA) has initiated a program to formulate methodology for commercial
farming of the giant South American river turtle and other species (Vogt 1995).

TRANSLOCATION AND REINTRODUCTION

Translocation, the introduction of a species into areas not previously inhabited
by the species, has been tried in at least a few instances. Medem (1969) reported
that introduced giant South American river turtles had established a viable population above the rapids on the Caqueta River in the Colombian Amazon. N. J. H.
Smith (1975) reported that in 1950, a species of South American river turtle
(probably *P. expansa*) was introduced into Venezuela's Lake Valencia after a
10-month headstarting period. Apparently no significant nesting took place on
the lake's artificial beaches, however.

Alfinito et al. (1976) reported an effort to translocate adult giant South American river turtles from the Rio Trombetas to the Rio Tapajos in Brazil. The rationale for this was that the Trombetas was polluted due to bauxite mining, and unseasonal flooding was destroying much of the turtles' reproductive effort. From
1970 to 1974, 130 adult females were tagged and then translocated to the Rio Tapajos. The authors reported that since the introductions, nesting at Rio Tapajos
beaches had increased in proportion to the number of animals introduced and that
some marked turtles had been identified on the Tapajos nesting beaches. None
had been observed back at their original beach on the Trombetas, but marked
turtles did turn up in markets in the cities of Obidos, in Para, and Itacoatira, in
Amazonas (distances from the release site were not provided).

In a seemingly misguided effort reported by Thirakhupt and van Dijk (1994),
juvenile river and painted terrapins from the Thai Fisheries Department's Satun
Freshwater Fisheries Development Centre hatchery were being transported to
reservoirs throughout the country. Inasmuch as these species live in lotic and estuarine habitats, large, poorly vegetated reservoirs lacking sandbanks for nesting
appear unlikely to provide suitable habitat for these terrapins.

Pros and cons of translocations, reintroductions, and repatriation have been discussed by R. L. Burke (1991), Dodd and Seigel (1991; see also Seigel and Dodd,
Chapter 9), and Reinert (1991). The advantages of reintroducing species into formerly occupied habitats are obvious but must be weighed against possible consequences. Among the more serious problems are the low success rates observed
in previous projects, the potential for spreading disease, social disruption, and
genetic incompatibility. The Tortoise and Freshwater Turtle Specialist Group
cautioned against the reintroduction of captive-raised animals into the wild but
listed nine precautions to be followed should the method be deemed necessary
(IUCN 1989).

In Situ Techniques

The Tortoise and Freshwater Turtle Specialist Group (IUCN 1989) recommended in situ methods of habitat maintenance and controls on collection as preferred techniques for preserving chelonian populations. River turtles cannot exist in the wild without suitable habitat; hence habitat protection, acquisition, and maintenance should be basic priorities in conservation programs.

HABITAT PROTECTION

Protected areas are potentially one of the most effective means of conserving river turtles. However, the amount of protection provided varies considerably in existing programs. Some examples follow.

- Mississippi has designated a portion of the habitat of the ringed sawback turtle *(Graptemys oculifera)* along the Pearl River as a turtle sanctuary (G. George 1990).

- The Project Tuntung Sanctuary, established for river terrapin on the Perak River of Malaysia, could more accurately be called an extractive reserve, for while adult river terrapin are protected here, egg collectors are allowed to exploit all major nesting beaches and sand mining is allowed along the entire nesting region.

- On the Rio Trombetas in Brazil, certain sand nesting beaches are protected by armed guards throughout the period of nesting and incubation, but the turtles are not protected in feeding areas.

- The National Chambal River Gharial Sanctuary, one of several crocodile refuges in India, ostensibly protects all of its wildlife and habitat. However, areas within 3 km of an interstate bridge can be mined for sand. In recent years funding for protection of the sanctuary has dwindled, and sand mining operations have now extended well beyond the original limits. Also hunting and fishing have increased within the sanctuary boundaries. Nevertheless, the facility demonstrates the effectiveness of sanctuaries in protecting turtle populations. E. O. Moll (1990a) found the Chambal to be the second richest area for turtle diversity encountered during a year (1983 to 1984) of extensive river turtle surveys conducted within India.

- Religious sanctuaries at which turtles are fed and protected are also scattered throughout India. One such sanctuary exists along a stretch of temple-lined river at Bateshwar, Uttar Pradesh, India. Here, all animal life is protected. Turtles were unusually abundant here, including the otherwise rare painted roofed turtle, one of India's endangered species (E. O. Moll 1985b, 1990a).

• In the northern part of the country, Belize has designated a series of protected zones for the Central American river turtle in major waterways (Polisar and Horwich 1994). An effort was made to include all major habitats of the turtle within a protective zone.

E. O. Moll (1985a, 1990a) envisioned an ideal sanctuary as including a large breeding nucleus of the species of concern along with optimal nesting and feeding habitats. The object is to protect the breeding nucleus so that it can continually supply recruitment to the population both inside and outside the sanctuary. Ideally the protected population grows to a level at which population pressures force excess individuals out of the sanctuary, where they can continue to be harvested on a subsistence basis. So long as the breeding nucleus is left intact, the population will not be exterminated. However, genetic stagnation could be a potential problem, depending on the size of the breeding nucleus and whether there is gene flow from other areas.

For wide-ranging or migratory species, establishing sanctuaries that include both feeding and nesting grounds may be impractical. A more realistic solution for such species is to concentrate on protecting nesting beaches where both female and egg mortality is likely to be great. This approach is especially favored for the large, colonially nesting river turtles whose concentrations and predictable return to specific beaches make them highly vulnerable to human exploitation and predators.

On the negative side, sanctuaries can be expensive to establish and maintain even if they include only a nesting beach. Potential expenses include purchasing large tracts of land and hiring a permanent staff to enforce restrictions and protect the species from exploitation. Thus, what is perhaps the best technique for preserving a species may be too expensive for some countries to consider. Other problems include the necessity to eliminate, or at least reduce, human use of the area. For example, human disturbance, including boat traffic, disrupts and discourages nesting activity of the giant South American river turtle (Padua and Alho 1984; Mortimer et al. 1986). Boats are known to injure or kill river terrapins in periodic collisions (E. O. Moll 1984).

OTHER HABITAT-RELATED OPTIONS

Certain protective measures can be taken to protect turtle eggs at a nesting beach whether or not the area is protected. Patrolling beaches helps to discourage predators and poachers. Nest survivorship can be increased by transplanting eggs a few meters from the laying site (Stancyk 1982). We have also found that using a broom to sweep tracks and nesting sign from the beach is effective in deterring sight-oriented predators (especially humans).

Habitat improvement can be useful both in protected and unprotected areas. A variety of specific actions can be taken to improve chelonian habitat at the local level. G. George (1990) reported that Mississippi has adopted a policy in certain areas of the Pearl River to move dead trees and snags from the river channel to near the banks to supply basking sites and feeding areas for map turtles. In Brazil, IBAMA (1989) cleans debris from the nesting beaches of the giant South American river turtle to attract nesting turtles. In Malaysia, tropical grasses are removed prior to the nesting season of river terrapin for similar reasons (E. O. Moll 1984). At the landscape scale, river restoration projects repleat with erosion control, reduction of pollution, and re-creation of former flow patterns benefit turtles along with all other inhabitants of a river.

LEGAL REMEDIES

Protective laws and treaties range from international agreements such as the Convention on International Trade in Endangered Species of Wild Fauna and Flora (CITES 1973), which restrict international trade in listed species, to state laws that protect species on the local level. From a conservation perspective the best laws are those that provide total protection. V. J. Burke et al. (1994b) contend "that turtles may be especially vulnerable to population decline because they exhibit reproductive strategies incompatible with exploitation or significant loss of habitat." Demographic studies by Congdon et al. (1993, 1994) and Heppell et al. (1996) support this view. If these findings are applicable to river turtles generally, then most sustainable exploitation schemes may be destined for failure.

Nevertheless, as a first step to protect river turtles in developing nations, it may be more feasible politically to limit rather than to ban exploitation of a species. The conservation plan for the Central American river turtle discussed by Polisar and Horwich (1994) is an example of this approach. Incorporated into the plan are protected areas, closed seasons, banning of commercial exploitation, and possession limits.

Some countries offer federal protection to river turtles. For example, China gives the giant Asian softshell turtle its highest level of protection on its List of Important Protected Wild Animals (Zhao and Adler 1993). India protects eight river turtles in the schedules of the Indian Wildlife (Protection) Act of 1972 (Choudhury and Bhupathy 1993). In Thailand all turtle species except for the Asiatic softshell are officially protected by the 1992 Wildlife Conservation Act. In other countries control of turtle exploitation is a prerogative of the states. In Malaysia 5 of the 11 states have laws regulating exploitation of river terrapin; Perak protects not only river terrapin, painted terrapin, and the Malaysian giant turtle *(Orlitia borneen-*

sis) but also the crowned river turtle, which does not even occur in the country (E. O. Moll 1984).

In the United States both federal and state levels of protection exist; however, except for the yellow-blotched map turtle *(Graptemys flavimaculata),* ringed saw-back turtle, and Alabama red-bellied turtle *(Pseudemys alabamensis),* which are federally protected, protection of river turtle populations is at the state level. Levell (1995) listed 34 states with legislation controlling exploitation of river turtles, including full protection, closed seasons, licenses, and possession and size limits.

Closed seasons usually protect species during periods when they are especially vulnerable, such as times of reproduction. E. O. Moll (1990a) outlined a bimodal system of closed seasons for Indian turtles, which would protect commercially exploited species while creating a minimum of hardship on the market vendors. In this scheme, softshell turtles could not be collected from August to mid-December (the peak reproductive period), whereas hard-shelled species would be protected from mid-December to May (their chief reproductive period). Market vendors could sell softshells during the closed season for hard-shelled turtles and vice versa. The yellow-spotted Amazon River turtle and savanna side-necked turtle *(Podocnemis vogli)* can be hunted from 1 February to 31 March in Venezuela (Prichard and Trebbau 1984). Eight states in the United States have closed seasons for river turtles (Levell 1995).

Licenses help to regulate exploitation but benefit conservation only when they limit the numbers to be taken or the areas that can be exploited. In Malaysia, collecting turtle eggs requires a license. In the state of Perak, the license stipulates that one-third of the eggs collected must be given to the Department of Wildlife and National Parks for conservation purposes. Unfortunately this requirement has not been strictly enforced, and eggs obtained for conservation purposes must be purchased at market prices. Twenty-four states in the United States require some type of license (usually a fishing license) in order to collect turtles (Levell 1995).

Possession limits for river turtles have been legislated in 13 states of the United States (Levell 1995). However, when the daily bag limit is 100 turtles, as in West Virginia, or the possession limit is 12 dozen, as in South Dakota, the conservation value of the law is insignificant. Size limits for river turtles exist in seven states. Typically the philosophy has been to protect small individuals and harvest the large. This philosophy is flawed, however, because larger, reproductive individuals are extremely important in maintaining the stability of populations of species having delayed maturity and great longevity, such as turtles (Crouse et al. 1987; Frazer 1989; Congdon et al. 1993, 1994; Heppell et al. 1996). Population models developed by these authors agree that all age- and size-classes of a turtle population must be protected to reverse population declines. However, if exploitation of turtle populations cannot be prevented, then protection should be provided in the following order of priority based on the value of each group to the population: adults, large juveniles, juveniles, and eggs.

RECOMMENDATIONS FOR RIVER TURTLE CONSERVATION

We conclude this chapter with our recommendations for methods that have the greatest potential to protect and rebuild river turtle populations at the least risk to the species. Inasmuch as any action may require one to several decades before the results will become apparent, we have avoided controversial or questionable procedures. Whereas these may be tried on an experimental basis, we caution against basing an entire conservation program for a threatened species on these questionable procedures. Should they prove unsuccessful after one or two decades, it may be too late to try something else. Consider the potential damage that could have resulted to conservation programs had use of Styrofoam boxes to incubate sea turtle eggs continued for two or three decades before the problem of masculinization of hatchlings had been discovered.

We thus promote a conservative methodology in endangered river turtle conservation, emphasizing natural and in situ approaches over ex situ techniques. The logic here is that turtles are the products of millions of years of evolution. Presumably their reproductive behavior has been fine-tuned by natural selection to the environments in which they live. Therefore, the more similar our management and conservation actions are to turtles' natural reproductive processes, the more likely we are to succeed. As stated above, complete protection of all size-groups is the most desirable of all conservation actions. Beyond this we recommend the following actions in order of priority.

1. *Establishment of sanctuaries and reserves.* With habitat destruction and exploitation being common causes of river turtle declines, the establishment of protected areas preserving as large a breeding nucleus as possible along with that population's feeding and nesting sites is potentially one of the most effective long-term conservation actions. This action has the advantage of protecting an entire ecosystem rather than only a single species. It should be emphasized, however, that protected areas of a river are not closed systems, and they are subject to habitat degradation (e.g., pollution and siltation) from upstream sites. Therefore, management of the watershed above the reserve should be an important component of planning a reserve.

2. *Nest area protection and hatcheries.* Exploitation and predation are often most intense at the nesting beaches. If entire reserves are not feasible, protect-

ing nesting areas is the next highest priority. Sweeping away nesting signs, transplanting nests, and patrolling beaches can increase hatching success. If the nesting beach cannot be secured, sand beach hatcheries should be established. Natural clutches should be carefully transplanted to the hatchery within 24 hours of deposition to minimize egg mortality. Artificial nests should duplicate the dimensions, depth, and exposure of natural nests. Young should be released immediately upon emergence from the nest and allowed to crawl from the nesting area to the water.

3. *Public education and involvement.* A vital component of any conservation effort must be educating the public in regard to the need and rationale for implementing the program and the program objectives. Involvement and cooperation by the public in attaining the program's goals is the desired result.

4. *Captive breeding.* Should wild populations be too depleted for natural reproduction to take place, captive breeding can serve as a last-resort measure. In order to be an effective conservation tool, this method should be used in conjunction with habitat protection or restoration and controls on exploitation. Captive breeding and maintenance programs (i.e., true farming) for the purpose of substituting captive-raised stock for wild-caught individuals in commercial markets should continue to be evaluated. Carefully controlled pilot studies such as Brazil's (IBAMA) program with South American river turtle aquaculture should be encouraged.

CONCLUSION

The ultimate goal of any conservation program is self-sustainability. To achieve this goal, conservation plans for river turtles require action at three key levels or scales. At the population level, all age-groups must be given adequate protection. At the habitat level, critical feeding and nesting areas must be set aside and maintained. At the landscape level, the entire river system including its watershed requires protection from channelization, damming, draining, erosion, and pollution. Only after all three levels receive adequate attention can the long-term survival of river turtles be assured.

ACKNOWLEDGMENTS
We thank Dale Jackson and John Iverson, whose comments and suggestions, along with those of M. Klemens, have helped to improve this contribution.

VINCENT J. BURKE, JEFFREY E. LOVICH,
AND J. WHITFIELD GIBBONS

6

CONSERVATION OF FRESHWATER TURTLES

Nonriverine freshwater turtles and semiaquatic turtles are commonly grouped together as those species that predominantly inhabit small streams, slow-flowing
tributaries, or **lentic** (nonflowing) freshwater habitats for substantial portions of
their life cycles. Turtle species in this category constitute a diverse assemblage that
contains 160 species, or almost 60% of the world's approximately 270 turtle species
(Iverson 1992a, as amended by descriptions of new species, e.g., Lovich and McCoy
1992; McCord et al. 1995). All of the species termed freshwater spend part of their
life cycles, generally the nesting and incubation phases, in terrestrial habitats.

For the sake of brevity, nonriverine freshwater turtles and semiaquatic turtles
will be collectively referred to as freshwater turtles throughout this chapter. Our
categorization of freshwater turtles is phylogenetically artificial because the grouping includes many unrelated lineages. In addition, several species can be argued to
be both riverine and freshwater turtles, for example, sliders (*Trachemys scripta* ssp.)
and alligator snapping turtles *(Macroclemys temminckii)*. Turtles that are more typically riverine are considered separately in Chapter 5, a logical distinction from the
standpoint of ecology and conservation because riverine and freshwater turtles
generally differ with regard to both habitat use and threats to their survival.

The goals of this chapter are threefold. First, we will define, classify, and provide basic background information on freshwater turtles through a discussion of
the families that contain such species. Second, we will discuss the concept of the
life cycle as it applies to freshwater turtles and their conservation. Finally, we will
generally and specifically describe the status of freshwater turtles, outline case
studies of conservation problems, and provide recommendations for future con-

servation efforts. Our taxonomy is largely based on Iverson (1992a), although there are some amendments and disagreements that are largely inconsequential from the standpoint of ecology and conservation.

GENERAL ECOLOGY AND CLASSIFICATION

Although freshwater turtles generally share a dependency on slow-moving or stagnant freshwater habitats, they are composed of a variety of distinct taxonomic lineages. Both turtle suborders, Cryptodira and Pleurodira, contain freshwater species. Several families of cryptodirans are represented exclusively or almost so by freshwater turtles. However, no freshwater turtles occur in five cryptodiran families: Cheloniidae (hard-shelled sea turtles), Dermochelyidae (leatherback sea turtle), Carettochelyidae (pig-nosed or New Guinea plateless turtle), Dermatemydidae (Central American river turtle), and Testudinidae (tortoises).

The snapping turtle family, Chelydridae, contains two species of freshwater turtles, the snapping turtle *(Chelydra serpentina)* and the alligator snapping turtle. Both are generally carnivorous, opportunistic foragers (Ernst et al. 1994; Sloan et al. 1996) confined to the New World. Snapping turtles are relatively large (carapace length to 47 cm), lay 30 or more round, soft-shelled eggs, and predominantly inhabit marshes and similar types of wetlands. However, snapping turtles are also commonly found in rivers and can survive in estuaries for substantial periods of time. Alligator snapping turtles attain sizes exceeding 100 kg, lay up to 44 round eggs, and inhabit a variety of aquatic habitats, including rivers, swamps, and estuarine waters (Ernst et al. 1994). This species is the world's largest freshwater turtle.

All 22 species of mud *(Kinosternon* spp.) and musk *(Sternotherus* spp.) turtles in the family Kinosternidae contain populations that are either aquatic or semiaquatic. This family contains small- and moderate-sized carnivorous turtles that lay clutches which contain from 2 to 10 hard-shelled, ovoid eggs. Kinosternids generally inhabit lentic habitats, but some species prefer slow-flowing streams. Diet in this family generally consists of small prey items such as insects, amphibians, and small fishes. Two species, common mud turtle *(Kinosternon subrubrum)* and yellow mud turtle *(Kinosternon flavescens),* are known to spend extensive amounts of time on land during nesting forays (V. J. Burke et al. 1994a); the yellow mud turtle nests underground and remains with the eggs for up to 38 days (Iverson 1990). Several species, including the common and yellow mud turtles, overwinter in upland habitats (Bennett 1972; Christiansen et al. 1985; V. J. Burke and Gibbons 1995). Some mud turtle species may feed on land, but clear evidence of terrestrial foraging has not been established (however, see evidence presented in D. Moll 1979).

The sole species of the family Platysternidae, the big-headed turtle *(Platysternon megacephalum)*, is thought to be a semiaquatic species and has been reported to feed along streambanks in addition to streambeds. It is a small- to moderate-sized carnivore that usually lays two ovoid, soft-shelled eggs and inhabits cool mountain streams in southeastern Asia.

Softshell turtles of the family Trionychidae contain several freshwater species that are carnivorous and highly aquatic. All trionychids lay round, hard-shelled eggs; the number of eggs per clutch range from 15 to over 25. The freshwater trionychid species inhabit a variety of habitats such as marshes, drainage ditches, irrigation canals, streams, ponds, and lakes. Softshells are moderate- to large-sized turtles that feed on a variety of faunal prey. Modern softshell turtles are indigenous to Asia, Africa, New Guinea, and North America and appear to have descended from a lineage that once inhabited most of the temperate world.

The most diverse turtle family, the Emydidae, contains approximately 97 species (including species sometimes assigned to the separate family Bataguridae) of temperate, tropical, and subtropical turtles that are indigenous to Asia, Africa, Europe, and North and South America. The family includes many terrestrial and riverine species but is primarily composed of freshwater species. Most of the freshwater species are omnivorous at some point during their life cycle. Clutch size among freshwater emydids varies from about 2 eggs to over 20. Most species lay soft-shelled eggs, but some lay hard-shelled eggs. The freshwater emydid species range from being strongly aquatic (e.g., map turtles [*Graptemys* spp.], diamondback terrapin *[Malaclemys terrapin]*, and cooters [*Pseudemys* spp.]) to being primarily terrestrial but still dependent on aquatic habitats to complete their life cycles (e.g., wood turtle *[Clemmys insculpta]*).

Although river-dwelling turtles are common in the second turtle suborder, Pleurodira, some species inhabit lentic waters. Pleurodirans include two turtle families, the Chelidae and the Pelomedusidae. Chelids are indigenous to Australia, New Guinea, and South America. Clutch sizes for chelids range from 1 egg per nest to over 20. The eggs may be spherical or ovoid and hard shelled or soft shelled depending on the species. Most chelids appear to be primarily carnivorous, although several species are known to consume fruits and plant matter. Most of the chelid species inhabit slow-flowing nonriverine habitats, and many are strongly aquatic.

The Pelomedusidae are restricted to South America, Africa, and Madagascar. Pelomedusid clutches range from 6 to over 20 leathery-shelled eggs. The freshwater pelomedusids generally appear to be carnivorous; however, the habits of some species are poorly known. They occupy a wide variety of habitats; however, most species are riverine. Many of the tropical freshwater pelomedusids estivate during the dry season. Species of the diverse pelomedusid genus *Pelusios* (African mud turtles) occupy lentic marsh waters, flowing tributaries, and rivers depending on the species or population.

LIFE CYCLE REQUIREMENTS

The success of any conservation effort is dependent on a variety of factors. Perhaps the most critical factor in the maintenance of self-sustaining, free-living populations is the preservation of habitat and conditions required for completion of the life cycle (V. J. Burke and Gibbons 1995; Lovich and Gibbons 1997). In general terms, life cycle requirements include any elements needed by an organism to proceed from hatching (or birth) to reproduction.

Life cycles of freshwater turtles span years and involve multiple habitats (Congdon et al. 1993, 1994; V. J. Burke and Gibbons 1995). Because freshwater turtles are long lived, disruption of the life cycle may not be immediately obvious. Thus, proactive recognition of life cycle requirements and preservation of required habitats and conditions is clearly the most prudent method of conserving populations and species. Here, we outline the components of the life cycles of freshwater turtles. We include recommendations on ways of addressing these components during conservation efforts.

Eggs

The developing egg represents the beginning of the turtle life cycle. Eggs of many freshwater turtles for which we understand nesting patterns are laid in upland habitats within a few hundred meters of aquatic habitats. For example, a study of nest sites of three freshwater turtle species in a southeastern U.S. wetland suggested that all nests were in upland habitats within 275 m of the wetland (V. J. Burke and Gibbons 1995). In contrast, however, Blanding's turtles (*Emydoidea blandingii*) in Michigan regularly nest substantial distances (>1 km) from the aquatic habitats used by the nesting females (Congdon et al. 1983). Conversely, in some regions, eggs of the Northern Australian snake-necked turtle *(Chelodina rugosa)* are oviposited underwater in marshes that are subject to periodic drying (Kennett et al. 1993). It should, however, be noted that we have reliable documentation of nest site selection patterns for only a small subset of freshwater turtles.

As the above examples demonstrate, protecting nesting grounds for some species may be accomplished by simply protecting habitats adjacent to aquatic habitats. However, prudent conservation at the nest site requires a species-specific, and perhaps a population-specific, understanding of nest site patterns.

To develop, many, and perhaps most, freshwater turtle eggs require some exposure to sunlight at the nest site (Congdon and Gibbons 1990). Sun exposure can be attained in a variety of natural microhabitats, but turtles often make use of human-altered habitats as nest sites. Although freshwater turtles exploit periodic human disturbances at nesting sites, high levels of human activity in terrestrial habitats adjacent to aquatic habitats can be deleterious to freshwater turtle populations. This is particularly true for turtles such as the spotted turtle *(Clemmys guttata)* and the bog turtle *(Clemmys muhlenbergii),* which live in shallow wetland complexes (Lovich 1990). Populations inhabiting wetlands may be isolated from each other by surrounding croplands or pastures (Lovich 1989). Although some agricultural fields may provide suitable sites for developing eggs, the effects of plowing may doom nests and, ultimately, populations. Thus, small-scale human activities near freshwater habitats may be relatively benign to turtle eggs, but large-scale agricultural and urban development may be destructive. Kaufmann (1992) suggested that some agricultural activities were beneficial to wood turtle populations because they provided a mixture of different cover types and food sources near wooded streams.

Several laboratory and field studies have examined the effects of nest site microclimate (Bull and Vogt 1979; G. C. Packard and Packard 1988; Bodie et al. 1995). Prolonged inundation by water (Ewert 1985), lack of moisture (Ewert 1985), and exposure to subfreezing temperatures (Obbard and Brooks 1981) are probably the most common climate-related causes of embryo mortality for freshwater turtles. However, predation appears to account for the vast majority of egg mortality for many species. Predation rates of nests in freshwater turtle populations studied for three or more years can be very high, with up to 100% of observed nests destroyed in some years (Congdon et al. 1983, 1987, 1994; V. J. Burke 1995).

Human-related activities have increased the size of some predator populations (i.e., subsidized predators; see Mitchell and Klemens, Chapter 1) and, as a consequence, apparently have increased predation rates on some turtles. Boarman (1993) documented an increase in raven *(Corvus corax)* populations and discussed the potential impact on desert tortoise *(Gopherus agassizii)* populations due to high rates of predation on juveniles. W. S. Clark (1982) has documented that freshwater turtles are preyed upon by bald eagles *(Haliaeetus leucocephalus),* and it is possible that recovery efforts for bald eagles in the United States could increase predation pressures on some turtle populations. For most freshwater species it is unknown if similar scenarios are being played out in their populations, but many traditional predators of turtle eggs and hatchlings are widely considered to have increased in abundance in many areas due to human activities (Goodrich and Buskirk 1995). Congdon et al. (1993, 1994) suggested that decreased trapping of furbearers in Michigan was correlated with increased predation rates for two turtle species living in a preserve. Similarly, Lovich (1989) noted the coincidence between an increase in raccoon *(Procyon lotor)* numbers and a decrease in spotted turtle numbers over a period of several decades at a preserve in Ohio. Thus, even species within the protected confines of preserves may be subject to high rates of predation, particularly in the nest (Congdon et al. 1993, 1994). In any case, perpetual control of egg predators is costly, does not address root causes (i.e., the human-related causes of artificially high predator densities), and, in the absence of data concerning historic predator abundances, may result in unforeseen and unwanted consequences on other components of the ecosystem (Goodrich and Buskirk 1995; Ratnaswamy 1995). However, limiting predator subsidization (i.e., the root of the problem) would appear to be a low-cost method to reduce the threat of increased predation on incubating eggs. Examples of such a method would be locking lids on refuse dumpsters and covering trash at landfills.

Neonates

Upon hatching, neonate freshwater turtles either leave the nest or remain in the nest until the following year (Gibbons and Nelson 1978). Many populations display either prompt emergence or delayed emergence, but some populations may exhibit both patterns (e.g., the common musk turtle *[Sternotherus odoratus]*; Gibbons and Nelson 1978). The period of time that resource managers must be concerned about disturbances to nest sites is prolonged for neonates that remain in the nest. For example, autumn plowing may be benign to species that exhibit prompt emergence but may doom populations that display delayed emergence. Similar concerns may also apply to forestry activities such as prescribed burns and harvest.

Little is known about the behavior of freshwater turtle neonates immediately after leaving the nest, but it is generally assumed that most species proceed directly to aquatic habitats (Anderson 1958; B. O. Butler and Graham 1995; see E. O. Moll and Legler 1971 and Jansen 1993 for alternative strategies). Neonates may inhabit different portions of the same aquatic habitat that is occupied by juveniles and adults (e.g., common slider *[Trachemys scripta]*, Hart 1983; diamondback terrapin, Lovich et al. 1991; painted turtle *[Chrysemys picta]* and snapping turtle, Congdon et al. 1992; Blanding's turtle, Pappas and Brecke 1992). However, the paucity of data on this life cycle stage makes reliable inferences impossible. Turtle studies focusing on the first year after emergence would greatly enhance our understanding of turtle life cycles, habitat requirements, and conservation issues. The recent advances in telemetry, coupled with diligent trapping and searching efforts, could help fill this enormous gap in our understanding of turtle ecology in the same way that Witherington and his colleagues (Witherington and Salmon 1992; Witherington 1994b) have done for early life stages of sea turtles.

Juveniles

The onset of the juvenile stage can be arbitrarily assigned as 1 year after emergence from the nest (i.e., after the neonate stage). For freshwater turtles the juvenile stage may persist from 3 years (e.g., common mud turtle; Frazer et al. 1991) to more than 15 years (e.g., Blanding's turtle; Congdon et al. 1993). Early juvenile years may be subject to high predation risk, but this risk often diminishes with increased body size (Frazer et al. 1990; Iverson 1991b; Congdon et al. 1994).

Juveniles of some freshwater turtle species are known to change habitat use patterns as body size increases (Congdon et al. 1992) and consume different prey items than are consumed by adults (Georges 1982; Parmenter and Avery 1990). These two findings indicate that spatially heterogeneous freshwater ecosystems may be critical to the functioning of self-perpetuating populations of freshwater turtles. The transformation of much of the world's freshwater habitats into relatively homogeneous reservoirs, agricultural ponds, and channelized rivers may be a serious threat to the developmental habitats required for completion of freshwater turtle life cycles. For example, the Missouri River, located in the central United States, was once a meandering, braided **lotic** (flowing) system that fed numerous lentic wetlands within the floodplain. Humans transformed the river into a series of reservoirs (upper Missouri River) and an extremely fast-flowing channel (lower Missouri River). Currently, extensive and costly efforts are being discussed that would reestablish some of the complex wetland and lentic components of the floodplain (Galat et al. 1996). Increasing the heterogeneity of aquatic habitats such as the Missouri River could provide needed developmental habitats for many species, including freshwater turtles.

Understanding the shifting habitat needs of juvenile freshwater turtles can be a daunting task. However, a simple method of managing for complexity may be available if two steps are followed: (1) document the habitat components in ecosystems and landscapes containing self-perpetuating populations, and (2) assure that those components are not destroyed in ecosystems occupied by other turtle populations. In altered habitats, restoration of damaged components of the ecosystem or landscape based on historical observations or healthy ecosystems may be the only viable method of restoring freshwater turtle populations.

Adults

Maturity in freshwater turtles is caused by and coincident with a number of physiological and behavioral changes. For some species, the onset of maturity marks the first time since hatching that females venture into terrestrial habitats. Maturation may also induce males to move overland to other freshwater habitats in search of females (Morreale et al. 1984). In addition, adults of some species hibernate in upland habitats (Netting 1936; Bennett 1972). Thus, the conservation of suitable terrestrial habitats again appears to be critical to the maintenance of self-perpetuating turtle populations.

The amount and types of terrestrial habitats that adult freshwater turtles require certainly vary among species and landscapes. For example, the observation that seemingly self-sustaining populations of freshwater turtles inhabited a wetland within a successional old-field landscape led V. J. Burke and Gibbons (1995) to suggest that agricultural and real estate development within 275 m of similar wetlands should be minimized. Most semiaquatic turtles use terrestrial habitats for nesting, overwintering, and, occasionally, foraging. During terrestrial activities, semiaquatic species are vulnerable to high frequencies of encounters with humans. These encounters increase the probability that free-ranging freshwater turtles will be collected as pets (Garber and Burger 1995) or killed on roadways by vehicles. While overwintering and estivating, semiaquatic populations may be particularly vulnerable to disturbances in any of several habitat types. For example, draining of aquatic habitats or plowing or paving of terrestrial habitats both have serious negative impacts on a population.

In summary, each component of a freshwater turtle's life cycle is at risk in human-dominated landscapes. The reliance of freshwater turtles on heterogeneous landscapes (Kaufmann 1992) necessitates integrated conservation efforts. Failing to protect a single life cycle stage will ultimately doom the entire population to extinction. Conservation of freshwater turtles, from a life cycle perspective, does not mean that complete understanding of the life cycle is needed before any conservation action can be taken. However, it is obviously preferable to have as much species- and population-specific information as possible.

THREATS TO FRESHWATER TURTLES

Turtles in general are poor candidates for sustainable-harvesting programs and, like many long-lived species, are especially vulnerable to population declines if exploited (Congdon et al. 1993, 1994; V. J. Burke et al. 1994b). A large number of freshwater turtle species appear on conservation and regulatory lists of threatened and vulnerable species (Lovich 1995). Thus, freshwater turtles appear to be faring poorly in the modern world. Of the 160 turtle species that can be considered aquatic or semiaquatic (i.e., at least some populations are freshwater turtles), 62 (including species in which only a certain population or race is classified as sensitive) have been designated as requiring some conservation action. These 62 species include 33 species or populations rated as sensitive on the International Union for

Conservation of Nature and Natural Resources' (IUCN) "Red List" (IUCN 1996); 50 species listed in the action plan of the IUCN's Species Survival Commission (IUCN 1989); 18 species (or populations thereof) listed under the U.S. Endangered Species Act of 1973 (16 U.S.C. §§ 1531 to 1544); and 14 species listed in the Convention on International Trade in Endangered Species of Wild Fauna and Flora (CITES 1973). (Note that summing the numbers listed above does not total to 62 because many species are listed in more than one of the conservation designations.)

Compared with the other groups of turtles, freshwater species have received much less attention from conservation organizations than their numbers dictate. In part this situation may have resulted from freshwater turtles being of lesser economic importance than are river turtles and having less charisma than do tortoises and sea turtles.

Habitat Alteration

The reasons for the high proportion of freshwater species that are in need of conservation are varied. Alteration and exploitation of freshwater habitats are major causes of decline for many species. For example, Buhlmann (1995) found that isolated populations of chicken turtles (Deirochelys reticularia) in Virginia were threatened with extinction due to the loss of 80% of the interdunal bald cypress (Taxodium distichum) habitat that represents its historical range. The interdunal habitat was converted into residential housing and a four-lane highway. The presence of a four-lane highway further complicated matters because the remaining populations were subject to high levels of traffic-related mortality (Mitchell 1994; Buhlmann 1995).

Gibbs (1993) predicted widespread extinctions of turtle populations to be likely if only large wetlands were preserved. Gibbs used computer simulations to predict the effects of the loss of small wetlands in the northeastern United States. He suggested that many turtle species in the study region have established populations in wetlands smaller than those protected by legal statutes (wetland habitats less than 0.4 ha are not protected by federal statutes in the United States). In general, loss of habitat has been a major threat to most, if not all, threatened and endangered turtles, including the western pond turtle (Clemmys marmorata) (Brattstrom 1988), the spotted turtle (Lovich 1989), and the western swamp turtle (Pseudemydura umbrina) (Burbidge et al. 1990), to name only a few documented cases.

Disease

A new and growing threat to turtle populations worldwide is disease-induced mortality (Dodd 1988; Herbst 1994; E. R. Jacobson 1994a; E. H. Williams et al. 1994;

Flanagan, Chapter 3). Lovich et al. (1996) noted that 35% of a sample of common sliders from Lake Blackshear, Georgia, were affected by a severe shell disease characterized by necrotic lesions. The exact cause of the disease is unknown, but toxic or immunosuppressive chemicals may be predisposing factors. The existence of relatively large numbers of dead common sliders along the shoreline of the impoundment suggests that this shell disease may be fatal.

Human Exploitation of Turtles

Although direct exploitation of turtles as a food resource is mainly thought of as a threat to riverine and marine species, it is also a threat to many of the larger freshwater species and to generally riverine species that contain lentic populations. The Madagascan big-headed turtle *(Erymnochelys madagascariensis)*, an endemic turtle species that inhabits lakes, slow-moving rivers, and marshes of Madagascar, has suffered dramatic declines in numbers due to local exploitation as a food source (Kuchling 1988; Kuchling and Mittermeier 1993). In Bangladesh, local consumption has added to the depletion of many freshwater turtle species (M. A. R. Khan 1982), and Kuchling (1995b) observed several turtle species for sale in South China markets, generally for use as food.

In the United States and Canada, members of the freshwater turtle family Chelydridae have been heavily exploited for years, and in many places the exploitation continues. H. W. Clarke and Southall (1920) reported that the wholesale market in Chicago handled 10,000 snapping turtles per year. Demand continues to be very high as evidenced by data summarized by Brooks et al. (1988), who noted that the annual commercial catch in Minnesota alone is estimated at 36,000 to 40,800 kg, or approximately 6,000 to 6,800 average-sized adults. Brooks et al. (1988) reported that in southern Ontario annual catch was 30,000 to 50,000 kg, or 5,000 to 8,300 snapping turtle adults (based on estimates from a 1982 Ontario Ministry of Natural Resources report). In Virginia, approximately 1,350 snapping turtles are slaughtered annually at the state's only known processing center, and an unknown number of Virginia snapping turtles may be processed in other states (J. Mitchell, personal communication). However, the snapping turtle remains an abundant species in Virginia. The alligator snapping turtle has also been heavily exploited as a food source, particularly in Louisiana. Sloan and Lovich (1995) noted that a single wholesale buyer in Louisiana purchased 17,117 kg of alligator snapping turtle from 1984 through 1986.

The overall scenario of exploitation has been the same for most freshwater turtles around the world (Thorbjarnarson et al., Chapter 2). Heavy exploitation is rapidly followed by stock depletion and market collapse. For example, freshwater turtles in the Amazon were once part of a thriving turtle meat industry, but overexploitation has reduced turtle numbers to the point that the industry has collapsed (Alho 1985; Klemens and Thorbjarnarson 1995).

Exploitation of turtles for the pet trade is a serious threat to the persistence of many freshwater turtle species. The trade in freshwater turtles is a worldwide phenomenon that is part of the larger fashion of keeping exotic animals as pets. As pets, turtles are generally marketed in economically developed countries such as the United States, Japan, and those of Western Europe. One need only log on to the Internet and search for "turtle" to understand how extensive the marketing of turtles as pets has become. It should be recognized, however, that the Internet represents only a small portion of the marketing efforts.

The Humane Society of the United States (HSUS 1994) summarized existing knowledge on the live turtle trade in the United States, reporting that U.S. Fish and Wildlife Service records documented the export of at least 25 million turtles through U.S. ports between 1989 and mid-1994. Common sliders, destined for the pet trade, made up the bulk of these exports with an estimated value of over US$17 million (HSUS 1994). During 1993, South Korea imported over one million hatchling common sliders from the United States, followed by Italy and Japan (the latter importing over 600,000).

In terms of numbers, the red-eared slider *(Trachemys scripta elegans)*, a species indigenous to the southern United States (Ernst et al. 1994), appears to be the most heavily exploited species for the pet trade. Annual exports of this species from the United States number between three and ten million individuals depending on the year (Feehan 1986; Warwick 1986; Warwick et al. 1990; Ernst et al. 1994). Red-eared sliders have been the focus of captive-breeding efforts in an attempt to economize the trade and make it more conservation oriented (Warwick 1986; Pritchard 1993). However, the breeding efforts have never been demonstrated to replace collection from free-ranging populations, and there is widespread concern among turtle ecologists that red-eared slider populations are becoming rapidly depleted (Warwick 1986). In general, turtles do not fit the criteria established for candidate species for aquaculture (Webber and Riordan 1976). An additional problem is the establishment of red-eared slider populations as a result of releases in nonnative habitats (e.g., Israel, Bouskila 1986; Singapore, Ng et al. 1993; South Africa, Newbery 1984; South Korea, Platt and Fontenot 1992; Spain, da Silva and Blasco 1995). Although introductions of slider turtles have been cast as a threat to the continued existence of turtles native to the areas where sliders have been introduced (D. C. Holland 1994; da Silva and Blasco 1995), little scientific evidence is available to support the claim.

Although the pet trade represents a large share of the traffic in freshwater turtles, many are also sold for cosmetic and purported medicinal purposes (E. O. Moll 1982; Alho 1985). Das (1990) suggested impetuses for turtle export from Bangladesh were food and medicinal markets.

General solutions to the problems of exploitation of and trade in freshwater turtles have not been satisfactorily offered. The paucity of general solutions may be, in part, the result of a lack of consensus among turtle biologists regarding the desirability of comprehensive action. The idea put forth by Das (1990), that turtle populations should be surveyed first to determine if they are suitable candidates for collection, is one method of more tightly controlling exploitation. His method, if applied, could relieve pressure on populations that have been negatively affected by the trade in both products and pets. However, monitoring such collection is often difficult. During an international conference on the conservation, restoration, and management of turtles and tortoises (Van Abbema 1997), numerous accounts of the deleterious effects of collection for the pet trade were voiced. An eloquent argument against exploitation of turtles, because they are made so vulnerable by their life history strategies, was given by Congdon et al. (1994). They suggested that sustainable exploitation of animals that take years to mature and have long generation times is probably an unrealistic goal. Given the widespread belief among turtle ecologists that the pet trade is detrimental to many freshwater species, the authors of this chapter can find no compelling reasons to support its continuance as presently regulated. Perhaps turtle conservationists should consider the words of Bartlett (1997) on the subject: "The time for a change has come. Let us all have the foresight and courage to begin that change."

There have been several specific attempts to deal with conservation problems faced by freshwater turtles. The remainder of this chapter will describe those efforts for selected species and conclude with conservation recommendations.

CASE STUDIES

We devote this section to examining the conservation status of examples that represent particular situations faced by freshwater turtles. The case studies chosen were selected because they represent particular species or groups for which adequate and reliable data and data analyses are available from which reasonable conclusions can be drawn. Throughout this section, we have avoided building scenarios based largely on speculation.

Madagascan Big-Headed Turtle: Conservation of Taxonomic Relicts

Found only in Madagascar, the Madagascan big-headed turtle is the sole extant Old World member of the subfamily Podocneminae. The species attains a size of up to 43.5 cm and lives in slow-flowing rivers, swamps, lagoons, and marshes (Ernst and Barbour 1989). In western Madagascar, the Madagascan big-headed turtle is heavily exploited as a subsistence by-catch by fishermen who slaughter any turtle caught (Kuchling 1992).

The conservation biology of the species in western Madagascar was reviewed by Kuchling (1988). Considered to be very abundant formerly, its use as a food source by native peoples appears to have caused serious population declines. In fact, the best-studied population of the species was extirpated between 1987 and 1991 (Kuchling 1992). Although large females can produce more than 60 eggs per year (Kuchling 1988), the Madagascan big-headed turtle may not be able to maintain a stable population due, in part, to a possibly biennial reproductive cycle (Kuchling and Mittermeier 1993).

Cast against the rapid population growth of Madagascar, the prospects for survival of this endemic species are dim. A conservation strategy incorporating elements of public education, law enforcement, research and monitoring, habitat protection, and development of less damaging fishery practices has been proposed, but successful implementation will be difficult (Kuchling 1997b).

Diamondback Terrapin: A Coastal Species

The diamondback terrapin is a turtle that resides primarily in tidal creeks of estuaries along the Atlantic and Gulf of Mexico coastlines of the United States. It inhabits only brackish waters, which differentiates it from other freshwater species, but in many respects its behavior and morphology appear similar to those of some map turtles. According to R. Conant (1975), diamondback terrapin are the "most celebrated of [North] American turtles." Conant's comment was based on the fact that the diamondback terrapin has long been exploited as a source of food by all classes and cultures within the species' range. According to Carr (1952) tidewater slaves in the United States once went on strike to protest a diet too heavy in diamondback terrapin. Sometime after that incident the diamondback terrapin found a place on the table of the privileged members of society. With increased demand for diamondback terrapin by epicures, prices soared, and a market was born to supply the big eastern cities of Baltimore, Philadelphia, and New York. The diamondback terrapin became one of the most economically important reptiles in the world.

Records kept in the state of Maryland suggest that the legal trade in diamondback terrapin ranged from 13,608 kg during 1880 to a high of 40,438 kg during 1891 (Figure 6.1). Between 1880 and 1936, the Maryland trade processed over 139,706 kg of diamondback terrapin (McCauley 1945), which translates into the processing of approximately 200,000 diamondback terrapin. Females were the most coveted because of their relatively larger size (adult female mass averages about 700 g; Lovich and Gibbons 1990).

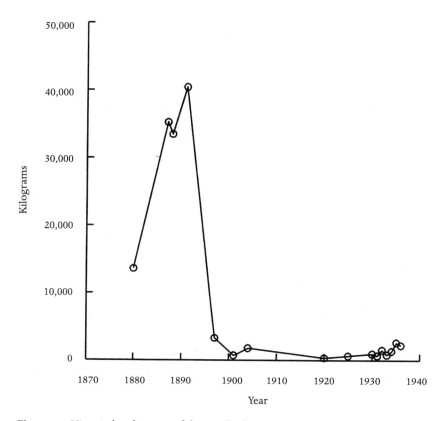

Figure 6.1. Historical exploitation of diamondback terrapin in Maryland (data from McCauley 1945). The *y*-axis represents the weight of the known commercial diamondback terrapin catch.

In recognition of the demand for diamondback terrapin, in 1878 the state of Maryland enacted a law providing a closed season and a size limit for the species (McCauley 1945). As demand increased, prices soared, and wild stocks became depleted. In response, the United States government initiated studies of captive propagation (Coker 1906; Hildebrand and Hatsel 1926; Hildebrand 1929). Eventually the diamondback terrapin fad died out, and populations recovered from the several decades of exploitation. In addition, the vast salt marshes in which diamondback terrapin lived provided them with a level of protection due to their relative inaccessibility.

Today the diamondback terrapin faces new threats, including mortality by drowning in blue crab *(Callinectes sapidus)* traps (Bishop 1983; Roosenburg 1990), habitat degradation (past and present), and detrimental interactions associated with human recreation. Burger and Garber (1995) documented a negative relationship between human beach use in New Jersey and both the number of nests and number of nesting females. Their studies suggested that heavy beach use may reduce nesting by diamondback terrapin. They also noted increased rates of propeller injury on nesting females as boat use increased in the study area. As a result of human impacts, diamondback terrapin populations are declining in some areas (Seigel and Gibbons 1995). Significant local declines have been documented in Florida (Seigel 1993) and some parts of South Carolina (Lovich and Gibbons, unpublished).

A market still exists for diamondback terrapin, particularly in the Chinese restaurants of New York City. Vendors admitted to selling between 2,000 and 3,000 diamondback terrapin in a single year. Most were collected in Virginia, the Carolinas, Maryland, and New Jersey, but some were collected from local areas, including Jamaica Bay and other parts of Long Island, New York. It is conservatively estimated that over 10,000 diamondback terrapin are sold in New York each summer, with females retailing for up to $20 each (Garber 1988). Continued exploitation, coupled with all the other problems the diamondback terrapin faces in the modern world, bodes poorly for the future of the "most celebrated of American turtles."

Coahuilan Box Turtle: Threats to Species with Restricted Ranges

The genus *Terrapene* contains four species of predominantly terrestrial emydid turtles. Only one, the Coahuilan box turtle *(Terrapene coahuila)*, is truly aquatic. Although historically not uncommon in its remote habitat, it is perhaps one of the most endangered turtle species in the world by virtue of its extremely small geographic range. Found only in an isolated intermountain basin in the northern Chihuahuan Desert of Mexico, its entire range is confined to no more than 800 km². Virtually everything that is known of this unusual species is the result of research conducted by W. S. Brown (1974).

Unfortunately, the isolated nature of the Coahuilan box turtle's habitat is no hedge against endangerment. Water is a priceless commodity in arid regions and is often exploited to the detriment of wildlife. Researchers cited in W. S. Brown (1974) suggested that extensive habitat was destroyed in 1964 by canals that carried water away from Coahuilan box turtle habitat for irrigation. The surface area of one studied marsh–pool complex reportedly decreased from about 10 km² to less than 0.2 km², virtually eliminating the entire population of the Coahuilan box turtle. W. S. Brown considered the amount of habitat lost to be an exaggeration and suggested that only 0.25 to 0.50 km² of habitat was lost. The amount is still significant when considering the number of turtles affected. Assuming a population density of 148 turtles per hectare, then 3,700 to 7,400 Coahuilan box turtles died or emigrated.

W. S. Brown (1974) proposed several conservation measures for the Coahuilan box turtle: (1) adopting measures to review the feasibility of planned irrigation projects in prime aquatic habitats, (2) restricting the indiscriminate construction of canals to drain major aquatic habitats, and (3) establishing special protection for the species in the form of legislation that limits collecting to scientific purposes only. The continued survival of this species ultimately depends on protection of the wetlands in which it occurs.

Clemmys: Conservation Concerns at the Genus Level

Turtles of the genus *Clemmys* have long been popular with reptile fanciers. They are hardy, intelligent, and attractive species. However, the attraction has been fatal from the standpoint of the survival of many turtle populations. Combined with habitat destruction and other modern threats, overcollecting has had a serious impact on these turtles. For example, they are among the most popular species of turtles exported from the United States: 4,692 specimens were shipped overseas between 1989 and mid-1994 at an estimated value of $102,658 (HSUS 1994).

The spotted turtle is widely distributed in shallow wetland habitats across the Great Lakes region southward, east of the Appalachians, and southward to northern Florida (Ernst et al. 1994). Lovich (1989) listed several probable reasons for the decline of spotted turtles, including (1) overcollecting by the pet trade, (2) habitat destruction, (3) predation by subsidized predators (see Mitchell and Klemens, Chapter 1), (4) overgrazing by livestock, (5) agricultural cultivation, and possibly (6) pollution. Populations are often patchily distributed in shallow wetlands, which are highly susceptible to ecological succession (Lovich and Jaworski 1988; Graham 1995). Once the habitat becomes overgrown with successional species of plants, it may be unsuitable for spotted turtles. If impediments such as large distances or human developments prevent the turtles from migrating to acceptable habitats once their former habitat becomes unsuitable (Netting 1936; Ward et al. 1976; Lovich 1990), the species may become extirpated from a local area. Population declines have been noted even in the protected confines of nature reserves (Lovich and Jaworski 1988; Lovich 1989).

The wood turtle has also suffered serious declines in many portions of its range. Although the species was exploited for food in the past (Harding and Bloomer 1979), the most serious threats to the long-term survival of wood turtle populations are habitat destruction and collection for the pet trade. As populations are protected in some states, collectors have started "laundering" specimens by claiming that the wood turtles were collected in adjoining states, states not even occupied by the species (A. Salzberg, personal communication). For example, several specimens recently offered for sale were supposedly from Ohio, a state that does not protect wood turtles because none live there (Ernst et al. 1994). The literature does contain several old and dubious records of wood turtles in Ohio (R. Conant 1951; F. G. Thompson 1953) that have been perpetuated in some accounts (e.g., Iverson 1992a), but the evidence strongly suggests that these individuals originated from populations in Pennsylvania or the release of captives (R. Conant 1951).

The best study to document declining wood turtle populations was conducted over 20 years by Garber and Burger (1995). They studied two **allopatric** populations (i.e., not overlapping) in a fenced-off and presumably undisturbed (by humans) area in Connecticut. During the first 9 years of the study the area was closed to recreation, and both populations were stable with a mean of 94 turtles. In 1982 the area was opened to recreation (fishing and hiking), and both wood turtle populations declined 87% over the next 9 years. Despite a constant level of collecting effort, no wood turtles were collected during the last 2 years of the study. Throughout the investigation forest size remained the same, road building was restricted, and air and water quality remained constant. The authors suggested that people may have removed turtles from the area. Whatever the cause, it appears obvious that wood turtle populations are extremely sensitive to increased human presence (Burger and Garber 1995).

The bog turtle is one of the smallest and most secretive turtles in North America. Although it is found from eastern New York and western Massachusetts south to Georgia, it is common nowhere, often existing in disjunct small populations of only 38 to 250 individuals (Herman 1994). Like other members of the genus, bog turtle populations have been declining due to habitat destruction and overcollecting for the pet trade. Destruction and modification of wetlands have particularly devastated bog turtle populations. For example, Torok (1994) documented the extirpation of a New Jersey population within 1 year following construction of a storm water outfall into bog turtle habitat and subsequent discharges of storm runoff.

A detailed survey in North Carolina located only 48 populations statewide (Herman 1994). Of these, 11 (23%) were considered to be viable, 18 (37%) were potentially viable, 10 (21%) were nonviable, and 9 (19%) were of unknown status. Populations were judged to be viable if the population supported 30 or more turtles, sufficient core habitat was available, and evidence of reproduction or recruitment was observed. The estimated statewide population is between 1,260 and 2,500 bog turtles. Only about one-half of the populations from Virginia to Georgia are considered to be viable (Tryon and Herman 1990). A similar survey of eight historic bog turtle sites in western New York found only a single viable population (Collins 1990).

As with other eastern members of the genus *Clemmys,* habitat succession is a problem for bog turtles. Tryon and Herman (1990) and Herman (1994) discussed the beneficial value of cattle and horse grazing in removing "nuisance" vegetation and keeping bog habitats in early-seral stages favorable to the bog turtle. Invasion of bogs by dense thickets of exotic pest plant species, such as multiflora rose *(Rosa multiflora)* and honeysuckles *(Lonicera* spp.), is also perceived as a threat to southern bogs and the bog turtle (Herman 1994). In New York and New England, the exotic Eurasian pest plant purple loosestrife *(Lythrum salicaria)* is a threat to bog turtle habitat (Bury 1979a; Klemens 1993a).

In recognition of the isolated nature of bog turtle habitats, emphasis should be placed on creating and protecting wetland networks that allow movement and gene flow among populations to prevent local extinctions (Chase et al. 1989; Buhlmann et al. 1997). Connecting bog turtle habitats will not be possible in every area due to the widely scattered nature of some populations. Buhlmann et al. (1997) suggested that long-term protection of bog turtle populations in Virginia will require involvement of all affected groups (e.g., landowners, developers, and conservation biologists) to develop effective management plans.

The western pond turtle is found along the west coast of North America from Washington to northern Baja California, Mexico. Although not as popular in the pet trade as its eastern congeners, the western pond turtle has its share of conservation problems. The western pond turtle was used as a source of food in San Francisco until at least World War II. With the development of agriculture in California's Central Valley, vast wetlands containing populations of western pond turtles were drained or channelized (Buskirk 1990). Urban development in southern California destroyed most populations of western pond turtle late in the twentieth century. In 1960 there were 87 known localities for the species in California south of Ventura County. By 1970 these were reduced to 57. As of 1988, viable populations of the species were found in only 20 or fewer localities in southern California (Brattstrom 1988). Populations have also experienced significant declines in the northern portion of the range, including the Willamette drainage of Oregon (D. C. Holland 1994). An additional complication in the conservation of the species is the recent recognition that northern populations exhibit low genetic diversity (Gray 1995), a possible consequence of habitat fragmentation and isolation.

Yellow Mud and Red-Bellied Turtles: Disjunct Populations

Extralimital populations (i.e., those outside the primary range of the species) and **disjunct populations** (separated by large areas) of wide-ranging species have long been considered to be at risk. Quite often they are also the subject of taxonomic controversy. The Illinois mud turtle *(Kinosternon flavescens spooneri)* provides a classic example of such a situation. Originally described as a new subspecies by P. W. Smith (1951), the Illinois mud turtle is restricted to isolated relict populations in the central Midwest of the United States (Seidel 1978). These **relict populations** appear to be the remnants of a once larger species range. Originally reported from 13 localities, by the late 1970s only three populations were considered to be extant, having an estimated total population size of 650 or fewer individuals (L. E. Brown and Moll 1979). Habitat destruction associated with agriculture, industry, and recreation contributed to the suggestion to list the species as endangered under the U.S. Endangered Species Act (L. E. Brown and Moll 1979; Dodd 1982b).

The proposal to list the Illinois mud turtle was met with considerable opposition by members of the industrial community. Their challenge was based on the contention that populations were not thoroughly surveyed and that the subspecies was not taxonomically valid (Dodd 1982b). In his review of the systematics of the yellow mud turtle *(Kinosternon flavescens)*, Iverson (1979) recognized the validity of *K. f. spooneri*, but later investigators (Houseal et al. 1982; J. F. Berry and Berry 1984) found *K. f. spooneri* to be indistinguishable from, and synonymous with, the yellow mud turtle. Amidst the controversy the U.S. Fish and Wildlife Service decided against listing the turtle (Dodd 1982b). However, the Illinois mud turtle did receive protection from each of the three states encompassing its range (T. Johnson, personal communication).

Although there are several examples of specific turtle populations being listed under the U.S. Endangered Species Act (e.g., Plymouth populations of the red-bellied turtle *[Pseudemys rubriventris]* and western populations of the desert tortoise), such was not the fate of the Illinois mud turtle. Fortunately, the state governments encompassing its range had the wisdom to act without the collaboration of federal agencies.

Each species of red-bellied turtle can itself be considered a disjunct member of what has been termed a natural grouping of allopatric species (Alabama red-bellied turtle *[Pseudemys alabamensis]*, red-bellied turtle, and Florida red-bellied turtle *[Pseudemys nelsoni]*) (Seidel 1994). This group seems to have evolved from a more wide-ranging species but is now composed of three species, some of which have disjunct populations themselves. A relict population of the red-bellied turtle in Massachusetts, the so-called Plymouth red-bellied turtle, was described as a separate subspecies *(P. r. bangsi)* by Babcock (1937). The taxonomic distinctiveness of the group was questioned for many years (see review by Browne et al. 1996), and recent research has demonstrated that the Massachusetts populations are no different from others of the red-bellied turtle (Iverson and Graham 1990; Browne et al. 1996).

Regardless of its taxonomic status, in 1980 the Plymouth red-bellied turtle was listed as an endangered "species" (the U.S. Endangered Species Act allows the listing of populations). Presently, it is estimated that there are about 300 individuals restricted to 17 ponds and one river site in Plymouth County, Massachusetts (Amaral 1994). Threats to the continued survival of the relict populations include genetic isolation and habitat alteration. This situation underscores the importance of maintaining populations in our efforts to maintain species. Some would hold that there is no need to conserve Plymouth red-bellied turtles because the same turtle can be found elsewhere. However, in evolutionary terms, extralimital populations can be a first step in the evolutionary process, and they are components of the local biodiversity. It seems more appropriate to consider efforts to protect the extralimital population of the red-bellied turtle as a model of how conservation should work.

At the southwestern limit of the red-bellied turtle distribution, the Alabama red-bellied turtle was listed as an endangered species in 1987 (Dobie and Bagley 1990). The species is restricted to the Mobile Bay of Alabama (C. J. McCoy and Vogt 1985), which is at the mouth of the Alabama River. This species may be the result of allopatric speciation, demonstrating the evolutionary importance of disjunct populations. Predation on nests by pigs *(Sus scrofa)* and fish crows *(Corvus ossifragus)* and impacts of human recreation in this coastal area are cited causes of decline of this species (Dobie and Bagley 1990).

Western Swamp and Black Softshell Turtles: The Rarest Turtles in the World

The western swamp turtle and the black softshell turtle *(Aspideretes nigricans)* are the two freshwater species with the most restricted ranges. These are arguably the most endangered turtles in the world. The former is restricted to a small nature reserve in western Australia and by 1980 was reduced to a population of 20 to 30 turtles (Burbidge 1981; Kuchling and Dejose 1989; Kuchling et al. 1992). An intensive population manipulation was instituted during 1987, and the captive and wild stock was increased to well over 100 individuals. There are current plans to begin a second population of the species.

The black softshell turtle is restricted to a pond associated with a religious shrine in Bangladesh, but its historic range is completely unknown, and it is assumed to be extinct in the wild. The entire species is represented by only about 300 individuals (Ahsan et al. 1991). Although some details of its biology are known (Ahsan and Saeed 1992), much more is unknown regarding this enigmatic relict.

Efforts to deal with conservation issues related to the black softshell and western swamp turtles have generally encouraged establishment of additional populations. Unfortunately, the impacts of such translocations on other species, including other turtle species, are unknown. The western swamp turtle was likely restricted to its present habitat primarily as a result of ecological factors (Groves and Ride 1982), including drought and increased predation by an introduced predator (Burbidge et al. 1990). Issues related to the advisability of captive breeding are discussed by Kuchling and Dejose (1989) and Kuchling et al. (1992), and translocations are discussed in other chapters of this volume (e.g., Seigel and Dodd, Chapter 9). We advise extreme caution when establishing populations in areas not known to be part of the species' historic range (see Dodd and Seigel 1991).

Leyte Pond and Cochin Forest Cane Turtles: Poorly Known and "Rediscovered" Species

Other freshwater turtles have relatively small distributions or are exceedingly poorly known (Lovich and Gibbons 1997). For example, the Leyte pond turtle (*Heosemys leytensis; Geoemyda* fide McCord et al. 1995) is known from only a single surviving neotype (Buskirk 1989). The original specimens from which the species was described were collected from the Philippine island of Leyte near Cabalian but were destroyed during World War II. Subsequent searches have failed to find additional living specimens. The conservation status of this species is obviously a mystery, if it even survives in the ravaged ecosystems of the Philippines. The plight of these and other "covert" species was discussed by Lovich and Gibbons (1997).

Another poorly known but "rediscovered" species is the Cochin forest cane turtle *(Geoemyda silvatica)*. Described in 1912 from two specimens collected near Kerala, India, the species remained virtually unknown to science until 1982, when additional specimens were collected (E. O. Moll et al. 1986). The rarity of the Cochin forest cane turtle is difficult to ascertain given that individuals are difficult to find even when present in an area. However, the small range of the species, coupled with deforestation of its habitat and local use of the turtle for food, does not enhance its prospects for long-term survival (Groombridge et al. 1983).

CONCLUSIONS AND RECOMMENDATIONS

One challenge to those involved in freshwater turtle conservation will be finding conservation solutions that are neither costly nor difficult to implement. Unlike turtles with broad charismatic appeal (sea turtles and tortoises) or economic impact (e.g., river turtles), it is unlikely that many freshwater species will engender substantial funding. Two examples of simple solutions are those proposed by Mount (1976) and at the Conservation of Florida Turtles Conference in 1993 (Eckert College, St. Petersburg, Florida). The shooting of turtles is a problem that has been recognized in many areas of the United States (e.g., Missouri; Johnson 1982).

Mount suggested that conservation of the Alabama red-bellied turtle would be greatly enhanced by going beyond bans on shooting turtles. He encouraged banning the possession of 0.22-caliber rifles by boaters. Recreational shooting is an unnecessary and common source of human-related mortality for Alabama red-bellied turtles. The threat of citation and weapon confiscation could quite likely deter possession of these firearms by anglers and recreational boaters and thus remove the temptation to shoot turtles for "fun."

During the Conservation of Florida Turtles Conference, a simple solution was proposed to the problem of abandoned or underchecked **trot lines,** which are baited fishing lines tied to overhanging branches. The trot lines often incidentally kill turtles, especially when the lines are abandoned or infrequently checked. The proposal born at the meeting would require identification tags on all trot lines. This practice is already in place in some states such as Missouri. Under the proposal, untagged lines would be cut and destroyed by wildlife rangers during routine patrols. Tagged lines that were obviously abandoned or underchecked (i.e., those with rotting carcasses or excessive debris) would be confiscated, and the owner would be fined. Both of these solutions are low cost and could even generate revenue (via fines). The recommendations also address root causes of problems, a primary goal of conservation solutions (Frazer 1992; Lovich 1996; Seigel and Dodd, Chapter 9).

In this chapter we have endeavored to describe the various types of freshwater and semiaquatic turtle species, discuss their life cycle requirements, and outline general and specific conservation issues related to them. The freshwater turtles represent a broad spectrum of species and concomitantly face varying levels and types of threats. Because many species take several years or more to mature, recovery efforts may be costly and the effectiveness of such efforts may be difficult to justify on time scales relevant to political consensuses. In general, late-maturing animals such as freshwater turtles are poor candidates for both harvest and aquaculture. Therefore, the best conservation strategy may be a proactive stance that prevents them from becoming depleted in the first place.

Surveys of freshwater turtle populations are critical, both to determine if populations are in decline and to identify any human-related causes of the decline early. The foundation of any conservation effort for a specific taxonomic group is, based on the best available data, establishment of whether a population or species is in decline, is in imminent danger of decline, or is greatly reduced below historic levels. It is now safe to say that the best available data suggest that large-scale exploitation of freshwater turtles will eventually lead to dramatic population declines. Thus, we warn against exploitation of freshwater species that exceeds small-scale collections for local use by indigenous peoples.

For already reduced stocks, efforts to reestablish populations should be organized such that self-perpetuating populations are the ultimate goal. Of course, reestablishment is aided by some knowledge of the population's life cycle, life history, and natural history, including adult sex ratios (Lovich 1996). Local causes of the depletion should be identified, albeit they are sometimes difficult to establish clearly. In such cases, identification of likely human-induced mortality factors should be identified, and attempts should be made to eliminate them. Of course, such prescriptions are more easily written about than implemented. However, the collected chapters in this volume provide the information needed to frame arguments for freshwater turtle conservation.

A few specific steps may greatly enhance the long-term outlook for freshwater turtle populations. First, we encourage strong consideration of an elimination of the pet trade based on wild-caught turtles. Turtle farming has yet to achieve a convincingly high degree of success, or even independence from wild populations (Klemens and Thorbjarnarson 1995). However, if tightly controlled and monitored, farming may be a potential alternative to the wholesale collection of wild turtles. Although our recommendation will not be enforceable everywhere, we consider the elimination or tight regulation of the turtle trade to be clearly preferable to the open-market system in operation today. There is certain to be an underground trade in turtles following any ban on open-market trade, but the number of individuals traded should decline dramatically. One has only to look at the decline in trade of sea turtle products that resulted from a wide-ranging ban to realize that legal protection can have impacts. In addition to being prudent, a move to restrict the pet trade in turtles severely would greatly increase public notice of their plight and would allow a more public forum for discussion of the many issues that turtles face.

The second step involves increasing awareness about the importance of slow-moving (lentic) waters to nongame wildlife. Wherever and whenever marshes, sloughs, swamps, and similar habitats are threatened, conservationists must take a strong stand against unbridled development and misuse. Turtle biologists must make conservationists, educators, community leaders, and politicians aware of and sympathetic to the habitat needs of freshwater turtles and their aquatic associates. Even fish and game departments, which would seem to be logical allies, may need to be educated regarding the effects of fisheries practices on turtles. With regard to the public, arguments based on aesthetics and awareness that the turtles are part of the local culture (e.g., Sloan and Lovich 1995) and history may be the most convincing (see also Leopold 1949:201–226).

Finally, development of cheap, simple, and optimistic solutions to local conservation problems must be encouraged. In this sense, many sea turtle biologists have excelled. For example, in Mexico one researcher established a "Festival of Turtles" in an effort to reduce egg exploitation (G. Ruiz, personal communication).

She collected a few eggs and incubated them. During the festival, the hatchlings were released into the waves. After a few short years of the festival, local children refused to allow the adults to exploit the local sea turtles. As demonstrated by several other chelonian conservation efforts worldwide, similar efforts hold great promise for freshwater turtle conservation. Currently there is very little sympathy for freshwater species in many quarters. Hands-on experiences with hatchlings could engender needed sympathy.

Simple and inexpensive laws will help in many areas but may be ineffective in others. Legal solutions must be considered as part of the arsenal used to decrease exploitation of freshwater turtle stocks. We are optimistic about the future of freshwater turtle species because the interest and effort that has long been needed are becoming commonplace. However, there is no time to be lost, and turtle biologists and conservationists must vigilantly find and implement solutions to the dilemmas faced by freshwater and semiaquatic turtle species. Nature centers and conservation educators throughout the world are the most important vehicle for spreading information related to conservation efforts. Biologists studying freshwater turtles must join forces with such entities to garner the public support needed to parlay the conservation needs of freshwater turtles into meaningful actions.

ACKNOWLEDGMENTS

Research and manuscript preparation were supported by contract DE-AC09-76SR00819 between the U.S. Department of Energy and the University of Georgia's Savannah River Ecology Laboratory and by support from the U.S. Geological Survey, Biological Resource Division's Midwest Science Center. We thank Tracey Tuberville, Terry Graham, Dennis Herman, and Rod Kennett for their assistance and advice. Tom Johnson, Michael Klemens, Joseph Mitchell, and Don Moll kindly provided critical reviews of drafts of the manuscript.

JAMES McDOUGAL

7

CONSERVATION OF TORTOISES AND TERRESTRIAL TURTLES

Among the most charismatic and relatively well studied group of chelonians are the tortoises. Tortoises constitute the family Testudinidae, a geographically widespread taxa consisting of 11 genera and approximately 40 species (Iverson 1992a). All are strictly terrestrial and have unwebbed toes, elephantine hind feet with never more than two phalanges in each digit, and, usually, **osteoderms** (bony scales) present on the forelimbs (Iverson 1992a). Morphologically and ecologically tortoises are a diverse group. In size they range from the meter-or-more-long, 80- to 185-kg giants of the islands of the Galápagos and Indian Ocean (Pritchard 1979; Ernst and Barbour 1989) to the diminutive species of the genera *Homopus* and *Psammobates,* found in the deserts and veldt of southern Africa. The smallest, the speckled cape tortoise *(Homopus signatus),* rarely exceeds an adult carapace length of 100 mm (Boycott and Bourquin 1988; Boycott 1989).

Tortoises are distributed throughout many of the tropical regions of the world, including South America and the Galápagos Islands, Africa, Madagascar and Aldabra Atoll in the Indian Ocean, India, and Southeast Asia. Some tortoises, including the Chaco tortoise *(Geochelone chilensis), Gopherus* spp., and *Testudo* spp., have a more temperate distribution, inhabiting, respectively, southern South America, southern North America, and southern Europe, northern Africa, and the Sinai Peninsula east to western Asia. Tortoises are absent from all other temperate regions, Australia and New Guinea, the Philippine Archipelago, and most of the islands of the Sunda Shelf. In the past tortoises were more widespread than they are today, occurring in northern Europe and England, central Asia, the West Indies, and in North America as far north as southern Canada. They also occurred on various islands in the Indian Ocean, where some species have become extinct in historical times (Ernst and Barbour 1989). Within this extensive distribution tortoises inhabit a wide variety of habitats. In tropical regions they may be found in evergreen forest, mesic and dry deciduous woodlands, shrublands, savannas, grasslands, and deserts—habitats that range from extremely humid to arid. Habitats used by tortoises in temperate regions are also quite diverse. The only tortoise genus that occurs in North America is *Gopherus*. Representatives of this genus are found in all three major deserts (Mojave, Sonoran, and Chihuahuan), and one species, the gopher tortoise *(G. polyphemus)*, is found in the southeastern United States from South Carolina to Louisiana. The Palearctic genus *Testudo* is restricted to regions with a Mediterranean climate in southern Europe and to steppe and desert regions in western and central Asia, North Africa, and the Middle East.

There are also a number of turtle species that are not tortoises but are in some respects similar to tortoises in that they are exclusively or primarily terrestrial and lay small clutches of relatively large eggs. Ecologically they differ from tortoises by being restricted to relatively mesic habitats, whereas at least some tortoise species are found in extremely dry regions. Also terrestrial turtle species often depend on invertebrate prey as an important component of their diet, whereas tortoises are mainly herbivorous. In many ways these differences are unimportant, however, because the threats that face tortoises and terrestrial turtles are alike in many cases.

Terrestrial turtles are a diverse group made up of various species in the family Emydidae (subfamilies Batagurinae and Emydinae). The best-known representatives of this group are the North American box turtles *(Terrapene* spp.). This genus comprises four species, one of which, the Coahuilan box turtle *(T. coahuila)*, has an extremely limited distribution (see V. J. Burke et al., Chapter 6). The common box turtle *(T. carolina)* and ornate box turtle *(T. ornata)* are widely distributed throughout the eastern and central United States, with subspecies of both forms ranging into parts of Mexico (Ernst and Barbour 1989; Iverson 1992a). North American box turtle populations are threatened by many of the factors discussed in this chapter, including habitat alteration (see Mitchell and Klemens, Chapter 1). They have long been used for food, medicine, and ceremonial purposes by at least some of the aboriginal populations in North America, and it has been suggested that box turtle populations were severely reduced in western New York due to these uses (Adler 1970). More recently box turtles have been extensively collected for sale in both the domestic and international pet trade. They are now listed on Appendix II (allowing trade if a permit from country of origin is obtained) of the Convention on International Trade in Endangered Species of Wild Fauna and Flora (CITES 1973). Exports of North American box turtles from the United States have effectively ceased. (Trade in North American box turtles is discussed more fully by Thorbjarnarson et al., Chapter 2.)

Other terrestrial turtle species include the Neotropical wood turtles, brown wood turtle *(Rhinoclemmys annulata)*, furrowed wood turtle *(R. areolata)*, painted wood turtle *(R. pulcherrima)*, and Mexican spotted wood turtle *(R. rubida)* (Ernst and Barbour 1989), and a variety of Southeast Asian species including the tricarinate hill turtle *(Melanochelys tricarinata)*, keeled box turtle *(Pyxidea mouhotii)*, black-breasted leaf turtle *(Geoemyda spengleri)*, Cochin forest cane turtle *(Geoemyda silvatica)*, and Indochinese box turtle *(Cuora galbinifrons)*. This list is not meant to be comprehensive, and, as the ecology of many of the species listed here is little known, others may be added in time. The factors that threaten populations of these species are not well known in most cases. The black-breasted leaf turtle has been quite common in the pet trade since the 1990s, and the Indochinese box turtle has also frequently been offered for sale. Habitat destruction is probably the greatest threat to the Cochin forest cane turtle, a species restricted to a limited area in southwestern India. An even greater threat to turtle species in Southeast Asia may be the great, and apparently growing, demand for turtles for food and medicines, especially in China. Because the threats that face box turtle populations are addressed in other chapters in this volume (Mitchell and Klemens, Chapter 1; Thorbjarnarson et al., Chapter 2), and there is little specific information on many of the other terrestrial turtle species, the remainder of this chapter will be devoted to tortoises specifically.

Tortoises have figured prominently in many cultures for a variety of reasons. They have long been used as food and medicines. Their shells have been used as household and ceremonial implements and as curios for tourists. They have served as symbols of longevity, strength, and perseverance. More recently they have become popular pets, being brought into homes as objects of interest. All of these interactions between human cultures and tortoises have had effects, mainly negative, on tortoise populations. These negative effects continue today and, in fact, have accelerated and intensified as the interactions responsible continue, depleting tortoise populations even further and making recovery or even stability of these populations less and less likely.

The future of many tortoise populations is uncertain. Although there is little information regarding the status of most populations, at least some are declining in numbers, and several species are threatened with extinction. Indeed, this is a conservative statement because many species that today seem to exist in sufficient numbers to ensure long-term viability are beset by problems that, if unchecked, could rapidly and drastically reduce their numbers. These threats include those that have brought some tortoise species to (or over) the brink of extinction in the past and include threats that have not been clearly recognized until recently. The goal of this chapter is to examine those factors that threaten the survival of tortoise populations and species worldwide and to look at what is being done and what might be done to mitigate these problems as the ecosystems of the world continue to be fragmented and degraded, species continue to decline and disappear, and the Earth becomes increasingly dominated by humans.

THREATS TO THE SURVIVAL OF TORTOISE POPULATIONS

There are three primary factors that are responsible for the decline in many tortoise populations and species. The direct exploitation of tortoise populations for food and their purported medicinal qualities and to supply a burgeoning demand for pets involves the removal of individuals from populations and in many instances has taken place on a large scale (see Thorbjarnarson et al., Chapter 2). The destruction or degradation of tortoise habitat results in either the elimination of tortoise habitat or the alteration of tortoise habitat to the extent that the local population will be reduced and sometimes extirpated (see Mitchell and Klemens, Chapter 1). Habitat loss and degradation have been major factors in the reduction of some tortoise populations during the twentieth century. Disease may threaten the continued existence of tortoise populations, a problem that has been little studied in wild tortoise populations and the implications of which for the conservation of tortoise populations and species are not well understood (see Flanagan, Chapter 3). As tortoise populations are progressively reduced by the deterministic factors mentioned above, they become increasingly susceptible to stochastic and catastrophic events. These events may be especially significant in very small populations and may be responsible for the ultimate demise of these populations.

These threats to survival are certainly not unique to tortoises as a group. Throughout history the overexploitation of many animal species for food has resulted in drastically reduced population sizes and, in some cases, extinction. The negative effects of habitat destruction and degradation are well known, and today they are considered some of the most important factors leading to species extinction. Likewise, the effects of disease on wild animal populations has been well documented. What makes these threats of such importance to tortoise populations is that most tortoises are generally long-lived organisms, characterized by delayed sexual maturity, relatively low fecundity, and high adult survival (Wilbur and Morin 1988; Congdon et al. 1993). Congdon et al. (1993) found that given this suite of life history characteristics, very high annual survivorship in juvenile freshwater turtles was required to maintain a stable population. What this means is that posthatching, most individuals are important to the continued survival of the population. Although specific, long-term demographic data are unavailable for most tortoise species, data gathered by Turner et al. (1987) on reproduction in the desert tortoise *(Gopherus agassizii)* indicated that this species exhibits similar demographic constraints to those discussed by Congdon et al. (1993). It is certainly not unreasonable to assume that these constraints apply to many (if not most) tortoise species worldwide. Therefore, the drastic reduction in size that many tortoise populations have experienced may have dire implications for their recovery. Below, I present a more detailed overview of the major threats to tortoise populations. Much attention is given to the use of tortoises as food, a topic about which little is known in most cases but which is potentially a major conservation concern in some regions. Therefore this threat is reviewed by region.

Exploitation for Food

Archaeological evidence indicates that tortoises have long been used for food by human cultures in many parts of the world (e.g., Wu 1943; R. W. Taylor 1982; Boycott and Bourquin 1988; Schneider and Everson 1989). Today tortoises continue to be a part of the diet in many cultures, although the level and importance of this use varies both regionally and by species. Tortoises may be an important protein source in some parts of South America, Africa, India, and Asia, whereas their use as food is presently minor and localized in most parts of Europe and North America (Klemens and Thorbjarnarson 1995). In some cases, tortoises are used on a subsistence basis and are occasional additions to a diet based primarily on other sources of nutrition. Recently, however, with improving economic conditions and reduced trade barriers, the demand for tortoises (and other turtle species) for food and medicine has been growing rapidly, particularly in China. To meet this demand, the exploitation of tortoise populations has increased and may now be a serious threat to some species.

Where human population density is relatively low and tortoise habitat is intact, the use of tortoises as food may not be sufficient to reduce local populations seriously. Where tortoises supply a large amount of the protein consumed by the local human population, or when the exploitation of tortoises for food (or some byproduct) changes from subsistence use to supplying a market system, major and relatively rapid declines in tortoise populations may occur. A number of historic (and possibly some prehistoric) examples exist that illustrate the consequences of the overexploitation of tortoise populations for food. One example comes from the island of Madagascar, where at least two species of giant tortoises *(Geochelone* spp.) have been identified from subfossil remains. Both *Geochelone grandidieri* and *Geochelone abrupta* (which date from 2290 to 2060 and 2850 to 1910 before the present, respectively) seem to have overlapped both spatially and temporally with the initial period of human colonization of Madagascar, and the extinction of both of these species is hypothesized to have been a result of overhunting (Mahe and

Sourdat 1973). A number of large bird and mammal species also became extinct on Madagascar during this period, possibly lending credence to the hypothesis that nonsustainable hunting levels by an expanding human population led to the extinction of many of the larger vertebrates of Madagascar (P. S. Martin 1966), although Dewar (1997) presented caveats to accepting this theory uncritically.

Other events in the same region of the Indian Ocean provide a more unequivocal example of the overexploitation of tortoise populations resulting in extinction or at least severe reduction of tortoise population size (Arnold 1979; Stoddart and Peake 1979; Swingland 1989b). Many isolated islands, including those of the Mascarenes, Comoros, Seychelles, and Aldabra Atoll, previously supported dense populations of giant tortoises of a number of species. From the early seventeenth century, these populations were decimated by uncontrolled hunting of the giant tortoises for their meat and oil. Settlers took large numbers for their own use, and many were later used to provision sailing vessels. By the early nineteenth century, most of these species were extinct, and today only the Aldabra tortoise *(Geochelone gigantea)* still exists, found in a wild state on only Aldabra Atoll. A similar pattern of events took place during the nineteenth century in the Galápagos Islands of the eastern Pacific Ocean, though most populations of Galápagos tortoise *(Geochelone nigra)* are still extant, if only barely so in some cases (see "Giant Tortoises: The Overharvesting of Vulnerable Populations," Thorbjarnarson et al., Chapter 2).

Certainly the exploitation of tortoises for food can reduce their populations significantly, in some cases to the point of extinction. Below is a brief regional overview of the exploitation of tortoises for food.

NORTH AMERICA

In North America, tortoises have been an important food source to some cultures. Prehistorically, the use of tortoises as food may have been widespread, and overhunting by Paleo-Indians during the Pleistocene has been hypothesized to have been a factor in the dramatic range contraction of the Bolson tortoise *(Gopherus flavomarginatus)* (Bramble in Morafka et al. 1989). The desert tortoise has also been used as a food source for thousands of years (Luckenbach 1982; Bury and Corn 1995), and Kroeber (1925) documented the use of the desert tortoise as food in some Native American cultures in the twentieth century.

R. W. Taylor (1982) reported that the gopher tortoise has been exploited in Florida for over 4,000 years. The gopher tortoise has long been known as a food item in rural parts of the southeastern United States (Auffenberg 1978; Auffenberg and Franz 1982; Diemer 1986), and Carr (1952:339) pointed out that "the importance of this animal in the lives of the poorer rural people of Florida and south Georgia, since the days of initial colonizations, would not be easily overestimated."

The exploitation of the gopher tortoise for food appears to have been a significant factor in its decline in the Florida Panhandle (Auffenberg and Franz 1982). Diemer (1986) reported that tortoise hunters in the Panhandle had to travel to Georgia or other parts of Florida to obtain gopher tortoises. The use of tortoises for food, at least in the United States, appears to have declined. It probably still exists at relatively low levels in certain rural areas of the Southeast, though it is not generally considered a conservation concern.

In contrast, the use of tortoises as food has been an important factor in historic population declines in Mexico, at least for the Bolson tortoise. Morafka et al. (1989) consider use as food the primary factor in the decline of this species. Although they note that the Bolson tortoise has probably been a source of food since pre-Columbian times, it is the drastic increase in predation by humans that has decimated populations of this species in the twentieth century. Two main factors seem to have been responsible for this increase in use. First is the construction of a railroad during the 1940s, which ran through the center of the range of the Bolson tortoise. Bolson tortoises were gathered by railroad crews for local use and reportedly for shipment to Pacific coast cities, where they were sold as a delicacy (Morafka 1982). The presence of the railroad led to an increase in the local human population, resulting in the extirpation of Bolson tortoise populations in proximity to the railroad. The second factor that has substantially increased predation levels is Mexico's land reform program, which resettled people in cooperative farms on undeveloped land, including some within the range of the Bolson tortoise. Morafka (1982) reported that these cooperative farms were expanding, even in the Mapimi Biosphere Reserve in Durango, a stronghold for the species. Obvious signs of predation were found (scattered shells and excavated tortoise burrows) even in areas of relatively low human population density. See Bury et al. (1988) for a detailed discussion of this species.

The desert tortoise is apparently still commonly consumed in parts of Mexico (Lowe 1990). Fritts and Jennings (1994) documented people in the state of Sonora who reported eating desert tortoise, though infrequently. Those interviewed considered desert tortoise suitable for food but said that it was only irregularly available. The same study found two moderate-sized settlements where desert tortoise populations had been reduced, probably by exploitation for food. The use of tortoises for food, though localized, must be considered a potentially important threat to the species found in Mexico.

SOUTH AMERICA

Tortoises have probably always been a common food item for aboriginal peoples in South America. Today all three species found on the continent are used for food to some extent. The yellow-footed tortoise (Geochelone denticulata) is a relatively large species and is exploited for food in some regions (P. Walker 1989b). Dixon and Soini (1986) reported that large numbers are consumed by the rural population in the Iquitos region of Peru, and Pritchard and Trebbau (1984) stated that it is commonly consumed by Indians and others living in the rainforests of northern South America. In many parts of the yellow-footed tortoise's range, human population densities are low and large areas of habitat (evergreen tropical forest) are intact and relatively inaccessible, making commercial exploitation unlikely. The yellow-footed tortoise is generally considered secure at present, but as human populations grow within the range of this species, local populations are likely to decline.

In contrast, the red-footed tortoise *(Geochelone carbonaria)* has long been used for food by both the aboriginal inhabitants of the regions in which it occurs and European colonists. At present, human predation is considered to be a major threat to this species. According to P. Walker (1989c) it is under pressure over much of its range and apparently declining in some areas. Pritchard and Trebbau (1984) reported that casual but frequent collection of red-footed tortoises whenever they are encountered has depleted or eliminated many populations in proximity to human settlements. One reason for this species' vulnerability to predation is associated with its preferred habitat. It is generally a species of moist savannas and woodlands adjacent to drier grasslands (Pritchard and Trebbau 1984), which are areas far more accessible to tortoise hunters than are interior forests. This species is sold in many South American markets (Pritchard 1979). Large numbers are sold and consumed during the Holy Week prior to Easter because the Catholic Church classifies turtles as fish, thus allowing their consumption during this period (Pritchard and Trebbau 1984; P. Walker 1989c).

The status of the Chaco tortoise as a food item is less clear. Human populations within its range apparently use this species as food (Pritchard 1979; P. Walker 1989a), and Richard (1987 *in* P. Walker 1989a) stated that gravid females are preferred. Waller (1997) stated that the use of this species as food is related to cultural factors rather than subsistence needs, and that although consumption may not be widespread, the impact on tortoise populations may be locally significant.

EUROPE, NORTH AFRICA, AND WESTERN ASIA

The tortoises of these regions all belong to the genus *Testudo*. Although in many cases these tortoises live in areas long populated by humans, few reports exist regarding their use as food. One exception is that of Beshkov (1993), who reported that the collection in Bulgaria of the spur-thighed tortoise *(Testudo graeca)* and Hermann's tortoise *(Testudo hermanni)* for food has eliminated these tortoises in some locations and has led to a rapid decline in population numbers in other locations. In some areas within the European–north African–west Asian region, the exploitation of tortoises for food may exist on a local level (i.e., they may occa-

sionally be a part of the diet), but widespread collection for food is apparently unknown, and this type of exploitation is not considered an important conservation
concern in this region.

SUB-SAHARAN AFRICA, MADAGASCAR, AND ISLANDS OF THE INDIAN OCEAN

The exploitation of tortoises for food in sub-Saharan Africa varies greatly by both
species and region. The leopard tortoise *(Geochelone pardalis)* and the African
spurred tortoise *(Geochelone sulcata)* both reach large sizes and are consumed over
much of their respective ranges. The leopard tortoise, found throughout much of
eastern and southern Africa, is reportedly rare in regions of high human population density due to overhunting (Boycott and Bourquin 1988; Broadley 1989c; Lambert 1995a); in areas of low human population densities and within the various reserves it inhabits, populations of the leopard tortoise are apparently secure
(Broadley 1989c; Baard 1994). The African spurred tortoise is found in the Sahel
region of southern Mauritania, northern Senegal, and east to Ethiopia. Broadley
(1989b) suggested that because Moslems are the main human inhabitants of the
region, this species is less exploited for food than is the leopard tortoise within its
range (the presumption being that religious constraints on the consumption of
tortoises protects the African spurred tortoise to some degree). Lambert (1993)
felt that historical cultural differences account for the observed variations in levels
of exploitation. In Mali, local inhabitants reported seeing African spurred tortoises
stockpiled in three locations in March 1990, and tortoises were confiscated from
a dealer who was transporting them to Ghana for sale as food and for shipment
abroad (Lambert 1993). These reports suggest that this species is exploited for food;
however, the level of exploitation remains unclear.

At least some species of hinge-back tortoises *(Kinixys* spp.) are used as food in
some parts of their range (Klemens and Thorbjarnarson 1995). Broadley (1989d)
reported that Bell's hinge-back tortoise *(K. belliana)* is eaten throughout most of
its range, although due to its relatively small size it can remain common even in
densely populated areas. Schmidt (1919) reported the use of dogs *(Canis domestica)*
to track serrated hinge-back tortoises *(K. erosa)* by scent in what was then the Belgium Congo. The pancake tortoise *(Malacochersus tornieri)* may be consumed in
some parts of its range; however, this use is not intensive and apparently not a conservation concern (Klemens and Moll 1995). Likewise, the small species of the genera *Homopus* and *Psammobates,* inhabitants of the deserts, grasslands, and heath-
lands of extreme southern Africa, do not seem to be exploited for food to any
appreciable degree (Baard 1994). The South African bowsprit tortoise *(Chersina angulata)* was exploited for food prehistorically, and its remains are common at some
archaeological sites (Branch 1989a). There are recent reports of the consumption

of this species by rural inhabitants on the west coast of South Africa (E. Baard, personal communication); however, this consumption does not seem to be a serious threat to these populations.

In Madagascar, four extant, endemic tortoise species are currently recognized. Two of these, the common spider tortoise *(Pyxis arachnoides)* and the flat-tailed spider tortoise *(Pyxis planicauda)*, are relatively small species with localized distributions. Durrell et al. (1989d) reported that at least the common spider tortoise is apparently rarely used for food. Levels of exploitation of the flat-tailed spider tortoise, if any, are unknown. The remaining two species, the radiated tortoise *(Geochelone radiata)* and the ploughshare tortoise, or angonoka *(Geochelone yniphora)*, are large species that have been intensively exploited for food both historically and, in the case of the radiated tortoise, at present. During the eighteenth and nineteenth centuries, populations of the radiated tortoise were severely reduced around a number of port towns in southern Madagascar due to commercial exploitation. Large numbers were shipped to the Mascarene Islands to be used as food (Honegger 1979). This species is still exploited by certain groups in Madagascar, and in some areas it is commonly sold in markets (Juvik 1975; Durrell et al. 1989b; Goodman et al. 1994). Gonzalez-Gonzalez (1993) reported that the inhabitants of Réunion Island have imported radiated tortoises from Madagascar for many years, sometimes keeping large numbers in backyard pens. Similarly, from at least the seventeenth century onward, the angonoka was collected in large numbers for shipment to the Comoro Islands (Durrell et al. 1989c). More recently this species was regularly collected to sell to Europeans as food, even though it has been officially protected since 1931 (Decary 1954). The angonoka is apparently not generally eaten by the local population at present (Durbin et al. 1996); however, the long history of exploitation for food has taken its toll on angonoka populations, which remain critically low at this time.

The destruction wrought on the various species of giant tortoises that inhabited many of the islands in the western Indian Ocean has been discussed above. The most important factor in their decline was gross overexploitation for food and oil, and a number of species were driven to extinction. For detailed reviews of tortoise populations in this region and their decline see Arnold (1979), Stoddart and Peake (1979), and Swingland (1989b).

INDIAN SUBCONTINENT

Tortoises have commonly been used as food in many parts of India. The Indian star tortoise *(Geochelone elegans)* is eaten by various cultural groups throughout its range, including the Jogi in western Rajasthan, the Vagris in Saurashtra, the Irula in Tamil Nadu, and Palaiyars of North Travancore (Frazier 1987; Das 1991).

Hutton (1837) reported that the Bhil tribes of western India were expert trackers of this species. The elongated tortoise *(Indotestudo elongata)* and Travancore tortoise *(Indotestudo forstenii)* are consumed in many parts of their respective ranges. Exploitation of the elongated tortoise by the Chakma occurs in the Chittagong Hills of Bangladesh (M. A. R. Khan 1982) and the Chitwan area of Nepal (Dinerstein et al. 1987). The Travancore tortoise is limited in distribution to the western Ghats of southwestern India as well as Sulawesi and Halmahera Islands of Indonesia. Within its range, this species is used for food and may provide an important source of protein for local human populations (E. O. Moll 1989b; Das 1991). It should be noted that the taxonomic status of the two allopatric populations of the Travancore tortoise is unclear. They originally were considered distinct species (the Travancore tortoise *[Indotestudo travancorica]* in southwestern India and Forsten's tortoise *[Indotestudo forstenii]* in Sulawesi and Halmahera Islands, Indonesia). However, based on their inability to distinguish the two forms by means of morphological characteristics, Hoogmoed and Crumly (1984) considered *I. forstenii* a senior synonym of *I. travancorica*. Recent investigations, based on genetic and morphological data, into the relationships between the Indian and Indonesian forms indicate that these populations are, in fact, taxonomically distinct (M. Klemens and G. Amato, personal communications).

The Asian brown tortoise *(Manouria emys)* is captured for food throughout its range on the Indian subcontinent; however, it seems not to be common anywhere (Das 1991). It may be that the use of tortoises for food on the Indian subcontinent has been of a subsistence rather than a commercial nature. Whether or not this use has led to serious historical population declines in any species is unclear; however, continued exploitation for food by an expanding human population is likely to have negative impacts on all species if it has not already.

SOUTHEAST ASIA AND CHINA

The use of tortoises for food in Southeast Asia is great and an important conservation concern. All species are probably threatened to some degree, both from past exploitation levels as well as more recent, greatly increased exploitation levels. At least four species of tortoise occur in the region. The little-known Burmese star tortoise *(Geochelone platynota)* is apparently extremely rare, and as early as 1863, Blyth reported that live specimens were difficult to obtain because the local inhabitants were so fond of eating them. In 1868, Theobold mentioned large numbers taken for food. Today the status of this species is unclear. It is virtually unknown in collections, at least in the West, and few field surveys have been conducted to date. There are recent reports of this species showing up in food markets in China. The impressed tortoise *(Manouria impressa)* and the Asian brown tortoise are both used for food, although they are localized in distribution and apparently nowhere common. A very long history of exploitation may be a factor in the present scarcity of both of these species. Wu (1943) reported that remains of the Asian brown tortoise were found in archaeological excavations at the city of Anyang, China, dating from the Shang Dynasty (1300 to 1000 before the common era) (W. H. McNeill 1963). Anyang is located near the northern border of Henan in the Huang He (Yellow) River valley, far outside the known range of the Asian brown tortoise, which indicates a long history of trade in this species. The much more widely distributed and common elongated tortoise is frequently consumed throughout its range. It is found in markets in China where turtles and tortoises are in demand as a source of food and medicine (Kuchling 1995b).

Exploitation for Medicines

The use of tortoises for their purported medicinal qualities is widespread in India and parts of Asia. The literature on this topic is limited, so similar uses in other parts of the world may be underrepresented. The medicinal use of turtle shell (not tortoise exclusively) was found to be widespread in India (Choudhury and Bhupathy 1993) and was recorded in almost all parts of the country. The same authors also noted that, at least in parts of Assam and West Bengal, the use of turtle meat for its medicinal properties is found in affluent urban populations, not just rural ones. The flesh, shell, gall bladder, and blood of turtles may be consumed to cure disorders as diverse as stomach ailments, skin diseases, headache, and piles (Das 1991; Choudhury and Bhupathy 1993). Shibata (1975) reported that in Asia both the elongated tortoise and the impressed tortoise are exported from Thailand to Hong Kong, where they are used in the manufacture of a popular Chinese drug called *gui ban*. Beshkov (1993) stated that since the 1960s in Bulgaria there has been a great increase in the use of the blood, meat, eggs, and other products of spur-thighed and Hermann's tortoises as cures for cancer and leukemia.

Exploitation for the Pet Trade

The exploitation of tortoise populations to supply the pet trade has existed for hundreds of years at least, and there is no doubt that it has been responsible for significant reductions to tortoise populations in many parts of the world. As early as 1802, Daudin reported that geometric tortoises *(Psammobates geometricus)* were popular pets (Baard 1990). This form of exploitation seems to have begun in earnest during the late 1800s, when spur-thighed tortoises began to be exported from North Africa, mainly Algeria and Morocco, to markets in France and the United Kingdom (Lambert 1995b). Trade apparently began on a small scale, on the order of a few hundred specimens per year (e.g., Sowerby and Lear 1872), but the volume of exports seems to have accelerated through the later years of the nineteenth century. Bateman (1897:44) mentioned that occasionally in the establishments of the larger animal dealers, tortoises might be found "crowding, as thickly as possible, the floor of some upper room," and that a seller of these tortoises headed his advertisement with the announcement "10,000 Tortoises." During the twentieth century the demand for tortoises grew, and the numbers of specimens being imported into Europe grew as well until, by 1937, several hundred thousand were arriving at the London docks each summer. World War II interrupted this trade for some years, but after the war it was back in force, with hundreds of thousands of tortoises being imported by France, Germany, and Great Britain annually (Lambert 1995b). The Central Asian tortoise *(Testudo horsfieldii)* was also being collected in large numbers during the early decades of the twentieth century. For example, in 1932 some 27,000 Central Asian tortoises were collected in Kazakhstan alone (Shnitnikov 1932 *in* Kubykin 1995). Along with the various species of *Testudo,* thousands of South African bowsprit tortoises were being imported into Great Britain from South Africa (Baard 1990). During the early 1960s, the United States also began importing large numbers of spur-thighed and Hermann's tortoises, adding to the drain on tortoise populations. The result of this trade was the severe depletion of populations of these tortoises over large areas of their ranges.

In the United States the desert tortoise was the first species subjected to high levels of exploitation, by both people who casually collected specimens for pets and commercial collectors who supplied the booming tourist trade. Early on, Archie Carr expressed concern over the large number of these animals captured for sale to tourists, "who in most cases would be hard put to show any need at all for a desert tortoise" (Carr 1952:328). Also, well-known desert tortoise populations have been repeatedly visited by groups from colleges and universities, and specimens apparently often returned home with these groups. The Utah population described in the classic study by Woodbury and Hardy (1948) declined from approximately 300 to 40 after repeated visits of this type (Luckenbach 1982). Coombs (1974, 1977) reported that other populations in Utah were also reduced by this type of collecting pressure. Notwithstanding laws protecting the desert tortoise from casual collection over much of its range, estimates and anecdotal accounts of the number of desert tortoises in captivity in certain regions of the western United States suggest a phenomenal loss to desert tortoise populations, especially in the Mojave Desert of southern California (USFWS 1993b). Commercial trade in this species today is insignificant, but illegal, casual collecting may be a threat to at least some populations.

During the early 1960s, other tortoise species began to enter the pet trade, some in large numbers. One of the first to appear on the market in the United States, usually next to the familiar species of *Testudo,* was the Texas tortoise *(Gopherus berlandieri).* Large numbers were shipped out of southern Texas until concern for the future of this species prompted passage of legislation in 1967 to protect it (F. L. Rose and Judd 1982). Virtually no Texas tortoises are seen in the pet trade today.

Later in the 1960s and into the 1970s, the number of tortoise species available in the pet trade began to grow. Large numbers of red-footed tortoises from Colombia and Brazil, star tortoises from India, elongated tortoises from Thailand, and leopard, hinge-back, and pancake tortoises from Africa were imported to supply the rapidly growing demand, particularly in the United States, Japan, and a number of European countries. Although exact figures are few and difficult to assess, the trade was certainly substantial by any standards. For example, Honegger (1980) recorded 2,744 elongated tortoises imported in 1978 by countries that were parties to CITES, and Das (1991) reported an annual figure of 10,000 Indian star tortoises sold in Calcutta's New Market alone in the late 1970s. More recently, populations of the Egyptian tortoise *(Testudo kleinmanni)* were decimated by collection for the pet trade, especially during the 1980s (Buskirk 1985; Geffen and Mendelssohn 1989; Baha el Din 1994; Mendelssohn and Geffen 1995). Klemens and Moll (1995) documented unsustainable levels of trade in populations of the pancake tortoise in Tanzania (see "Pancake Tortoise: Exploitation for the Pet Trade," Thorbjarnarson et al., Chapter 2).

Restrictions placed upon the export of certain tortoise species have changed the species composition of those readily available today, as well as making illegal trade in some species relatively common. For example, a number of large confiscations of Indian star tortoises occurred during the 1990s (Choudhury and Bhupathy 1993; J. Ventura, personal communication). Another relatively recent change in the market for tortoises as pets is the availability of captive-bred specimens of many species, although some species are still so inexpensive to import that captive breeding is not an economically viable alternative.

Habitat Destruction and Degradation

Habitat destruction is one of the primary factors responsible for the extinction and extirpation of many species today. Although effects of the outright destruction of habitat are obvious and well known, other forms of habitat degradation that are more subtle and harder to observe may also negatively affect populations of organisms. For example, the phenomenon of habitat fragmentation is of major concern for biological conservation today and indeed has been called the primary cause of the present extinction crisis (Wilcox and Murphy 1985). **Fragmentation** may be understood as the progressive reduction of a species' required habitat to the point at which the habitat area exists as a number of remnant patches surrounded by and separated from each other by a matrix of suboptimal or nonusable space (Forman and Godron 1981). Fragmentation, as it is occurring today, is essentially an anthropogenic process. Habitats can be fragmented by the building and expansion of human settlements, either rural or urban–suburban, and the associated infrastructure (such as roads); by intensive agricultural development and expansion; by deforestation; or by any other processes that subdivide an organism's habitat into smaller and smaller areas. Fragmentation of ecosystems and biological communities has many ecological consequences, and fragmented landscapes are characterized by changes in microclimate and some degree of isolation between component patches (Saunders et al. 1991). Fragmentation leads to smaller population sizes for a species, which potentially increases the importance of stochastic demographic and genetic factors (see Gibbs and Amato, Chapter 8) as well as catastrophic environmental factors to the future viability of these populations (M. L. Shaffer 1981; Gilpin and Soulé 1986).

Roads and highways not only fragment tortoise habitat but also can be a significant source of mortality to a population. This population reduction can occur when tortoises are killed by passing traffic or taken by a predator (including humans). Some desert tortoise populations have experienced significant mortality on roads and highways (Luckenbach 1982; Boarman et al. 1997). The multiple factors that can affect a tortoise population when a new road is constructed through its habitat were clearly illustrated by Goodman et al. (1994). They described high levels of mortality in a population of radiated tortoises in the Karimbola Plateau region of southern Madagascar. Radiated tortoises were trapped after falling down a steep embankment on the side of an unfinished road. Some died due to exposure to the intense sun or by drowning during periods of heavy rains; others may have been collected by passersby for use as food or for later sale in local markets.

Edge effects may also affect tortoise populations. These effects are a direct result of habitat fragmentation; the **edge** refers to the transition zone between the original habitat and the matrix of altered habitat that borders it. In the context of tortoise conservation probably the most significant factor resulting from these ecological edges is the potential for increased populations of generalist predators, often subsidized predators (see Mitchell and Klemens, Chapter 1), which may increase mortality rates for incubating eggs and juvenile tortoises. Although little information exists on edge effects that is specific to tortoise populations, there is some evidence that edges can be of importance. For example, Temple (1987) found that predation rates on the eggs of North American box turtles (*Terrapene* spp.) increased near an ecological edge.

It is well known that introduced animal species, particularly mammals, can adversely affect native plant and animal populations (Coblentz 1990; Westman 1990; L. Bowen and Van Vuren 1997). These effects have been clearly demonstrated in a number of island ecosystems, for example, the Galápagos Islands and many of the islands of the western Indian Ocean, where the introduction of rats (*Rattus* spp.), cats *(Felis catus)*, dogs, pigs *(Sus scrofa)*, and goats (*Capra* spp.) has played an important role in the decimation of giant tortoise populations through predation of eggs and juveniles, competition for food, and destruction of habitat through overgrazing and trampling (Arnold 1979; Swingland 1989b; Cayot et al. 1994). Increased levels of predation by native predators have also been observed in some tortoise populations. This is most often associated with increases in the population size of the native predator species due to some change, such as human settlement and attendant refuse dumps or changes in land use, which leads to the elimination of what were formerly limiting factors for the predator populations (see Mitchell and Klemens, Chapter 1). Some examples are the increase in feral pig populations in Bulgaria, leading to increases in predation on smaller size-classes of both the spur-thighed tortoise and Hermann's tortoise (Beshkov 1993), and raven *(Corvus corax)* predation on desert tortoises in the western United States (Boarman 1997). An interesting example of the interaction of a number of types of habitat degradation leading to increased predation rates is reported by Mendelssohn and Geffen (1995) for the Egyptian tortoise. Overgrazing has led to a shortage of cover for Egyptian tortoises, thus making them more vulnerable to dogs, crows (*Corvus* spp.), and ravens. In addition, overbrowsing of shrubs under which rodents burrow has led to the disappearance of certain rodent species and a shortage of burrows for tortoises to take refuge in during the long and extremely hot summer months. In this case, overgrazing of tortoise habitat has led to a reduction of cover for the tortoises, compromising their ability to avoid both adverse environmental conditions and predators.

Overgrazing can lead to increased levels of competition for food, reduced plant productivity, and altered species composition of the local plant community. These changes can lead to decreased availability of food, shelter, and nesting areas for tortoises and disrupt social interactions in tortoise populations. Overgrazing has apparently affected some populations of the desert tortoise (e.g., Luckenbach 1982; Avery and Neibergs 1997), though Oldemeyer (1994) cautioned that this has not been conclusively demonstrated. Overgrazing has also been implicated in the decline of some populations of the Chaco tortoise in Argentina (P. Walker 1989a), the spur-thighed tortoise in North Africa (Bayley and Highfield 1996), and the Egyptian tortoise in Egypt and the Middle East (Mendelssohn and Geffen 1995). Overgrazing can be a particularly acute problem in arid regions where recovery by the vegetation is difficult or impossible.

Exotic and invasive plant species can also negatively affect tortoise populations; however, there is little specific information available on this topic (but see Jennings 1997b). Exotic and invasive plants may displace native plant communities, which are usually far more diverse. This replacement may, in turn, disrupt ecologically critical factors such as food availability and the physical structure of the habitat, which, in turn, may affect thermoregulatory ability, successful nesting and critical incubation temperatures, and the availability of shelter from predators. The spread of red brome *(Bromus rubens)*, an introduced species, was reported to be a possible threat to desert tortoise populations in the Pakoon Basin of northwestern Arizona (T. Duck *in* Bury et al. 1994). This species facilitates the spread of fire, and these fires can destroy the native perennial shrubs that desert tortoises require for cover. In South Africa, Baard (1990, 1993) reported that introduced Australian *Acacias* and grasses such as *Bromus* and *Briza* spp. have degraded large portions of the habitat of the geometric tortoise. An interesting case of an introduced plant providing an important resource for a tortoise species was reported by Bayley and Highfield (1996). In this case an introduced opuntia cactus *(Opuntia ficus indica)* now provides shelter and food for the spur-thighed tortoise in an area of otherwise degraded habitat in Morocco.

In some regions changes in the frequency or intensity of fire events can significantly reduce tortoise populations. Fire can affect tortoise populations through direct mortality. For example, in March 1982 in South Africa, fire swept through the single largest known population of the critically endangered geometric tortoise. It is estimated that 80% of the geometric tortoise population was destroyed (Boycott and Bourquin 1988). Fire has also been reported to have affected populations of some species of *Testudo* (e.g., Hermann's tortoise, Stubbs et al. 1985; marginated tortoise *[Testudo marginata]*, Willemsen 1995). Fire can also affect tortoise populations by changing tortoise habitat and lowering its carrying capacity. Although fire may be a normal occurrence within the ecosystem, fire suppression may result in increased fire intensity when a fire does occur (due to the accumulation of available fuel). Human presence in a region may increase fire frequency or intensity to an extent that fire decreases tortoise populations. Interestingly enough, a decrease in fire frequency may also reduce tortoise populations. In ecosystems that experience regular fire events, the cessation of fire leads to changes in plant species composition and ecological structure. Such habitat changes have been observed in the longleaf pine *(Pinus palustris)* forests of the southeastern United States, habitat of the gopher tortoise (Auffenberg and Franz 1982), and in the oak forests of southern France, habitat of the Hermann's tortoise (Stubbs 1995).

Changes in agricultural practices, specifically the change from low-technology polycultures to industrial monocultures with high inputs of fertilizers and pesticides, have reduced tortoise populations in some regions. This can be the result of both outright habitat destruction and possibly chemical poisoning, though the importance of the latter is unclear at present (e.g., Inozemtsev and Pereshkolnik 1994; Bayley and Highfield 1996).

Finally, the use of off-road recreational vehicles and the staging of military training activities are significant problems for some tortoise populations. Most information on the effects of these activities is available for the desert tortoise in the
North American West (Bury et al. 1977) and the Egyptian tortoise in Israel
(Mendelssohn and Geffen 1995); however, there is no reason to believe that they
cannot be significant factors elsewhere as well.

Disease

The presence of various diseases in natural and captive populations of many organisms is well known, and disease processes have presumably been important
agents of natural selection and evolution throughout the history of life on Earth
(Real 1996). Disease has been, and continues to be, a significant problem in conservation programs targeting endangered species, especially those with critically
low populations (E. R. Jacobson 1993). Comparatively little is known about disease organisms or processes in wild populations of tortoises, although there is a
growing body of literature based on captive populations. To what extent wild
populations of tortoises are exposed to disease and what effects disease might have
on the structure and viability of these populations in the future are just beginning
to be investigated (see Flanagan, Chapter 3).

One of the first indications that natural tortoise populations could indeed be severely affected by disease came to light in 1988. At that time desert tortoises from
the Desert Tortoise Natural Area in Kern County, California, were found to have
an upper respiratory tract disease (URTD) (E. R. Jacobson et al. 1991). A 1989 survey showed 43% of the 468 desert tortoises exhibited clinical signs of the disease
(Knowles 1989). This population declined catastrophically, and this decline was, in
part, responsible for populations of this species north and west of the Colorado
River being listed as threatened by the U.S. government (USFWS 1990b). Infected
desert tortoises have also been found in the Las Vegas valley of Nevada (E. R. Jacobson et al. 1995), on the Beaver Dam slope of Utah and Arizona, and in the
Sonoran Desert (E. R. Jacobson 1993). Subsequent investigations have shown the
microorganism *Mycoplasma agassizii* to be the causal agent of URTD (M. B. Brown
et al. 1994; E. R. Jacobson et al. 1995). Lowe (1990) discussed the occurrence of
URTD in Sonoran populations of the desert tortoise.

The origin of the pathogen is difficult to determine. Because URTD is often
seen in captive desert tortoises, it is possible that a pathogenic strain of *Mycoplasma*
sp. was introduced into the wild population via release of infected captive specimens (E. R. Jacobson et al. 1995). Based on the rapid decline of the population of
tortoises at the Desert Tortoise Natural Area, this disease would seem to be highly
infectious. E. R. Jacobson et al. (1991) reported that URTD has been observed in

red-footed, leopard, Indian star, radiated, and gopher tortoises and that *Mycoplasma* sp. have been isolated from spur-thighed and leopard tortoises. The occurrence of URTD is often associated with the presence of the bacterium *Pasteurella testudinis* (Snipes and Biberstein 1982) and herpesvirus particles (Pettan-Brewer et al. 1996); however, their relationships to the disease or each other are unclear. Predisposing and synergistic factors are likely to be involved in the development and spread of the disease (E. R. Jacobson et al. 1991; Pettan-Brewer et al. 1996). Herpesvirus has also been implicated in the mortality of imported Argentine Chaco tortoises (E. R. Jacobson et al. 1985) and captive spur-thighed tortoises (Cooper et al. 1988).

The studies cited above have resulted in a clearer understanding of this very important topic in the conservation of tortoises. Further investigations into the health of tortoise populations worldwide are likely to result in new pathogens and disease processes being recognized, along with their associated problems for conservation strategies and planning.

The Vulnerability of Small Populations

Critically low population levels in some tortoise species already exist. Some forms of Galápagos tortoises, the angonoka, and the geometric tortoise are well-known examples. In some other species, the evidence for low population levels is mainly anecdotal, though it is often compelling. For example, Thirakhupt and van Dijk (1994) reported on the status of three tortoise species in western Thailand—elongated tortoise, Asian brown tortoise, and impressed tortoise. They reported that habitat degradation (especially through anthropogenic fires converting tropical evergreen forest into floristically poor, fire-climax dipterocarp forests) and long-term predation by humans have apparently reduced tortoise populations significantly. In the case of the elongated tortoise, considered common in much of its range in Southeast Asia, populations appear to have crashed since the mid-1980s in western Thailand, and it is now nowhere common. The remaining two species were reported to be rare. Further, Thirakhupt and van Dijk noted that even professional turtle gatherers admit that searching for tortoises is no longer worth the effort. Das (1995) reported that inhabitants of certain areas of Bangladesh recalled that one to three Asian brown tortoises might be captured per year in the 1950s, whereas now they are rarely seen. The situation seems to be similar in other parts of Southeast Asia as well, at least for the two species of *Manouria* (E. H. Taylor 1970; Wirot 1979; Das 1991; Espenshade and Buskirk 1994; Chan-ard et al. 1996). These reports indicate that populations of these species may be well below historic levels. It is likely that the present rarity of these species is due, in large part, to a long history of exploitation for food and, to some extent, the pet trade. In light of the above, it is interesting to note that both the Asian brown tortoise and impressed tortoise are still regularly imported into the United States, although the numbers seen are relatively small.

Whatever the deterministic causes of low population levels in a tortoise species (e.g., habitat destruction or overhunting), the potential consequences are the same. As tortoise populations are progressively reduced to low levels, stochastic demographic, environmental, and possibly genetic factors become increasingly important. For example, in populations characterized by very low population densities, individuals may have lower and lower probabilities of finding a mate. **Demographic stochasticity** (the chance variation in individual birth and death) can result in a skewed sex ratio or age structure. In a nonreproductive population, or a population with very low or no recruitment, the population may be functionally extinct even though adults are still present. **Environmental stochasticity** (catastrophic environmental events) may have dire consequences for a species with a highly localized distribution and poor dispersal ability. These factors operate independent of population density and can be serious factors for species that exist in only a few isolated populations. Finally, stochastic genetic processes (e.g., genetic drift) may be a problem in some small populations. In long-lived species, such as tortoises (and turtles generally), that exhibit relatively long generation times, however, these processes are likely to be of less importance because the population will be affected by other factors before genetic problems become manifest.

CONSERVATION OF TORTOISE POPULATIONS

Given the threats facing tortoise populations worldwide, what can be done to protect them and ensure their survival? Superficially this is an easy question to answer. If habitat destruction is reducing the numbers of a tortoise species, protect at least some of its habitat. If it is the exploitation of a tortoise population for food or the pet trade, prevent that exploitation. Realistically, of course, neither the problems nor the solutions are quite so straightforward. Conservation generally is an extremely complex process, one that must integrate the need for biologically sound strategies for the recovery and protection of a species with the needs (real and perceived) of human populations. Conservation decisions are often based on incomplete information on the ecology of the target organism, the ecosystem of which it is a part, and the social context in which the conservation effort will be taking place. With these constraints in mind we can examine what strategies might be useful in mitigating the threats outlined above.

Habitat Protection

The most cost-effective and nonmanipulative method of protecting a species is to protect its habitat. Ideally this presumes that a large enough area is protected so that the physical and biological processes that are critical to the maintenance of the ecosystem are also conserved and that populations of the target organism(s) are large enough to be genetically and demographically viable in some consensually determined future. It should be recognized, however, that this situation may be the exception rather than the rule.

In many cases, some degree of habitat management may be necessary to optimize habitat for the tortoise species of interest. Improving or maintaining habitat might be accomplished by removing predators (e.g., rats, pigs, or dogs) or competitors (e.g., goats) or perhaps by initiating an appropriate fire regime to maintain habitat suitable for tortoise foraging and nesting. In other cases, management may entail managing human activities, such as restricting access to all-terrain vehicles or preventing collection of tortoises for food or the pet trade. Whatever the management strategy, management itself needs to be flexible and able to change as ecological monitoring of the system and the species of interest suggests (or dictates) that it should. Managers also need to recognize that in few cases do we understand the long-term results of our actions, and that in many, if not most, cases we are managing human actions and the results of those actions rather than ecological or evolutionary processes (Orr 1990; Ehrenfeld 1991; Stanley 1995).

Fortunately, some tortoise species today exist in large, relatively intact ecosystems, and when human population densities are low, it is these species that have the least need for conservation measures. The yellow-footed tortoise in much of its range in South America, the Texas tortoise in the United States, and many of the small tortoise species of southern Africa (e.g., *Chersina, Homopus,* and *Psammobates*) are examples of species that are secure in at least part of their respective ranges. Some species have had large or small areas set aside specifically to protect local populations. The Mapimi Biosphere Reserve in Durango, Mexico, is a multiple-use area that was established to protect the Bolson tortoise and other local resources (Kaus 1993). In Cape Province of the Republic of South Africa, a number of small preserves have been set aside to protect the critically endangered geometric tortoise (Baard 1993).

Other species are protected in certain parts of their range but need some sort of management activity to ensure the viability of their populations. For example, periodic burning of longleaf pine forests inhabited by the gopher tortoise in the southeastern United States maintains the presence of herbaceous plant species used by the gopher tortoises for food and cover and prevents the forest understory from overgrowing potential breeding, nesting, and foraging sites (Lohoefener and

Lohmeier 1980; Auffenberg and Franz 1982). In the Massif des Maures, the last stronghold of the Hermann's tortoise in France, grazing by sheep (*Ovis* spp.) and goats used to keep the understory open and created suitable habitat for Hermann's tortoise feeding and nesting. With the post–World War II decline in rural human inhabitants, grazing has existed at a much reduced level and less suitable habitat has existed for Hermann's tortoise populations. This is one of the factors cited as important in the decline of this species in France (Stubbs 1995).

Some of the most intense management of any tortoise species is found at the Charles Darwin Research Station in the Galápagos Islands, where since 1965 researchers have been attempting to restore viable populations of Galápagos tortoises to islands where they have been severely reduced in numbers. Management activities have included control and eradication of introduced mammal species as well as captive breeding and headstarting programs and the protection of nest sites (Cayot et al. 1994).

Regulation of Trade

Unfortunately, the creation and management of protected areas does not ensure protection to tortoise populations if they are still exploited for food, medicines, and the pet trade. Legislation and international agreements have been effective in controlling trade in at least some tortoise species previously seen in the pet trade; however, many are still exported in large numbers. The use of tortoises as food and medicines often takes place on a local or national level and is very difficult to assess, much less control. Recently there have been reports of elongated tortoises being imported into China, apparently to be used as medicines (J. Ventura, personal communication). Such trade is impossible to control through legal means if the countries involved are not signatories of any conservation trade agreements. International censure or political pressure is probably the only alternative. Given the lack of importance of turtles in international politics, however, this alternative seems highly unlikely.

Captive Breeding

In cases in which a population has reached critically low numbers and is unlikely to recover, or for which the factors responsible for the species decline continue to operate, captive breeding of the species of concern may be needed to ensure its survival. The goal of captive-breeding programs should be well defined at the outset. In cases in which it is feasible, the goal should be a short-term program intended to augment numbers in the wild population or to reestablish an extirpated population (but see below). Efforts to protect the species habitat should take place concurrently and be a major component of the species recovery plan. Whenever possible, breeding facilities should be located in the country where the releases will occur. When this is not logistically feasible, facilities should be located in an area where the species of interest is not exposed to related taxa. To reduce the risk of disease transmission the breeding group should not be located in a diverse zoological collection in most cases. For detailed reviews of captive breeding as a conservation strategy, see Conway (1995), Balmford et al. (1996), Hutchins and Conway (1996), and Snyder et al. (1996).

Repatriation, Relocation, and Release Programs

Tortoises are charismatic creatures, loved by many for many reasons, not the least of which is their placid demeanor and disposition. Because so many people care about tortoises and their welfare, it is relatively easy to obtain support for conservation actions that, superficially at least, seem to benefit them. Unfortunately, in many instances, these efforts concentrate on the individual organism rather than the population or species as a whole. This has led to well-meaning manipulative strategies that may not address the real problems facing the tortoise population involved but only some of the symptoms (see Frazer 1992; Seigel and Dodd, Chapter 9).

One set of these strategies includes the repatriation, relocation, and translocation of tortoises. These terms refer to actions by which tortoises (or any organism) are released into an area formerly or presently occupied by the species (**repatriation**), animals are moved away from an area in which they are threatened to an area where they are less threatened (**relocation**), and individuals are released into areas not historically occupied by that species (**translocation**) (Dodd and Seigel 1991). In the case of tortoises, specimens may have been obtained as a result of confiscations or removed from land that is to be destroyed by development projects. Small-scale cases of all three of these actions take place when people release unwanted captive tortoises into the wild. Of all chelonians, tortoises are most frequently the subjects of these "conservation" actions. For example, a survey of repatriation, relocation, and translocation programs by Dodd and Seigel (1991) found that the gopher tortoise was the most frequent subject of these programs of any reptile or amphibian species. This species is found in the southeastern United States, and thousands of animals have been moved from one area to another, especially in Florida, in efforts to mitigate the negative effects (i.e., habitat destruction) of development projects. According to Dodd and Seigel (1991), these efforts have met with little success, although R. L. Burke (1991) offers a different perspective.

Some international repatriation, relocation, and translocation projects have taken place on a large scale as well. For example, Klemens (1995) reported on several hundred pancake tortoises that were seized by customs officials in the Nether-lands. The shipment originated in Tanzania and was destined for the United States. Due to the publicity surrounding the seizure (especially the poor conditions in which the tortoises were being shipped), Dutch authorities shipped the pancake tortoises back to Tanzania to be released. Much praise was received for this "hu-manitarian" gesture, notwithstanding the fact that throughout the process the Tor-toise and Freshwater Turtle Specialist Group of the International Union for Con-servation of Nature and Natural Resources had advised against releasing the pancake tortoises back into the wild.

What could possibly be wrong with releasing tortoises back into the wild to resume their lives in nature? Assuming that the animals are released in appropri-ate habitat, there are at least three major problems that face these kinds of activi-ties, which are well meaning but potentially disruptive or even lethal to the popu-lations involved. These problems are dispersal, genetic incompatibility, and disease (see Seigel and Dodd, Chapter 9, for a more complete discussion of this topic). Tortoises often do not remain where they are released, which can render repatri-ation, relocation, and translocation schemes pointless unless large enough tracts of tortoise habitat exist in which most individuals will eventually end up as in-habitants, even after dispersing from the point of release. Even then, are enough individuals being released so that densities will be high enough for successful re-production? Are native tortoise populations present? If not, why? If native tortoise populations no longer occur in the area, are the factors that caused their extirpa-tion understood and are the causal factors still potentially a threat? If a native popu-lation is present, how genetically similar are the native population and the animals to be released into that population? If the native population is large relative to the number of animals to be released, this may be a minor concern. If, however, the native population is very small (e.g., such as the angonoka in Madagascar), then genetic considerations may be far more important. Last, and perhaps most im-portant, is the possibility of disease transmission from tortoises being released into wild populations (e.g., E. R. Jacobson 1993). Tortoises held in captivity have ample opportunity to acquire various forms of pathogens. The introduction of these pathogens into immunologically naive or physiologically stressed wild populations may result in morbidity and mortality. The spread of URTD in certain areas of the Mojave Desert is thought to have originated with the release of infected captive specimens into the wild population (E. R. Jacobson et al. 1995).

It is clear that adequate baseline data on wild tortoise populations are required, against which to compare potential donor animals before a realistic assessment of a repatriation, relocation, and translocation project is possible. This can be il-lustrated by the case of the almost repatriated pancake tortoises mentioned above. With commendable caution, Tanzanian authorities decided to delay the release of these animals while a health assessment of two native populations of pancake tortoises was conducted. Comparisons of the wild populations against those being held for release showed that blood and nasal mucous samples from the wild populations differed little in key health parameters across a wide geographic range. Samples collected from the pancake tortoises returned to Tanzania (which had been housed in various animal holding facilities and zoos in Western Europe) were quite variable, and many showed signs of disease. On the basis of these findings Tanzanian authorities decided against the release of these animals. What is important here is that without comparative data from wild populations, these pancake tortoises and their pathogens would most likely have been released into the wild (see "Integrate New Information and Techniques into Conservation Programs," Klemens, Chapter 10). Rarely do adequate data exist.

Unfortunately, in some cases today, assessment data are not given adequate attention before repatriation, relocation, and translocation programs are implemented. Much of the effort devoted to the gopher tortoise in Florida may be a waste of effort. But repatriation, relocation, and translocation programs can be highly visible and make people feel that something good is being done, that animals are being saved, and, indeed, we do know what we are doing. This illusion of effectiveness may be as important a danger to effective conservation as the biological considerations mentioned above are to the tortoises themselves. Fortunately, many now realize the risks and complexities inherent in using repatriation, relocation, and translocation as conservation strategies. For example, one well-conducted, ongoing gopher tortoise repatriation, relocation, and translocation project is being conducted by the Wildlife Conservation Society in New York. Displaced gopher tortoises are relocated to a barrier island off the coast of Georgia for release. No native gopher tortoise population presently occurs on the island, although the habitat is similar to that which occurs on the mainland. All gopher tortoises undergo a thorough health assessment prior to release, as well as periodic follow-ups. The released population is carefully monitored for habitat use, territoriality, and reproduction (which has occurred). In conclusion, if a proposed repatriation, relocation, and translocation project is based on a sound analysis of a particular situation, biologically realistic assumptions, and adequate information, it may be worthwhile to attempt. However, potential problems and limitations must be recognized.

SUMMARY AND CONCLUSION

Protection of the world's tortoise species will no doubt be difficult, even though the goal is worthwhile. The continued use of many tortoise species for food and medicines, regionally at accelerated rates, will be extremely difficult to control in the world as it exists today. It is possible—likely—that many populations will be extinct before exploitation levels are stabilized, if they ever are. Control of the exploitation of tortoise populations to supply the international pet trade may be somewhat more attainable. As national legislation and international trade treaties (e.g., CITES) have made trade in tortoise species more restrictive, there has been an effort in the herpetocultural community to produce captive-born specimens of many of the more desirable species. Although many of the less-expensive species (e.g., Bell's hinge-back tortoise and Central Asian tortoise) are still priced too low to generate interest in commercial propagation, other species are produced in large numbers and, in some cases, are nearly able to supply the domestic demand (e.g., the African spurred tortoise in the United States). Commercial captive breeding has different goals than do conservation breeding programs; however, by reducing collecting pressure on wild populations, commercial captive breeding may be able to make a contribution to conservation efforts.

Habitat destruction and degradation will continue to affect tortoise species, and close monitoring of tortoise populations is required. In many cases such monitoring will be difficult to achieve because there are relatively few people working in the field and resources are limited. There is a paucity of information on the ecology, distribution, and status of many tortoise species. Efforts must be made to ensure the protection of substantial areas of tortoise habitat. At least in some cases, habitat conservation may not be as daunting a task as it sounds because conservation areas set aside for other species, particularly mammalian megafauna, also provide habitat for tortoise (and many other) species. The problem may then become preventing the exploitation of tortoise populations in these areas (e.g., Thirakhupt and van Dijk 1994). When possible, the formulation and institution of policy measures designed to discourage habitat destruction should be supported.

Finally, the specter of little-known disease processes needs to be addressed. This will require extreme care in instituting manipulative or ex-situ programs (e.g., captive breeding and repatriation, relocation, and translocation) as well as continued awareness of, and research into, the issue of disease in wild and captive populations.

In this chapter I have attempted to outline briefly what the threats are to tortoise and terrestrial turtle species today and how these threats can be addressed. Proximately, the problem is how to protect populations of these species for the immediate future and ensure their viability in some unknown future. Of course we plan our strategies within the context of the world as it exists today. There are, however, two intimately related issues that would seem to be rather large flies in the ointment of our potential successes, and, in fact, they are the central issues in all of conservation today. One is the unprecedented level of population growth exhibited by humans, and the other is the enormous level of resource consumption associated with this growth. Although this is far too large, complicated, and contentious a topic to address in a chapter on tortoise conservation, I think that it is extraordinarily important for those involved in efforts to maintain and restore biological diversity to be acutely aware of the global context in which our efforts are framed and how global issues threaten to undermine even our most cherished successes.

ACKNOWLEDGMENTS
Michael Klemens was kind enough to offer me the opportunity to be part of this effort. I thank Ernst Baard, R. Bruce Bury, and Jeffrey Lovich for providing critical comments and suggestions for the improvement of this chapter.

JAMES P. GIBBS AND
GEORGE D. AMATO

8

GENETICS AND DEMOGRAPHY IN TURTLE CONSERVATION

The application of genetics and demography to conservation has proceeded rapidly in the 1990s. Conservation genetics has come to encompass issues broadly related to population genetics and systematics of endangered taxa (Amato and Gatesy 1994; Avise and Hamrick 1996). Studies in conservation genetics range from investigating higher-level relationships and the degree of evolutionary novelty represented by particular lineages (R. L. Burke et al. 1996; H. B. Shaffer et al. 1997) to elucidating inter- and intrapopulation genetic diversity (Lamb et al. 1989). A related discipline, molecular ecology, uses genetic markers to reveal information about mating systems and dispersal that can be particularly useful in developing management strategies for threatened taxa (Galbraith et al. 1995). From the perspective of turtle conservation, developments in conservation genetics have provided many important insights into the design of effective management strategies (e.g., B. W. Bowen and Avise 1996).

Similar strides have been made in the 1990s relative to demographic analyses for wildlife conservation (e.g., Burgman et al. 1993). New and powerful ways of examining population dynamics and management questions are now available. These advances have been particularly important for turtle conservation. Many long-term studies of turtle populations initiated a decade or more ago have recently come to fruition (e.g., Bjorndal and Carr 1989; Gibbons 1990b; Congdon et al. 1993, 1994; V. J. Burke et al. 1995). The data accumulated provide information on turtle demography that has been previously unavailable for these long-lived organisms. Furthermore, sophisticated, matrix-based demographic analyses have become widely accepted (Caswell 1989). These analytical techniques have been coupled with the newly available information on turtle demography, as well as with population projection models, to improve our understanding of ways to manage turtle populations effectively (e.g., Crouse et al. 1987).

Our goal here is to provide an overview of current genetic and demographic aspects of turtle conservation. Our focus is on describing how recent developments in the fields of conservation genetics and population biology can benefit efforts to conserve turtles.

GENETIC ISSUES IN TURTLE CONSERVATION

One generalization that has been suggested about the genetics of the order Testudines (Avise et al. 1992; H. B. Shaffer et al. 1997) is that its evolution is taking place at a slower rate than that of mammals and birds. Most studies have concentrated on mitochondrial DNA (mtDNA) divergence and have revealed a rate of divergence 2.5 to 3 times slower (B. W. Bowen et al. 1993). This generally slower rate may not be unique to turtles, as suggested by studies on other ectotherms (Caccone et al. 1997). Lack of interpopulation genetic differentiation in early studies of turtles was considered the result of this slow rate of evolution, but more recent studies have revealed significant geographic partitioning in many marine and terrestrial turtle species (e.g., Britten et al. 1997). Thus, differences in evolutionary rates do not significantly affect the application of current conservation genetic techniques to the order Testudines.

Systematics

Many questions remain regarding systematic relationships within the Testudines. H. B. Shaffer et al. (1997) provided an excellent review of the history and current state of **higher-level phylogenetics** of turtles (that is, evolutionary relationships among genera and families) based on morphology and molecules. One noteworthy result is the lack of resolution on these levels for major groups of cryptodires (the "hidden neck" turtles, which include the majority of turtle species). Whether this lack of resolution reflects a relatively rapid radiation of the major lineages some 100 million years ago or a current lack of identifiable characters evolving at a rate useful for such analyses is not yet clear. However, a knowledge of higher-level relationships can be useful in determining conservation priorities by revealing lineages of distinct evolutionary novelty (e.g., the relationship between the Kemp's ridley sea turtle [*Lepidochelys kempii*] and the olive ridley [*Lepidochelys olivacea*]; B. W. Bowen et al. 1993) and in area-based approaches that employ measures such as degree of endemism.

Research on **lower-level systematics** of turtles (that is, evolutionary relationships among species and subspecies) has more obvious conservation implications. For example, at the species level, genetic studies of the snapping turtle *(Chelydra serpentina)* support species-level distinctiveness for the Central American *(C. s. rossignonii)* and South American *(C. s. acutirostris)* subspecies (Phillips et al. 1996), correspondingly elevating the conservation status of these poorly known southern forms, which are more threatened (by overharvest) than are the northern subspecies. In contrast, molecular genetic analyses have corroborated traditional subdivision of the western pond turtle *(Clemmys marmorata)* into distinct northern and southern subspecies, emphasizing the need to augment populations of the strongly declining northern subspecies while preserving their genetic identity (Gray 1995). Other studies examining species' boundaries may result in management strategies that emphasize the distinctiveness of a population (e.g., Kemp's ridley; B. W. Bowen et al. 1991) or the use of a metapopulation model to manage an isolated population (e.g., Plymouth red-bellied turtle *[Pseudemys rubriventris]*; Browne et al. 1996). For examining evolutionary novelty, recent examples suggesting **paraphyly** (separate evolutionary origins) of species in such genera as *Clemmys* (Bickham et al. 1996) and *Geochelone* (Caccone et al. 1997) demonstrate that current taxonomy may be an inadequate basis for conservation decisions.

Population Structure and Migration

Some of the most important applications of genetic techniques to issues in turtle conservation relate to population management. This has been particularly true in the case of marine turtles, for which population genetic studies have addressed key questions of direct relevance to conservation: population structure, rookery longevity, and the composition of mixed-stock populations in foraging areas. Most notably, substantial differences in mitochondrial genotype frequencies have been observed among conspecific nesting rookeries of green *(Chelonia mydas)*, loggerhead *(Caretta caretta)*, and hawksbill *(Eretmochelys imbricata)* turtles (B. W. Bowen et al. 1992, 1994; Broderick et al. 1994). Nesting populations within each of these species are effectively differentiated by maternal lineage, and rookeries are therefore demographically independent, at least over the ecological time frames that most concern conservationists. For management purposes, depleted colonies cannot be expected to be readily replenished, nor extirpated colonies recolonized, via recruitment from other rookeries. An extension of these results is that rookeries are apparently very long-lived entities, with persistence times ranging from thousands to tens of millions of years (B. W. Bowen and Avise 1996).

Rookery-specific genetic markers have been applied to identify the origins of marine turtles found on mixed-stock foraging grounds and to identify migration routes between nesting and foraging areas (B. W. Bowen et al. 1996). These stud-ies have detected considerable overlap among rookeries on foraging grounds in all species of marine turtles. Thus, although rookeries are largely independent enti-ties in terms of female reproduction, they may nevertheless be jointly affected by mortality sources in coastal and oceanic foraging areas, including those associated with human activities such as fishing. Rookery-specific markers have also been used to determine that nesting and foraging areas for marine turtles can be ex-tremely remote from one another, as in the case of loggerheads of Japanese and Australian origin that forage in the North Pacific Ocean (B. W. Bowen et al. 1995).

Although this discussion has focused thus far on marine turtles, molecular ge-netic data have also been used to elucidate population structures in freshwater and terrestrial turtles of conservation concern. For example, Britten et al. (1997) used allozymes, mtDNA restriction sites, and morphological data to delineate man-agement units for the desert tortoise *(Gopherus agassizii)*. Genetically based popu-lation units showed a surprisingly high degree of concordance with management units previously designated based on ecological criteria. Similarly, genetic analy-ses have uncovered spatial subdivisions that were not perceptible by traditional morphological analyses in populations of common slider *(Trachemys scripta)* (Scrib-ner et al. 1986). Analysis of mtDNA variation in the loggerhead musk turtle *(Ster-notherus minor)* has identified fixed genetic differences between nearly all local populations sampled in the southeastern United States (D. Walker et al. 1995), sug-gesting strong restriction on contemporary gene flow between locales, including between sites widely separated within the same drainage. Similar analyses have examined levels of genetic variation in fragmented and isolated versus more wide-spread populations of turtles of conservation concern (Parker and Whiteman 1993; Gray 1995). Many of the genetic partitions thus far identified in turtle popu-lations correspond to distinct landforms (e.g., river drainages for freshwater turtles, intermontane basins for terrestrial turtles, and islands for marine turtles), an indi-cation of how genetic analyses can yield information to guide habitat protection programs for turtle conservation.

Molecular Ecology and Quantitative Genetics

Application of modern genetic techniques to questions concerning turtle ecology has been limited. However, the methods developed by Galbraith et al. (1995) for genetically fingerprinting individual turtles hold much promise for bolstering our knowledge of reproductive and social behavior in wild turtles and for improving management strategies for captive populations. Another promising, and under-utilized, area of genetic analysis for turtle conservation is quantitative genetics. Rather than focusing on distributions of discrete genetic markers among individuals and taxa as most genetic approaches do, **quantitative genetics** is a group of techniques used to study variation in continuously distributed traits, such as body size, shape, or some physiological measurement. In particular, estimation of variation in quantitative genetic characters can provide valuable information for understanding how well turtles can adapt to environmental stresses. For example, Janzen (1994) evaluated heritability of temperature thresholds for sex determination in painted turtles *(Chrysemys picta)*. In the context of global warming scenarios, phenotypic change of six standard deviations from the mean would be required in each generation to track predicted temperature changes. This quantitative genetics perspective highlights the extremely remote possibility that turtles can evolve quickly enough to track such environmental change and maintain balanced sex ratios in the wild.

DEMOGRAPHIC ISSUES IN TURTLE CONSERVATION

Data accumulated from several long-term studies published since the 1980s (E. C. Williams and Packer 1987; Gibbons 1990b; Congdon et al. 1993, 1994; V. J. Burke et al. 1995) have provided an understanding of the demography of turtles that was previously unavailable for these long-lived organisms. In particular, recent analyses of turtle populations have highlighted several aspects of turtle demography that make turtle populations especially sensitive to human impacts, particularly overexploitation. These aspects of turtle demography, in turn, pose special challenges for management of turtle populations. In this section, we provide an overview of turtle demographics and close with a discussion of the implications of these demographic attributes for the conservation of turtle populations.

Key Biological Traits of Turtles That Influence Demography

High adult survivorship rates and delayed sexual maturity are two key traits of the population biology of turtles. These traits have coevolved along with the distinctive chelonian morphology that typically features a rigid shell (Wilbur and Morin 1988). The shell provides protection from predators but does so only after a size threshold has been attained. Consequently, young turtles allocate considerable resources to growth and development of the protective shell. Allocation of these scarce resources in young turtles, however, causes reproduction to be delayed. The cost of delayed reproduction associated with early growth are offset to some extent by the opportunity for an extended reproductive life afforded by the protective value of the shell. In addition to longevity and delayed sexual maturity, another important aspect of turtle population biology relates to reproductive mode.

Virtually all turtle species undergo repeated cycles of reproduction that involve migrations of widely varying distances to lay eggs at select terrestrial sites. This is true for all turtles despite extensive adaptive radiations within the group into marine, freshwater, and terrestrial habitats (although one species, the Northern Australian snake-necked turtle *[Chelodina rugosa]*, was recently determined to deposit its eggs in underwater nests; Kennett et al. 1993).

There are several important demographic consequences of the distinctive suite of biological traits that characterizes turtles. Because early development of the shell confers effective protection against predators, larger juvenile and adult turtles experience high survival rates relative to those of other reptiles (Congdon et al. 1994). In contrast, reproduction among turtles is substantially delayed, with the age of first breeding in both terrestrial and aquatic species typically a decade or more (Congdon et al. 1993). Furthermore, virtually all turtles lay their eggs on land, where the mortality of eggs and hatchlings is generally high (Wilbur and Morin 1988).

Turtle demography can be characterized as follows: (1) low egg and hatchling survival, (2) high rates of juvenile and adult survival and consequent longevity, (3) delayed reproductive maturation, and (4) **iteroparity,** that is, repeated cycles of reproduction once adulthood has been reached. Life table analysis indicates that the contributions by each demographic parameter to population growth, however, are skewed. Generally speaking, population stability is most strongly influenced by changes in adult and juvenile survival, whereas changes in fecundity, nest survival rates, and age at first reproduction exert substantially less influence on population stability (Congdon et al. 1993, 1994; Doak et al. 1994). This is not to suggest, however, that chronic, widespread failure of egg and hatchling stages cannot jeopardize an entire species (see, for example, Spotila et al. 1996).

Age Structure of Populations

One of the most important demographic considerations for turtle conservation is the age structure that typifies turtle populations, which is unusual among vertebrate animals. Both Crouse et al. (1987) and Congdon et al. (1993, 1994) have described how a consequence of delayed maturity is a predominance of juveniles and subadults in any stable turtle population. Studies of loggerheads by Crouse et al. (1987) indicate that a ratio of eggs and juveniles to adults of nearly 400 to 1 is required to maintain a stable population. For common snapping turtles *(Chelydra serpentina serpentina),* this value is approximately 18 to 1 (Congdon et al. 1994). Considering that many other species of vertebrates with rapid maturation exhibit ratios of nonreproductives to reproductives near parity in any population (Caughley 1977), turtle age distributions appear unusually skewed.

The unusual age structures of turtle populations have several important management implications. First, given the ratios of eggs and juveniles to reproductive individuals in turtle populations (which may well range from 10:1 to 1,000:1), observation of even large numbers of immatures during a population census may not indicate that a population is stable or self-sustaining (Crouse and Frazer 1995). Thus, caution must be exercised in making inferences about population status from estimates of population size. Careful inspection of a turtle population's age structure must be made to determine the expected number of reproductives present if the population were stable and the degree of fit between this expectation and the observed age structure (Klemens 1989).

Second, the disparate ratios of eggs and juveniles to reproductive individuals in turtle populations indicate that few eggs and juveniles will reach maturity despite the relatively high posthatchling survival rates experienced by turtles. Thus, protecting even large numbers of nests and eggs as a management strategy will typically have only a marginal eventual impact on the size of adult populations (Crouse and Frazer 1995). Increased egg and hatchling survival through management activities on nesting beaches can augment adult populations only when adult and juvenile survival rates are at high levels; increased egg and hatchling survival cannot compensate for losses when adult and juvenile survival rates are reduced (Heppell et al. 1996). This underlies the primary biological argument against making expensive conservation investments in headstarting, nest protection, or other strategies of increasing juvenile survival as a means of bolstering populations of adult turtles (but see Spotila et al. 1996 for a counterperspective). A third implication of turtle population age structure for management is that whereas adults form the reproductive component of any population, they constitute only a small proportion numerically in most turtle populations. Management or protection focused on only those comparatively rare individuals in the adult stage will do less to change the trajectory of a population than will increasing the survivorship of the much larger fraction of the population composed by juveniles (Crouse and Frazer 1995).

Survival Rates

In two related papers, Congdon et al. (1993, 1994) combined long-term field data with life table analysis to explore the sensitivity of population growth in two freshwater turtles (the common snapping turtle and Blanding's turtle [*Emydoidea blandingii*]) to life history traits. These studies indicated that high survival rates are necessary at each life stage, except in the egg stage, to ensure that enough individuals survive to reproduce and maintain populations in these species. Furthermore, small increases in mortality rates of adults, such as might be expected from modest exploitation of turtle populations, could lead to strong declines in populations (see also Brooks et al. 1991a; Doak et al. 1994). Field corroboration of this conclusion has been provided by Garber and Burger (1995), who observed that a population of wood turtles *(Clemmys insculpta)* protected in a restricted-access watershed collapsed shortly after the area was opened to recreational use. The population decline apparently occurred solely because of modest, occasional removal of turtles by recreationalists. Further illustration of the sensitivity of turtle populations is provided by the striking contrast in density and diversity of turtle communities inside versus outside the strictly protected lands associated with the Savannah River Plant in South Carolina (Gibbons 1990b).

Thus, the suite of demographic traits that characterizes most turtle species effectively constrains their populations' capacity to absorb any human-induced increases in mortality rates. The models employed by Congdon et al. (1993, 1994) tend to be quite robust in their predictions, and sensitivity analysis indicates that predictions from these models are stable despite the sampling errors that may occur in estimating model parameters (Crouse and Frazer 1995). Together, these analyses (Crouse et al. 1987; Congdon et al. 1993, 1994) suggest that even modest harvests (intentional or incidental) of long-lived, late-maturing turtle species are likely to result in declining populations.

This conclusion has sober implications for turtle conservation because many turtle populations are used intensively for food and other purposes in various parts of the world (e.g., Kuchling 1988; Klemens and Moll 1995; Thorbjarnarson et al., Chapter 2) or are subject to significant by-catch in fisheries operations (e.g., Roosenburg et al. 1997). Prohibition or extremely modest harvest of adults is likely the only way to ensure the persistence of turtle populations. Rapid declines of turtle populations subjected to commercial exploitation are commonplace (e.g., Alho 1985; Kuchling 1988; Polisar and Horwich 1994; Klemens and Moll 1995), and no sustainable harvest system for wild turtle populations has yet been reported.

Population Turnover Rates

Extended intervals between generations in most turtle populations present a further complication to the management of turtle populations. Even in freshwater turtles, two to four decades may lapse, on average, between a turtle hatching and its offspring hatching (Congdon et al. 1993). This "sluggishness" in turtle population dynamics presents special challenges to managers because long delays may occur before population responses to disturbances or to management actions can be detected. For example, Crouse et. al. (1987) have suggested that conservation measures for loggerhead populations may take 70 years or more to effect any substantial increase in the number of turtles appearing at beaches to nest. This presents obvious difficulties for biologists operating within the policy arena because immediate returns as a result of conservation investments are generally expected by policy makers.

The extended generation times of turtles also complicate the nature of the observed response of turtle populations to management. For loggerheads, prolonged low survival during a period of exploitation, followed by increased survival of adults resulting from implementation of some conservation measure, will likely result in an increase in nesting activity for a few decades. However, this nesting activity will likely decrease again, despite maintenance of the conservation measure, because a paucity of offspring produced decades earlier during the period of exploitation may cause a delayed drop in recruitment into the population of reproductively active adults (Crouse and Frazer 1995). A related situation occurs with the giant Galápagos tortoise *(Geochelone nigra),* for which several island populations have experienced no recruitment for decades (Pritchard 1996). Conservation measures for these populations, even if enacted immediately, will not compensate for the inevitable, although perhaps temporary, future drop in the adult populations that will occur as a result of the earlier decades of failed recruitment.

Finally, turtle populations may persist for decades at high levels of abundance owing only to the longevity of surviving individuals. Apparently healthy populations may in fact already be imperiled because of long-term, chronic reproductive failure. The situation may be hidden to managers if they measure only abundance as an index of population status, as is commonly done. Abundance assessments can be particularly deceiving when the only readily censused component of a population is the adults, as is the case for many aquatic turtles. Thus, reproductive rates and age structure in turtle populations must be monitored, in addition to abundance, to assess population status reliably. The most important implication of long intergeneration intervals is, therefore, that managers cannot afford to wait until turtle populations are greatly reduced before initiating conservation measures because recovery will then be difficult or impossible to effect.

Migrations

Most turtles undergo substantial movements during at least some part of their annual life cycle. Virtually all turtles undergo migration to terrestrial sites for egg laying. Migrations range from extremely local movements by terrestrial turtles to preferred nesting areas, to short-distance migrations by freshwater turtles to upland nesting habitats adjacent to home ranges in wetland areas, to cross-global migrations by marine turtles between foraging areas and nesting beaches. Some terrestrial turtles also undergo annual migrations simply to exploit ephemeral food sup-

plies or undergo episodic migrations to escape drought (Gibbons et al. 1983; Morreale et al. 1984; Graham 1995). Furthermore, seasonal home ranges of turtles can
be quite extensive, for example, as large as 10 ha in some terrestrial species (e.g.,
the ornate box turtle *[Terrepene ornata]*; Doroff and Keith 1990) and several kilometers in length in stream-dwelling species (e.g., the alligator snapping turtle
[Macroclemys temminckii]; Harrel et al. 1996).

Turtle movements are of conservation concern when human activities disrupt
the habitat continuity upon which migrating turtles depend (see also Mitchell and
Klemens, Chapter 1). Development of uplands adjacent to wetlands destroys the
habitat interface critical for turtles that migrate between wetland and upland habitats to breed (see V. J. Burke et al., Chapter 6). Furthermore, although conservation measures for wetland habitats important to aquatic turtles often are quite effective, adjacent upland areas, critical to those turtles for nesting, are frequently
neglected (V. J. Burke and Gibbons 1995). Reductions in the connectivity among
wetland habitats, for example, by construction of roads, levees, and dams, block
the migration routes of turtles and can lead to local population extinctions (Dodd
1990). For terrestrial species with large home ranges (e.g., the ornate box turtle;
Doroff and Keith 1990), habitat fragmentation in conjunction with road construction may be particularly inimical to populations (see also McDougal, Chapter 7). Roads in particular can represent a significant, additive source of mortality
to which turtle populations likely cannot adjust (Congdon et al. 1993, 1994) unless
elaborate management activities accompany road construction, such as fencing
roads and building underpasses (e.g., Guyot and Clobert 1996).

The interactions between habitat alteration, turtle movement, turtle mortality,
and population persistence are poorly appreciated and clearly need to be investigated in greater detail. Nevertheless, our current knowledge is sufficient to state
that turtle habitat conservation plans must accommodate both local movements
and nesting migrations if populations are to be successfully protected. Given the
size of home ranges and the relatively low population densities of terrestrial
turtles, substantial areas of continuous habitat, on the order of 10^3 to 10^4 km^2,
likely need to be protected to conserve populations of this group of turtles. In contrast, modest areal combinations of upland and wetland habitat may suffice for
aquatic turtles (V. J. Burke and Gibbons 1995), although a long-term (26-year) study
by V. J. Burke et al. (1995) observed that a metapopulation of freshwater-dwelling
common sliders required an area of perhaps 1,000 ha. Riverine and marine turtles
pose special problems for conservation biologists because foraging and nesting
areas are often disjunct and connected by migratory routes that can span multiple
international political jurisdictions.

CONCLUSIONS

The distinctive suite of attributes that characterizes turtle life histories severely constrains the capacity of turtle populations to cope with additive mortality sources caused by human alteration of turtle habitats. Thus, turtle populations are vulnerable to overexploitation in a manner unusual among vertebrate animals. Managers charged with protecting turtle populations must realize that turtle demography is unlike that of most other vertebrates and that management of turtle populations is therefore quite problematic. In particular, managers should consider the implications of age structure, extended generation times, characteristic high survival rates, and movements in order to conserve turtle populations successfully. Perhaps most importantly, notions of sustainable commercial or recreational exploitation of turtle populations should be discarded because they are likely biologically infeasible. Managers should also be aware of the unique perspectives that molecular genetic analyses can provide on questions related to turtle systematics, population structure, movements, social behavior, and potential for responses to environmental stresses. Finally, the interactions between habitat continuity, turtle migration, mortality levels, and population persistence must be recognized and understood by the makers of environmental policy if turtle populations are to remain viable in a world increasingly dominated by human activities.

To conclude, it is worth reiterating Frazer's (1992) message concerning setting appropriate goals for turtle conservation efforts. Many novel management mechanisms have been suggested (and in some cases implemented) to conserve threatened turtle populations. These include headstarting hatchlings in captivity in an attempt to rebuild depleted populations, implementing devices on fishing gear to reduce incidental capture, and installing special lights on nesting beaches to reduce the disorienting effects of artificial lights on hatchlings and nesting females. Frazer (1992) warns, however, that such a focus on short-term, reactive management techniques distracts from the most critical issue in turtle conservation—provision of clean, productive, and intact environments in which turtles can complete their life cycles. Demographic and genetic analyses of problems in turtle conservation must contribute directly to this long-term, overarching goal if turtle populations are to persist in the wild.

RICHARD A. SEIGEL AND
C. KENNETH DODD, JR.

9
MANIPULATION OF TURTLE POPULATIONS FOR CONSERVATION
Halfway Technologies or Viable Options?

There are two distinct approaches to maintaining biological diversity: the traditional resource management approach and the conservation biology approach. The former is often associated with game and fisheries management in Europe and North America (Meine 1994; Noss and Cooperrider 1994). Among the characteristics of this approach is a heavy reliance on manipulation of species and their habitats (the high-tech management of Noss and Cooperrider 1994). Manipulation includes altering habitats to benefit selected species (e.g., establishing food plots by planting specific crops or using herbicides to remove undesirable vegetation), controlling predator populations, increasing population sizes of target species through captive breeding, and reintroducing species into areas where they have been extirpated. In essence, the traditional resource management approach is a strategy to maintain, increase, or restore the numbers of a target species regardless of the direct or indirect effects of these management practices on non-target species (J. McDougal, personal communication).

By contrast, the conservation biology approach is largely nonmanipulative, relying only minimally on high-tech solutions to conservation issues. This approach emphasizes (1) maintaining functional ecosystems, (2) monitoring population and ecosystem processes, and (3) maintaining viable populations (Noss and Cooperrider 1994). Basically, the conservation biology approach is one in which scientific information is gathered to make an informed plan for recovery. Manipulation of habitats or populations may be considered, but any manipulation is intended primarily to restore natural ecosystem conditions rather than simply to benefit target species.

Traditional manipulative programs have achieved considerable success for many game species, for example, whitetail deer *(Odocoileus virginianus)* and wild turkeys *(Meleagris gallopavo)* in the United States (Dickson 1995; Storm and Palmer 1995). However, other attempts at manipulation of nongame species have resulted in failure and have generated a considerable debate concerning the ethics and efficiency of manipulation of nongame species (S. Conant 1988; Griffith et al. 1989; Frazer 1992; Meffe 1992; Myers 1994). The criticisms of Frazer (1992) and Meffe (1992) are especially appropriate; they considered many (but not all) high-tech solutions to complex conservation issues halfway technologies, that is, solutions that address only the symptoms of the problem rather than the causes. Such solutions give the appearance that a problem is being solved without actually addressing the causes of the problem in the first place. Consequently, high-tech solutions are usually ineffective and often costly.

Attempts to use manipulative methodologies to restore declining populations of turtles have taken three main approaches, listed in order of increasing manipulation: (1) protection of freshly laid nests in order to reduce predation rates, either at the actual nest site or nearby (WATS 1983), (2) **headstarting** programs by which hatchling turtles are raised to a certain size in captivity and then released into the wild at or near the original nesting sites (e.g., Byles 1993), and (3) **repatriation, relocation,** or **translocation** programs (herein referred to as release programs; see definitions in "Repatriation, Relocation, and Release Programs," McDougal, Chapter 7), in which individual turtles are moved from one locality to a site where populations have either been extirpated or are in need of augmentation. See Dodd and Seigel (1991) and Reinert (1991) for a further discussion of these terms.

In this chapter we will discuss the constraints involved in initiating a manipulative program as a turtle conservation technique, briefly review the success or failure of existing programs, and make specific recommendations concerning the role of manipulative programs in conserving turtle populations. While not opposed to manipulative projects per se, we believe that the majority of projects conducted in the past have been poorly planned and executed. As such, they have been halfway technologies rather than effective conservation options. A review of manipulative programs undertaken to date is presented in Appendix 9.1 (found at the end of this chapter).

BIOLOGICAL CONSTRAINTS ON MANIPULATIVE PROGRAMS

The tendency for many biologists and wildlife managers (those in academia, government, and nongovernmental agencies) to "default" to manipulation as a solution to declining populations is striking. We have been in numerous meetings where the only solution suggested to help endangered or threatened amphibians or reptiles was to manipulate populations by reintroduction or headstarting, without any consideration of what factors precipitated a population's decline. In one case, a representative of a federal agency suggested that a good management option to reverse declining populations of yellow-blotched map turtles (*Graptemys flavimaculata*) in the southeastern United States was to establish vegetable food plots along sandbars. Because the yellow-blotched map turtles are aquatic and feed mainly on mollusks and sponges, this strategy would clearly have been ineffective.

Our goal in this section is not to disparage well-intentioned biologists and resource managers. Rather, our contention is that there is a predisposition to use manipulation as a quick and easy solution to complex conservation issues, without first (1) collecting ecological data to make informed decisions, (2) considering the constraints involved in starting such a program, or (3) considering what other alternatives are available. Below, we review some of the basic biological constraints that need to be taken into account before manipulative programs are initiated.

Life History Characteristics

Although the longevity of turtles has been recognized for some time, quantitative studies of the unique population consequences of long-lived species are more recent (e.g., Crouse et al. 1987; Gibbons 1987; Congdon et al. 1993, 1994; Heppell et al. 1996; see also "Demographic Issues in Turtle Conservation," Gibbs and Amato, Chapter 8). These studies showed that an important consequence of the life history traits of long-lived organisms is a high degree of vulnerability to changes in patterns of survival, especially changes in the survival rates of older juveniles and adults (Crouse et al. 1987; Congdon et al. 1993, 1994; Heppell et al. 1996). Unless there is a compensatory relationship between the number of adults and juvenile survival rates (i.e., as the number of adults decreases, juvenile survival increases), increases in adult mortality may result in sharp decreases in population size. For example, Congdon et al. (1994) showed that a harvest pressure as low as 10% per year could result in a 50% reduction in adult snapping turtles (*Chelydra serpentina*) within 15 years. Furthermore, Brooks et al. (1991a) found that juvenile snapping turtles showed no compensatory response to increased adult mortality.

We argue that one of the consequences of increased longevity is that turtles are poor candidates for most manipulative programs. For example, Crouse et al. (1987) used a sensitivity analysis to show that the time and resources of conservation programs for sea turtles should be focused at protecting subadults and adults, not hatchlings, because the effects of changes in mortality rates of hatchlings were limited compared with the effects of changes in adult and subadult mortality. Thus, nest protection and headstarting programs would appear to have only limited value for long-lived species such as turtles (but see Grand and Beissinger 1997). This point has been repeatedly emphasized by Frazer (1992), Congdon et al. (1993, 1994), Congdon and Dunham (1994), and Heppell et al. (1996).

Increased longevity may have important implications for release programs as well. A successful release program (or any conservation program, for that matter) should be defined as one that establishes a viable population, not simply one in which reproduction has been found to occur (Dodd and Seigel 1991). One mechanism of predicting the success of a release program is through the use of a population viability analysis. Although such analysis has been used only rarely for turtles (e.g., Cox et al. 1987), it is a widely used technique for other taxa (Lindenmayer 1994; M. L. Shaffer 1994).

The gopher tortoise (Gopherus polyphemus) is one of the species most frequently subjected to release programs; over 10,000 individual gopher tortoises were relocated in Florida in the 1990s alone (J. Diemer-Berish, personal communication; see Dodd and Seigel 1991 for review). Most of these relocations involve taking groups of adult gopher tortoises (hatchlings and small juveniles frequently cannot be located due to their small size) from a habitat slated for development and moving them to an undisturbed site (Diemer et al. 1989). Dodd and Seigel (1991) argued that the success of the vast majority of these efforts has been limited (but see R. L. Burke 1991 for another view). Most adult gopher tortoises brought to a new habitat simply leave after only a few hours or days, despite intensive efforts to keep them on site (Diemer et al. 1989).

We pose a straightforward question that, to us, should have been answered before gopher tortoise relocation programs were ever implemented: what proportion of tortoises relocated to a new site would have to remain there in order to establish a viable population? If the required proportion is high, then relocations likely are doomed to fail; conversely, if the proportion is low, relocations may be successful under some circumstances.

We conducted a simple population viability analysis to answer this question, using two widely available computer programs: Popdyn (Greir 1990) and Vortex (Lacy and Kreeger 1992). The basic parameters used to create our model are listed in Table 9.1. Most of the values applied are from studies conducted by R. A. Seigel and his students in Mississippi and Louisiana (K. R. Smith et al. 1997) and from the literature. In order to determine what proportion of gopher tortoises need to remain at the site of a release to establish a viable colony, we varied the adult survival rate from 80 to 95% annually. In this context, the adult survival rate is equivalent to the retention rate of gopher tortoises at a colony. Clearly, if a gopher tortoise leaves a colony, it is "dead" with respect to that population. We then ran each model 10 times at each retention rate and determined the average number

Table 9.1

Parameters and values for population viability analysis of relocated gopher tortoises

Parameter	Value	Source(s)
Initial number	50 adults	
Age at maturity[a]	15 years	Ernst et al. 1994
Maximum clutch size	8	K. R. Smith et al. 1997
Mean clutch size	5.6	K. R. Smith et al. 1997
Number of clutches	1	
Reproductive frequency[b]	90%	K. R. Smith et al. 1997
First-year survival	10%	K. R. Smith et al. 1997; J. Butler, unpublished
Adult survival	Variable in model	

[a]Data for age at maturity were near the median of ages summarized in Ernst et. al. (1994).
[b]Reproductive frequency is the number of clutches laid per year; in this case, not all females are reproductively active.

of gopher tortoises remaining at the release site after 30 years and the probability the colony would go extinct within the same period.

Our results are shown in Figures 9.1 and 9.2. We found that when annual adult retention rates (survival) fell below about 90%, colonies declined rapidly and went

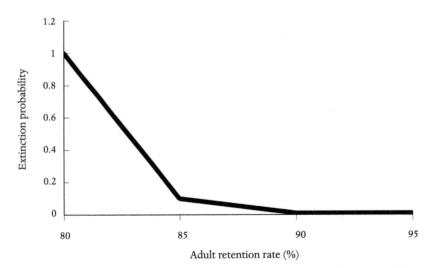

Figure 9.1. Probability of extinction for relocated gopher tortoises as a function of adult retention rate (see Table 9.1 for model parameters). Note that although the probability of extinction is less than 0.2 when adult retention rate is greater than 85%, this result is mainly an artifact of running the model for only 30 years. When adult retention rate is less than 90%, populations gradually decrease in size and would eventually go extinct.

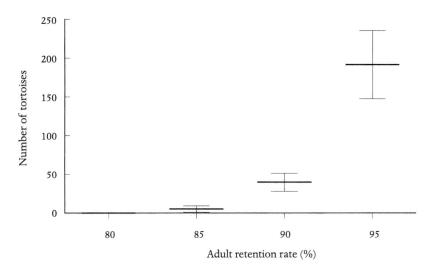

Figure 9.2. Population sizes after 30 years for relocated gopher tortoises as a function of adult retention rate (see Table 9.1 for model parameters). Means (±1 SD) are shown. Note that these simulations start with 50 released adults; thus, only the 95% retention level showed a stable or increasing population.

extinct within 30 years or sooner. The extinction results are conservative in that we ran the models for only 30 years; in several cases, population sizes after 30 years were reduced to less than 10 individuals, and such populations would have been projected to go extinct had we run the models for a slightly longer period.

Although theoretical models and projections such as these are often viewed with suspicion by empirical ecologists, these analyses provide strong support for the arguments of Crouse et al. (1987), Frazer (1992), Scott and Seigel (1992), Congdon et al. (1993, 1994), and Congdon and Dunham (1994) that turtle populations are highly sensitive to changes in adult and subadult survival. In the case of gopher tortoise relocations, few (if any) attempts have managed to retain even 50% of adults after just a few years. For example, R. L. Burke (1989) found that only 35 of 85 relocated gopher tortoises remained on the release site after 2 years. Other studies have experienced even lower success (see Diemer et al. 1989 for summary).

Some researchers have argued that our models are inadequate because we assume that low retention rates continue after the first 2 years; they suggest that retention rates may become stable after some point (J. Demuth, personal communication). However, because most releases are monitored for only a short period, there is no published evidence to support the contention that retention rates become stable over time. At one long-term release site in Louisiana, only about 30% of 40 gopher tortoises released over 7 years are still within 1 km of the release site, and no successful reproduction has occurred (S. Shivley, personal communication). Based on the data available, we conclude that release programs for turtles and other long-lived species are likely to have only limited success; only if a very high proportion of adults are retained on the release site on an annual basis are release programs likely to be anything more than a halfway technology.

Behavior, Social Structure, and Spacing

There is scant information in the literature on chelonian social behavior in general, much less on the behavior of turtles that have undergone headstarting, repatriation, relocation, or translocation. Turtles are not considered social animals in the sense that they have cooperative interaction or social aggregations (e.g., Plotkin et al. 1995). However, the presence of a defensible structure, such as a burrow, suggests a potential for territoriality, and the use of common feeding or nesting areas suggests the potential for competitive or social interactions. K. H. Berry (1986) hypothesized that relocated desert tortoises (Gopherus agassizii) might disrupt the social structure of resident populations through displacement or that they might be driven away by residents. Stewart (1993) could not verify adverse effects over a short duration of time after relocation of desert tortoises at a power plant site.

Some turtles are known to be aggressive toward conspecifics, and the presence of conspecifics may alter foraging (Formanowicz et al. 1989) or basking (Flaherty and Bider 1984) behavior. There is some indication that turtles are capable of individual recognition (Kramer 1989) and that familiarity may mediate aggressive behavior (M. Davis 1981). Such observations suggest that behavioral repertoires are more complex than often realized. The potential for altering resident social structure by releasing animals that have undergone headstarting, repatriation, relocation, or translocation, and the potential that social behaviors will deter released animals from taking up residency, should be considered prior to initiating intensive manipulative programs.

Some behavioral questions surrounding headstarting and release programs are quite complex and lead directly to some of the most important and contentious issues in chelonian biology. For example, before the initiation of the Kemp's ridley (Lepidochelys kempii) headstarting program in the late 1970s, questions arose concerning whether hatchlings return to natal beaches and, if so, whether imprinting or socially facilitated behavior is involved. Where might imprinting occur and what cues might be involved? What behavioral mechanisms might be involved in migration? Might feeding behaviors and preferences be altered by captivity? The lack of answers to such important behavioral questions led, in part, to the recognition that the Kemp's ridley headstarting program was an experiment rather than a proven recovery technique. These questions also pointed the direction for future research, the need for which and the results of which were incorporated into the project's study plan.

Incubation Temperature, Sex Determination, and Sex Ratios

The effect of temperature on sex determination, body size, and other phenotypic traits within a species is a vital biological characteristic that should be known prior to undertaking headstarting or release programs. Most turtles studied to date have environmental sex determination; that is, the sex of the individual is determined by a complex interaction between the proportion of embryonic development above or below a certain threshold temperature and by the effects of hormones (primarily estrogens) on gonadal differentiation (Ewert and Nelson 1991; Wibbels et al. 1991b, c). Patterns are variable among species, however. In some instances low temperatures result in males, whereas in other species both low and high temperatures yield only or mostly females (Ewert et al. 1994). The estrogenic action of environmental contaminants, such as PCBs (Bergeron et al. 1994), may influence or even reverse temperature-dependent sex determination. A few groups (e.g., Trionychidae, Chelidae, and Staurotypinae) and species such as the wood turtle *(Clemmys insculpta)* have true genotypic sex determination.

Serious problems may result from incubating eggs at constant temperatures. For example, previously sea turtle biologists often artificially incubated eggs in Styrofoam boxes at constant, relatively low, temperatures. As a result, thousands of male hatchlings were released as part of nest protection or headstarting programs (Mrosovsky and Yntema 1980; Mrosovsky 1982). Females, which develop at higher temperatures, were largely absent from these early releases. Depending upon the goals of a project, release of large numbers of hatchlings of one sex could be counterproductive; however, current methods have largely corrected these early mistakes.

A more important question, perhaps, is what the sex ratio of turtles released in headstarting or release programs should be. This question only recently has been debated (Vogt 1994; Mrosovsky and Godfrey 1995; Lovich 1996). There are no simple answers because the determination of natural sex ratios in turtle populations is fraught with difficulty and the desired skewed sex ratios of animals released may hinge more on the immediate goals of the release program than on some theoretical ideal. Turtle sex ratios in nature are often quite variable (Bury 1979b), and reports in the literature may be biased by collecting techniques or other factors. A beach may produce different sex ratios of hatchlings within a season (Mrosovsky et al. 1984), or a population's sex ratio may be skewed in any one year but at parity over a relatively long time span (e.g., Gibbons 1983). On the other hand, releasing large numbers of females might be thought to yield a better chance of quickly increasing population size.

If budgets or time constraints prevent an accurate experimental assessment of the effect of temperature on sex ratios, eggs should be incubated either at a variety of constant incubation temperatures that mirror the range of nest temperatures found in nature or at fluctuating temperatures that mimic daily or seasonal cycles from undisturbed nests. Keep in mind, however, that mimicking temperatures found in natural nests is not easy because the temperature of natural nests will vary with season and location (e.g., in shade versus sun).

In addition to altering the sex ratio, incubation temperatures may also have other important effects on an individual's phenotype and fitness. A number of recent studies have shown that incubation conditions (temperature and hydric environment) significantly affect a variety of phenotypic traits of turtles, including incubation time, body size at hatching, and hatchling growth, survival, and endurance (Gutzke et al. 1987; K. Miller et al. 1987; Brooks et al. 1991b; Janzen 1993a, b). Moving eggs to an artificial environment may have important life history consequences with unknown implications for population viability. This subject needs further attention from researchers considering manipulative projects that alter incubation conditions of eggs.

Habitat Requirements

Many turtles have rather specific habitat requirements. In this context, we prefer to extend the concept of habitat to include not only space for the immediate needs of a species or individuals, particularly food and shelter, but also a spatial element on a community and landscape scale (see Harris and Kangas 1988). As we have already pointed out (Dodd and Seigel 1991), habitat requirements include a three-dimensional set of physical and biological parameters that permit feeding, reproducing, finding cover, and having social interaction for all size-classes. In addition, temporal variation in habitat use may be quite complex. For example, sea turtles, often the subjects of headstarting and release projects, use different types of habitats (nesting, foraging, developmental, and migratory) that cover vast stretches of ocean and vary with different life stages (see Meylan and Ehrenfeld, Chapter 4). Some freshwater turtles (e.g., chicken turtle [*Deirochelys reticularia*]) may spend parts or all of the winter in terrestrial habitats far from their normal aquatic sites (Buhlman 1995; V. J. Burke et al., Chapter 6).

Prey or forage should be available for all life stages. For example, many freshwater turtles switch diets between juvenile (often carnivorous) and adult (largely herbivorous) stages. Other species have specific food requirements (e.g., mollusks for map turtles [*Graptemys* spp.] and fruits for South American river turtles [*Podocnemis* spp.]). Food must be available in sufficient quantity and quality (in terms of nutrient content) on a seasonal basis. Knowledge of a turtle's food habits and the availability of prey or forage in environments scheduled to receive turtles undergoing headstarting or release programs is essential.

All turtles lay eggs and, therefore, nesting habitats should be available to animals to be released from headstarting, repatriation, relocation, or translocation programs. Nesting areas should be large enough to minimize intraspecific disturbance, be nearby or somehow recognizable to the turtles, contain appropriate nesting media (e.g., friable soils for digging and soils or sands of appropriate texture or grain size for proper gas exchange, moisture retention, and protection from excessive temperature extremes), not be subject to destruction from short-term environmental effects, and not be in close proximity to large predator concentrations.

Adequate and immediately available cover sites are especially critical for turtles undergoing headstarting and release programs because they are unfamiliar with the new habitats. Sites selected for the release of such turtles must include habitats with cover where turtles may seek shelter from predators, environmental perturbations (fire, floods, cold and heat, and catastrophic storms), and human activity. Each of these requirements has spin-off corollaries. For example, whereas cover sites should allow for predator protection, released turtles should not be placed into environments that contain concentrations of overabundant natural (i.e., subsidized, as described by Mitchell and Klemens, Chapter 1) predators (e.g., ravens [Corvus corax] and raccoons [Procyon lotor] in North America) (Garrott et al. 1993) or in close proximity to concentrations of exotic or feral predators (e.g., dogs [Canis domestica], cats [Felis catus], mongooses, and feral pigs [Sus scrofa]).

Cover requirements may be quite specific, such as the narrow crevices used by pancake tortoises (Malacochersus tornieri) (Klemens and Moll 1995; D. Moll and Klemens 1996) and flattened musk turtles (Sternotherus depressus) or the hibernacula required by tortoises in cool climates (e.g., Bailey et al. 1995). The timing of release programs is also critical; for example, individuals released late in the year in temperate zone areas may have insufficient time to locate suitable hibernation sites before the onset of winter (M. Plummer, personal communication).

Turtles are ectotherms that require external heat sources to maintain proper physiological activity and to ward off disease. Basking sites are often vital to their well-being. Basking sites must be of good quality and in sufficient quantity in habitats scheduled to receive animals from headstarting and release programs. In addition, basking sites must be free of excessive human disturbance.

Likewise, habitats selected for releasing turtles from headstarting or release programs should be free from human disturbances, such as roads and areas with excessive human recreation (e.g., shooting, boating and waterskiing, and driving off-road vehicles), and in areas not likely to be subject to toxic contaminants.

Consideration of habitat on a landscape scale may be very important for headstarting and release programs. Required habitats may be physically separated by extensive areas that are used as migratory or movement corridors. For example, many freshwater turtles travel between temporary and permanent wetlands, sometimes using the same migratory pathways (e.g., the Australian snake-necked turtles [*Chelodina* spp.]), or between wetlands and adjacent uplands (e.g., the spotted turtle [*Clemmys guttata*], chicken turtle, and mud turtles [*Kinosternon* spp.]; V. J. Burke and Gibbons 1995). Males, especially among tortoises (e.g., gopher tortoise), travel between females who are widely scattered. Female turtles may travel distances greater than 1,000 km between nesting beaches and feeding grounds (sea turtles) or several hundred meters across upland habitats in search of nesting locations (e.g., Blanding's turtle [*Emydoidea blandingii*]; Congdon et al. 1983). Clearly, the propensity and need for both long- and short-distance movements must be considered if headstarting or release programs are planned. A priori, it seems reasonable that there should be an inverse correlation between the extent of movement and the potential success of a headstarting or release program to establish or augment a local population.

Population Genetics

Biologists generally agree that in order to conserve biodiversity, genetic variation must be considered at both the species and population level in management programs. Headstarting and release programs must take into consideration whether the introduction of animals into unfamiliar environments will lessen or increase extinction probabilities or simply prevent the loss of individuals on a short-term temporal scale. After all, if the headstarting or release programs are unsuccessful in establishing new or augmenting declining populations, genetic variation certainly is lost. Even if a program is pronounced a success, the consequences on long-term genetic variability may not always be positive.

The manner in which genetic constraints will affect within-species diversity (e.g., through local population fitness or stochastic demographic processes) must be considered (see Reinert 1991). Mixing genetic populations may result in decreased fitness of locally coadapted individuals, a loss of unique alleles and a concomitant loss of overall variability, or an inability to maintain local adaptation. The genetic breakdown resulting from the loss of both coadaptation and local adaptation is termed **outbreeding depression** (Templeton 1994).

Local populations have coevolved within a framework that includes both biological (e.g., food, predators, and parasites) and nonbiological (e.g., weather, ocean currents, and other physical factors) components. In some areas, even groups of spatially **sympatric** (occurring in the same area) individuals, such as in feeding populations, are composed of individuals from rather genetically different breeding populations (e.g., hawksbills [*Eretmochelys imbricata*] in northern Australia;

Broderick et al. 1994). Likewise, certain spatially close populations of a single species separated by a physical barrier may be different genetically (Lamb et al. 1989). Because of the importance of locally adapted gene pools, the success of headstarting and release programs may be inversely proportional to the distance animals are moved. Unfortunately, many turtles will attempt to home when displaced (see Swingland 1994), especially if distances between home range and release site are not far.

The degree of or the potential for outbreeding depression may determine how animals released from headstarting, repatriation, relocation, and translocation programs fit into the new environment and thus the chances for success. Therefore, turtle headstarting and release programs need to incorporate information on the genetic population structure of both the donor animals as well as any animals in the area where releases are proposed. If animals to be released are genetically very different from resident animals, headstarting and release programs probably are not justified. The question becomes more difficult if differences are very slight or if few resident animals are present on repatriation sites.

Disease

Management to prevent and treat disease has been an integral part of captive programs ever since zoos started to care for reptiles. However, the study of disease in wild turtle populations virtually has been neglected, with the recent exception of the massive programs under way to understand upper respiratory tract disease (URTD) in North American (E. R. Jacobson et al. 1991, 1995; E. R. Jacobson 1993) and European tortoises and fibropapillomas in sea turtles (Herbst 1994). Dodd (1988) previously noted that disease can have severe effects on a declining wild turtle population, at least on a short-term basis.

It is interesting to note that the focus on disease in wild turtle populations results, in part, from the suspected transmission of URTD from repatriated captive tortoises released into natural habitats. The introduction of infected gopher tortoises on Sanibel Island, Florida, and desert tortoises in the Mojave Desert, California, may be the prime agent in the rapid decline of some tortoise populations (USFWS 1989). Although URTD is known to be present in many gopher tortoise populations, the Florida Game and Fresh Water Fish Commission has allowed the relocation of literally thousands of gopher tortoises without examination for disease. As yet (December 1999), disease-related repatriation, relocation, and translocation guidelines are still not available despite the potential effects that URTD may have on the declining gopher tortoise populations.

Prior to initiating headstarting and release programs, investigators should be aware of known or potential disease problems and plan accordingly. E. R. Jacobson (1994b) suggested that animals scheduled for release should be quarantined in a facility apart from other herpetological specimens. Physical separation in different locations, rather than in the same building, is recommended. In addition, the health status of animals to be released requires rigorous review; animals should be screened by veterinarians familiar with the evaluation and treatment of reptile diseases. No animals showing health problems should be released. Should disease problems be found, animals must be quarantined and the disease treated.

SOCIOLOGICAL AND ECONOMIC CONSIDERATIONS

Although biological constraints set the boundaries within which headstarting and release projects must operate, human psychology, societal values, and the limitations of human organizations are often just as important in predicting whether such projects will succeed or fail.

Motivation and Public Perceptions

We are aware of programs and organizations that have polished brochures that promote all sorts of wonderful conservation actions for critically endangered turtles and tortoises. These brochures make interesting reading because they invariably endorse highly manipulative but unproven headstarting and release programs. In certain instances, these programs have been touted as *the* way to save a species despite the almost total lack of distributional and life history information on wild populations and the lack of any documentation detailing research protocols and project justification. This lack of information and justification is an intolerable situation when dealing with what may be critically endangered species.

As we and other authors have lamented (Dodd and Seigel 1991; Swingland 1994), headstarting and release programs often are surrounded by extensive publicity designed to solicit public and political support for the project, the conservation of the species in question, or both. Although we are not opposed to publicity per se, we are concerned (1) that publicity gives a false sense of success or accomplishment, especially at the start of a headstarting or release project, and (2) that the perceived need for publicity overrides sound conservation biology. Hatchling sea turtles running to the sea make good photo opportunities for headstarting programs, and news stories about saving tortoises by relocating them make good press. However, the follow-up stories 20 or 30 years hence may not be so positive; by then, the public's recollection will long have faded, and public concern may be diverted from real problems and solutions.

Publicity can lure the public and even resource agency officials into a false sense of security in the belief that the methods undertaken actually are having a positive effect on the conservation of the species. For nearly all headstarting and release projects, however, the success or effectiveness of the project will be measured years or even decades from its initiation. In essence, the public comes to believe that halfway technologies can solve an extremely complex problem when they may not. Simple and cost-effective techniques are likely to be overlooked if more favorable publicity can be generated by high-visibility programs. Public support and individual egos sometime influence the selection and continuation of headstarting and release programs to the exclusion of a well-thought-out recovery plan based upon scientific data (e.g., Taubes 1992).

We strongly take issue with individuals or organizations that advocate headstarting and release projects for their publicity or public awareness values to the sublimation of scientific considerations. Whereas these projects may "generate excellent publicity and have a role to play in raising awareness of the local people" of problems affecting species (Bloxam and Tonge 1995), a scientific consideration of conservation options should be the sole basis for undertaking highly manipulative actions. Headstarting, repatriation, relocation, and translocation should be considered as strategies of last resort, when less manipulative projects have failed or are not feasible.

Habitat

An assessment of the habitat into which animals are released from headstarting, repatriation, relocation, or translocation programs is very important. Above, we briefly mentioned some of the factors to be considered, such as the availability of prey or forage, the availability of basking and hibernation sites, and freedom from predators and human disturbance. Habitats into which animals are released need to be protected via a long-term (i.e., essentially in perpetuity) commitment. It does not benefit the survival of individuals of a long-lived taxon, such as tortoises, to relocate them into areas subject to the same problems as the areas from which they were taken. Management plans must include temporal as well as spatial scales. A corollary to this requirement is the determination of who will manage the land, how it will be managed, and who will pay for it through time.

It must be remembered that turtles and tortoises are sometimes integral or keystone components of their ecosystems. This is especially true of burrowing species. For example, gopher tortoises dig extensive burrow systems that are inhabited by more than 360 obligate and facultative commensals (species of vertebrates and invertebrates that rely on tortoise burrows for shelter or feeding) (D. R. Jackson and

Milstry 1989). If burrowing tortoises are relocated, provisions need to be made to assure the survival of commensals, especially obligate, endangered, threatened, or rare species. Single-species management should be avoided if possible.

Human Impacts

Habitats into which animals are placed must be free from human poaching and encroachment. For example, one would not relocate gopher tortoises into areas where they were once depleted by poaching (R. W. Taylor 1982) unless the threat was removed. This could be accomplished by a combination of education and strict law enforcement, but without a commitment to carrying out these nonbiological management actions, the relocation program likely would fail. Similarly, placing sea turtles from headstarting programs into areas with shrimp trawling, without restrictions on the shrimping seasons and methodologies (i.e., requiring the use of turtle excluder devices), would be a waste of time and money.

Some very visible release projects, such as the translocation of the Aldabra tortoise *(Geochelone gigantea)* in the Seychelles, have not been successful, in part due to inadequate attention to human-related habitat questions. In the case of the Seychelles' Aldabra tortoise, human poaching has seriously jeopardized chances of establishing a population on a long-term basis (Hambler 1994). In another case, gopher tortoises held prior to release in a relocation project in Florida were stolen, presumably to be used as food. Security before, during, and after headstarting and release projects needs to be addressed. On small preserves, a community watch might be organized using local volunteers to ensure turtles are not harassed or vandalized; on larger reserves, security personnel may be necessary.

Technical Expertise and Long-Term Monitoring

Given some of the considerations discussed above, a certain degree of technical expertise is required prior to initiating headstarting and release programs. Whereas the need for technical expertise may foster cross-disciplinary cooperation, accumulating necessary data may be expensive and time consuming. Failure to incorporate a wide spectrum of technical expertise, however, may cause biologists to overlook important considerations (e.g., specialized dietary requirements or disease control) that will hasten the failure of the project. In some regions of the world, technical expertise is simply not available.

Headstarting and release projects involving turtles and tortoises cannot be evaluated on a short-term basis (Dodd and Seigel 1991). Long-term monitoring is necessary to determine population persistence and stability, reproduction, habitat quality, and demographic patterns that affect the population's status. Monitoring turtles from headstarting and release programs for only a mere fraction of the time it takes them even to reach sexual maturity is of very limited value, although it may show an immediate failure of the project (e.g., large-scale dispersion off the site intended for population establishment). Success cannot be measured without observations continuing through generational times of the species in question, which imposes serious logistic and management questions that must be addressed at the start of a project. If there is no long-term commitment to population monitoring (and habitat protection, as discussed above), headstarting and release projects are doomed to failure and cannot be supported.

Funding

Manipulating turtle populations by means of headstarting and release methods can be an expensive proposition. For example, the 15-year headstarting project involving Kemp's ridley (see Meylan and Ehrenfeld, Chapter 4), including airlifting eggs to the United States from Mexico, headstarting and releasing turtles into appropriate habitat, and monitoring the results, cost more than US$4 million (Taubes 1992). An additional $2 million was spent developing turtle excluder devices to prevent turtles that had been released, as well as other sea turtles, from drowning in shrimp trawls. Although the Kemp's ridley project represents an extreme in funding, even small-scale release projects need to assess costs for habitat protection, management, security, transport, disease prevention and treatment, monitoring of released turtles, temporary holding centers, and other facets of the project. In Palau, "low-budget" headstarting projects for green turtles (Chelonia mydas) and hawksbills cost greater than $150,000 and $388,000, respectively (Donnelly 1994). Given such costs and the sometimes small chance of success, are such projects the best way to use conservation resources?

A GRADIENT OF APPROACHES TO TURTLE CONSERVATION: AN ILLUSTRATIVE EXAMPLE

The yellow-blotched map turtle is endemic to the Pascagoula River and its tributaries in southeastern Mississippi. The species has declined rapidly in recent years and was listed as threatened under the U.S. Endangered Species Act (16 U.S.C. §§ 1531 to 1544) in 1991 (USFWS 1993a). Major threats to this species include an unusually low reproductive rate (perhaps the result of dioxin contamination), the loss of basking sites, very high nest predation rates, and direct impacts from humans via wanton shooting of adults, collection for the pet trade, disturbance to nesting beaches, and boat propeller wounds (USFWS 1993a). Under current demographic

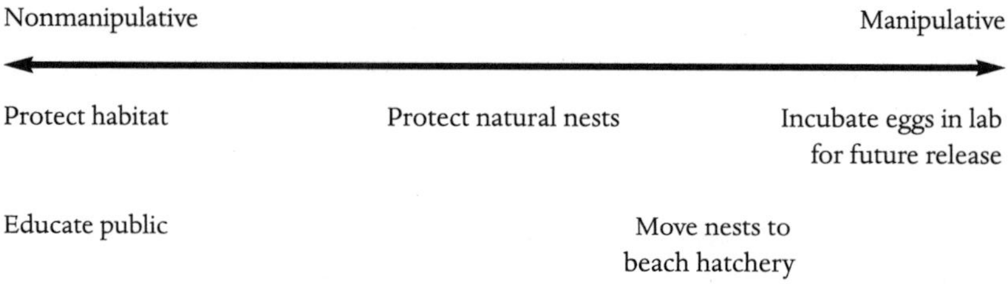

Nonmanipulative   Manipulative

←——→

Protect habitat   Protect natural nests   Incubate eggs in lab
                                                              for future release

Educate public   Move nests to
                                            beach hatchery

Figure 9.3. A gradient of approaches to the conservation of the yellow-blotched map turtle. This gradient of approaches can be applied to any species.

and reproductive conditions, a preliminary population viability analysis showed that there is a high probability of extinction of this species within 50 years (Seigel and Brauman, unpublished).

Figure 9.3 illustrates a gradient of possible actions for preventing the extinction of this turtle, ranging from completely nonmanipulative to highly manipulative. Although some of these actions are not mutually exclusive, there is clearly a wide range of potential costs and benefits associated with these approaches. In the case of the yellow-blotched map turtle the nonmanipulative approaches have the lowest costs, both in terms of funding and impacts on the population. Because the federal and state governments have acquired considerable land within the range of this species, purchasing additional lands is probably not needed. Public education and enhanced law enforcement would have relatively low costs and might alleviate problems such as the shooting of adults, injuries resulting from collisions with powerboats, and human disturbance of nesting beaches. Naturally, the success of these measures is unpredictable, but few negative results can be foreseen.

By contrast, most of the manipulative approaches carry both higher costs and a higher probability of negative impacts. Protecting natural nests would have no negative consequences in terms of alteration of phenotypes or sex ratios but would be expensive in terms of personnel. Additionally, the effectiveness of protecting nests as a means of increasing population size is questionable (Heppell et al. 1996). The same objections, magnified, are true for moving nests to beach hatcheries, where alterations of phenotypes and sex ratios are likely to occur. The most extreme manipulations, lab incubation of eggs and relocations, carry very high personnel and funding costs and the same potential impacts on phenotypes and sex ratios as noted above. Thus, we conclude that implementation of manipulative management of this species is both premature and inappropriate and that nonmanipulative approaches should be implemented first.

Clearly, any approach to the conservation and management of turtles (or any other species) can span the range from manipulative to nonmanipulative. Because the needs of every species are different, each species probably requires a unique conservation plan. However, it is our position that manipulative approaches to turtle conservation should represent a mechanism of last resort and should be used only when three conditions are met: (1) nonmanipulative approaches have been attempted and have been shown to fail, (2) the manipulative approaches under consideration have been tested (at least with similar species) and have been shown to be effective, and (3) the results of the experimental manipulations are incorporated into ongoing evaluations of the techniques applied. Some may consider these conditions extreme and limiting, but we do not share that belief. For example, we do not object to experimental tests of manipulative approaches to conservation. In fact, we welcome such tests, with the only caveats being that these tests be treated as experiments rather than tried and tested conservation methods and that the results of these tests be published in the peer-reviewed literature so that others can judge the results. In the absence of such evidence, we suggest that approaches to the conservation of turtles should proceed from nonmanipulative to manipulative, rather than in the opposite direction, as is too often the case.

CONCLUSIONS

Highly manipulative programs such as headstarting, repatriation, relocation, and translocation are, at best, unproven conservation techniques for the majority of turtles for which they might be undertaken. The lack of success in many of these programs results from a failure to address a complex interaction of biological and socially based constraints. Headstarting and release programs rely on a considerable amount of technology that is expensive and logistically difficult to implement. While we do not suggest that such programs should never be considered, we recommend that they be undertaken only as a last resort; headstarting and release projects are experimental rather than proven conservation or mitigation techniques. If, after careful consideration, manipulative programs are deemed necessary, we recommend they be as unobtrusive as possible. For example, if protection of nests is considered essential, then consideration should be given to protecting the actual nest site via predator-proof cages. Although not as media-friendly or convenient as beach hatcheries, protecting natural nests increases hatchling survival while at the same time avoiding manipulation of incubation conditions.

Conservation programs that rely on the half-way technologies reviewed here give a false sense of immediate well-being and fail to address directly the problems facing species and ecosystems. Research programs must address the root causes of turtle population declines rather than seek short-term solutions that do not prevent long-term declines.

ACKNOWLEDGMENTS

For critical comments on the manuscript, we thank Jeff Demuth, Nat Frazer, J. Whitfield Gibbons, Michael Klemens, Jim McDougal, and Michael Plummer. This research was supported by Department of Energy contract number DE-FC09-96SR18546 with the University of Georgia, by the Faculty Research Participation Program of the Oak Ridge Institute for Science and Education (ORISE), and by a Travel Contract with ORISE. R. Seigel's research on map turtles and gopher tortoises was supported by funding from the U.S. Fish and Wildlife Service, the Army Corps of Engineers, and the Mississippi Department of Wildlife, Fisheries, and Parks. Additional funding was provided by Southeastern Louisiana University's Faculty Development Fund.

Appendix 9.1

Review of Intensive Manipulative Programs for Turtles

Program type and species	Location and dates	Result	Source(s)
Combination of headstarting and repatriation			
Chelonia mydas	Florida (1959–1989)	18,000 green turtles released, but there was no way to evaluate	Donnelly 1994
	Cayman Islands (1980–1991)	10,573 yearling green turtles released; turtles survived and migrated, but there was no evidence of reproduction	F. Wood and Wood 1993
Eretmochelys imbricata	Palau Islands (1982–1991)	Poor hatching prior to release; 2,364 hawksbills released, 7 recaptured; project failed	Donnelly 1994
Geochelone nigra	Galápagos Islands (1970–present)	1,415 Galápagos tortoises released in 1970–1992; majority of these tortoises have survived, but very little reproduction has been observed (first in 1990)	Márquez et al. 1991; Cayot et al. 1994
Lepidochelys kempii	Mexico and United States (1978–1992)	More than 18,000 Kemp's ridleys released, but there was no measure of success; project terminated	Taubes 1992; Byles 1993; P. Williams 1993; Donnelly 1994
Pseudemys rubriventris	Massachusetts (1984–present)	823 red-bellied turtles released in 17 ponds in 1985–1993; small turtles have low survivorship, and large turtles have survivorship similar to that of subadults	A. Haskell, personal communication; Amaral 1994

Appendix 9.1 continued

Program type and species	Location and dates	Result	Source(s)
Pseudemydura umbrina	Australia (1994)	Project newly initiated; status unknown	Burbidge and Kuchling 1994
Repatriation, relocation, and translocation			
Caretta caretta	Virginia (mid-1970s)	Informal and unsuccessful	Dodd and Seigel 1991
Emys orbicularis[a]	Italy (1989–1990)	45 European pond turtles moved; monitoring continued until 1992; no reproduction was observed	Gariboldi and Zuffi 1994
Geochelone gigantea	Seychelles (1978–1982)	Attempts to start new population on Curieuse Island; 250 Aldabra tortoises moved, but only 117 remained by 1990; new colony not established and effort disappointing	Hambler 1994
Geochelone radiata	Madagascar (1994)	165 radiated tortoises moved from Réunion to Berenty Reserve	Boullay 1995
Geochelone sulcata	Senegal (1995)	8 adult African spurred tortoises moved from Europe to Senegal	Anonymous 1995
Gopherus agassizii	California (1977–1995)	No good long-term results; some projects ongoing	Dodd and Seigel 1991; Stewart 1993
Gopherus polyphemus	Florida and Georgia (1970s–present)	Thousands of gopher tortoises involved; no guidelines yet available	Dodd and Seigel 1991; D. Rostal, personal communication
Malacochersus tornieri	Tanzania (1992)	Approximately 300 pancake tortoises confiscated in Europe; they had been exposed to disease in holding facilities, so repatriation was not allowed by Tanzanian authorities	Klemens 1995
Testudo hermanni[a]	France (1985–1988)	850 Hermann's tortoises repatriated	Devaux 1990
	Greece (1991)	275[b] Hermann's tortoises repatriated from northern Europe to Greece via Italy	Ballasina 1992; RANA International Foundation 1994

Continued on next page

Appendix 9.1 continued

Program type and species	Location and dates	Result	Source(s)
Testudo hermanni[a]	Greece and Tunisia (1994)	446 Hermann's tortoises (55 to Tunisia, 391 to Greece) repatriated	RANA International Foundation 1994

Note: Other repatriation, relocation, and translocation projects are proposed or under way in Brazil *(Podocnemis expansa, Podocnemis unifilis,* and *Trachemys dorbignyi),* Lithuania *(Emys orbicularis),* Madagascar *(Geochelone yniphora),* Mexico and the United States *(Gopherus flavomarginatus),* Russia *(Testudo graeca nikolskii),* and Tanzania *(Malacochersus tornieri).*

[a]Centers in France (SOPTOM), Italy (CARAPAX), and Spain (Ebro Delta Natural Park; C.R.T.-L'Albera) are involved in repatriation of this and other European and North African species.

[b]RANA International Foundation (1994) reported 289 repatriated.

MICHAEL W. KLEMENS

10

FROM INFORMATION TO ACTION
Developing More Effective Strategies to Conserve Turtles

The preceding chapters have provided a comprehensive overview of both the challenges and specific issues that must be addressed in order to conserve the world's dwindling populations of turtles effectively. These challenges are both complex and interrelated, necessitating a new operational paradigm to reverse the current trajectory of population extirpations that will ultimately result in the extinction of many turtle species. Those concerned with the future of turtles must take a hard and critical look at current conservation programs, evaluating their effectiveness in the light of the information synthesized from the preceding chapters. Only by first looking backward can we effectively begin to move forward. To move forward we need to consider several broad categories of turtle conservation issues as outlined below.

CONSIDER ECOLOGICAL AND POPULATION ISSUES ACROSS A BROAD RANGE OF GEOGRAPHIC SCALES

A limitation of vision is one of the most fundamental challenges to surmount in creating programs that will effectively conserve turtles. Poorly designed and ill-conceived conservation programs, that is, the halfway technologies discussed in some of the previous chapters (e.g., Seigel and Dodd, Chapter 9), justify their existence by keeping the scope of their conservation actions, and follow-up monitoring, relatively narrow. By maintaining this narrow focus it is quite easy, and therefore extremely appealing, to engage in heavy-handed intervention and manipulation. The temporary effects of these actions erode when the long-term con-

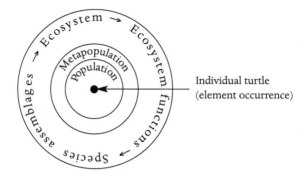

Individual turtle
(element occurrence)

Figure 10.1. Successful conservation efforts require a scope broader than the protection of the location of an individual turtle (element occurrence) or local population of a single species. This schematic represents the broader contexts within which the individual turtle occurs.

servation benefits of these programs are reviewed in ever-larger concentric rings that extend beyond the individual animal, to the population, metapopulation, and ecosystem (see Figure 10.1).

Actions taken to conserve turtles are often limited in both scope and scale, due in large part to a lack of ecosystem perspective. Expanding the geographical and ecological scope of turtle conservation projects is a high priority. With few exceptions, conservation actions for turtles remain tightly focused on local populations of single species, largely ignoring metapopulation or ecosystem ramifications. Single-species approaches do have both validity and importance in conservation. However, to result in long-term conservation gains, they must be embedded in a larger vision that conserves ecosystem function, integrity, and diversity. Although these caveats may be intuitively understood, a review of many ongoing turtle conservation projects indicates that too little emphasis is placed upon the larger picture.

The conservation history of the bog turtle *(Clemmys muhlenbergii)* provides a worst-case scenario of what can, and did, happen when conservation attention and efforts are narrowly focused on the local scale without the benefit of critical scientific evaluation and peer review. The bog turtle is sparsely distributed over a discontinuous geographic range in the eastern United States from Massachusetts to Georgia. The range is divided into two **allopatric populations** (occurring in geographically separated areas), from Massachusetts south to Maryland and from southern Virginia to Georgia. These two populations were at one time considered to be taxonomically distinct (Dunn 1917). Bog turtles inhabit small habitat patches consisting of open-canopy, shallow, spring-fed wetlands, meadows, and fens. These patches of habitat occur as part of much larger wetland and drainage basin complexes. Historically, as succession caused canopy closure, bog turtles moved to other open-canopy wetland patches within large, dynamic wetland complexes (Klemens 1989).

Beginning in the 1970s, through the development of individual (state-based) Natural Heritage Programs by The Nature Conservancy, each state began to gather presence versus absence data on the occurrence of rare species. These efforts included not only accumulation of historical presence information from the literature and museum collections but also field work targeted at discovering new localities for rare species. These programs were very successful at pinpointing many new occurrences for bog turtles, as well as extending the known range of this species southward into Georgia. In the late 1970s, the U.S. Fish and Wildlife Service (USFWS) issued a "Notice of Review," requesting that states within the bog turtle's range gather additional information to evaluate the status of this species (C. K. Dodd, personal communication). The resultant flush of new records of bog turtle occurrences led first to speculation (e.g., Arndt 1982; Chase et al. 1989) and then to acceptance (e.g., Bourg 1992) that the bog turtle was not rare but secretive, and that this species was much more secure than previously considered.

These findings, however, were flawed by being based upon the smallest scale of bog turtle occurrence, the individual turtle, with little information concerning populations, metapopulation dynamics, or patterns of ecosystem fragmentation and degradation that were occurring throughout much of the bog turtle's range. By focusing on presence data generated by single turtles, a rangewide pattern of noncyclical population decline was obscured. Although bog turtle biologists raised serious challenges to the findings that the bog turtle was doing well, including evidence of what appeared to be precipitous declines in the viability of many bog turtle populations, these concerns were largely ignored. The increasingly large amount of bog turtle geographic point data, that is, **element occurrences,** primarily collected by entry-level biologists and college students (i.e., nonspecialists), was considered both robust and sufficiently conclusive to cement the secretive-rather-than-rare argument (Bourg 1992).

The most important effect that the Bourg report had upon bog turtle conservation was that it galvanized researchers to present an alternative point of view more effectively, an alternative that not only considered the local level but the metapopulation and ecosystem status of the bog turtle. Fortunately, the USFWS was sufficiently skeptical about some of the conclusions presented in the secretive-rather-than-rare-argument to investigate the metapopulation and ecosystem issues. The USFWS funded research that led to the creation of a matrix (Klemens 1993b) that, for the first time, allowed amalgamation of bog turtle occurrences into metapopulations, greatly decreasing the actual number of bog turtle sites. For example, although 178 bog turtle occurrences were reported in Maryland, a series of performance criteria that factored in wetland connectivity and turtle move-ments amalgamated these into a final count of 90 metapopulations, of which 25 had been lost in the last 15 years (USFWS 1997).

The second step in the USFWS matrix reviewed the viability of bog turtle popu-lations by examining the size-class structure (which corresponds to age-class) and recruitment structure of each metapopulation. After reviewing the results of these dual analyses, the USFWS (1997) determined that the northern allopatric popu-lation was a threatened species, as defined by the U.S. Endangered Species Act (16 U.S.C. §§ 1531 to 1544), and the southern allopatric population threatened by simi-larity of appearance. The USFWS listing of the bog turtle reversed what had be-come one of the greatest ironies of turtle conservation—that a system designed to monitor vulnerable species by tracking individual sightings was unable to de-tect a serious decline in the health of the overall population. The case of the bog turtle provides a valuable lesson to those who may place undue reliance on an un-critical review of databases. Absent critical, scientific interpretation of individual data points, database systems have the distinct potential to hinder rather than help conservation. Admittedly, the case of the bog turtle is extreme, and the chances for a large number of such "false positive" results is small. However, in the case of the bog turtle, reliance upon a narrowly defined data set, the absence of criti-cal review, and the lack of attention to the larger population and ecosystem is-sues all contributed to a two-decade delay in obtaining much-needed federal pro-tection for North America's rarest turtle.

INTEGRATE NEW INFORMATION AND TECHNIQUES INTO CONSERVATION PROGRAMS

The 1990s have witnessed an explosion of knowledge in the realm of applied and theoretical conservation and the mainstreaming of conservation as a scientifically informed discipline. In this book, I have endeavored to present, through a multiple-contributor approach, the most up-to-date thinking on turtle conservation. I have asked each of the chapter contributors to review the effectiveness of current con-servation efforts critically, in light of the most up-to-date research, information, and technologies that they were presenting. Turtles are evolutionarily conserva-tive creatures; however, we cannot allow the conservation of turtles to be guided by outdated technologies and approaches, parochial interests, and resistance to new discoveries and information.

In 1993, I chaired an international conference of tortoise and freshwater turtle specialists, land managers, and policy makers to discuss the emerging problem of a global turtle decline and to facilitate the exchange of information and technologies (see Van Abbema 1997). The impetus for this conference was severalfold, but one of the driving forces was the realization that approaches and technologies that had long been discarded in the United States as ineffective were being exported and promoted overseas. In one Asian country, a U.S. agency-funded program was promoting the removal of turtles from the wild to be captively bred in local zoos, even though ample opportunity existed for habitat protection and nonmanipulative techniques. When I asked personnel of the U.S. agency sponsoring this program why they advocated this approach of last resort as the first line of response, I was advised that this program was what the host country wanted, and it was better to do this than to do nothing! Is doing something, no matter how ill advised, better than doing nothing? Is the quid pro quo for heightening concern for turtles to hasten their trajectory toward extinction? Surely, we are capable of doing better.

Despite an ample (and growing) body of scientific evidence arguing against reintroductions and translocations without rigorous health and genetic screenings, as well as an assessment of the effects upon the existing population, these activities continue (see Seigel and Dodd, Chapter 9). Why does the state of Florida, for example, continue the expensive, biologically unsound, and rarely effective relocation of gopher tortoises *(Gopherus polyphemus)* from development sites? Why do many Western European countries continue to repatriate confiscated tortoises to their countries of origin, without any regard for the impacts of these repatriated tortoises on existing wild populations or any financial provision to insure that these repatriations are conducted in a responsible scientific manner?

Such conscience-clearing expediency (Klemens 1995) is increasingly replacing sound wildlife management and obviates any necessity for society to account fully for the ecological impacts that are caused by our lack of environmental stewardship. We have a strong, empirical basis upon which to argue effectively against these ill-conceived activities, promoted under the guise of responsible conservation. However, despite ample evidence that these activities are not in the best interests of the species, politically motivated public relations activities to repatriate confiscated tortoises continue. Several trusts and foundations in Europe exist almost entirely to repatriate confiscated tortoises without regard for the effects of these repatriations upon wild populations or regard for the wildlife management programs of other sovereign states.

In March 1991, a shipment of several hundred pancake tortoises *(Malacochersus tornieri)* was seized by customs authorities in the Netherlands, en route from Tanzania to the United States (see "Pancake Tortoise: Exploitation for the Pet Trade," Thorbjarnarson et al., Chapter 2). Although this was only one shipment in a flourishing trade, the publicity surrounding this seizure, including the inhumane and illegal method of shipment, set in motion a chain of events for which political and public relations considerations took precedence over sound wildlife management practices. After holding these pancake tortoises for an extended period of time, the Dutch authorities shipped them back to Tanzania, to be "released into the wild."

Throughout this confiscation process, the scientific community had unequivocally advised against releasing these pancake tortoises back into the wild. The reasoning was quite clear: captive tortoises frequently harbor pathogens acquired from a variety of sources, both chelonian and nonchelonian. Although these pathogens may persist with only minor clinical symptoms in tortoises that are well fed and amply watered (as captives often are), if these pathogens were to be introduced into wild populations the results could be devastating. The epidemic of upper respiratory tract disease that is sweeping through populations of the desert tortoise *(Gopherus agassizii)* in the western United States is thought to have originated from captive desert tortoises released into the wild (see Flanagan, Chapter 3; McDougal, Chapter 7). The seized pancake tortoises had been exported from Tanzania and subsequently housed at various animal holding facilities and zoos in Western Europe; consequently, they posed a significant health threat if released into the wild.

Despite minimal advance notice of the impending return of the pancake tortoises, the Tanzanian wildlife authorities decided that holding facilities should be constructed and the pancake tortoises quarantined until the various management issues and controversies surrounding repatriation had been fully investigated. In February 1993, at the request of the Tanzanian government, I initiated a research program designed to obtain the data required to make an informed decision as to the feasibility of repatriating these tortoises back into the wild. In order to evaluate the health of the pancake tortoises being returned to Tanzania from the Netherlands, it was necessary to first create a baseline of health parameter data from free-ranging pancake tortoises to determine what was, in fact, a healthy pancake tortoise. Two widely separated sites were sampled, Tarangire National Park in northern Tanzania and Ruaha National Park in south-central Tanzania. Sampling free-ranging populations was followed by sampling a subset of the pancake tortoises that had recently been returned to Tanzania.

Each tortoise in the study received a complete physical exam. A fecal sample was collected, a nasal flush was conducted, and a blood sample drawn (see Raphael et al. 1994). Analysis of these samples in the field and at the Wildlife Conservation Society's Animal Health Center in New York revealed that the blood and nasal mucous samples from wild populations were quite consistent in key health parameters across a wide geographic range (Raphael et al. 1994). These values served as a baseline against which we measured samples collected from the pancake tortoises returned to Tanzania. The health parameters of the returned pancake tortoises were quite variable, and many tortoises showed clinical signs of debilitation and disease that were borne out by their blood chemistry. In addition, four animals had an upper-respiratory-tract-disease–like pathogen in their nasal mucous (Karesh et al. 1993). Based on these data, the Tanzanian authorities concluded that it was not prudent to release these animals into the wild. Had these animals been healthy, there were still many other factors that would have required study prior to releasing them. These factors included, but were not limited to, whether the returned pancake tortoises were genetically compatible with those at the release site, whether the release site could absorb additional tortoises, and, if so, what number, sex, and age-classes. If these studies had indicated that repatriation was feasible, protocols would then have had to be developed to monitor the effectiveness of the release over time.

With increasing confiscations of tortoises (the entire family of 40 or more species is on either Appendix II or Appendix I of the Convention on International Trade in Endangered Species of Wild Fauna and Flora [CITES 1973]), customs and wildlife authorities in importing countries are faced with an ever-increasing dilemma. As zoos and similar facilities begin to reach a saturation point for the accommodation of confiscated wildlife, the option of simply returning the shipment to the country of origin becomes an increasingly attractive and expedient alternative. For example, in the United States a consistent policy on how to deal with this issue is lacking. At present, the decision on how to dispose of confiscated wildlife rests with the discretion of the individual customs inspectors and agents. Paradoxically, it is the poorer exporting countries that are most often blamed for creating this problem, although it is generally the more affluent Western nations that generate the demand for this burgeoning traffic in live tortoises. Although exporting countries should be encouraged to fulfill their obligations under CITES, importing countries must recognize their responsibilities in this matter. By returning confiscated tortoises to the country of origin, without providing either the financial or technical assistance to ensure that repatriation is carried out in a scientifically sound and humane manner, the importing countries continue to cast a blind eye to their responsibility in the creation as well as the solution of this problem.

APPLY RIGOROUS COST-BENEFIT ANALYSES TO CONSERVATION PROGRAMS

The United States has expended millions of dollars to conserve certain turtle species, specifically those listed under the provisions of the U.S. Endangered Species Act as well as various state-listed endangered and threatened species. As this book is targeted at an international audience, it is not unreasonable to ask whether the U.S. experience can provide insight or have relevance to turtle conservation worldwide. It is precisely because the United States (which contains approximately 20% of the world's turtle species) has invested so heavily in expensive manipulative conservation programs for certain turtle species (e.g., the Kemp's ridley turtle [*Lepidochelys kempii*] and Plymouth red-bellied turtle [*Pseudemys rubriventris*]) with such limited successes that analysis of U.S. conservation efforts is instructive. If the world's wealthiest country has made such limited progress in conserving turtles by means of these expensive methodologies, can we reasonably expect developing countries, burdened by poverty and a rapidly expanding human population striving for a higher standard of living, to achieve conservation goals using these methods? Yet it is precisely these types of expensive methodologies that continue to drive turtle conservation efforts around the world.

For example, wetland habitat restoration, if done correctly, is an expensive proposition. This is not widely recognized because most **mitigation wetlands** (wetlands constructed to replace wetlands lost during construction) and wetland restorations are simplified wetlands (basically the excavation of a depression and creation of a generalized pond habitat) as opposed to structurally complex fens, bogs, and shrub swamps that have a deep layer of organic muck and various layers of vegetation. The labor-intensive construction, monitoring, and costs involved in correctly mitigating (i.e., replacing) a small section of structurally complex wetland that was critical habitat for a threatened turtle can be considerable if done correctly, as illustrated by a recent project in New York (E. Kiviat, personal communication). This mitigation project was triggered by the expansion of a public school located at the edge of a complex of wetland and upland communities that supported a population of Blanding's turtle *(Emydoidea blandingii)*, a legally protected species in New York. The proposed expansion included filling a 0.7-ha shrubby wetland used by juvenile and nesting Blanding's turtles. Rather than reconfiguring the footprint of building, the school board applied to the New York State Department of Environmental Conservation for a permit to fill this small wetland. Although creating a generalized replacement wetland (i.e., a pond) would have been quite inexpensive, the Department of Environmental Conservation required that the replacement wetland be designed to recreate, as quickly as possible, a well-functioning, structurally complex wetland ecosystem to minimize impacts to the Blanding's turtle population. Prior to any habitat alteration, a baseline study of the turtles on site was conducted using mark–recapture, radiotelemetry, and nest monitoring. Analysis of vegetation and soils in the "donor" wetland (the wetland to be filled) and in three preexisting reference wetlands used by Blanding's turtles was conducted. A groundwater monitoring system was installed at the restoration site. Turtles and other small animals were live trapped and collected from the donor wetland and moved to a preexisting "holding" wetland.

Wetland, upland nesting areas, and a drought refuge pool were built in the autumn of 1996 and spring of 1997. A barrier was constructed to separate turtle habitats from school facilities. A 1.2 m by 2.4 m flat spatula was mounted on a excavator to lift and separate entire sod horizons from the donor wetland. These large sod wedges included mature sedge and fern tussocks, woody hummocks, mature shrubs, and trees up to 10 cm in diameter, as well as organic sediments to a depth of 38 cm. These sods were translocated to the restoration area 200 to 400 m away. Remaining organic soil was excavated from the donor wetland and used to fill in between the sods and to create a bottom substrate for the newly created wetland. Stumps and logs from larger trees were moved into the restoration area to increase microhabitat diversity and create basking sites for the Blanding's turtles. In addition to salvaging thousands of mature plants, by moving entire chunks of sod, the microbial and invertebrate communities were also translocated.

In the spring of 1997, 11 Blanding's turtles nested in the upland habitats of the restoration site. At least three nesting females used the constructed wetlands during the nesting season, as did other species of turtles. Frogs, salamanders, snakes, birds, and mammals have used these new wetlands. The habitat restoration has been integrated into the overall school expansion, with educational materials and monitoring protocols being prepared. Intensive monitoring of vegetational restoration will be required for 5 years, and monitoring of Blanding's turtles will continue, minimally, for several decades. The initial construction costs for the wetland was US$1,300,000; however, this figure is low because certain related costs were absorbed in the overall school construction budget. Intensive monitoring, and adaptations to the management protocol when required, could easily double the cost of this project over the next decade. With the benefit of hindsight, the school would have been well advised to have more seriously considered redesigning their building as opposed to filling in the structurally complex wetland habitat of a threatened species and then recreating it less than 400 m away.

CONTROL EXPLOITATION

Based upon the discussion of biological characteristics intrinsic to turtles (Gibbs and Amato, Chapter 8) and the patterns of human exploitation (Thorbjarnarson et al., Chapter 2), it is clear that turtles are extremely vulnerable to being overhunted and overcollected. Most species are also under pressure from additional threats, such as the loss of habitat. Therefore it is often hard to assess the effects of harvest regimes without understanding the entire range of existing (and projected) impacts to turtle populations. In the long term, habitat loss is the most permanent threat; however, in the short term, overcollection can eliminate or severely reduce a population of turtles to critical levels. Collection of the pancake tortoise

(Klemens and Moll 1995) and the Egyptian tortoise *(Testudo kleinmanni)* (Baha el Din 1994) are two recent examples of overcollection that severely affected wild populations. As is the case for these two tortoises, species that have narrow habitat requirements and limited geographic ranges are especially vulnerable.

If turtle populations are to recover from overexploitation and to be protected from suffering decline from human use, one fundamental aspect of managing human use of turtles will be the precautionary principle; that is, harvest levels must be set well below what is considered to be sustainable. Recent research (e.g., Congdon et al. 1994) has demonstrated that the concept of sustainedly harvesting turtles is extremely difficult to put into practice. The level of sustainable harvest for many turtle species is so low that when exploitation is permitted, the sustainable level is invariably exceeded. The bottom line is that despite promotion by many leading conservation groups that sustainable-use programs are the key to maintaining wildlife resources, turtles are not biologically appropriate candidates for most wild-harvest programs as currently practiced, whether for food, shell products, or pets. The sustainable-use movement champions the concept of "use it or lose it"; in short, unless there is some useful aspect attached to an animal or plant, it will ultimately not be saved. In the case of turtles, the reality is too often "use it, lose it." What biological information does exist on levels of harvest is based on experiences of overharvest, indicating negative effects on turtle populations. What is lacking are targeted studies on what may be, if any, acceptable levels of harvest of certain commercially important species. Using these data one could propose programs, on a case by case basis, that might reduce and limit exploitation of turtles.

Sustainable-use programs do offer great promise for certain groups of reptiles, including crocodilians and some of the larger lizards, for example, iguanas (Klemens and Thorbjarnarson 1995; see "Options for Management of Turtles," Thorbjarnarson et al., Chapter 2). I suggest that we begin to place greater emphasis on the sustainable use of ecosystems and on gaining an understanding of which species are exploitable and which are not. Certainly, turtles have an important role in maintaining ecosystems. For example, turtles can be important dispersal agents for a variety of temperate forest plants (Rust and Roth 1981; Braun and Brooks 1987); the role of frugivorous tortoises in both dispersal and germination of rainforest plants has not been adequately studied. (See also "The Role of Turtles in the Riverine Ecosystem," E. O. Moll and Moll, Chapter 5.) Even if many species themselves are not candidates for harvest, they are part of an overall ecosystem structure that allows for the extraction of natural products and the exploitation of species that are biologically amenable to allow harvest.

If exploitation is not controlled, we can look forward to ecosystems in which turtles are so rare that they have greatly diminished ecological and economic importance. This is already the case for several species of large, commercially important river turtles, including the river terrapin *(Batagur baska)* in Southeast Asia and the giant South American river turtle *(Podocnemis expansa)* and yellow-spotted Amazon River turtle *(Podocnemis unifilis)* in the Brazilian Amazon. Some other, more targeted remedies to address overexploitation follow.

Impose a Moratorium on Trade

Given the escalating worldwide exploitation of turtles for meat, traditional medicines, consumer goods, and pets, a moratorium on the harvest and trade in wild-caught chelonians should be considered. A moratorium would give individual countries time to develop management programs for turtle populations. Scientific data could be gathered to determine if harvest is sustainable and, if so, at what level and at what life stage; it could also be determined whether setting up farming programs would be feasible. Although a worldwide ban may be difficult to achieve, consumer countries such as the United States and members of the European Economic Community could easily consider a total ban on all imports and exports of wild-caught turtles. Such a ban might also serve to stimulate commercial captive propagation of turtles by eliminating wild-caught turtles from the market, though it would be essential to develop controls to ensure that the captive-bred turtles are not being augmented by wild-caught animals.

Improve Regulatory Frameworks at National and International Levels

Other mechanisms to control trade could be instituted, including improving and harmonizing trade regulations and replacing the hodgepodge of laws and regulations at the local, regional, state, and international levels. The existing patchwork of regulations creates a sieve through which it is relatively easy to traffic in turtles and turtle products by taking advantage of regulatory loopholes and windows of opportunity. For example, protection of a species in one country frequently heightens the exploitation of the same species in another country. Species protected in one country are often smuggled across international borders and then exported "legally" from that country. This "laundering" of wildlife is also prevalent within countries in which states and provinces have varying protection standards for the same species. This problem was a major motivation to obtain national protection in the United States for the bog turtle. Well-designed legislation to regulate trade and curtail exploitation of turtles is predicated upon effective enforcement. Too often, laws that protect turtles are not enforced because of the low priority given to protecting small, nongame species by law enforcement agencies. In many countries, enforcement efforts are understaffed and underfunded, and officers lack basic training and equipment to carry out inspections, interdictions, and enforcement effectively.

Reduce Mortality Rates of Turtles in Trade

The trade in turtles is generally a high-volume trade. Individual turtles are undervalued; therefore, it is financially acceptable to lose a portion of each shipment due to mortality from poor and inhumane shipping conditions. Humane considerations aside, this type of volume market fosters rapid depletion of turtles. The treatment of animals in the turtle trade, as well as in the trade in other reptiles and amphibians, is more often than not simply barbaric. From the original point of collection to the exporter, importer, wholesaler, and individual pet shop, the most basic standards of care, not to mention ethical responsibilities, are abrogated. By the time a single turtle reaches a pet shop, many more have perished en route. Humans are able to empathize with the suffering of dogs and cats, but concern quickly evaporates further "down" the evolutionary ladder. In New York City, it is not uncommon to walk into a pet shop and see a cage of turtles (or other reptiles) that includes dead, decomposing, and emaciated animals mixed in with active, apparently healthy creatures. Imagine the public outcry if there was a single dead or dying puppy in a pet store! By extending the reach of human compassion to include the "lesser creatures" we can begin to argue (and to demand) that inhumane and ecologically wasteful conditions be eliminated in the live animal trade.

Shift the Burden of Proof in Evaluating Exploitation

Currently, the major tenet of wildlife protection and management legislation presumes that exploitation is nondetrimental unless proven otherwise. Regulatory authorities should approach the management of turtle exploitation with the presumption that it poses a threat to wild populations, thereby shifting the burden of proof to rigorously demonstrating that the use of turtles would be nondetrimental to wild populations.

Research the Impacts of Trade and Harvest and Translate into Policy

Applied research, including market studies and comparative demographic studies between exploited and nonexploited populations, is needed to evaluate better the impacts of turtle trade and harvest. Based on a research approach, studies could evaluate **sustainable harvest** (harvest from wild populations that is not detrimental to the long-term health of a population or species), **ranching** (captive breeding that relies on seed stock [especially eggs] from wild populations and requires some continued input of wild turtles or eggs into the system), **closed-cycle farming** (captive breeding that requires wild-caught adult stock but produces all eggs and young from that stock), and other types of management programs. For example, experimental management programs could work toward improving the performance of subsistence-use turtle projects while eliminating the commercial-use aspects that are inherent in many of these subsistence programs. It is essential that any programs that are established to harvest or manage turtles sustainedly be supported by data that demonstrate such programs are indeed truly effective at conserving turtles and are not simply exploiting turtles and disguising that exploitation as sustainable use. There is a need to develop programs that reinforce the value of turtles in local communities, replacing the perception of turtles as common property not to be conserved with programs that promote stewardship of community resources.

Reduce and Reorient the Market for Turtles and Turtle Products

The demand for wildlife and wildlife by-products is the driving force behind exploitation, though it is rarely the focus of conservation efforts. Consumer campaigns against spotted cat furs, ivory, and tortoiseshell in Europe and the United States have drastically reduced consumer demand. Approaches to affecting demand can take various forms depending upon the use of turtles and by-products. Reorienting consumer demand to purchase turtles and turtle products originating from captive-bred animals (closed-cycle production systems) is one approach. The concept that an educated consumer can shift product production is fundamental to the success of eco-labeling programs, such as those that seek to identify products prepared from only sustainably harvested tropical hardwoods. Improving the husbandry skills of purchasers of pet turtles is a complementary angle, with the intent of reducing mortality and therefore replacement demand. All these efforts would, in theory, reduce overall demand for turtles and redirect demand toward individuals who supply turtles from approved use programs. This approach would be most effective if combined with a greatly reduced supply of cheap, wild-caught turtles, which tend to undercut the market in closed-cycle production systems. Reorienting turtle by-product demand, especially for meat and medicine, could be approached in a similar manner. To date, there has been little effort in targeting consumer populations outside the United States and Europe. Thus, studies on consumer motivation and attachments to various by-product uses are essential to developing a strategy to reduce consumer demand.

REDEFINE THE ROLE OF CAPTIVE BREEDING IN TURTLE CONSERVATION

Though much has been written about the role of captive breeding for conservation (mainly as the zoo serving as an ark), most current captive-breeding programs are not producing turtles that will be able to be released in the wild. In most instances, captive-breeding programs are producing specimens of unknown genetic and geographic provenance that are maintained in conditions which do not allow the development of natural physiological cycles or behaviors and that are unfit for release. Many of these captive-bred animals have been exposed to diseases that do not occur in the wild and may, as suspected of captive desert tortoises released into the Mojave Desert, be carriers of lethal diseases. What, then, is the role of the ever-increasing number of captive-bred animals residing in zoos and private collections? To answer this question one must first distinguish between two distinct types of captive-breeding activity.

Captive breeding efforts are broadly defined in two categories, in situ and ex situ (see also "Overview of Conservation and Management Methods," E. O. Moll and Moll, Chapter 5). Ex situ programs are predicated on a highly manipulative, often costly strategy of producing captive-born turtles under completely artificial conditions, often in a country far removed from the actual wild population. These types of captive-breeding programs produce animals that may resemble the wild ancestral stock but are physiologically, behaviorally, and genetically constructs of artificial propagation and have little chance of actually being able to survive in the wild. In situ programs have a distinct advantage as they produce young that have some chance of survival. These programs are located within the actual range (not just the country of origin) of the target species. Here breeding adults are subject to natural circadian and yearly cycles, forage for natural foods, and ideally are confined in large areas of native habitat and vegetation with minimal human intervention.

There are very few conservation programs that are strictly in situ. This may be in part due to the sponsors of captive-breeding programs, which are primarily Western institutions that often need to see a tangible benefit from their conservation actions, that is, exhibits. Only a few of the very largest zoos have the resources to invest heavily in field projects that will never be seen by their visiting public. Another drawback to in situ programs is the lack of control, which is inexorably linked to most hands-on, manipulative projects. To yield any long-term conservation gains, in situ breeding programs must be integrated with habitat conservation initiatives and accompanied by monitoring programs that provide feedback on the overall effectiveness of the species recovery and conservation efforts. Therefore, in situ projects are correctly viewed as tools to achieve a larger conservation goal, not an end unto themselves. As in situ projects require devolving control to local, in-country institutions, they present additional challenges in requiring the formation of partnerships between institutions that all too often have very different approaches to habitat conservation as well as different approaches to maintaining, breeding, and reintroducing captive-bred animals.

Clearly, there are but a very few species for which the expense and effort of captive breeding will be required to bolster and restore wild populations. Habitat protection and the management of wild turtle populations hold much greater promise (and much lower cost) than do captive-breeding programs. Putting concepts of habitat and wild population protection into actual practice is often more difficult than intellectually embracing them. For many, accepting these concepts involves discarding long-cherished notions that captive-bred turtles will one day return to the wild. Yet, these captive-bred animals do not have to be free ranging to have a tremendous impact in reversing the worldwide decline of turtles.

Zoos, aquaria, and other live animal collections inspire enthusiasm, interest, and compassion for wildlife and their habitats in a manner that is truly unique to those institutions. Observing live animals in natural settings fosters an emotional connection to wildlife that inspires conservation action in a manner that cannot be duplicated on television, in film, or by visiting a museum of natural history. Zoological parks draw their attendance from a wide cross section of society and through their exhibits and educational programs are able to influence public attitudes toward wildlife. In short, they educate and rally political and financial support for conservation programs in their backyard and around the world. These exhibits, as well as many private collections, will require living animals for years to come. Unfortunately, the current turtle exploitation scenario undercuts captive-bred stock with cheap, wild-caught animals. However, it is my hope that with increasing control over wildlife trade, and heightened public consciousness about the impacts of the trade in wild-caught turtles, captive-bred turtles will replace wild-caught animals in zoos as well as in the pet trade. Substituting captive-bred stock for wild-caught turtles will help conserve dwindling populations of wild turtles around the world.

DEVELOP INTEGRATED LANDSCAPE CONSERVATION PROGRAMS

As mentioned earlier in this discussion, turtle conservation efforts have been largely limited to single species. Likewise, habitat conservation has often focused on a rather small, local scale. The results, as discussed in the earlier chapters of this book, have not been very effective at conserving turtles. Despite heightened concern for turtles, including the publication of action and recovery plans and entire journals and books devoted to turtles and turtle conservation, populations and entire species are rapidly sliding toward extinction.

To conserve turtles effectively over the long term will require reorienting conservation efforts to reach far beyond individual species and small habitat patches by placing protection efforts into a much larger context of metapopulations and ecosystems. Large landscape areas (mosaics of habitat) are required to maintain metapopulations and to support the full range of dynamic ecosystem processes required to maintain turtle habitat. Preserves for turtles, such as those inhabited by the geometric tortoise (Psammobates geometricus) in South Africa and the western swamp turtle (Pseudemydura umbrina) in Australia, require expensive, intensive management to function. Such preserves are so divorced from natural ecosystem processes that the management needs of both the habitat and the turtles are more akin to a zoo than an ecosystem. These expensive management regimes are not a viable option for most turtle species. Therefore, conservationists must become adept and conversant with a much broader range of land use and development considerations. By embedding turtle conservation into a much larger picture, we have the ability to begin to halt, and reverse, the trajectory toward extinction that is affecting so many turtle species.

Although large-scale habitat plans are necessary to conserve turtles, it is still necessary to monitor the health of turtle populations in these systems. For example, human exploitation can decimate turtle populations in protected areas. At Tarangire National Park in Tanzania, pancake tortoises disappeared from a large portion of this 260,000-ha savanna system because collection for the pet trade was not detected (Klemens and Moll 1995). Also, umbrella ecosystem protection often fails to address the life history and conservation requirements of marine and river turtles, species that cross political and jurisdictional boundaries as part of their life history cycles. Many protected systems also are held hostage to outside ecosystem inputs, including pollution, siltation, and water diversions. Watershed management plans are excellent mechanisms to review the totality of inputs and outputs of aquatic systems, thereby conserving ecosystem functions. However, the complexities and difficulties in implementing such plans are directly correlated with the size of a drainage basin and its catchment.

The Great Swamp, which lies in New York's Harlem Valley, is where the Wildlife Conservation Society has been working in partnership with a wide range of civic, conservation, and municipal groups to develop a locally driven, scientifically informed landscape conservation plan. The Great Swamp drainage basin is part of the Hudson River estuarine system, which contains one of the world's most diverse assemblages of turtles: the loggerhead turtle (Caretta caretta), Kemp's ridley, common snapping turtle (Chelydra serpentina serpentina), eastern mud turtle

(Kinosternon subrubrum subrubrum), common musk turtle *(Sternotherus odoratus)*, midland painted turtle *(Chrysemys picta marginata)*, eastern painted turtle *(Chrysemys picta picta)*, spotted turtle *(Clemmys guttata)*, wood turtle *(Clemmys insculpta)*, bog turtle, Blanding's turtle, common map turtle *(Graptemys geographica)*, diamondback terrapin *(Malaclemys terrapin)*, and eastern box turtle *(Terrapene carolina carolina)*. The value of the real estate here, lying in a rapidly urbanizing suburban corridor, is increasing, as are large-scale development pressures. Estimates are that the human population in the southern section of the Great Swamp (Putnam County) will increase by 40% by the year 2015 while that of the northern section (Dutchess County) will increase by 28% (Regional Plan Association 1991). With such challenges to the landscape, and with inadequate local and state regulatory wetland protection, the future of the Great Swamp's biological integrity will rely upon strong and well-informed local decision makers equipped with both ecological data and the knowledge of how to apply those data to negotiate effectively land use decisions that will protect ecosystem integrity.

In the Great Swamp, scientists have moved beyond merely going on record as stating that greatly expanded protection needs are required to actually working with local decision makers so that nonscientists experience firsthand the biological requirements of the Great Swamp ecosystem. For example, I have involved community members, including local politicians and members of regulatory boards and commissions, in biological survey work that includes locating and monitoring populations of threatened turtle species. Through several roundtable meetings, the Wildlife Conservation Society has begun to communicate effectively with local decision makers who are charged with balancing environmental concerns with community development and the rights of property owners. Through these dialogues, all of the project participants have learned a great deal about how local people view this wetland resource and the pressures on their land and way of life as well as their vision of the future for their communities.

Through involvement with the Great Swamp project, members of the communities have begun to recognize the incredible natural values that many of them had taken for granted. By accompanying scientists into the field, members of local zoning and planning boards have observed turtles moving hundreds of feet from wetlands into upland forested areas. Equipped with this knowledge, local decision makers have begun to argue effectively for mechanisms that protect the Great Swamp with upland buffer zones large enough to protect turtles. These mechanisms include downsizing and clustering development activities as well as creating other incentives to achieve protection of habitat through the development process. There is strong local interest in protecting the scenic, recreational, and ecological values of the Great Swamp and its watershed, and a large consortium of local groups, both municipal and nongovernmental, have formed an umbrella organization called FrOGS (Friends of the Great Swamp) to address the dual goals of protecting the ecological integrity of the 1,620-ha wetland and its 25,515-ha catchment while allowing for economic development.

Drainage basin plans such as that for the Great Swamp depend upon scientific information upon which to base land use plans that balance economic development with environmental protection. Even when the information exists, there is a tremendous dissonance between the providers of information (scientists) and the users of those data (planning agencies). Scientists are well positioned to serve as the catalytic link, providing information and advice to decision makers that can result in better-informed land use planning. However, scientists are usually detached from the process, and this detachment is frequently self-imposed. Why? In some instances it stems from a self-absorbed interest to study species or systems without a sense of greater obligation to use those data for the public good. In many cases, the reluctance to become involved in applying data stems from the realities of planning—the need to make important decisions based on often incomplete data and the need to monitor implementation.

The scientist working outside the community has the luxury of conducting additional sampling, to be absolutely assured that the data are clean and support or refute a hypothesis. The scientist that works within the community, applying data to real-life decisions of land use planning, must approach problems by asking a fundamentally different set of questions. Do we have enough data to make a prudent judgement about the course of a project? What are the risks of making decisions with incomplete data versus the risks of inaction? To conserve turtles (and other organisms) effectively we need to develop a cadre of scientists who have the technical ability to frame research questions that have both ecosystem management and public policy implications, to develop the research projects that address those questions, and to communicate effectively research findings by actively engaging decision makers who represent a diversity of interests and governmental levels.

There is an urgent need to synthesize and disseminate what is already known. There already exists a large body of information on some issues, such as wetland buffers, invasive species, and threatened and endangered species, yet it is not readily accessible to decision makers. In order to maximize the impact of scientific studies, they have to be interpretable in a readily understood, consistent, and logical manner so they can be used in a land use decision-making context. This is more than cobbling conservation recommendations onto scientific papers. It requires being able to design applied research studies and disseminate information in a strategically targeted manner in order to influence the decision-making and policy process.

Conservation organizations increasingly engage communities in a participatory process, thereby greatly increasing the effectiveness of top-down, government-led conservation actions. In the United States and elsewhere, large-scale planning and ecosystem conservation efforts were traditionally considered to be largely within the purview of federal, state, and county government. Those individuals and communities that have had the most to gain or lose as a result of these mandates are all-too-frequently disenfranchised in the decision-making process. Not surprisingly, local communities may be resistant to top-down initiatives and often derail or severely restrict their implementation unless community members see that they, too, have a stake in the success of these programs. The current backlash against environmental regulation in the United States may be directly attributable to decades of top-down conservation and management dicta, imposed on an ever-growing group of stakeholders who have viewed themselves, quite correctly, as totally outside the decision-making process.

But the need to involve local communities in land use planning and implementation is more than a public relations game, more than just winning acceptance of a conservation plan. Local planning boards, wetland commissions, tribal councils, villages, and other municipal agencies have the ability to achieve, through the adoption of local ordinances, procedures, and management plans, a more comprehensive ecosystem protection than prescribed by higher levels of government. These local entities, if provided with the proper information and the ability and political will to use that information, can be highly effective at protecting ecosystems as part of the land use planning, subdivision, and development processes. It is also important that local interest groups and nongovernmental organizations be similarly empowered by becoming well informed and articulate in land use planning and conservation issues. These groups often serve as catalysts for better planning by lobbying and applying political pressure to officials.

The issue of wetland regulation is an excellent example of how the citizen–scientist can provide information to the local community, which, in turn, can use that information to achieve a higher level of ecosystem protection than is required by state statute. For example, New York State law prescribes a 100-foot (30-m) buffer zone around state-regulated wetlands (those that are greater than 12.4 acres [5 ha] or that contain state-listed endangered or threatened species). There are two basic problems with this approach. First, many significant wetlands and wetland complexes that are less than 12.4 acres are totally without protection; second, even if a wetland is protected by a 100-foot buffer, most wetland-dependent species have extensive upland habitat requirements, much greater than 100 feet from the edge of a wetland. Clearly, state law is unable to protect the ecological vitality of a wetland, even one that contains rare species. The adoption of local wetland ordinances, which regulate small wetlands, are important tools in protecting wetland ecosystems. However, like all tools, unless used correctly they will not yield the desired results.

Alternative strategies have been employed in some communities. The Town of East Hampton on the east end of Long Island, New York, has added value to its local environmental and zoning ordinances by creatively planning to protect natural resources through the creation of open-space reservations that correspond to ecosystem realities, not arbitrary legislative mandates. To create these open-space reservations, the town planner, as well as the planning and zoning boards, sought out technical expertise from scientists to gain knowledge of ecosystem functions within the community. This knowledge provided them with not only the information upon which to create these open-space reservations but the ability to communicate effectively the rationale behind those planning decisions to other town officials, the electorate, and the development community.

Last, but by no means least, I see an urgent need to expand and enhance avenues for formal and informal public education regarding two key issues: we need to address the limited, often disconnected view that many people have of how ecosystems function, and we must begin to dispel the widely held notion that a community must choose either conservation or economic development. A better understanding of the full range of options that communities can exercise to balance environmental stewardship with economic well-being is required. These educational efforts should focus not only on appreciating the complexity of ecosystems and the effects of cumulative impacts upon them but on evaluating the short- and long-term costs and benefits of various types of land use scenarios. In terms of understanding the spectrum of choices available, curricula for the general public and decision makers could be developed that make a clear distinction between economic growth, measured by short-term productivity, and more sustainable development, measured by a set of qualitative standards that place a higher premium on long-term benefits, such as overall quality of life.

CONCLUSION

Today we face a tremendous challenge—to save the world's 260 or more species of turtles from the specter of extinction. I remain optimistic that we can build upon the experiences of the past, using those hard-learned lessons to chart a more secure and sustainable future for the world's turtles. This is the driving force that motivates those who seek, through this book and other avenues, to reorient our approach to turtle conservation.

ACKNOWLEDGMENTS
This concluding chapter has drawn heavily upon the preceding chapters and has especially benefited from input, discussion, and critical review from my colleagues, Dorene Bolze (overexploitation) and Erik Kiviat-Hudsonia (cost-benefit analysis of wetland restoration), as well as Jim McDougal and John Thorbjarnarson, who reviewed the entire chapter and made valuable suggestions for focus and improvement.

LITERATURE CITED

Acronyms used herein include IUCN (International Union for Conservation of Nature and Natural Resources) and NOAA (National Oceanic and Atmospheric Administration).

Adler, K. K. 1970. The influence of prehistoric man on the distribution of the box turtle. Annals of the Carnegie Museum of Natural History 41:263–280.

Agassiz, L. 1868. A Journey in Brazil, 5th edn. Ticknor and Fields, Boston.

Aguilar, R., J. Mas, and X. Pastor. 1995. Impact of Spanish swordfish longline fisheries on the loggerhead sea turtle, *Caretta caretta*, population in the western Mediterranean. Pages 1–6 in J. I. Richardson and T. H. Richardson (compilers). Proceedings of the Twelfth Annual Workshop on Sea Turtle Biology and Conservation. NOAA Technical Memorandum NMFS-SEFSC-361.

Ahsan, M. F., M. N. Haque, and C. M. Fugler. 1991. Observations on *Aspideretes nigricans*, a semi-domesticated endemic turtle from eastern Bangladesh. Amphibia-Reptilia 12:131–136.

Ahsan, M. F., and M. A. Saeed. 1992. Some aspects of the breeding biology of the black softshell turtle, *Aspideretes nigricans*. Hamadryad 17:28–31.

Alfinito, J., C. M. Vianna, M. M. F. da Silva, and H. Rodriques. 1976. Transferencia de tartarugas do Rio Trombetas para o Rio Tapajos. Brasil Florestal 7 (26): 49–53.

Alho, C. J. R. 1985. Conservation and management strategies for commonly exploited Amazonian turtles. Biological Conservation 32:291–298.

Alho, C. J. R., T. M. S. Danni, and L. F. M. Padua. 1984. Influência da temperatura de ineubacao do sexo da tartaruga da Amazônia *Podocnemis expansa* (Testudinata: Pelomedusidae). Revista Brasileira de Biologia 44:305–311.

———. 1985. Temperature-dependent sex determination in *Podocnemis expansa* (Testudinata: Pelomedusidae). Biotropica 17:75–78.

Allen, C. 1992. It's time to give Kemp's ridley head-starting a fair and scientific evaluation! Marine Turtle Newsletter 56:21–24.

Allen, W. H. 1992. Increased dangers to Caribbean marine ecosystems. BioScience 42:330–335.

Alvarado, J., A. Figueroa, and R. Byles. 1990. Alternative conservation methods used for marine turtles in Michoacan, Mexico. Pages 183–184 in T. H. Richardson, J. I. Richardson, and M. Donnelly (compilers). Proceedings of the Tenth Annual Workshop on Sea Turtle Biology and Conservation. NOAA Technical Memorandum NMFS-SEFSC-278.

Alvarez del Toro, M., R. A. Mittermeier, and J. B. Iverson. 1979. River turtle in danger. Oryx 15:170–173.

Amaral, M. 1994. Plymouth Redbelly Turtle *(Pseudemys rubriventris)* Recovery Plan. 2nd rev. U.S. Fish and Wildlife Service, Hadley, Mass.

Amato, G., and J. Gatesy. 1994. PCR assays of variable nucleotide sites for identification of conservation units. Pages 215–226 in B. Schierwater, B. Streit, G. Wagner, and R. DeSalle (eds.). Molecular Approaches to Ecology and Evolution. Birkhauser, Basel, Switzerland.

Anderson, P. K. 1958. The photic responses and water-approach behavior of hatchling turtles. Copeia 1958:211–215.

Anonymous. 1988. Small starts can reap big results. Focus (July/August): 4.

Anonymous. 1995. *Geochelone sulcata;* le retour! La Tortue International 30:26–27.

Aranda A., C., and M. W. Chandler. 1989. Las tortugas marinas del Perú y su situación actual. Herpetologo 62:77–86.

Araúz Almengor, M., C. L. Mo, and E. Vargas M. 1993. Marine Turtle Newsletter 63:10–13.

Aridjis, H. 1990. Mexico proclaims total ban on harvest of turtles and eggs. Marine Turtle Newsletter 50:1–3.

Arndt, R. G. 1982. The bog turtle—an endangered species? Pages 99–103 in P. Wray (ed.). Proceedings Northeast Endangered Species Conference, May 9–11, 1980, Provincetown, MA. Center for Endangered Species, Ayer, Mass.

Arnold, E. N. 1979. Indian Ocean giant tortoises: Their systematics and island adaptations. Philosophical Transactions of the Royal Society of London, Series B, Biological Sciences 286:127–145.

———. 1980. Recently extinct reptile populations from Mauritius and Réunion, Indian Ocean. Journal of Zoology 191:33–47.

Atatür, M. K. 1979. Investigations on the morphology and osteology, biotope and distribution in Anatolia of *Trionyx triunguis* (Reptilia, Testudines) with some observations on its biology. Ege Üniversitesi, Fen Fakultesi Monografiler Serisi 18:1–75.

Auffenberg, W. 1978. Gopher tortoise. Pages 33–35 in R. W. McDiarmid (ed.). Rare and Endangered Biota of Florida. Vol. 3, Amphibians and Reptiles. University Presses of Florida, Gainesville.

Auffenberg, W., and R. Franz. 1982. The status and distribution of the gopher tortoise *(Gopherus polyphemus)*. Pages 95–126 in R. B. Bury (ed.). North American Tortoises: Conservation and Ecology. U.S. Fish and Wildlife Service, Wildlife Research Report 12.

Avery, H. W., and A. G. Neibergs. 1997. Effects of cattle grazing on desert tortoise, *Gopherus agassizii:* Nutritional and behavioral interactions. Pages 13–20 in J. Van Abbema (ed.). Proceedings: Conservation, Restoration, and Management of Tortoises and Turtles—an International Conference, July 1993, State University of New York at Purchase. New York Turtle and Tortoise Society, New York.

Avise, J. C., B. W. Bowen, T. Lamb, A. B. Meylan, and E. Bermingham. 1992. Mitochondrial DNA evolution at a turtle's pace: Evidence for low genetic variability and reduced microevolutionary rate in the Testudines. Molecular Biology and Evolution 9:457–473.

Avise, J. C., and J. L. Hamrick (eds.). 1996. Conservation Genetics: Case Histories from Nature. Chapman and Hall, New York.

Baard, E. H. W. 1989a. The status of some rare and endangered endemic reptiles and amphibians of the southwestern Cape Province, South Africa. Biological Conservation 49:161–168.

———. 1989b. *Psammobates geometricus*, geometric tortoise (English), Suurpootjie (Afrikaans). Pages 85–87 *in* I. R. Swingland and M. W. Klemens (eds.). The Conservation Biology of Tortoises. Occasional Papers of the IUCN Species Survival Commission, no. 5. Gland, Switzerland.

———. 1990. Biological aspects and conservation status of the geometric tortoise, *Psammobates geometricus* (Linnaeus, 1758) (Cryptodira: Testudinidae). Doctoral dissertation, University of Stellenbosch, Republic of South Africa.

———. 1993. Distribution and status of the geometric tortoise *Psammobates geometricus* in South Africa. Biological Conservation 63:235–239.

———. 1994. Cape Tortoises: Their Identification and Care. Cape Nature Conservation, Cape Town.

Babcock, H. L. 1919. Turtles of New England. Memoirs of the Boston Society of Natural History 8:325–431.

———. 1937. A new subspecies of the red-bellied terrapin *Pseudemys rubriventris* (Le Conte). Occasional Papers of the Boston Society of Natural History 8:293–294.

Bacon, P., F. Berry, K. Bjorndal, H. Hirth, L. Ogren, and M. Weber (eds.). 1984. Proceedings of the Western Atlantic Turtle Symposium, vols. 1 and 3. RSMAS Printing, Miami.

Baha el Din, S. M. 1994. Status of the Egyptian Tortoise *Testudo kleinmanni* in Egypt. Report to the Wildlife Conservation Society, Turtle Recovery Program, Bronx, New York.

Bailey, S. J., C. R. Schwalbe, and C. H. Lowe. 1995. Hibernaculum use by a population of desert tortoises *(Gopherus agassizii)* in the Sonoran Desert. Journal of Herpetology 29:361–369.

Baillie, J., and B. Groombridge (eds.). 1996. IUCN Red List of Threatened Animals. International Union for Conservation of Nature and Natural Resources, Gland, Switzerland.

Balazs, G. H. 1982a. Status of sea turtles in the central Pacific Ocean. Pages 243–252 *in* K. A. Bjorndal (ed.). Biology and Conservation of Sea Turtles. Smithsonian Institution Press, Washington, D.C.

———. 1982b. Growth rates of immature green turtles in the Hawaiian Archipelago. Pages 117–125 *in* K. A. Bjorndal (ed.). Biology and Conservation of Sea Turtles. Smithsonian Institution Press, Washington, D.C.

———. 1985. Impact of ocean debris on marine turtles: Entanglement and ingestion. Pages 1–40 *in* R. S. Shomura and H. O. Yoshida (eds.). Proceedings of the Workshop on the Fate and Impact of Marine Debris. NOAA Technical Memorandum NMFS-SWFC-54.

———. 1986. Fibropapillomas in Hawaiian green turtles. Marine Turtle Newsletter 39:1–3.

Balée, W. 1985. Ká apor ritual hunting. Human Ecology 13:485–510.

Ballasina, D. 1992. Report on repatriation of tortoises to Greece. British Herpetological Society Bulletin 40:2–4.

262LITERATURE CITED

Ballou, J. D. 1993. Assessing the risks of infectious diseases in captive breeding and reintroduction programs. Journal of Zoo and Wildlife Medicine 24 (3): 327–335.
Balmford, A., G. M. Mace, and N. Leader-Williams. 1996. Designing the ark: Setting priorities for captive breeding. Conservation Biology 10:719–727.
Barr, C. 1992. Current status of trade and legal protection of sea turtles in Indonesia. Pages 11–13 in M. Salmon and J. Wyneken (compilers). Proceedings of the Eleventh Annual Workshop on Sea Turtle Biology and Conservation. NOAA Technical Memorandum NMFS-SEFSC-302.
Bartlett, R. D. 1997. The impact of the pet trade on populations of protected turtles (with brief notes on other reptile species). Pages 50–53 in T. Tyning (ed.). Status and Conservation of Turtles of the Northeastern United States. Serpents Tale, Lanesboro, Minn.
Bateman, Rev. G. C. 1897. The Vivarium: Being a Practical Guide to the Construction, Arrangement, and Management of Vivaria. L. Upcott Gill, London.
Bates, H. W. 1863. The Naturalist on the River Amazons. John Murray, London.
Bayley, J. R., and A. C. Highfield. 1996. Observations on ecological changes threatening a population of Testudo graeca graeca in the Souss Valley, southern Morocco. Chelonian Conservation and Biology 2:36–42.
Beck, R. H. 1903. In the home of the giant tortoise. Pages 1–17 in Seventh Annual Report of the New York Zoological Society, New York.
Belkin, D. A., and C. Gans. 1968. An unusual chelonian feeding niche. Ecology 49:768–769.
Bellrose, R. C., R. Sparks, F. L. Paveglio, Jr., D. Steffeck, R. Thomas, R. Weaver, and D. Moll. 1977. Fish and wildlife changes resulting from the construction of a nine foot navigation channel in the Illinois Waterway from LaGrange Lock and Dam upstream to Lockport Lock and Dam. U.S. Army Corps of Engineers, Chicago District, Contract Report DACW 23-76-C-0066.
Bennett, D. H. 1972. Notes on the terrestrial wintering of mud turtles (Kinosternon subrubrum). Herpetologica 28:245–247.
Benson, A. J., and C. P. Boydstun. 1995. Invasion of the zebra mussel in the United States. Pages 445–446 in E. T. LaRoe, G. S. Farris, C. E. Puckett, P. D. Doran, and M. J. Mac (eds.). Our Living Resources: A Report to the Nation on the Distribution, Abundance, and Health of U.S. Plants, Animals, and Ecosystems. National Biological Survey, Washington, D.C.
Bergeron, J., D. Crews, and J. A. McLachlan. 1994. PCBs as environmental estrogens: Turtle sex determination as a biomarker of environmental contamination. Environmental Health Perspectives 102:780–781.
Berry, J. F. 1975. The population effects of ecological sympatry on musk turtles in northern Florida. Copeia 1975:692–701.
Berry, J. F., and C. M. Berry. 1984. A re-analysis of geographic variation and systematics in the yellow mud turtle, Kinosternon flavescens (Agassiz). Annals of the Carnegie Museum 53:185–206.
Berry, J. F., and R. Shine. 1980. Sexual size dimorphism and sexual selection in turtles (Order Testudines). Oecologia (Berlin) 44:185–191.
Berry, K. H. 1985. Avian predation on the desert tortoise in California. Bureau of Land Management report to Southern California Edison Co., Riverside, Calif.

————. 1986. Desert tortoise *(Gopherus agassizii)* relocation: Implications of social behavior and movements. Herpetologica 42:113–125.

————. 1989. *Gopherus agassizii,* desert tortoise. Pages 5–7 *in* I. R. Swingland and M. W. Klemens (eds.). The Conservation Biology of Tortoises. Occasional Papers of the IUCN Species Survival Commission, no. 5. Gland, Switzerland.

Berry, K. H., and P. Medica. 1995. Desert tortoises in the Mojave and Colorado deserts. Pages 135–137 *in* E. T. LaRoe, G. S. Farris, C. E. Puckett, P. D. Doran, and M. J. Mac (eds.). Our Living Resources: A Report to the Nation on the Distribution, Abundance, and Health of U.S. Plants, Animals, and Ecosystems. National Biological Survey, Washington, D.C.

Beshkov, V. A. 1993. On the distribution, relative abundance and protection of tortoises in Bulgaria. Chelonian Conservation and Biology 1:53–62.

Bhadauria, R. S., A. Pai, and D. Basu. 1990. Habitat, nesting and reproductive adaptations in narrow-headed soft-shell turtle *Chitra indica* (Gray) (Reptilia, Chelonia). Journal of the Bombay Natural History Society 87:364–367.

Bickham, J. W., T. Lamb, P. Minx, and J. C. Patton. 1996. Molecular systematics of the genus *Clemmys* and the intergeneric relationships of Emydid turtles. Herpetologica 52:89–97.

Bishop, J. M. 1983. Incidental capture of diamondback terrapins by crab pots. Estuaries 6:426–430.

Bjorndal, K. A. (ed.). 1982. Biology and Conservation of Sea Turtles. Smithsonian Institution Press, Washington, D.C.

————. 1995. Biology and Conservation of Sea Turtles. Rev. edn. Smithsonian Institution Press, Washington, D.C.

Bjorndal, K. A., A. Bolten, and C. Lagueux. 1993. Decline of the nesting population of hawksbill turtles at Tortuguero, Costa Rica. Conservation Biology 7:925–927.

Bjorndal, K. A., and A. Carr. 1989. Variation in clutch size and egg size in the green turtle nesting population at Tortuguero, Costa Rica. Herpetologica 45:181–189.

Bloxam, Q. M. C., and S. J. Tonge. 1995. Amphibians: Suitable candidates for breeding-release programmes. Biodiversity and Conservation 4:636–644.

Blyth, E. 1863. A collection of sundries from different parts of Burma. Journal of the Asiatic Society of Bengal 32:73–90.

Boarman, W. I. 1993. When a native predator becomes a pest: A case study. Pages 191–206 *in* S. K. Majumdar, E. W. Miller, D. E. Baker, E. K. Brown, J. R. Pratt, and J. F. Schalles (eds.). Conservation and Resource Management. Pennsylvania Academy of Science, Philadelphia.

————. 1997. Predation on turtles and tortoises by a "subsidized predator." Pages 103–104 *in* J. Van Abbema (ed.). Proceedings: Conservation, Restoration, and Management of Tortoises and Turtles—an International Conference, July 1993, State University of New York at Purchase. New York Turtle and Tortoise Society, New York.

Boarman, W. I., and K. H. Berry. 1995. Common ravens in the southwestern United States, 1968–1992. Pages 73–75 *in* E. T. LaRoe, G. S. Farris, C. E. Puckett, P. D. Doran, and M. J. Mac (eds.). Our Living Resources: A Report to the Nation on the Distribution, Abundance, and Health of U.S. Plants, Animals, and Ecosystems. National Biological Survey, Washington, D.C.

Boarman, W. I., M. Sazaki, and W. B. Jennings. 1997. The effect of roads, barrier fences, and culverts on desert tortoise populations in California, USA. Pages 54–58 *in* J. Van Abbema (ed.). Proceedings: Conservation, Restoration, and Management of Tortoises and Turtles—an International Conference, July 1993, State University of New York at Purchase. New York Turtle and Tortoise Society, New York.

Bodie, J. R., K. R. Smith, and V. J. Burke. 1995. Comparisons of diel temperature patterns from nests of two sympatric turtle species. American Midland Naturalist 136:181–186.

Bodmer, R. E. 1994. Managing wildlife with local communities in the Peruvian Amazon: The case of the Reserva Comunal Tamshiyacu-Tahuayo. Pages 113–134 *in* D. Western and R. M. Wright (eds.). Natural Connections: Perspectives in Community-Based Conservation. Island Press, Washington, D.C.

Bolten, A. B., and G. H. Balazs. 1995. Biology of the early pelagic stage—the "lost year." Pages 579–581 *in* K. A. Bjorndal (ed.). Biology and Conservation of Sea Turtles. Rev. edn. Smithsonian Institution Press, Washington, D.C.

Bolton, M. 1989. The management of crocodiles in captivity. FAO Conservation Guide 22. Food and Agricultural Organization of the United Nations, Rome.

Bolze, D. 1992. The Wild Bird Trade: When a Bird in the Hand Means None in the Bush. Wildlife Conservation Society, Bronx, New York.

Boullay, S. 1995. Repatriation of radiated tortoises, *Geochelone radiata*, from Réunion Island to Madagascar. Chelonian Conservation and Biology 1:319–320.

Bourg, N. A. 1992. Status of the bog turtle *(Clemmys muhlenbergii)* in North America. The Nature Conservancy Pennsylvania Science Office report to the U.S. Fish and Wildlife Service, Middletown, Pa.

Bouskila, A. 1986. On the danger of the red-eared terrapin, *Chrysemys scripta*, in natural habitats in Israel. Hardun 3:63.

Bowen, B. W., F. A. Abreu-Grobois, G. H. Balazs, N. Kamezaki, C. J. Limpus, and R. J. Ferl. 1995. Trans-Pacific migrations of the loggerhead turtle *(Caretta caretta)* demonstrated with mitochondrial DNA markers. Proceedings of the National Academy of Sciences of the USA 92:3731–3734.

Bowen, B. W., and J. C. Avise. 1996. Conservation genetics of marine turtles. Pages 190–237 *in* J. C. Avise and J. L. Hamrick (eds.). Conservation Genetics: Case Histories from Nature. Chapman and Hall, New York.

Bowen, B. W., A. L. Bass, A. Garcia-Rodriguez, C. E. Diez, R. Van Dam, A. Bolten, K. A. Bjorndal, M. M. Miyamoto, and R. J. Ferl. 1996. Origin of hawksbill turtles in a Caribbean feeding area as indicated by genetic markers. Ecological Applications 6:566–572.

Bowen, B. W., N. Kamezaki, C. J. Limpus, G. R. Hughes, A. B. Meylan, and J. C. Avise. 1994. Global phylogeography of the loggerhead turtle *(Caretta caretta)* as indicated by mitochondrial DNA haplotypes. Evolution 48:1820–1828.

Bowen, B. W., A. B. Meylan, and J. C. Avise. 1991. Evolutionary distinctiveness of the endangered Kemp's ridley sea turtle. Nature 352:709–711.

Bowen, B. W., A. B. Meylan, J. Perran Ross, C. J. Limpus, G. H. Balazs, and J. C. Avise. 1992. Global population structure and natural history of the green turtle *(Chelonia mydas)* in terms of matriarchical phylogeny. Evolution 46:865–881.

Bowen, B. W., W. S. Nelson, and J. C. Avise. 1993. A molecular phylogeny for marine turtles: Trait mapping, rate assessment, and conservation relevance. Proceedings of the National Academy of Sciences of the USA 90:5574–5577.

Bowen, L., and D. Van Vuren. 1997. Insular endemic plants lack defenses against herbivores. Conservation Biology 11:1249–1254.

Boycott, R. C. 1989. *Homopus signatus,* Namaqualand speckled padloper; Peer's padloper (for southern race) (English), gifskilpadjie; klipskilpadjie; Namaqualand-klipskilpadjie (Afrikaans). Pages 82–84 *in* I. R. Swingland and M. W. Klemens (eds.). The Conservation Biology of Tortoises. Occasional Papers of the IUCN Species Survival Commission, no. 5. Gland, Switzerland.

Boycott, R. C., and O. Bourquin. 1988. The South African Tortoise Book. A Guide to South African Tortoises, Terrapins and Turtles. Southern Book Publishers, Johannesburg.

Branch, W. 1989a. *Chersina angulata,* angulate tortoise; bowsprit tortoise (English), rooipensskilpad; bontskilpad (Afrikaans). Pages 68–71 *in* I. R. Swingland and M. W. Klemens (eds.). The Conservation Biology of Tortoises. Occasional Papers of the IUCN Species Survival Commission, no. 5. Gland, Switzerland.

———. 1989b. *Homopus femoralis,* greater padloper; Karoo tortoise (English), Vlakskilpad; Bergskilpadjie; groter padloper (Afrikaans). Pages 80–81 *in* I. R. Swingland and M. W. Klemens (eds.). The Conservation Biology of Tortoises. Occasional Papers of the IUCN Species Survival Commission, no. 5. Gland, Switzerland.

Brattstrom, B. H. 1988. Habitat destruction in California with special reference to *Clemmys marmorata:* A perspective. Pages 13–24 *in* H. F. DeLisle, P. R. Brown, B. Kaufman, and B. M. McGurty (eds.). Proceedings of the Conference on California Herpetology. Southwestern Herpetologists Society, Van Nuys, Calif.

Brattstrom, B. H., and D. F. Messer. 1988. Current status of the southern Pacific pond turtle, *Clemmys marmorata pallida,* in southern California. Final Report (Contract C-2044) to California Fish and Game, San Diego.

Braun, J., and G. R. Brooks, Jr. 1987. Box turtles *(Terrapene carolina)* as potential agents for seed dispersal. American Midland Naturalist 117:312–318.

Brito, W. L. S., and M. Ferreira. 1978. Fauna Amazônica preferida como alimento uma análise regional. Brasil Florestal 9 (35): 11–17.

Britson, C. A., and W. H. Gutzke. 1993. Antipredator mechanisms of hatchling freshwater turtles. Copeia 1993:435–440.

Britten, H. B., B. R. Riddle, P. F. Brussard, R. Marlow, and T. E. Lee, Jr. 1997. Genetic delineation of management units for the desert tortoise, *Gopherus agassizii,* in Northeastern Mojave Desert. Copeia 1997:523–530.

Broadley, D. G. 1989a. *Kinixys natalensis,* Natal hinged tortoise. Pages 60–61 *in* I. R. Swingland and M. W. Klemens (eds.). The Conservation Biology of Tortoises. Occasional Papers of the IUCN Species Survival Commission, no. 5. Gland, Switzerland.

———. 1989b. *Geochelone sulcata,* spurred tortoise (English), Abu gatta, Abu gefne (Arabic). Pages 47–48 *in* I. R. Swingland and M. W. Klemens (eds.). The Conservation Biology of Tortoises. Occasional Papers of the IUCN Species Survival Commission, no. 5. Gland, Switzerland.

———. 1989c. *Geochelone pardalis,* leopard tortoise (English), Bergskilpad (Afrikaans). Pages 43–46 *in* I. R. Swingland and M. W. Klemens (eds.). The Conservation Biology of Tortoises. Occasional Papers of the IUCN Species Survival Commission, no. 5. Gland, Switzerland.

———. 1989d. *Kinixys belliana,* Bell's hinged tortoise. Pages 49–55 *in* I. R. Swingland and

M. W. Klemens (eds.). The Conservation Biology of Tortoises. Occasional Papers of the IUCN Species Survival Commission, no. 5. Gland, Switzerland.

Broderick, D., C. Moritz, J. D. Miller, M. Guinea, R. I. T. Prince, and C. J. Limpus. 1994. Genetic studies of the hawksbill turtle *Eretmochelys imbricata:* Evidence for multiple stocks in Australian waters. Pacific Conservation Biology 1:123–131.

Brongersma, L. D. 1982. Marine turtles of the eastern Atlantic Ocean. Pages 407–416 *in* K. A. Bjorndal (ed.). Biology and Conservation of Sea Turtles. Smithsonian Institution Press, Washington, D.C.

Brooks, R. J., M. L. Bobyn, D. A. Galbraith, J. A. Layfield, and E. G. Nancekivell. 1991b. Maternal and environmental influences on growth and survival of embryonic and hatchling snapping turtles *(Chelydra serpentina)*. Canadian Journal of Zoology 69:2667–2676.

Brooks, R. J., G. P. Brown, and D. A. Galbraith. 1991a. Effects of a sudden increase in natural mortality of adults on a population of the common snapping turtle *(Chelydra serpentina)*. Canadian Journal of Zoology 69:1314–1320.

Brooks, R. J., D. A. Galbraith, E. G. Nancekivell, and C. A. Bishop. 1988. Developing guidelines for managing snapping turtles. Pages 174–179 *in* R. C. Szaro, K. E. Severson, and D. R. Patton (technical coordinators). Management of Amphibians, Reptiles, and Small Mammals in North America. U.S. Forest Service General Technical Report RM-166.

Brown, J. H., and A. Kodric-Brown. 1977. Turnover rates in insular biogeography: Effect of immigration on extinction. Ecology 58:445–449.

Brown, L. E., and D. Moll. 1979. The status of the nearly extinct Illinois mud turtle with recommendations for its conservation. Milwaukee Public Museum, Special Publications in Biology and Geology 3:1–49.

Brown, M. B., I. M. Schumacher, P. A. Klein, K. Harris, T. Correl, and E. R. Jacobson. 1994. *Mycoplasma agassizii* causes upper respiratory tract disease in the desert tortoise. Infection and Immunity 62:4580–4586.

Brown, W. S. 1974. Ecology of the Aquatic Box Turtle, *Terrapene coahuila* (Chelonia, Emydidae), in Northern Mexico. Bulletin of the Florida State Museum, Biological Science 19.

Browne, R. A., N. A. Haskell, C. R. Griffin, and J. W. Ridgeway. 1996. Genetic variation among populations of the redbelly turtle *(Pseudemys rubriventris)*. Copeia 1996:192–195.

Bryan, A. M., P. G. Olafsson, and W. B. Stone. 1987. Disposition of low and high environmental concentrations of PCBs in snapping turtle tissues. Bulletin of Environmental Contamination and Toxicology 38:1000–1005.

Buhlmann, K. A. 1995. Habitat use, terrestrial movements, and conservation of the turtle *Deirochelys reticularia* in Virginia. Journal of Herpetology 29:173–181.

Buhlmann, K. A., J. C. Mitchell, and M. G. Rollins. 1997. New approaches for the conservation of bog turtles, *Clemmys muhlenbergii,* in Virginia. Pages 359–363 *in* J. Van Abbema (ed.). Proceedings: Conservation, Restoration, and Management of Tortoises and Turtles—an International Conference, July 1993, State University of New York at Purchase. New York Turtle and Tortoise Society, New York.

Bull, J. J. 1980. Sex determination in reptiles. Quarterly Review of Biology 55:3–21.

Bull, J. J., and R. C. Vogt. 1979. Temperature-dependent sex determination in turtles. Science (Washington, D.C.) 206:1186–1188.

Burbidge, A. A. 1981. The ecology of the western swamp tortoise *Pseudemydura umbrina* (Testudines: Chelidae). Australian Wildlife Research 8:203–223.

Burbidge, A. A., and G. Kuchling. 1994. Western swamp tortoise recovery plan. Western Australia Wildlife Management Program, no. 11. Department of Conservation and Land Management, Western Australia.

Burbidge, A. A., G. Kuchling, P. J. Fuller, G. Graham, and D. Miller. 1990. The western swamp tortoise. Western Australia Wildlife Management Program, no. 6:i–v, 1–14. Department of Conservation and Land Management, Western Australia.

Burger, J. 1977. Determinants of hatching success in diamondback terrapins, *Malaclemys terrapin*. American Midland Naturalist 97:444–464.

Burger, J., and S. Garber. 1995. Risk assessment, life history strategies, and turtles: Could declines be prevented or predicted? Journal of Toxicology and Environmental Health 46:483–500.

Burgman, M. A., S. Ferson, and H. R. Akcakaya. 1993. Risk assessment in conservation biology. Chapman and Hall, London.

Burke, R. L. 1989. Florida gopher tortoise relocation: Overview and case study. Biological Conservation 48:295–309.

———. 1991. Relocations, repatriations, and translocations of amphibians and reptiles: Taking a broader view. Herpetologica 47:350–357.

Burke, R. L., T. E. Leuteritz, and A. J. Wolf. 1996. Phylogenetic relationships of emydine turtles. Herpetologica 52:572–584.

Burke, V. J. 1995. Ecological and conservation implications of terrestrial habitat use by aquatic turtles. Doctoral dissertation, University of Georgia, Athens.

Burke, V. J., N. B. Frazer, and J. W. Gibbons. 1994b. Conservation of turtles: The chelonian dilemma. Pages 35–39 *in* B. A. Schroeder and B. E. Witherington (compilers). Proceedings of the Thirteenth Annual Workshop on Sea Turtle Biology and Conservation. NOAA Technical Memorandum NMFS-SEFSC-341.

Burke, V. J., and J. W. Gibbons. 1995. Terrestrial buffer zones and wetland conservation: A case study of freshwater turtles in a Carolina bay. Conservation Biology 9:1365–1369.

Burke, V. J., J. W. Gibbons, and J. L. Greene. 1994a. Prolonged nesting forays by common mud turtles *(Kinosternon subrubrum)*. American Midland Naturalist 131:190–195.

Burke, V. J., J. L. Greene, and J. W. Gibbons. 1995. The effect of sample size and study duration on metapopulation estimates for slider turtles *(Trachemys scripta)*. Herpetologica 51:451–456.

Bury, R. B. 1979a. Review of the ecology and conservation of the bog turtle, *Clemmys muhlenbergii*. U.S. Fish and Wildlife Service, Special Scientific Report-Wildlife, no. 219.

———. 1979b. Population ecology of freshwater turtles. Pages 571–602 *in* M. Harless and H. Morlock (eds.). Turtles: Perspectives and Research. Wiley-Interscience, New York.

Bury, R. B., and P. S. Corn. 1995. Have desert tortoises undergone a long-term decline in abundance? Wildlife Society Bulletin 23:41–47.

Bury, R. B., T. C. Esque, and L. A. DeFalco. 1994. Distribution, habitat use, and protection of the desert tortoise in the eastern Mojave Desert. Pages 57–72 *in* R. B. Bury and D. J. Germano (eds.). Biology of North American Tortoises. National Biological Survey, Washington, D.C.

Bury, R. B., R. A. Luckenbach, and S. D. Busack. 1977. Effects of off-road vehicles on vertebrates in the California desert. U.S. Fish and Wildlife Service, Wildlife Research Report 8.

Bury, R. B., D. J. Morafka, and C. J. McCoy. 1988. Distribution, abundance and status of the Bolson tortoise. Annals of the Carnegie Museum of Natural History 57:5–30.

Bush, M., B. B. Beck, and R. J. Montali. 1993. Medical considerations of reintroduction. Pages 24–26 in M. E. Fowler (ed.). Zoo and Wild Animal Medicine, Current Therapy. W. B. Saunders, Philadelphia.

Buskirk, J. R. 1985. The endangered Egyptian tortoise *Testudo kleinmanni*: Status in Egypt and Israel. Pages 35–52 in S. McKeown, F. Caporaso, and K. H. Peterson (eds.). Proceedings of the Ninth International Herpetological Symposium on Captive Husbandry and Breeding. University of San Diego, San Diego.

———. 1989. A third specimen and neotype of *Heosemys leytensis* (Chelonia: Emydidae). Copeia 1989:224–227.

———. 1990. An overview of the western pond turtle, *Clemmys marmorata*. Pages 16–23 in K. R. Beaman, F. Caporaso, S. McKeown, and M. D. Graff (eds.). Proceedings of the First International Symposium on Turtles and Tortoises: Conservation and Captive Husbandry. California Turtle and Tortoise Club, Los Angeles, Calif.

Bustard, H. R. 1980. Should sea turtles be exploited? Marine Turtle Newsletter 15:3–5.

Butler, B. O., and T. E. Graham. 1995. Early post-emergent behavior and habitat selection in hatchling Blanding's turtles, *Emydoidea blandingii*, in Massachusetts. Chelonian Conservation and Biology 1:187–196.

Butler, J. A., and E. Shitu. 1985. Uses of some reptiles by the Yoruba people of Nigeria. Herpetological Review 16:15–16.

Butler, M. J., IV, J. H. Hunt, W. F. Herrnkind, M. J. Childress, R. Bertelsen, W. Sharp, T. Matthews, J. M. Field, and H. G. Marshall. 1995. Cascading disturbances in Florida Bay, USA: Cyanobacteria blooms, sponge mortality, and implications for juvenile spiny lobsters *Panulirus argus*. Marine Ecology Progress Series 129:119–125.

Byles, R. 1993. Head-start experiment no longer rearing Kemp's ridleys. Marine Turtle Newsletter 63:1–3.

Caccone, A., M. Milinkovitch, V. Sbordoni, and J. R. Powell. 1997. Phylogeny, biogeography, and molecular rates in European newts (genera *Euproctus* and *Triturus*), inferred from mitochondrial DNA sequences. Systematic Biology 46:126–144.

Cahill, T. 1978. The shame of Escobilla. Outside Magazine (February).

Cahn, A. R. 1937. The Turtles of Illinois. Illinois Biological Monographs 16 (1/2): 1–218.

Caillouet, C. W., Jr. 1995. Egg and hatchling take for the Kemp's ridley headstart experiment. Marine Turtle Newsletter 68:13–15.

Caillouet, C. W., Jr., C. T. Fontaine, S. A. Manzella-Tirpak, and D. J. Shaver. 1995a. Survival of head-started Kemp's ridley sea turtles *(Lepidochelys kempii)* released into the Gulf of Mexico or adjacent bays. Chelonian Conservation and Biology 1:285–292.

Caillouet, C. W., Jr., C. T. Fontaine, S. A. Manzella-Tirpak, and T. D. Williams. 1995b. Growth of head-started Kemp's ridley sea turtles *(Lepidochelys kempii)* following release. Chelonian Conservation and Biology 1:231–234.

Caldwell, D. K. 1960. Sea turtles of the United States. Fishery Leaflet 492. U.S. Fish and Wildlife Service, Washington, D.C.

———. 1963. The sea turtle fishery of Baja California, Mexico. California Fish and Game 49 (3): 140–151.

Caldwell, D. K., and A. Carr. 1957. Status of the sea turtle fishery in Florida. Pages 457–462 in Transactions of the Twenty-Second North American Wildlife Conference, 4–7 March 1957. Wildlife Management Institute, Washington, D.C.

Campbell, L. M. 1997. International conservation and local development: The sustainable use of marine turtles in Costa Rica. Doctoral dissertation, University of Cambridge, United Kingdom.

———. 1998. Use them or lose them? Conservation and the consumptive use of marine turtle eggs at Ostional, Costa Rica. Environmental Conservation 25:305–319.

Cann, J., and J. M. Legler. 1994. The Mary River tortoise: A new genus and species of short-necked chelid from Queensland, Australia (Testudines; Pleurodira). Chelonian Conservation and Biology 1:81–96.

Cantarelli, V. H. 1997. The Amazon turtles—conservation and management in Brazil. Pages 407–410 in J. Van Abbema (ed.). Proceedings: Conservation, Restoration, and Management of Tortoises and Turtles—an International Conference, July 1993, State University of New York at Purchase. New York Turtle and Tortoise Society, New York.

Cantor, T. E. 1847. Catalogue of reptiles inhabiting the Malayan Peninsula and islands. Chelonia. Journal of the Asiatic Society of Bengal 16:607–620. Reprint, A. Asher, Amsterdam, 1966.

Carr, A. F. 1952. Handbook of Turtles: The Turtles of the United States, Canada, and Baja California. Cornell University Press, Ithaca, N.Y.

———. 1954. The passing of the fleet. AIBS (American Institute of Biological Sciences) Bulletin 4 (5): 17–19.

———. 1967. So Excellent a Fishe: A Natural History of Sea Turtles. Natural History Press, Garden City, N.Y.

———. 1972. Great reptiles, great enigmas. Audubon 74 (2): 24–35.

———. 1973. The Everglades. The American Wilderness Series. Time-Life Books, New York.

———. 1979. Encounter at Escobilla. Marine Turtle Newsletter 13:10–13.

———. 1982. Notes on the behavioral ecology of sea turtles. Pages 19–26 in K. A. Bjorndal (ed.). Biology and Conservation of Sea Turtles. Smithsonian Institution Press, Washington, D.C.

———. 1984. The voice of the turtle. Interview by T. Knipe. Calypso Log 11:2–5.

———. 1987a. Impact of nondegradable marine debris on the ecology and survival outlook of sea turtles. Marine Pollution Bulletin 18:352–356.

———. 1987b. New perspectives on the pelagic stage of sea turtle development. Conservation Biology 1:103–121.

Carr, A. F., and M. H. Carr. 1972. Site fixity in the Caribbean green turtle. Ecology 53:425–429.

Carr, A. F., M. H. Carr, and A. B. Meylan. 1978. The ecology and migrations of sea turtles. VII. The West Caribbean green turtle colony. Bulletin of the American Museum of Natural History 162:1–46.

Carr, A. F., and R. M. Ingle. 1959. The green turtle (Chelonia mydas mydas) in Florida. Bulletin of Marine Science of the Gulf and Caribbean 9:315–320.

Carvajal, F. 1956. Relación del descubrimiento del río Apure hasta su ingreso en el Orinoco. Grandes Linros Venezolanos, Caracas.

Castro, Z. 1986. Geografía histórica de la tortuga del Orinoco. Licenciatura thesis, Universidad Central de Venezuela, Caracas.

Caswell, H. 1989. Matrix population models: Construction, analysis, and interpretation. Sinauer, Sunderland, Mass.

Cato, J. C., F. J. Prochaska, and P. C. H. Pritchard. 1978. An analysis of the capture, marketing, and utilization of marine turtles. Report (Contract 01-7-042-11283) to the National Marine Fisheries Service, Environmental Assessment Division, St. Petersburg, Fla.

Caughley, G. 1977. Analysis of Vertebrate Populations. Wiley, New York.

Caughley, G., and A. Gunn. 1996. Conservation Biology in Theory and Practice. Blackwell Scientific Publications, Cambridge, Mass.

Causey, M. K., and C. A. Cude. 1978. Feral dog predation of the gopher tortoise, *Gopherus polyphemus* (Reptilia, Testudines, Testudinidae), in southeast Alabama. Herpetological Review 9:94–95.

Cayot, L. J., H. L. Snell, W. Llerena, and H. M. Snell. 1994. Conservation biology of Galápagos reptiles: Twenty-five years of successful research and management. Pages 297–305 in J. B. Murphy, K. Adler, and J. T. Collins (eds.). Captive Management and Conservation of Amphibians and Reptiles. Society for the Study of Amphibians and Reptiles, Athens, Ohio.

Chan, E. H., and H. C. Liew. 1995. An offshore sanctuary for the leatherback turtles of Rantau Abang, Malaysia. Pages 18–20 in J. I. Richardson and T. H. Richardson (compilers). Proceedings of the Twelfth Annual Workshop on Sea Turtle Biology and Conservation. NOAA Technical Memorandum NMFS-SEFSC-361.

Chan-ard, T., K. Thirakhupt, and P. P. van Dijk. 1996. Observations on *Manouria impressa* at Phu Luang Wildlife Sanctuary, northeastern Thailand. Chelonian Conservation and Biology 2:109–113.

Chapman, J. A., and G. A. Feldhamer (eds.). 1982. Wild Mammals of North America: Biology, Management, and Economics. Johns Hopkins University Press, Baltimore, Md.

Chase, J. D., K. R. Dixon, J. E. Gates, D. Jacobs, and G. J. Taylor. 1989. Habitat characteristics, population size, and home range of the bog turtle, *Clemmys muhlenbergii,* in Maryland. Journal of Herpetology 23:356–362.

Chessman, B. C. 1978. Ecological studies of freshwater turtles in southeastern Australia. Doctoral dissertation, Monash University, Australia.

Chin, L. 1968. Notes on orang-utans, bird ringing project and turtles. Sarawak Museum Journal 16 (32/33): 249–252.

———. 1969. Notes on turtles and orang-utans. Sarawak Museum Journal 17 (34/35): 403–404.

———. 1970. Notes on orang-utan and marine turtles. Sarawak Museum Journal 18 (36/37): 414–415.

———. 1975. Notes on marine turtles *(Chelonia mydas).* Sarawak Museum Journal 23 (44): 259–265.

Choudhury, B. C., and S. Bhupathy. 1993. Turtle trade in India: A study of tortoises and freshwater turtles. World Wildlife Fund-India, New Delhi.

Christiansen, J. L. 1981. Population trends among Iowa's amphibians and reptiles. Proceedings of the Iowa Academy of Science 88:24–27.

Christiansen, J. L., and R. M. Bailey. 1988. The lizards and turtles of Iowa. Iowa Department of Natural Resources, Nongame Technical Series 3:1–19.

Christiansen, J. L., J. A. Cooper, J. W. Bickham, B. J. Gallaway, and M. D. Springer. 1985. Aspects of the natural history of the yellow mud turtle, *Kinosternon flavescens* (Kinosternidae), in Iowa: A proposed endangered species. Southwestern Naturalist 30:413–425.

Christiansen, J. L., and B. J. Gallaway. 1984. Raccoon removal, nesting success, and hatchling emergence in Iowa turtles with special reference to *Kinosternon flavescens* (Kinosternidae). Southwestern Naturalist 29:343–348.

CITES (Convention on International Trade in Endangered Species of Wild Fauna and Flora). 1973. [Text of the Convention.] CITES Secretariat, Châtelaine-Genève, Switzerland. (For more information, go to *www.wcmc.org.uk/CITES.*)

CITES Secretariat. 1995. Ninth meeting of the conference of the parties: Resolution of the conference of the parties. Marine Turtle Newsletter 69:4–8.

———. 1996. Export quotas for 1996. Notification to the parties, no. 916. CITES Secretariat, Châtelaine-Genève, Switzerland.

Clark, C. W. 1976. Mathematical Bioeconomics: The Optimum Management of Renewable Resources. Wiley-Interscience, New York.

Clark, D. B., and J. W. Gibbons. 1969. Dietary shift in the turtle *Pseudemys scripta* (Schoepff) from youth to maturity. Copeia 1969:704–706.

Clark, H. W., and J. B. Southall. 1920. Fresh water turtles: A source of meat supply. U.S. Bureau of Fisheries Document 889:3–20.

Clark, W. S. 1982. Turtles as a food source of nesting bald eagles in the Chesapeake Bay region. Journal of Field Ornithology 53:49–51.

Cliffton, K., D. O. Cornejo, and R. S. Felger. 1982. Sea turtles of the Pacific coast of Mexico. Pages 199–209 *in* K. A. Bjorndal (ed.). Biology and Conservation of Sea Turtles. Smithsonian Institution Press, Washington, D.C.

Coblentz, B. E. 1990. Exotic organisms: A dilemma for conservation biology. Conservation Biology 4:261–265.

Coblentz, B. E., and D. W. Baber. 1987. Biology and control of feral pigs on Isla Santiago, Galápagos, Ecuador. Journal of Applied Ecology 24:403–418.

Coker, R. E. 1906. The natural history and cultivation of the diamondback-terrapin with notes on other forms of turtles. North Carolina Geological Survey Bulletin 14:1–69.

Colborn, T., D. Dumanoski, and J. P. Myers. 1996. Our Stolen Future. Dutton Publishers, New York.

Cole, G. A., and W. L. Minckley. 1966. *Speocirolana thermydronis,* a new species of cirolanid isopod crustacean from central Coahuila, Mexico. Tulane Studies in Zoology 13:17–22.

Collie, J. 1995. Protection of endangered marine turtles in the Republic of Seychelles. Report submitted to United Nations Environment Programme, Nairobi, and University of Adelaide, Adelaide, Australia.

Collins, D. E. 1990. Western New York bog turtles: Relics of ephemeral islands or simply elusive? Pages 151–153 *in* R. S. Mitchell, C. J. Sheviak, and D. J. Leopold (eds.). Ecosystem Management: Rare Species and Significant Habitats. Proceedings of the Fifteenth Annual Natural Areas Conference. New York State Museum Bulletin, no. 471. Albany.

Conant, R. 1951. The Reptiles of Ohio. University of Notre Dame Press, Notre Dame, Ind.

———. 1975. A Field Guide to Reptiles and Amphibians of Eastern and Central North America. Houghton Mifflin, Boston.

Conant, R., and J. T. Collins. 1991. A Field Guide to Reptiles and Amphibians, Eastern and Central North America. 3rd edn. Houghton Mifflin, Boston.

Conant, S. 1988. Saving endangered species by translocation. BioScience 38:254–257.

Congdon, J. D., G. L. Breitenbach, R. C. van Loben Sels, and D. W. Tinkle. 1987. Reproduction and nesting ecology of snapping turtles *(Chelydra serpentina)* in southeastern Michigan. Herpetologica 43:39–54.

Congdon, J. D., and A. E. Dunham. 1994. Contributions of long-term life history studies to conservation biology. Pages 181–182 *in* G. K. Meffe and C. R. Carroll (eds.). Principles of Conservation Biology. Sinauer, Sunderland, Mass.

Congdon, J. D., A. E. Dunham, and R. C. van Loben Sels. 1993. Delayed sexual maturity and demographics of Blanding's turtles *(Emydoidea blandingii)*: Implications for conservation and management of long-lived organisms. Conservation Biology 7:826–833.

———. 1994. Demographics of common snapping turtles *(Chelydra serpentina)*: Implications for conservation and management of long-lived organisms. American Zoologist 34:397–408.

Congdon, J. D., and J. W. Gibbons. 1989. Biomass productivity of turtles in freshwater wetlands: A geographic comparison. Pages 583–592 *in* R. R. Sharitz and J. W. Gibbons (eds.). Freshwater Wetlands and Wildlife. DOE Symposium Series, no. 61. U.S. Department of Energy, Office of Scientific and Technical Information, Oak Ridge, Tenn.

———. 1990. Turtle eggs: Their ecology and evolution. Pages 109–123 *in* J. W. Gibbons (ed.). Life History and Ecology of the Slider Turtle. Smithsonian Institution Press, Washington, D.C.

Congdon, J. D., S. W. Gotte, and R. W. McDiarmid. 1992. Ontogenetic changes in habitat use by juvenile turtles, *Chelydra serpentina* and *Chrysemys picta*. Canadian Field Naturalist 106:241–248.

Congdon, J. D., J. L. Greene, and J. W. Gibbons. 1986. Biomass of freshwater turtles: A geographic comparison. American Midland Naturalist 115:165–173.

Congdon, J. D., D. W. Tinkle, G. L. Breitenbach, and R. C. van Loben Sels. 1983. Nesting ecology and hatching success in the turtle *Emydoidea blandingii*. Herpetologica 39:417–429.

Constable, J. D. 1982. Visit to Vietnam. Oryx 16:249–254.

Conway, W. 1995. Wild and zoo animal interactive management and habitat conservation. Biodiversity and Conservation 4:573–594.

Coombs, E. M. 1974. Utah cooperative desert tortoise study, *Gopherus agassizii*. Report to the Bureau of Land Management, Salt Lake City, Utah, and the Utah Division of Wildlife Resources, Salt Lake City.

———. 1977. Status of the desert tortoise, *Gopherus agassizii*, in the state of Utah. Proceedings of the Desert Tortoise Council 1977:95–101.

Cooper, J. E. 1989. The role of pathogens in threatened populations: An historical review. ICBP (International Council for Bird Preservation) Technical Publication, no. 10.

Cooper, J. E., S. Gschmeissner, and R. D. Bone. 1988. Herpes-like virus particles in necrotic stomatitis of tortoises. Veterinary Record 123:554.

Corn, P. S. 1994. Recent trends of desert tortoise populations in the Mojave Desert. Pages 85–93 *in* R. B. Bury and D. J. Germano (eds.). Biology of North American Tortoises. National Biological Survey, Washington, D.C.

Cornelius, S. E. 1982. Status of sea turtles along the Pacific coast of Middle America. Pages 211–219 *in* K. A. Bjorndal (ed.). Biology and Conservation of Sea Turtles. Smithsonian Institution Press, Washington, D.C.

———. 1985. Update on Ostional. Marine Turtle Newsletter 33:5–8.

Cornelius, S. E., M. Alvarado Ulloa, J. C. Castro, M. Mata del Valle, and D. C. Robinson. 1991. Management of olive ridley sea turtles *(Lepidochelys olivacea)* nesting at Playas Nancite and Ostional, Costa Rica. Pages 111–135 *in* J. G. Robinson and K. H. Redford (eds.). Neotropical Wildlife Use and Conservation. University of Chicago Press, Chicago.

Cornelius S. E., and D. C. Robinson. 1981. Abundance, distribution, and movements of olive ridley sea turtles in Costa Rica. Report (Contract 14-16-0002-80-225) to U.S. Fish and Wildlife Service, Endangered Species Office, Albuquerque, N.Mex.

———. 1982. Abundance, distribution, and movements of olive ridley sea turtles in Costa Rica. Report (Contract 14-16-0002-80-225) to U.S. Fish and Wildlife Service, Endangered Species Office, Albuquerque, N.Mex.

———. 1983. Abundance, distribution, and movements of olive ridley sea turtles in Costa Rica. Report (Contract 14-16-0002-80-225) to U.S. Fish and Wildlife Service, Endangered Species Office, Albuquerque, N.Mex.

———. 1984. Abundance, distribution, and movements of olive ridley sea turtles in Costa Rica, IV. Report to U.S. Fish and Wildlife Service, Endangered Species Office, Albuquerque, N.Mex.

———. 1985. Abundance, distribution, and movements of olive ridley sea turtles in Costa Rica. Report (Contract 14-16-0002-80-225) to U.S. Fish and Wildlife Service, Endangered Species Office, Albuquerque, N.Mex.

Cox, J., D. Inkley, and R. Kautz. 1987. Ecology and habitat protection needs of gopher tortoise (Gopherus polyphemus) populations found on lands slated for large-scale development in Florida. Florida Game and Fresh Water Fish Commission, Nongame Wildlife Program Technical Report 4. Tallahassee.

Crain, D. A., A. Bolten, and K. Bjorndal. 1995. Effects of beach nourishment on sea turtles: Review and research initiatives. Restoration Ecology 3:95–104.

Creighton, M. S. 1995. Rites and Passages: The Experience of American Whaling, 1830–1870. Cambridge University Press, New York.

Crouse, D. T., L. B. Crowder, and H. Caswell. 1987. A stage-based population model for loggerhead sea turtles and implications for conservation. Ecology 68:1412–1423.

Crouse, D. T., and N. B. Frazer. 1995. Population models and structure. Pages 601–603 in K. A. Bjorndal (ed.). Biology and Conservation of Sea Turtles. Rev. edn. Smithsonian Institution Press, Washington, D.C.

Crowder, L. B., S. R. Hopkins-Murphy, and J. A. Royle. 1995. Effects of turtle excluder devices (TEDs) on loggerhead sea turtle strandings with implications for conservation. Copeia 1995:773–779.

Curl, D. 1986. The rarest tortoise on earth. Oryx 20:35–39.

Curl, D. A., I. C. Scoones, M. K. Guy, and G. Rakotoarisoa. 1985. The Madagascan tortoise Geochelone yniphora: Current status and distribution. Biological Conservation 34:35–54.

Curtin, C. G. 1997. Biophysical analysis of the impact of shifting land use on ornate box turtles, Wisconsin, USA. Pages 31–36 in J. Van Abbema (ed.). Proceedings: Conservation, Restoration, and Management of Tortoises and Turtles—an International Conference, July 1993, State University of New York at Purchase. New York Turtle and Tortoise Society, New York.

Dahl, T. E. 1990. Wetlands losses in the United States 1780's to 1980's. U.S. Fish and Wildlife Service, Washington, D.C.

Daly, T. 1990. The development of a regional sea turtle program in the South Pacific. Pages 169–172 in T. H. Richardson, J. I. Richardson, and M. Donnelly (compilers). Proceedings of the Tenth Annual Workshop on Sea Turtle Biology and Conservation. NOAA Technical Memorandum NMFS-SEFSC-278.

Darwin, C. 1845. The Voyage of the Beagle. Reprint, Doubleday, New York, 1962.

Das, I. 1986. The diversity and utilisation of land tortoises in tropical Asia. Tigerpaper 13:18–21.

———. 1990. The trade in freshwater turtles from Bangladesh. Oryx 24:163–166.

———. 1991. Colour Guide to the Turtles and Tortoises of the Indian Subcontinent. R. & A. Publishing, Avon, United Kingdom.

———. 1995. Turtles and Tortoises of India. Oxford University Press, Bombay.

da Silva, E., and M. Blasco. 1995. *Trachemys scripta elegans* in Southwestern Spain. Herpetological Review 26:133–134.

Davenport, J., T. M. Wong, and J. East. 1992. Feeding and digestion in the omnivorous estuarine turtle *Batagur baska* (Gray). Herpetological Journal 2:133–139.

Davis, G. E., and M. C. Whiting. 1977. Loggerhead sea turtle nesting in Everglades National Park, Florida, U.S.A. Herpetologica 33:18–28.

Davis, M. 1981. Aspects of the social and spatial experience of eastern box turtles, *Terrapene carolina carolina*. Doctoral dissertation, University of Tennessee, Knoxville.

Decary, R. 1950. La Faune Malgache. Payot, Paris.

———. 1954. Tortues terrestres de Madagascar. Revue de Madagascar 20 (3me tremestre): 40–44.

DeNardo, D. 1996. Reproductive biology. Pages 212–224 *in* D. R. Mader (ed.). Reptile Medicine and Surgery. W. B. Saunders, Philadelphia.

De Rooij, N. 1915. The Reptiles of the Indo-Australian Archipelago. Lacertilia, Chelonia, Emydosauria. E. J. Brill, Leiden, Netherlands.

De Silva, A. 1995. The status of *Geochelone elegans* in North Western Province of Sri Lanka: Preliminary findings. Pages 47–49 *in* Proceedings International Congress of Chelonian Conservation, July 1995, Gonfaron, France. Editions SOPTOM (Station d'observation et de protectiòn des tortues des maures), Gonfaron, France.

de Silva, G. S. 1982. The status of sea turtle populations in east Malaysia and the South China Sea. Pages 327–337 *in* K. A. Bjorndal (ed.). Biology and Conservation of Sea Turtles. Smithsonian Institution Press, Washington, D.C.

Devaux, B. 1990. Réintroduction de tortues d'Hermann *(Testudo hermanni hermanni)* dans le Massif des Maures. Revue d'Ecologie: La Terre et la Vie 5:291–297.

Dewar, R. E. 1997. Were people responsible for the extinction of Madagascar's subfossils, and how will we ever know? Pages 364–377 *in* S. M. Goodman and B. D. Patterson (eds.). Natural Change and Human Impact in Madagascar. Smithsonian Institution Press, Washington, D.C.

Diamond, J. M. 1984. Historic extinctions: A Rosetta stone for understanding prehistoric extinctions. Pages 824–862 *in* P. S. Martin and R. G. Klein (eds.). Quaternary Extinctions: A Prehistoric Revolution. University of Arizona Press, Tucson.

Díaz del Castillo, B. 1908. The conquest of New Spain. Hakluyt Society of London, new ser., 23.

Dickson, J. G. 1995. Return of wild turkeys. Pages 70–71 *in* E. T. LaRoe, G. S. Farris, C. E. Puckett, P. D. Doran, and M. J. Mac (eds.). Our Living Resources: A Report to the Nation on the Distribution, Abundance, and Health of U.S. Plants, Animals, and Ecosystems. National Biological Survey, Washington, D.C.

Diemer, J. E. 1986. The ecology and management of the gopher tortoise in the southeastern United States. Herpetologica 42:125–133.

———. 1989. *Gopherus polyphemus,* gopher tortoise. Pages 14–16 *in* I. R. Swingland and

M. W. Klemens (eds.). The Conservation Biology of Tortoises. Occasional Papers of the IUCN Species Survival Commission, no. 5. Gland, Switzerland.

———. 1992. Gopher tortoise, *Gopherus polyphemus* (Daudin). Pages 123–127 *in* P. E. Moler (ed.). Rare and Endangered Biota of Florida. Vol. 3, Amphibians and Reptiles. University Press of Florida, Gainesville.

Diemer, J. E., D. R. Jackson, J. L. Landers, J. N. Layne, and D. A. Wood (eds.). 1989. Gopher Tortoise Relocation Symposium Proceedings. Florida Game and Fresh Water Fish Commission, Nongame Wildlife Program Technical Report 5. Gainesville.

Dinerstein, E., G. R. Zug, and J. C. Mitchell. 1987. Notes on the biology of *Melanochelys* (Reptilia, Testudines, Emydidae) in the Terai of Nepal. Journal of the Bombay Natural History Society 84:687–688.

Dixon, J. R., and P. Soini. 1986. The Reptiles of the Upper Amazon Basin, Iquitos Region, Peru. Milwaukee Public Museum, Milwaukee, Wisc.

Doak, D., P. Kareiva, and B. Klepetka. 1994. Modeling population viability for the desert tortoise in the western Mojave Desert. Ecological Applications 4:446–460.

Dobie, J., and F. M. Bagley. 1990. Alabama Red-Bellied Turtle *(Pseudemys alabamensis)* Recovery Plan. U.S. Fish and Wildlife Service, Atlanta, Ga.

Dodd, C. K., Jr. 1982a. Does sea turtle aquaculture benefit conservation? Pages 473–480 *in* K. Bjorndal (ed.). Biology and Conservation of Sea Turtles. Smithsonian Institution Press, Washington, D.C.

———. 1982b. A controversy surrounding an endangered species listing: The case of the Illinois mud turtle. Smithsonian Herpetological Information Service, no. 55. Washington, D.C.

———. 1988. Disease and population declines in the flattened musk turtle *Sternotherus depressus*. American Midland Naturalist 119:394–401.

———. 1990. Effects of habitat fragmentation on a stream-dwelling species, the flattened musk turtle *Sternotherus depressus*. Biological Conservation 54:33–45.

———. 1995. Reptiles and amphibians in the endangered longleaf pine ecosystem. Pages 129–131 *in* E. T. LaRoe, G. S. Farris, C. E. Puckett, P. D. Doran, and M. J. Mac (eds.). Our Living Resources: A Report to the Nation on the Distribution, Abundance, and Health of U.S. Plants, Animals, and Ecosystems. National Biological Survey, Washington, D.C.

Dodd, C. K., Jr., K. M. Enge, and J. N. Stuart. 1988. Aspects of the biology of the flattened musk turtle, *Sternotherus depressus*, in Alabama. Bulletin of the Florida State Museum of Biological Sciences 34:1–64.

———. 1989. Reptiles on highways in north-central Alabama, USA. Journal of Herpetology 23:197–200.

Dodd, C. K., Jr., and R. Seigel. 1991. Relocation, repatriation, and translocation of amphibians and reptiles: Are they conservation strategies that work? Herpetologica 47:336–350.

Domantay, J. S. 1953. The turtle fisheries of the Turtle Islands. Bulletin of the Fisheries Society of the Philippines 3/4:3–27.

Donnelly, M. 1992. Cayman Turtle Farm cited for international trade infractions. Marine Turtle Newsletter 58:12–13.

———. 1994. Sea Turtle Mariculture: A Review of Relevant Information for Conservation and Commerce. Center for Marine Conservation, Washington, D.C.

Doroff, A. M., and L. B. Keith. 1990. Demography and ecology of an ornate box turtle *(Terrapene ornata)* population in south-central Wisconsin. Copeia 1990:387–399.

Drake, D. L. 1996. Marine turtle nesting, nest predation, hatch frequency, and nesting seasonality on the Osa Peninsula, Costa Rica. Chelonian Conservation and Biology 2:89–92.

Dunn, E. R. 1917. Reptile and amphibian collections from the North Carolina mountains, with especial reference to salamanders. Bulletin of the American Museum of Natural History 37:593–634.

Dunson, W. A. 1960. Aquatic respiration in *Trionyx spinifer asper.* Herpetologica 16:277–283.

Dunson, W. A., and H. Heatwole. 1986. Effect of relative shell size in turtles on water and electrolyte composition. American Journal of Physiology 250:R1133–R1137.

Dunson, W. A., and E. O. Moll. 1980. Osmoregulation in sea water of hatchling emydid turtles, *Callagur borneoensis,* from a Malaysian sea beach. Journal of Herpetology 14:31–36.

Dunson, W. A., and M. E. Seidel. 1986. Salinity tolerance of estuarine and insular emydid turtles *(Pseudemys nelsoni* and *Trachemys decussata).* Journal of Herpetology 20:237–245.

Durbin, J., V. Rajafetra, D. Reid, and D. Razandrizanakanirina. 1996. Local people and Project Angonoka—conservation of the ploughshare tortoise in north-western Madagascar. Oryx 30:113–120.

Durrell, L., B. Groombridge, S. Tonge, and Q. Bloxam. 1989a. *Acinixys planicauda,* Madagascar flat-tailed tortoise, Kapidolo. Pages 94–95 *in* I. R. Swingland and M. W. Klemens (eds.). The Conservation Biology of Tortoises. Occasional Papers of the IUCN Species Survival Commission, no. 5. Gland, Switzerland.

———. 1989b. *Geochelone radiata,* radiated tortoise, Sokake. Pages 96–98 *in* I. R. Swingland and M. W. Klemens (eds.). The Conservation Biology of Tortoises. Occasional Papers of the IUCN Species Survival Commission, no. 5. Gland, Switzerland.

———. 1989c. *Geochelone yniphora,* ploughshare tortoise, plowshare tortoise, angulated tortoise, angonoka. Pages 99–102 *in* I. R. Swingland and M. W. Klemens (eds.). The Conservation Biology of Tortoises. Occasional Papers of the IUCN Species Survival Commission, no. 5. Gland, Switzerland.

———. 1989d. *Pyxis arachnoides,* Madagascar spider tortoise; Tsakafy; Kapila. Pages 103–104 *in* I. R. Swingland and M. W. Klemens (eds.). The Conservation Biology of Tortoises. Occasional Papers of the IUCN Species Survival Commission, no. 5. Gland, Switzerland.

Eckert, K. L. 1993. The Biology and Population Status of Marine Turtles in the North Pacific Ocean. NOAA Technical Memorandum NMFS-SWFSC-186.

———. 1995. Anthropogenic threats to sea turtles. Pages 611–612 *in* K. A. Bjorndal (ed.). Biology and Conservation of Sea Turtles. Rev. edn. Smithsonian Institution Press, Washington, D.C.

Eckert, S. A., D. Crouse, L. B. Crowder, M. Maceina, and A. Shah. 1994. Review of the Kemp's ridley sea turtle headstart program. NOAA Technical Memorandum NMFS-OPR-3.

Egypt. 1994. *Testudo kleinmanni* from Appendix II to Appendix I. Conference of the Parties 9. CITES Secretariat, Châtelaine-Genève, Switzerland.

Ehrenfeld, D. W. 1974. Conserving the edible sea turtle: Can mariculture help? American Scientist 62:23–31.

————. 1980. Commercial breeding of captive sea turtles: Status and prospects. Pages 93–96 in J. B. Murphy and J. T. Collins (eds.). Reproductive Biology and Diseases of Captive Reptiles. Society for the Study of Amphibians and Reptiles, Athens, Ohio.

————. 1982. Options and limitations in the conservation of sea turtles. Pages 457–463 in K. A. Bjorndal (ed.). Biology and Conservation of Sea Turtles. Smithsonian Institution Press, Washington, D.C.

————. 1991. The management of diversity: A conservation paradox. Pages 26–39 in F. H. Bormann and S. R. Kellert (eds.). Ecology, Economics, Ethics: The Broken Circle. Yale University Press, New Haven, Conn.

Ehrlich, P. R. 1989. Attributes of invaders and the invading processes: Vertebrates. Pages 315–328 in J. A. Drake, M. A. Mooney, F. di Castri, R. H. Groves, F. J. Kruger, M. Rejmánek, and M. Williamson (eds.). Biological Invasions: A Global Perspective. Wiley, New York.

Ehrlich, P. R., and A. H. Ehrlich. 1981. Extinction: The Causes and Consequences of the Disappearance of Species. Random House, New York.

Eley, T. J. 1989. Sea turtles and the Kiwai, Papua New Guinea. Pages 49–51 in S. A. Eckert, K. L. Eckert, and T. H. Richardson (compilers). Proceedings of the Ninth Annual Workshop on Sea Turtle Biology and Conservation. NOAA Technical Memorandum NMFS-SEFSC-232.

Ernst, C. H. 1970. Reproduction in Clemmys guttata. Herpetologica 26:228–232.

Ernst, C. H., and R. W. Barbour. 1989. Turtles of the World. Smithsonian Institution Press, Washington, D.C.

Ernst, C. H., J. E. Lovich, and R. W. Barbour. 1994. Turtles of the United States and Canada. Smithsonian Institution Press, Washington, D.C.

Ernst, C. H., and J. F. McBreen. 1991. Wood turtle, Clemmys insculpta (Le Conte). Pages 455–457 in K. Terwilliger (coordinator). Virginia's Endangered Species. McDonald & Woodward Publishing, Blacksburg, Va.

Ernst, C. H., and B. S. McDonald, Jr. 1989. Preliminary report on enhanced growth and early maturity in a Maryland population of painted turtles, Chrysemys picta. Bulletin of the Maryland Herpetological Society 25:135–142.

Espenshade, W. H., and J. Buskirk. 1994. Manouria impressa (Günther 1882): A summary of known and anecdotal information. Tortuga Gazette 30 (5): 1–5.

Ewert, M. A. 1979. The embryo and its egg: Development and natural history. Pages 333–416 in M. Harless and H. Morlock (eds.). Turtles: Perspectives and Research. Wiley, New York.

————. 1985. Embryology of turtles. Pages 75–267 in C. Gans, F. Billett, and P. F. A. Maderson (eds.). Biology of the Reptilia. Vol. 14, Development A. Wiley, New York.

Ewert, M. A., and D. R. Jackson. 1994. Nesting ecology of the alligator snapping turtle, Macroclemys temminckii, along the lower Apalachicola River, Florida. Florida Game and Fresh Water Fish Commission, Nongame Wildlife Program Final Report. Tallahassee.

Ewert, M. A., D. R. Jackson, and C. E. Nelson. 1994. Patterns of temperature-dependent sex determination in turtles. Journal of Experimental Zoology 270:3–15.

Ewert, M. A., and C. E. Nelson. 1991. Sex determination in turtles: Diverse patterns and some possible adaptive values. Copeia 1991:50–69.

Fachin-Teran, A., R. C. Vogt, and M. D. S. Gomez. 1995. Food habits of an assemblage of five species of turtles in the Rio Guapore, Rondônia, Brazil. Journal of Herpetology 29:536–547.

Feehan, T. 1986. Turtle trade controversy re-ignited. TRAFFIC-USA 7:4–5.

Felger, R. S., and K. Cliffton. 1977. Conservation of the Sea Turtles of the Pacific Coast of Mexico. International Union for Conservation of Nature and Natural Resources and World Wide Fund for Nature, project no. 1471. Gland, Switzerland.

Ferreira, A. R. 1786. Viagem filosófica pelas capitanías do Grâo Pará, Rio Negro, Mato Grosso, e Cuibá, Memorias: Zoología, Botánica. Reprint, Conselho Federal de Cultura, Rio de Janeiro, 1972.

Fitch, H. S., and M. V. Plummer. 1975. A preliminary ecological study of the soft-shelled turtle *Trionyx muticus* in the Kansas River. Israel Journal of Zoology 24:28–42.

Fitzgerald, S. 1989. International Wildlife Trade: Whose Business Is It? World Wildlife Fund, Washington, D.C.

Fitzsimmons, N. N., A. D. Tucker, and C. J. Limpus. 1995. Long-term breeding histories of male green turtles and fidelity to a breeding ground. Marine Turtle Newsletter 68:2–4.

Flaherty, N., and J. R. Bider. 1984. Physical structures and the social factor as determinants of habitat use by *Graptemys geographica* in southwestern Quebec. American Midland Naturalist 111:259–266.

Forman, R. T. T., and M. Godron. 1981. Patches and structural components for a landscape ecology. BioScience 31:733–740.

Formanowicz, D. R., Jr., E. D. Brodie, Jr., and S. C. Wise. 1989. Foraging behavior of matamata turtles: The effects of prey density and the presence of a conspecific. Herpetologica 45:61–67.

Fosdick, P., and S. Fosdick. 1994. Last Chance Lost? Can and Should Farming Save the Green Sea Turtle? The Story of Mariculture, Ltd.—Cayman Turtle Farm. Irvin S. Naylor, York, Pa.

Fowler, L. E. 1979. Hatching success and nest predation in the green sea turtle, *Chelonia mydas*, at Tortuguero, Costa Rica. Ecology 60:946–955.

Frazer, N. B. 1989. Recent IUCN resolution less than ideal. Marine Turtle Newsletter 46:2–3.

———. 1992. Sea turtle conservation and halfway technology. Conservation Biology 6:179–184.

———. 1994. Sea turtle headstarting and hatchery programs. Pages 374–380 *in* G. K. Meffe and C. R. Carroll (eds.). Principles of Conservation Biology. Sinauer, Sunderland, Mass.

Frazer, N. B., J. W. Gibbons, and J. L. Greene. 1990. Life tables of a slider turtle population. Pages 183–200 *in* J. W. Gibbons (ed.). Life History and Ecology of the Slider Turtle. Smithsonian Institution Press, Washington, D.C.

———. 1991. Life history of the common mud turtle *Kinosternon subrubrum* in South Carolina, USA. Ecology 72:2218–2231.

Frazier, J. 1974. Sea turtles in Seychelles. Biological Conservation 6:71–73.

———. 1975. Marine turtles of the western Indian Ocean. Oryx 13:164–175.

———. 1979. Marine turtle management in Seychelles: A case-study. Environmental Conservation 6:225–230.

———. 1981. Oaxaca, 1980. Marine Turtle Newsletter 18:4–5.

———. 1982a. Subsistence hunting in the Indian Ocean. Pages 391–396 *in* K. A. Bjorndal (ed.). Biology and Conservation of Sea Turtles. Smithsonian Institution Press, Washington, D.C.

———. 1982b. Status of sea turtles in the central western Indian Ocean. Pages 385–389 *in* K. A. Bjorndal (ed.). Biology and Conservation of Sea Turtles. Smithsonian Institution Press, Washington, D.C.

———. 1987. Chelonians. The India Magazine 7 (10): 42–45, 47–49, 51.

Freeman-Grenville, G. S. P. 1962. The East Africa Coast: Select Documents from the First to the Earlier Nineteenth Century. Oxford University Press, New York.

Fritts, T. H., and R. D. Jennings. 1994. Distribution, habitat use, and status of the desert tortoise in Mexico. Pages 48–56 *in* R. B. Bury and D. J. Germano (eds.). Biology of North American Tortoises. National Biological Survey, Washington, D.C.

Fugler, C. M. 1984. The commercially exploited Chelonia of Bangladesh: Taxonomy, ecology, reproductive biology and ontogeny. Bangladesh Fisheries Information Bulletin 2:1–52.

Fuller, M. R., C. J. Henny, and P. B. Wood. 1995. Raptors. Pages 65–69 *in* E. T. LaRoe, G. S. Farris, C. E. Puckett, P. D. Doran, and M. J. Mac (eds.). Our Living Resources: A Report to the Nation on the Distribution, Abundance, and Health of U.S. Plants, Animals, and Ecosystems. National Biological Survey, Washington, D.C.

Gadgil, M., F. Berkes, and C. Folke. 1993. Indigenous knowledge for biodiversity conservation. Ambio 22:151–156.

Galat, D. L., J. W. Robinson, and L. W. Hesse. 1996. Restoring aquatic resources to the Lower Missouri River: Issues and initiatives. Pages 49–71 *in* D. L. Galat and A. G. Frazer (eds.). Overview of River–Floodplain Ecology in the Upper Mississippi River Basin. Vol. 3 of Science for Floodplain Management into the Twenty-First Century (J. A. Kelmelis, ser. ed.). U.S. Government Printing Office, Washington, D.C.

Galbraith, D. A., B. N. White, R. J. Brooks, J. H. Kaufmann, and P. T. Boag. 1995. DNA fingerprinting of turtles. Journal of Herpetology 29:285–291.

Gans, C. 1961. The feeding mechanism of snakes and its possible evolution. American Zoologist 1:217–227.

Garber, S. D. 1988. Diamondback terrapin exploitation. Plastron Papers (New York Turtle and Tortoise Society) 17:18–22.

Garber, S. D., and J. Burger. 1995. A 20-yr study documenting the relationship between turtle decline and human recreation. Ecological Applications 5:1151–1162.

Gariboldi, A., and M. A. L. Zuffi. 1994. Notes on the population reinforcement project for *Emys orbicularis* (Linnaeus, 1758) in a natural park of northwestern Italy (Testudines: Emydidae). Herpetozoa 7:83–89.

Garrott, R. A., P. J. White, and C. A. V. White. 1993. Overabundance: An issue for conservation biologists? Conservation Biology 7:946–949.

Gasith, A., and I. Sidis. 1984. Polluted water bodies, the main habitat of the Caspian terrapin *(Mauremys caspica rivulata)* in Israel. Copeia 1984:216–219.

Gates, C. E., R. A. Valverde, C. L. Mo, A. C. Chaves, J. Ballestero, and J. Peskin. 1996. Estimating *arribada* size using a modified instantaneous count procedure. Journal of Agricultural, Biological, and Environmental Statistics 1:275–287.

Geffen, E., and H. Mendelssohn. 1989. Activity patterns and thermoregulatory behavior of the Egyptian tortoise *Testudo kleinmanni* in Israel. Journal of Herpetology 23:404–409.

———. 1997. Avian predation on tortoises in Israel. Page 105 *in* J. Van Abbema (ed.). Proceedings: Conservation, Restoration, and Management of Tortoises and Turtles— an International Conference, July 1993, State University of New York at Purchase. New York Turtle and Tortoise Society, New York.

George, G. 1990. Status and conservation of *Graptemys barbouri, Graptemys flavimaculata, Graptemys oculifera,* and *Graptemys caglei.* Pages 24–30 *in* K. R. Beaman, F. Caporaso, S. McKeown, and M. D. Graff (eds.). Proceedings of the First International Symposium on Turtles and Tortoises: Conservation and Captive Husbandry. California Turtle and Tortoise Club, Los Angeles, Calif.

George, R. H. 1997. Health problems and diseases of sea turtles. Pages 363–385 *in* P. L. Lutz and J. A. Musick (eds.). The Biology of Sea Turtles. CRC Press, Boca Raton, Fla.

Georges, A. 1982. Diet of the freshwater turtle *Emydura krefftii* (Chelonia, Chelidae) in an unproductive lentic environment. Copeia 1982:331–336.

———. 1993. Setting conservation priorities for Australian freshwater turtles. Pages 49–58 *in* D. Lunney and D. Ayers (eds.). Herpetology in Australia—a Diverse Discipline. Transactions of the Royal Zoological Society of New South Wales, Mosmon.

Georges, A., and R. Kennett. 1989. Dry-season distribution and ecology of *Carettochelys insculpta* (Chelonia: Carettochelyidae) in Kakadu National Park, Northern Australia. Australian Wildlife Research 16:323–335.

Georges, A., and M. Rose. 1993. Conservation biology of the pig-nosed turtle, *Carettochelys insculpta.* Chelonian Conservation and Biology 1:3–12.

Ghirotti, M., and B. Mwanaumo. 1989. *Amblyomma marmoreum* on tortoises of Southern Province, Zambia. Journal of Wildlife Diseases 25 (4): 634–635.

Gibbons, J. W. 1967. Variation in growth rates in three populations of the painted turtle *Chrysemys picta.* Herpetologica 23:296–303.

———. 1970a. Reproductive dynamics of a turtle *(Pseudemys scripta)* population in a reservoir receiving heated effluent from a nuclear reactor. Canadian Journal of Zoology 48:881–885.

———. 1970b. Terrestrial activity and the population dynamics of aquatic turtles. American Midland Naturalist 83:404–414.

———. 1983. Reproductive characteristics and ecology of the mud turtle *Kinosternon subrubrum.* Herpetologica 38:254–271.

———. 1987. Why do turtles live so long? BioScience 37:262–269.

Gibbons, J. W. (ed.). 1990a. Life History and Ecology of the Slider Turtle. Smithsonian Institution Press, Washington, D.C.

Gibbons, J. W. 1990b. Turtle studies at SREL: A research perspective. Pages 19–44 *in* J. W. Gibbons (ed.). Life History and Ecology of the Slider Turtle. Smithsonian Institution Press, Washington, D.C.

Gibbons, J. W., J. L. Greene, and J. D. Congdon. 1983. Drought-related responses of aquatic turtle populations. Journal of Herpetology 17:242–246.

Gibbons, J. W., and J. E. Lovich. 1990. Sexual dimorphism in turtles with emphasis on the slider turtle *(Trachemys scripta).* Herpetological Monographs 4:1–28.

Gibbons, J. W., and D. H. Nelson. 1978. The evolutionary significance of delayed emergence from the nest by hatchling turtles. Evolution 32:297–303.

Gibbons, J. W., R. D. Semlitsch, J. L. Greene, and J. P. Schubauer. 1981. Variation in age and size at maturity of the slider turtle *(Pseudemys scripta).* American Naturalist 117:841–845.

Gibbs, J. P. 1993. Importance of small wetlands for the persistence of local populations of wetland associated animals. Wetlands 13:25–31.

Gilpin, M. E., and M. E. Soulé. 1986. Minimum viable populations: Processes of species extinction. Pages 19–34 in M. E. Soulé (ed.). Conservation Biology: The Science of Scarcity and Diversity. Sinauer, Sunderland, Mass.

Girgis, S. 1961. Aquatic respiration in the common Nile turtle, Trionyx triunguis (Forskal). Comparative Biochemistry and Physiology 3:206–217.

Glazebrook, J. S., and R. S. F. Campbell. 1990a. A survey of the diseases of marine turtles in northern Australia. II. Oceanarium-reared and wild turtles. Diseases of Aquatic Organisms 9:97–104.

———. 1990b. A survey of the diseases of marine turtles in northern Australia. I. Farmed turtles. Diseases of Aquatic Organisms 9:83–95.

Gonzalez-Gonzalez, J. 1993. Réunion Island—still a land of tortoises. Chelonian Conservation and Biology 1:51–52.

Goodman, S. M., M. Pidgeon, and S. O'Connor. 1994. Mass mortality of Madagascar radiated tortoise caused by road construction. Oryx 28:115–118.

Goodrich, J. M., and S. W. Buskirk. 1995. Control of abundant native vertebrates for conservation of endangered species. Conservation Biology 9:1357–1364.

Gordon, A. N., W. R. Kelly, and R. J. G. Lester. 1993. Epizootic mortality of free-living green turtles, Chelonia mydas, due to coccidiosis. Journal of Wildlife Diseases 29 (3): 490–494.

Graham, T. E. 1995. Habitat use and population parameters of the spotted turtle, Clemmys guttata, a species of special concern in Massachusetts. Chelonian Conservation and Biology 1:207–214.

Grand, J., and S. R. Beissinger. 1997. When relocation of loggerhead sea turtle (Caretta caretta) nests becomes a useful strategy. Journal of Herpetology 31:428–434.

Grassman, M. A., D. W. Owens, J. P. McVey, and R. Márquez M. 1984. Olfactory-based orientation in artificially imprinted sea turtles. Science (Washington, D.C.) 224:83–84.

Gray, E. M. 1995. DNA fingerprinting reveals a lack of genetic variation in northern populations of the western pond turtle (Clemmys marmorata). Conservation Biology 9:1244–1255.

Great Britain. Public Record Office. 1889, 1893, 1898. Calendar of State Papers, Colonial Series, American and West Indies, vols. 7, 9, 11. London.

Green, D., and F. Ortiz-Crespo. 1982. Status of sea turtle populations in the central eastern Pacific. Pages 221–233 in K. A. Bjorndal (ed.). Biology and Conservation of Sea Turtles. Smithsonian Institution Press, Washington, D.C.

Greir, J. W. 1990. Population dynamics modeling, version 4.5. North Dakota State University, Fargo, N.Dak.

Griffith, B., J. M. Scott, J. W. Carpenter, and C. Reed. 1989. Translocation as a species conservation tool: Status and strategy. Science (Washington, D.C.) 245:477–480.

Groombridge, B. 1990. Marine turtles in the Mediterranean: Distribution, population status, conservation. Council of Europe Environmental Conservation and Management Division, Nature and Environment Series 48. Strasbourg, France.

Groombridge, B., and R. Luxmoore. 1989. The Green Turtle and Hawksbill (Reptilia: Cheloniidae): World Status, Exploitation and Trade. CITES (Convention on International Trade in Endangered Species of Wild Fauna and Flora) Secretariat, Châtelaine-Genève, Switzerland.

Groombridge, B., E. O. Moll, and J. Vijaya. 1983. Rediscovery of a rare Indian turtle. Oryx 17:130–134.

Groombridge, B., and L. Wright. 1982. The IUCN Amphibia–Reptilia Red Data Book.

Pt. 1, Testudines, Crocodylia, Rhynchocephalia. International Union for Conservation of Nature and Natural Resources, Gland, Switzerland.

Groves, R. H., and W. D. L. Ride. 1982. Species at Risk: Research in Australia. Springer-Verlag, Berlin.

Gumilla, P. J. 1741. El Orinoco ilustrado y defendido. Reprint, Biblioteca de la Academia Nacional de Historia, Caracas, 1993.

Gutzke, W. H. N., G. C. Packard, M. J. Packard, and T. J. Boardman. 1987. Influence of the hydric and thermal environment on eggs and hatchlings of painted turtles (Chrysemys picta). Herpetologica 43:393–404.

Guyot, G., and J. Clobert. 1996. Conservation measures for a population of Hermann's tortoise Testudo hermanni in southern France bisected by a major highway. Biological Conservation 79:251–256.

Hall, E. R. 1981. The Mammals of North America, vols. 1 and 2. Wiley, New York.

Hambler, C. 1994. Giant tortoise Geochelone gigantea translocation to Curieuse Island (Seychelles): Success or failure? Biological Conservation 69:293–299.

Hanfee, F. 1995. Notes on freshwater turtle exploitation, Uttar Pradesh, India. TRAFFIC Bulletin 15 (3): 120–121.

Hardin, G. 1968. The tragedy of the commons. Science (Washington, D.C.) 162:1234–1248.

———. 1994. The tragedy of the unmanaged commons. Trends in Ecology and Evolution 9:199.

Harding, J. H., and T. J. Bloomer. 1979. The wood turtle, Clemmys insculpta: A natural history. Herp (Bulletin of the New York Herpetological Society) 15:9–26.

Harding, J. H., and J. A. Holman. 1990. Michigan Turtles and Lizards: A Field Guide and Pocket Reference. Michigan State University, Cooperative Extension Service, East Lansing, Mich.

Harrel, J. B., C. M. Allen, and S. J. Hebert. 1996. Movements and habitat use of subadult alligator snapping turtles (Macroclemys temminckii) in Louisiana. American Midland Naturalist 135:60–67.

Harris, L. D. 1984. The Fragmented Forest, Island Biogeography Theory and the Preservation of Biotic Diversity. University of Chicago Press, Chicago.

Harris, L. D., and P. Kangas. 1988. Reconsideration of the habitat concept. Pages 137–144 in Transactions of the Fifty-Third North American Wildlands and Natural Resources Conference.

Harris, L. D., and G. Silva-Lopez. 1992. Forest fragmentation and the conservation of biological diversity. Pages 197–237 in P. L. Fiedler and S. K. Jain (eds.). Conservation Biology: The Theory and Practice of Nature Conservation, Preservation, and Management. Chapman and Hall, New York.

Harrisson, T. 1951. The edible green turtle (Chelonia mydas) in Borneo. Pt. I. Breeding season. Sarawak Museum Journal 5 (3): 593–596.

———. 1954–59. The edible green turtle (Chelonia mydas) in Borneo, pts. II–VIII. Sarawak Museum Journal 6, no. 4 (1954): 126–128; 6, no. 6 (1955): 633–640; 7, no. 7 (1956): 233–239; 7, no. 8 (1956): 504–514; 8, no. 11 (1958): 481–486; 8, no. 12 (1958): 772–774; 9, nos. 13/14 (1959): 277–278.

———. 1962a. Notes on the green turtle (Chelonia mydas). Pt. XI. West Borneo numbers, the downward trend. Sarawak Museum Journal 10:614–623.

———. 1962b. Present and future of the green turtle. Oryx 6:1–11.

————. 1962c. Notes on the green turtle *(Chelonia mydas)*. Pt. XII. Monthly laying cycles. Sarawak Museum Journal 10:624–630.

————. 1964. Notes on marine turtles. Pt. XV. Sabah's Turtle Islands. Sarawak Museum Journal 11 (23/24): 624–627.

————. 1966. Notes on marine turtles. Pt. XVII. Sabah and Sarawak islands compared. Sarawak Museum Journal 14 (28/29): 335–340.

————. 1967. Notes on marine turtles. Pt. XVIII. A report on the Sarawak turtle industry with recommendations for the future. Sarawak Museum Journal 15 (30/31): 424–436.

Hart, D. R. 1983. Dietary and habitat shift with size of red-eared turtles *(Pseudemys scripta)* in a southern Louisiana population. Herpetologica 39:285–290.

Hays Brown, C., and W. M. Brown. 1982. Status of sea turtles in the southeastern Pacific: Emphasis on Peru. Pages 235–240 *in* K. A. Bjorndal (ed.). Biology and Conservation of Sea Turtles. Smithsonian Institution Press, Washington, D.C.

Helwig, D. D., and M. E. Hora. 1983. Polychlorinated biphenyl, mercury, and cadmium concentrations in Minnesota snapping turtles. Bulletin of Environmental Contamination and Toxicology 30:186–190.

Hendrickson, J. R. 1958. The green sea turtle, *Chelonia mydas* (Linn.), in Malaya and Sarawak. Proceedings of the Zoological Society of London 130:455–535.

Heppell, S. S., and L. B. Crowder. 1994. Is headstarting headed in the right direction? Pages 77–81 *in* B. A. Schroeder and B. E. Witherington (compilers). Proceedings of the Thirteenth Annual Workshop on Sea Turtle Biology and Conservation. NOAA Technical Memorandum NMFS-SEFSC-341.

Heppell, S. S., L. B. Crowder, and D. T. Crouse. 1996. Models to evaluate headstarting as a management tool for long-lived turtles. Ecological Applications 6:556–565.

Herbst, L. H. 1994. Fibropapillomatosis of marine turtles. Annual Review of Fish Disease 4:389–425.

Herbst, L. H., E. R. Jacobson, R. Moretti, T. Brown, J. P. Sundberg, and P. A. Brown. 1995. Experimental transmission of green turtle fibropapillomatosis using cell-free tumor extracts. Diseases of Aquatic Organisms 22(1).

Heriarte, M. 1662. Descricam do Estado do Maranham, Para, Corupa, Rio das Amazonas. Reprint, Akademische Druck, Austria, 1964.

Herman, D. W. 1994. The bog turtle, *Clemmys muhlenbergii,* in North Carolina: An action plan for its conservation and management. Final Report (1993 Nongame Wildlife Program Small Grant Contract 93 SG 06) to the North Carolina Wildlife Resources Commission. Raleigh, N.C.

Herman, D. W., and B. W. Tryon. 1997. Land use, development, and natural succession and their effects on bog turtle habitat in the southeastern United States. Pages 364–371 *in* J. Van Abbema (ed.). Proceedings: Conservation, Restoration, and Management of Tortoises and Turtles—an International Conference, July 1993, State University of New York at Purchase. New York Turtle and Tortoise Society, New York.

Highfield, A. C., and J. R. Bayley. 1995. Environmental and tourist impacts upon *Testudo graeca graeca* in Morocco: An integrated approach to habitat modification and education. Pages 107–109 *in* Proceedings International Congress of Chelonian Conservation, July 1995, Gonfaron, France. Editions SOPTOM (Station d'observation et de protectiòn des tortues des maures), Gonfaron, France.

Hildebrand, S. F. 1929. Review of experiments on artificial culture of diamond-back terrapin. Bulletin of the U.S. Bureau of Fisheries 45:25–70.

Hildebrand, S. F., and C. Hatsel. 1926. Diamond-back terrapin culture at Beaufort, N.C. U.S. Bureau of Fisheries, Economic Circular 60:1–20.

Hirth, H., and A. Carr. 1970. The green turtle in the Gulf of Aden and the Seychelles Islands. Verhandelingen der Koninklijke Nederlandse Akademie Van Wetenschappen 58 (5): 1–44.

Holland, D. C. 1994. The western pond turtle: Habitat and history. U.S. Department of Energy, Bonneville Power Administration, Portland, Oreg.

Holland, F. 1996. It moves? Sell it. BBC Wildlife (August): 4.

Honegger, R. E. 1979. Red Data Book. Vol. 3, Amphibia and Reptilia. International Union for Conservation of Nature and Natural Resources, Gland, Switzerland.

———. 1980. Reptilia, Amphibia, Pisces. Order Testudinata/Family Testudinidae. Vol. 3 of Identification Manual. International Union for Conservation of Nature and Natural Resources, Gland, Switzerland.

———. 1981. List of amphibians and reptiles either known or thought to have become extinct since 1600. Biological Conservation 19:141–158.

Hoogmoed, M. S., and C. R. Crumly. 1984. Land tortoise types in the Rijksmuseum van Natuurlijke Historie with comments on nomenclature and systematics (Reptilia: Testudines: Testudinidae). Zoologische Mededelingen Leiden 58 (15): 241–259.

Hornell, J. 1927. The Turtle Fisheries of the Seychelles Islands. His Majesty's Stationery Office, London.

Houseal, T. W., J. W. Bickham, and M. D. Springer. 1982. Geographic variation in the yellow mud turtle, *Kinosternon flavescens*. Copeia 1982:567–580.

HSUS (Humane Society of the United States). 1994. Preliminary Report: Live Freshwater Turtle and Tortoise Trade in the United States. Humane Society of the United States, Washington, D.C.

———. 1996. Proposal to US to propose inclusion of *Macroclemys temminckii* in Appendix II, in accordance with Article II 2(a). Humane Society of the United States, Washington, D.C.

Huff, J. A. 1989. Florida (USA) terminates 'headstart' program. Marine Turtle Newsletter 46:1–2.

Hughes, G. R. 1973. The survival situation of the hawksbill sea-turtle *(Eretmochelys imbricata)* in Madagascar. Biological Conservation 5:114–118.

———. 1975. Fano! The sea turtle in Madagascar. Defenders 50:159–163.

———. 1982. Conservation of sea turtles in the southern Africa region. Pages 397–404 *in* K. A. Bjorndal (ed.). Biology and Conservation of Sea Turtles. Smithsonian Institution Press, Washington, D.C.

———. 1989. Sea turtles. Pages 230–243 *in* A. I. L. Payne and R. J. M. Crawford (eds.). Oceans of Life off South Africa. Vlaeberg Publishers, Cape Town.

Humboldt, A. von. 1859. Von Orinoko zum Amazonas, Reise in die Äquinoktial-Gegenden des neuen Kontinents. F. A. Brockhaus, Wiesbaden, Germany.

———. 1861–62. Reise in die Aequinoctial-Gegenden des neuen Continents. Vol. 3. Translated into German by Hermann Hauff. J. G. Cotta'scher Verlag, Stuttgart, Germany.

Humphrey, S. L., and R. V. Salm (eds.). 1996. Status of sea turtle conservation in the western Indian Ocean. Regional Seas Reports and Studies, no. 165. International Union for Conservation of Nature and Natural Resources, East African Office, and the United Nations Environment Programme, Nairobi.

Hunter, M. L., Jr. 1996. Fundamentals of Conservation Biology. Blackwell Scientific Publications, Cambridge, Mass.

Hurtado G., M. 1982. The ban on the exportation of turtle skin from Ecuador. Marine Turtle Newsletter 20:1–4.

Hutchins, M., and W. Conway. 1996. Beyond Noah's Ark: The evolving role of modern zoological parks and aquariums in field conservation. International Zoo Yearbook 34:117–130.

Hutton, T. 1837. Geometric tortoises, *Testudo geometrica*. Journal of the Asiatic Society of Bengal 6:689–696.

IBAMA (Instituto Brasileiro do Meio Ambiente e dos Recursos Naturais Renováveis). 1989. Projeto quelônios da Amazonia—10 anos. Instituto Brasileiro do Meio Ambiente e dos Recursos Naturais Renováveis, Brasília, Brasil.

Ingle, R. M., and F. G. W. Smith. 1949. Sea Turtles and the Turtle Industry of the West Indies, Florida and the Gulf of Mexico, with Annotated Bibliography. University of Miami Press, Miami.

Inozemtsev, A. A., and S. L. Pereshkolnik. 1994. Status and conservation prospects of *Testudo graeca* L. inhabiting the Black Sea coast of the Caucasus. Chelonian Conservation and Biology 2:151–158.

Inskipp, T., and H. Corrigan (eds.). 1992. Review of Significant Trade in Animal Species Included in CITES Appendix II: Detailed Reviews of 24 Priority Species. World Conservation Monitoring Centre, Cambridge, United Kingdom.

IUCN (International Union for Conservation of Nature and Natural Resources). 1989. Tortoises and freshwater turtles, an action plan for their conservation. International Union for Conservation of Nature and Natural Resources, Species Survival Commission, Tortoise and Freshwater Turtle Specialist Group, Gland, Switzerland.

———. 1995. A global strategy for the conservation of marine turtles. International Union for Conservation of Nature and Natural Resources, Gland, Switzerland.

———. 1996. 1996 IUCN Red List of Threatened Animals. International Union for Conservation of Nature and Natural Resources, Gland, Switzerland.

Iverson, J. B. 1979. A taxonomic reappraisal of the yellow mud turtle, *Kinosternon flavescens* (Testudines: Kinosternidae). Copeia 1979:212–225.

———. 1982. Biomass in turtle populations: A neglected subject. Oecologia (Berlin) 55:69–76.

———. 1990. Nesting and parental care in the mud turtle, *Kinosternon flavescens*. Canadian Journal of Zoology 68:230–233.

———. 1991a. Patterns of survivorship in turtles (order Testudines). Canadian Journal of Zoology 69:385–391.

———. 1991b. Life history and demography of the yellow mud turtle, *Kinosternon flavescens*. Herpetologica 47:373–395.

———. 1992a. A Revised Checklist with Distribution Maps of the Turtles of the World. Privately printed, Richmond, Ind.

———. 1992b. Correlates of reproductive output in turtles (Order Testudines). Herpetological Monographs 6:25–42.

Iverson, J. B., C. P. Balgooyen, K. K. Byrd, and K. K. Lyddan. 1993. Latitudinal variation in egg and clutch size in turtles. Canadian Journal of Zoology 71:2448–2461.

Iverson, J. B., and T. E. Graham. 1990. Geographic variation in the redbelly turtle,

Pseudemys rubriventris (Reptilia: Testudines). Annals of the Carnegie Museum of Natural History 59:1–13.

Jackson, D. C., J. Allen, and P. K. Strup. 1976. The contribution of non-pulmonary surfaces to CO_2 loss in 6 species of turtles at 20°C. Comparative Biochemistry and Physiology A 55:243–246.

Jackson, D. R., and E. G. Milstry. 1989. The fauna of gopher tortoise burrows. Florida Game and Fresh Water Fish Commission, Nongame Wildlife Program Technical Report 5:86–98. Tallahassee.

Jackson, M. H. 1993. Galápagos, A Natural History. University of Calgary Press, Alberta, Canada.

Jacobson, E. R. 1993. Implications of infectious diseases for captive propagation and introduction programs of threatened/endangered reptiles. Journal of Zoo and Wildlife Medicine 24 (3): 245–255.

———. 1994a. Causes of mortality and diseases in tortoises: A review. Journal of Zoo and Wildlife Medicine 25 (1): 2–17.

———. 1994b. Veterinary procedures for the acquisition and release of captive-bred herpetofauna. Pages 109–118 in J. B. Murphy, K. Adler, and J. T. Collins (eds.). Captive Management and Conservation of Amphibians and Reptiles. SSAR (Society for the Study of Amphibians and Reptiles) Contributions to Herpetology, vol. 11. Athens, Ohio.

———. 1996. Marine turtle farming and health issues. Marine Turtle Newsletter 72:13–15.

Jacobson, E. R., M. B. Brown, I. M. Schumacher, B. R. Collins, R. K. Harris, and P. A. Klein. 1995. Mycoplasmosis and the desert tortoise *(Gopherus agassizii)* in Las Vegas Valley, Nevada. Chelonian Conservation and Biology 1:279–284.

Jacobson, E. R., S. Clubb, J. M. Gaskin, and C. Gardiner. 1985. Herpesvirus-like infection in Argentine tortoises. Journal of the American Veterinary Medical Association 187:1227–1229.

Jacobson, E. R., J. M. Gaskin, M. B. Brown, R. K. Harris, C. H. Gardiner, J. L. LaPointe, H. P. Adams, and C. Reggiardo. 1991. Chronic upper respiratory tract disease of free-ranging desert tortoises *(Xerobates agassizii)*. Journal of Wildlife Diseases 27 (2): 296–316.

Jacobson, E. R., J. Schumacher, S. Telford, E. C. Greiner, C. D. Buergelt, and C. H. Gardiner. 1994a. Intranuclear coccidiosis in radiated tortoises *(Geochelone radiata)*. Journal of Zoo and Wildlife Medicine 25 (1): 95–102.

Jacobson, E. R., T. J. Wronski, J. Schumacher, C. Reggiardo, and K. H. Berry. 1994b. Cutaneous dyskeratosis in free-ranging desert tortoises, *Gopherus agassizii*, in the Colorado Desert of southern California. Journal of Zoo and Wildlife Medicine 25 (1): 68–81.

Jacobson, S. K., and A. F. Lopez. 1994. Biological impacts of ecotourism: Tourists and nesting turtles in Tortuguero National Park, Costa Rica. Wildlife Society Bulletin 22:414–419.

Jansen, K. P. 1993. Ecology of the tropical freshwater turtle *Rhinoclemmys funerea* in Caribbean Costa Rica. Master's thesis, Southwest Missouri State University, Springfield.

Janzen, F. J. 1993a. An experimental analysis of natural selection on body size of hatchling turtles. Ecology 74:332–341.

———. 1993b. The influence of incubation temperature and family on the eggs, embryos, and hatchlings of the smooth softshell turtle *(Apalone mutica)*. Physiological Zoology 66:349–373.

———. 1994. Climate change and temperature-dependent sex determination in reptiles. Proceedings of the National Academy of Science of the USA 91:7487–7490.

Janzen, F. J., and G. L. Paukstis. 1991. A preliminary test of the adaptive significance of environmental sex determination in reptiles. Evolution 45:435–441.

Jenkins, M. D. 1995. Tortoises and Freshwater Turtles: The Trade in Southeast Asia. TRAFFIC International, Cambridge, United Kingdom.

Jennings, W. B. 1997a. Habitat use and food preferences of the desert tortoise, *Gopherus agassizii*, in the western Mojave Desert and impacts of off-road vehicles. Pages 42–45 in J. Van Abbema (ed.). Proceedings: Conservation, Restoration, and Management of Tortoises and Turtles—an International Conference, July 1993, State University of New York at Purchase. New York Turtle and Tortoise Society, New York.

———. 1997b. Invasions of exotic plants: Implications for the desert tortoise, *Gopherus agassizii*, and its habitat. Pages 10–12 in J. Van Abbema (ed.). Proceedings: Conservation, Restoration, and Management of Tortoises and Turtles—an International Conference, July 1993, State University of New York at Purchase. New York Turtle and Tortoise Society, New York.

Johnson, T. R. 1982. Missouri's Turtles. Conservation Commission of Missouri, Jefferson City.

Juvik, J. O. 1975. The radiated tortoise of Madagascar. Oryx 13:145–148.

Juvik, J. O., A. J. Andrianarivo, and C. P. Blanc. 1981. The ecology and status of *Geochelone yniphora:* A critically endangered tortoise in northwestern Madagascar, Malagasy Republic. Biological Conservation 19:297–316.

Juvik, J. O., A. R. Kiester, D. Reid, B. Coblentz, and J. Hoffman. 1997. The conservation biology of the angonoka, *Geochelone yniphora*, in northwestern Madagascar: Progress report. Pages 345–350 in J. Van Abbema (ed.). Proceedings: Conservation, Restoration, and Management of Tortoises and Turtles—an International Conference, July 1993, State University of New York at Purchase. New York Turtle and Tortoise Society, New York.

Kar, C. S., and S. Bhaskar. 1982. Status of sea turtles in the eastern Indian Ocean. Pages 365–372 in K. A. Bjorndal (ed.). Biology and Conservation of Sea Turtles. Smithsonian Institution Press, Washington, D.C.

Karesh, W. B., B. L. Raphael, M. W. Klemens, E. S. Dierenfeld, and P. D. Moehlman. 1993. Health survey of the pancake tortoise *(Malacochersus tornieri)*. Wildlife Conservation Society, Bronx, N.Y.

Kaufmann, J. H. 1992. Habitat use by wood turtles in central Pennsylvania. Journal of Herpetology 26:315–321.

Kaus, A. 1993. Environmental perceptions and social relations in the Mapimi Biosphere Reserve. Conservation Biology 7:398–406.

Kennett, R. M., K. Christian, and D. Pritchard. 1993. Underwater nesting by the tropical freshwater turtle, *Chelodina rugosa* (Testudinata: Chelidae). Australian Journal of Zoology 41:47–52.

Kennett, R. M., and O. Tory. 1996. The diet of two freshwater turtles, *Chelodina rugosa* and *Elseya dentata* (Testudines: Chelidae), from the wet-dry tropics of northern Australia. Copeia 1996:409–419.

Khan, M. A. R. 1982. Chelonians of Bangladesh and their conservation. Journal of the Bombay Natural History Society 79 (1): 110–116.

Khan, M. K. M. 1977. River terrapin. Nature Malaysiana 2 (3): 32–37.

Kiester, A. R., C. W. Schwartz, and E. R. Schwartz. 1982. Promotion of gene flow by transient individuals in an otherwise sedentary population of box turtles *(Terrapene carolina triunguis)*. Evolution 36:617–619.

King, F. W. 1978. The wildlife trade. Pages 253–271 *in* H. P. Brokaw (ed.). Wildlife and America. Contributions to an Understanding of American Wildlife and Its Conservation. U.S. Government Printing Office, Washington, D.C.

———. 1982. Historical review of the decline of the green turtle and the hawksbill. Pages 183–188 *in* K. A. Bjorndal (ed.). Biology and Conservation of Sea Turtles. Smithsonian Institution Press, Washington, D.C.

Klein, K. C., and R. Freed. 1989. Implementing the Massachusetts Wetlands Protection Act—the local perspective. Pages 499–507 *in* D. W. Fisk (ed.). Wetlands: Concerns and Successes. American Resources Association, Bethesda, Md.

Klemens, M. W. 1989. The methodology of conservation. Pages 1–4 *in* I. R. Swingland and M. W. Klemens (eds.). The Conservation Biology of Tortoises. Occasional Papers of the IUCN Species Survival Commission, no. 5. Gland, Switzerland.

———. 1990. The herpetofauna of southwestern New England. Doctoral dissertation, University of Kent, Canterbury, United Kingdom.

———. 1992. Letter from the field: Hunting and gathering among the Hadza. Rotunda 17:4–5.

———. 1993a. Amphibians and Reptiles of Connecticut and Adjacent Regions. State Geological and Natural History Survey of Connecticut Bulletin 112.

———. 1993b. Standardized bog turtle site-quality analysis. Report to U.S. Fish and Wildlife Service, State College, Pa.

———. 1995. Repatriation of confiscated tortoises: Conscience-clearing expediency *or* sound wildlife management? Re-Introduction News (Newsletter of the Re-Introduction Specialist Group of the IUCN's Species Survival Commission) 10:5–6.

Klemens, M. W., and D. Moll. 1995. An assessment of the effects of commercial exploitation on the pancake tortoise, *Malacochersus tornieri,* in Tanzania. Chelonian Conservation and Biology 1:197–206.

Klemens, M. W., and J. B. Thorbjarnarson. 1995. Reptiles as a food source. Biodiversity and Conservation 4:281–298.

Klemens, M. W., and J. L. Warner. 1983. The status of *Clemmys muhlenbergii* (Schoepff) in Connecticut. Herpetological Review 14:124–125.

Knight, A. W., and J. W. Gibbons. 1968. Food of a painted turtle, *Chrysemys picta,* in a polluted river. American Midland Naturalist 80:558–562.

Knowles, C. 1989. A survey for diseased desert tortoises in and near the Desert Tortoise Natural Area, Spring 1989. Report (Contract CA 950-[T9-23]) to the Bureau of Land Management, Riverside, Calif.

Kramer, M. 1989. Individual discrimination in juveniles of two turtles, *Pseudemys nelsoni* and *Pseudemys floridana* (Chelonia, Emydidae). Biology and Behavior 14:148–156.

Kroeber, A. 1925. Handbook of American Indians. Bureau of American Ethnology, Bulletin 78.

Kubykin, R. A. 1995. Population density of the steppe tortoise in some regions of the Almaty and Taldqorghan Districts, Kazakhstan. Chelonian Conservation and Biology 1:235–237.

Kuchling, G. 1988. Population structure, reproductive potential and increasing exploitation of the freshwater turtle *Erymnochelys madagascariensis*. Biological Conservation 43:107–113.

———. 1992. Distribution and status of *Erymnochelys madagascariensis* (Grandidier, 1867). Report to Conservation International and Ministère de la Production Anmale et des Eaux et Forêts. Conservation International, Washington, D.C.

———. 1995a. Ethics of manipulation—the western swamp tortoise *(Pseudemydura umbrina)* example. Pages 99–103 *in* Proceedings International Congress of Chelonian Conservation, July 1995, Gonfaron, France. Editions SOPTOM (Station d'observation et de protectiòn des tortues des maures), Gonfaron, France.

———. 1995b. Turtles at a market in western Yunnan: Possible range extensions for some southern Asiatic chelonians in China and Myanmar. Chelonian Conservation and Biology 1:223–226.

———. 1997a. Managing the last survivors: Integration of in situ and ex situ conservation of *Pseudemydura umbrina*. Pages 339–344 *in* J. Van Abbema (ed.). Proceedings: Conservation, Restoration, and Management of Tortoises and Turtles—an International Conference, July 1993, State University of New York at Purchase. New York Turtle and Tortoise Society, New York.

———. 1997b. Patterns of exploitation, decline, and extinction of *Erymnochelys madagascariensis:* Implications for conservation. Pages 113–117 *in* J. Van Abbema (ed.). Proceedings: Conservation, Restoration, and Management of Tortoises and Turtles—an International Conference, July 1993, State University of New York at Purchase. New York Turtle and Tortoise Society, New York.

Kuchling, G., and Q. M. C. Bloxam. 1988. Field-data on the Madagascan flat tailed tortoise *Pyxis (Acinixys) planicauda*. Amphibia-Reptilia 9:175–180.

Kuchling, G., and J. P. Dejose. 1989. A captive breeding operation to rescue the critically endangered western swamp turtle. International Zoo Yearbook 28:103–109.

Kuchling, G., J. P. Dejose, A. A. Burbidge, and S. D. Bradshaw. 1992. Beyond captive breeding: The western swamp tortoise *Pseudemydura umbrina* recovery programme. International Zoo Yearbook 31:37–41.

Kuchling, G., and R. A. Mittermeier. 1993. Status and exploitation of the Madagascan big-headed turtle, *Erymnochelys madagascariensis*. Chelonian Conservation and Biology 1:13–18.

La Condamine, C.-M. 1992. Viajem pelo Amazonas 1735–1745. Universidade de São Paulo, Edn. Nova Fronteira, Rio de Janeiro.

Lacy, R. C., and T. Kreeger. 1992. Vortex Users Manual. Chicago Zoological Society, Chicago.

Lagueux, C. J. 1991. Economic analysis of sea turtle eggs in a coastal community on the Pacific coast of Honduras. Pages 136–144 *in* J. G. Robinson and K. H. Redford (eds.). Neotropical Wildlife Use and Conservation. University of Chicago Press, Chicago.

———. 1998. Marine turtle fishery of Caribbean Nicaragua: Human use patterns and harvest trends. Doctoral dissertation, University of Florida, Gainesville.

Lamb, T., J. C. Avise, and J. W. Gibbons. 1989. Phylogeographic patterns in mitochondrial DNA of desert tortoise *(Xerobates agassizii),* and evolutionary relationships among the North American gopher tortoises. Evolution 43:76–87.

Lambert, M. R. K. 1983. Some factors influencing the Moroccan distribution of the western Mediterranean spur-thighed tortoise, *Testudo graeca graeca* L., and those precluding its survival in NW Europe. Zoological Journal of the Linnean Society 79:149–179.

———. 1984. Threats to Mediterranean (west Palaearctic) tortoises and their effects on wild populations: An overview. Amphibia-Reptilia 5:5–15.

———. 1993. On growth, sexual dimorphism, and the general ecology of the African spurred tortoise, Geochelone sulcata, in Mali. Chelonian Conservation and Biology 1:37–46.

———. 1995a. On the geographical size variation, growth, and sexual dimorphism of the leopard tortoise, Geochelone pardalis, in Somaliland. Chelonian Conservation and Biology 1:269–278.

———. 1995b. Tortoise situation in northern Africa. Pages 1–5 in D. Ballasina (ed.). Red Data Book on Mediterranean Chelonians. Edagricole-Edzioni Agricole, Bologna, Italy.

Landers, J. L., J. A. Garner, and W. A. McRae. 1980. Reproduction of gopher tortoises (Gopherus polyphemus) in southwestern Georgia. Herpetologica 36:353–361.

Lauckner, G. 1985. Diseases of Reptilia. Pages 554–626 in O. Kinne (ed.). Diseases of Marine Animals, vol. 4, pt. 2. Biologische Anstalt Helgoland, Hamburg, Germany.

Le Dien Duc, and S. Broad. 1995. Investigations into tortoise and freshwater turtle trade in Vietnam. International Union for Conservation of Nature and Natural Resources, Species Survival Commission, Gland, Switzerland.

Legler, J. M. 1960. Natural history of the ornate box turtle, Terrapene ornata ornata Agassiz. University of Kansas Publications, Museum of Natural History 11:527–669.

———. 1976. Feeding habits of some Australian short-necked tortoises. Victorian Naturalist 93:40–43.

———. 1978. Observations on behavior and ecology in an Australian turtle, Chelodina expansa (Testudines: Chelidae). Canadian Journal of Zoology 56:2449–2453.

———. 1985. Australian chelid turtles: Reproductive patterns in wide-ranging taxa. Pages 117–123 in G. Grigg, R. Shine, and H. Ehmann (eds.). Biology of Australasian Frogs and Reptiles. Transactions of the Royal Zoological Society of New South Wales, Mosman.

———. 1993. Morphology and physiology of the Chelonia. Pages 108–119 in C. J. Glasby, G. J. B. Ross, and P. L. Beesley (eds.). Fauna of Australia. Vol. 2A, Amphibia and Reptilia. Australian Government Publishing Service, Canberra.

Legler, J. M., and A. Georges. 1993. Family Chelidae. Pages 142–152 in C. J. Glasby, G. J. B. Ross, and P. L. Beesley (eds.). Fauna of Australia. Vol. 2A, Amphibia and Reptilia. Australian Government Publishing Service, Canberra.

Leong, J. K., D. L. Smith, D. B. Revera, J. C. Clary III, D. H. Lewis, J. L. Scott, and A. R. DiNuzzo. 1989. Health care and diseases of captive-reared loggerhead and Kemp's ridley sea turtles. Pages 178–201 in C. W. Caillouet, Jr., and A. M. Landry, Jr. (eds.). Proceedings of the First International Symposium on Kemp's Ridley Sea Turtle Biology, Conservation and Management. Texas A&M University Sea Grant College TAMU-SG-89-105, Galveston.

Leopold, A. 1949. A Sand County Almanac and Sketches Here and There. Special commemorative edn., Oxford University Press, New York, 1989.

Levell, J. P. 1995. A Field Guide to Reptiles and the Law. Serpent's Tale, Excelsior, Minn.

Lewis, C. B. 1940. The Cayman Islands and marine turtle. Bulletin of the Institute of Jamaica, Science Series 2:56–65.

Li Wenjun, T. K. Fuller, and Wang Sung. 1996. A survey of wildlife trade in Guangxi and Guandong, China. TRAFFIC Bulletin 16 (1): 9–16.

Licata, L. 1992. La Tortuga Arrau y su Conservació. Cuadernos Ecológicos, Corpoven, Caracas.

Limpus, C. J. 1982. The status of Australian sea turtle populations. Pages 297–303 *in* K. A. Bjorndal (ed.). Biology and Conservation of Sea Turtles. Smithsonian Institution Press, Washington, D.C.

———. 1992. Migration of green *(Chelonia mydas)* and loggerhead *(Caretta caretta)* turtles to and from eastern Australian rookeries. Wildlife Research 19:347–358.

———. 1993. The green turtle, *Chelonia mydas*, in Queensland: Breeding males in the southern Great Barrier Reef. Wildlife Research 20:513–523.

———. 1994. Current declines in south east Asian turtle populations. Pages 89–92 *in* B. A. Schroeder and B. E. Witherington (compilers). Proceedings of the Thirteenth Annual Workshop on Sea Turtle Biology and Conservation. NOAA Technical Memorandum NMFS-SEFSC-341.

———. 1995. Global overview of the status of marine turtles: A 1995 viewpoint. Pages 605–609 *in* K. A. Bjorndal (ed.). Biology and Conservation of Sea Turtles. Rev. edn. Smithsonian Institution Press, Washington, D.C.

Limpus, C. J., and D. Riemer. 1994. The loggerhead turtle, *Caretta caretta*, in Queensland: A population in decline. Pages 39–59 *in* R. James (compiler). Proceedings of the Australian Marine Turtle Conservation Workshop. Australian Nature Conservation Agency, Canberra.

Lindeman, P. V. 1992. Nest-site fidelity among painted turtles *(Chrysemys picta)* in northern Idaho. Northwestern Naturalist 73:27–30.

Lindenmayer, D. B. 1994. Some ecological considerations and computer-based approaches for the identification of potentially suitable release sites for reintroduction programmes. Pages 1–5 *in* M. Serena (ed.). Reintroduction Biology of Australian and New Zealand Fauna. Surrey Beatty and Sons, Chipping Norton, Australia.

Lohoefener, R., and L. Lohmeier. 1980. Comparison of gopher tortoise *(Gopherus polyphemus)* habitats in young slash pine and old longleaf pine areas of southern Mississippi. Journal of Herpetology 15:239–242.

Lovich, J. E. 1989. The spotted turtles of Cedar Bog, Ohio: Historical analysis of a declining population. Pages 23–28 *in* R. C. Glotzhober, A. Kochman, and W. T. Schultz (eds.). Cedar Bog Symposium II. Ohio Historical Society, Columbus.

———. 1990. Spring movement patterns of two radio-tagged male spotted turtles. Brimleyana 16:67–71.

———. 1995. Turtles. Pages 118–121 *in* E. T. LaRoe, C. E. Puckett, P. D. Doran, and M. J. Mac (eds.). Our Living Resources: A Report to the Nation on the Distribution, Abundance, and Health of U.S. Plants, Animals, and Ecosystems. National Biological Survey, Washington, D.C.

———. 1996. Possible demographic and ecologic consequences of sex ratio manipulation in turtles. Chelonian Conservation and Biology 2:114–117.

Lovich, J. E., and J. W. Gibbons. 1990. Age at maturity influences adult sex ratio in the turtle *Malaclemys terrapin*. Oikos 59:126–134.

———. 1997. Conservation of covert species: Protecting species we don't even know. Pages 426–429 *in* J. Van Abbema (ed.). Proceedings: Conservation, Restoration, and Management of Turtles and Tortoises—an International Conference, July 1993, State University of New York at Purchase. New York Turtle and Tortoise Society, New York.

Lovich, J. E., S. W. Gotte, C. H. Ernst, J. C. Harshbarger, A. F. Laemmerzahl, and J. W. Gibbons. 1996. Prevalence and histopathology of shell disease in turtles from Lake Blackshear, Georgia. Journal of Wildlife Diseases 32 (2): 259–265.

Lovich, J. E., and T. R. Jaworski. 1988. Annotated checklist of amphibians and reptiles reported from Cedar Bog, Ohio. Ohio Journal of Science 88:139–143.

Lovich, J. E., and C. J. McCoy. 1992. Review of the *Graptemys pulchra* group (Reptilia, Testudines, Emydidae), with descriptions of two new species. Annals of the Carnegie Museum of Natural History 61:293–315.

Lovich, J. E., A. D. Tucker, D. E. Kling, J. W. Gibbons, and T. D. Zimmerman. 1991. Behavior of hatchling diamondback terrapins released in a South Carolina salt marsh. Herpetological Review 22:81–83.

Lowe, C. H. 1990. Are we killing the desert tortoise with love, science, and management? Pages 84–106 *in* K. R. Beaman, F. Caporaso, S. McKeown, and M. D. Graff (eds.). Proceedings of the First International Symposium on Turtles and Tortoises: Conservation and Captive Husbandry. California Turtle and Tortoise Club, Los Angeles, Calif.

Luckenbach, R. A. 1982. Ecology and management of the desert tortoise *(Gopherus agassizii)* in California. Pages 1–37 *in* R. B. Bury (ed.). North American Tortoises: Conservation and Ecology. U.S. Fish and Wildlife Service, Wildlife Research Report 12.

Lutcavage, M. E., P. Plotkin, B. Witherington, and P. L. Lutz. 1997. Human impacts on sea turtle survival. Pages 387–409 *in* P. L. Lutz and J. A. Musick (eds.). The Biology of Sea Turtles. CRC Press, Boca Raton, Fla.

MacFarland, C. G., J. Villa, and B. Toro. 1974. The Galápagos giant tortoises *(Geochelone elephantopus)*. Pt. I. Status of the surviving populations. Biological Conservation 6:118–133.

Mack, D. 1983. Worldwide trade in wild sea turtle products: An update. Marine Turtle Newsletter 24:10–15.

Mack, D., N. Duplaix, and S. Wells. 1979. The sea turtle: An animal of divisible parts. International trade in sea turtle products. TRAFFIC-USA, Washington, D.C.

———. 1982. Sea turtles, animals of divisible parts: International trade in sea turtle products. Pages 545–563 *in* K. A. Bjorndal (ed.). Biology and Conservation of Sea Turtles. Smithsonian Institution Press, Washington, D.C.

Madson, J. 1990. On the Osage. Nature Conservancy Magazine (May/June): 7–15.

Mahe, J., and M. Sourdat. 1973. Sur l'extinction des vertebres subfossiles et l'aridification du climat dans le Sud-Ouest de Madagascar. Bulletin de la Societe Geologique de France 14:295–309.

Makeyev, V. M., S. Shammakov, A. T. Bozhanskii, R. W. Marlow, and K. von Seckendorff Hoff. 1997. Agricultural development and grazing as the major causes of population declines in Horsfield's tortoise in the Turkmen Republic. Page 20 *in* J. Van Abbema (ed.). Proceedings: Conservation, Restoration, and Management of Tortoises and Turtles—an International Conference, July 1993, State University of New York at Purchase. New York Turtle and Tortoise Society, New York.

Malecki, R. 1995. Purple loosestrife. Pages 458–459 *in* E. T. LaRoe, G. S. Farris, C. E. Puckett, P. D. Doran, and M. J. Mac (eds.). Our Living Resources: A Report to the Nation on the Distribution, Abundance, and Health of U.S. Plants, Animals, and Ecosystems. National Biological Survey, Washington, D.C.

Malecki, R., B. Blossey, S. Hight, D. Schroder, L. Kok, and J. Drea. 1993. Biological control of purple loosestrife. BioScience 43:680–686.

Manton, M., A. Karr, and D. W. Ehrenfeld. 1972. Chemoreception in the migratory sea turtle, *Chelonia mydas*. Biological Bulletin 143:184–195.

Manzella, S. A., C. W. Caillouet, Jr., and C. T. Fontaine. 1988. Kemp's ridley, *Lepidochelys kempii,* sea turtle head start tag recoveries: Distribution, habitat, and method of recovery. Marine Fisheries Review 50:24–32.

Marks, M., B. Lapin, and J. Randall. 1994. *Phragmites australis (P. communis):* Threats, management, and monitoring. Natural Areas Journal 14:285–294.

Márquez, C., G. Morillo, and L. J. Cayot. 1991. A 25-year management program pays off: Repatriated tortoises on Española reproduce. Noticias de Galápagos 50:17–18.

Márquez M., R. 1994. Synopsis of biological data on the Kemp's Ridley turtle, *Lepidochelys kempii* (Garman, 1880). NOAA Technical Memorandum NMFS-SEFSC-343.

Márquez M., R., R. A. Byles, P. Burchfield, M. Sanchez-P., J. Diaz-F., M. A. Carrasco-A., A. S. Leo-P., and C. Jimenez-O. 1996. Good news! Rising numbers of Kemp's ridleys nest at Rancho Nuevo, Tamaulipas, Mexico. Marine Turtle Newsletter 73:2–5.

Márquez M., R., A. Villanueva O., and C. Peñaflores S. 1976. Sinopsis de datos biologicos sobre la tortuga golfina, *Lepidochelys olivacea* (Eschscholtz, 1829). Instituto Nacional de Pesca, Secretaria de Industria y Comercio, Subsecretaria de Pesca, Mexico.

Martin, E. B., and M. Phipps. 1996. A review of the wild animal trade in Cambodia. TRAFFIC Bulletin 16 (2): 45–60.

Martin, P. S. 1966. Africa and Pleistocene overkill. Nature 212:339–342.

Martinez-Silvestre, A. 1995. Determinacion del contenido en contaminantes (DDTs y PCBs) en tehidos de *Caretta caretta* del Mediterraneo Espanol. Pages 169–172 *in* Proceedings International Congress of Chelonian Conservation, July 1995, Gonfaron, France. Editions SOPTOM (Station d'observation et de protectiòn des tortues des maures), Gonfaron, France.

Mascort, R. 1997. An overview of a threatened population of European pond turtles, *Emys orbicularis.* Page 312 *in* J. Van Abbema (ed.). Proceedings: Conservation, Restoration, and Management of Tortoises and Turtles—an International Conference, July 1993, State University of New York at Purchase. New York Turtle and Tortoise Society, New York.

Maxwell, F. D. 1911. Reports on inland and sea fisheries in the Thongwa, Myaungmya, and Bassein Districts, and turtle-banks of the Irrawaddy Division. Rangoon Government Printing Office.

May, P. H. 1992. Common property resources in the Neotropics: Theory, management progress, and an action agenda. Pages 359–378 *in* K. H. Redford and C. Padoch (eds.). Conservation of Neotropical Forests. Columbia University Press, New York.

McCauley, R. H., Jr. 1945. The reptiles of Maryland and the District of Columbia. Privately published, Hagerstown, Md.

McCord, W. P., J. B. Iverson, and Boeadi. 1995. A new batagurid turtle from Sulawesi, Indonesia. Chelonian Conservation and Biology 1:311–316.

McCoy, C. J., and R. C. Vogt. 1985. *Pseudemys alabamensis* Baur: Alabama red-bellied turtle. Catalog of American Amphibians and Reptiles 371.1–371.2. Society for the Study of Amphibians and Reptiles, Athens, Ohio.

McCoy, M. A. 1982. Subsistence hunting of turtles in the western Pacific: The Caroline Islands. Pages 275–280 *in* K. A. Bjorndal (ed.). Biology and Conservation of Sea Turtles. Smithsonian Institution Press, Washington, D.C.

McGehee, M. A. 1990. Effects of moisture on eggs and hatchlings of loggerhead sea turtles *(Caretta caretta).* Herpetologica 46:251–258.

McGoodwin, J. R. 1990. Crisis in the World's Fisheries. Stanford University Press, Stanford, Calif.

McNeely, J., K. R. Miller, W. V. Reid, R. A. Mittermeier, and T. B. Werner. 1990. Conserving the World's Biodiversity. International Union for Conservation of Nature and Natural Resources, Gland, Switzerland.

McNeill, F. 1955. Saving the green turtle of the Great Barrier Reef. Australian Museum Magazine 11:278–282.

McNeill, W. H. 1963. The Rise of the West. University of Chicago Press, Chicago.

Medem, F. 1969. Estudios adicionales sobre los Crocodylia y Testudinata del alto Caqueta y Rio Caguan. Caldesia 10 (48): 329–353.

Medina, J. T. (ed.). 1988. The Discovery of the Amazon. Dover Publications, New York.

Meffe, G. K. 1992. Techno-arrogance and halfway technologies: Salmon hatcheries on the Pacific Coast of North America. Conservation Biology 6:350–354.

Meffe, G. K., and C. R. Carroll (eds.). 1997. Principles of Conservation Biology. 2nd edn. Sinauer, Sunderland, Mass.

Meine, C. 1994. Conservation biology and wildlife management in America: A historical perspective. Pages 310–312 in G. K. Meffe and C. R. Carroll. Principles of Conservation Biology. Sinauer, Sunderland, Mass.

Mendelssohn, H., and E. Geffen. 1995. The Egyptian tortoise (Testudo kleinmanni). Pages 139–145 in D. Ballasina (ed.). Red Data Book on Mediterranean Chelonians. Edagricole-Edzioni Agricole, Bologna, Italy.

Meyers-Schöne, L., and B. T. Walton. 1994. Turtles as monitors of chemical contaminants in the environment. Pages 93–153 in G. W. Ware (ed.). Reviews of Environmental Contamination and Toxicology, vol. 135. Springer-Verlag, New York.

Meylan, A. B. 1982. Sea turtle migrations—evidence from tag returns. Pages 91–100 in K. A. Bjorndal (ed.). Biology and Conservation of Sea Turtles. Smithsonian Institution Press, Washington, D.C.

————. 1999. Status of the hawksbill turtle (Eretmochelys imbricata) in the Caribbean region. Chelonian Conservation and Biology 3:177–184.

Meylan, A. B., B. Bowen, and J. Avise. 1990. A genetic test of the natal homing versus social facilitation model for green turtle migration. Science (Washington, D.C.) 248:724–727.

Meylan, A. B., and M. Donnelly. 1999. Status justification for listing the hawksbill turtle (Eretmochelys imbricata) as critically endangered on the 1996 IUCN Red List of Threatened Animals. Chelonian Conservation and Biology 3:200–224.

Meylan, A. B., B. Schroeder, and A. Mosier. 1995. Sea turtle nesting activity in the state of Florida 1979–1992. Florida Marine Research Publications 52:1–51.

Miller, J. D. 1989. Marine turtles. Vol. 1, An assessment of the conservation status of marine turtles in the Kingdom of Saudia Arabia. MEPA (Meteorology and Environmental Protection Administration) Coastal and Marine Management Series, Technical Report no. 9.

Miller, K., G. C. Packard, and M. J. Packard. 1987. Hydric conditions during incubation influence locomotor performance of hatchling snapping turtles. Journal of Experimental Biology 127:401–412.

Milliken, T., and H. Tokunaga. 1987a. The Japanese Sea Turtle Trade 1970–1986. Report by TRAFFIC-JAPAN to the Center for Environmental Education, Washington, D.C.

————. 1987b. Observations of the hawksbill sea turtle headstart programme at the Micronesia Mariculture Demonstration Center (MMDC), Koror, Palau in October

1986. Report by TRAFFIC-JAPAN to the Center for Environmental Education, Washington, D.C.

Milne Edwards, A. 1874. Rescherches sur la faune éteinte des iles Mascareignes. Annales des Sciences Naturelles (Zoologie) 19:1–31.

Mitchell, J. C. 1994. The Reptiles of Virginia. Smithsonian Institution Press, Washington, D.C.

Mitchell, J. C., K. A. Buhlmann, and C. H. Ernst. 1991. Bog turtle, *Clemmys muhlenbergii* (Schoepff). Pages 457–459 *in* K. Terwilliger (coordinator). Virginia's Endangered Species. McDonald & Woodward Publishing, Blacksburg, Va.

Mittermeier, R. A. 1975. A turtle in every pot. Animal Kingdom 78 (2): 9–14.

———. 1978. South America's river turtles: Saving them by use. Oryx 14:222–230.

———. 1991. Hunting and its effect on wild primate populations in Suriname. Pages 93–107 *in* J. Robinson and K. Redford (eds.). Neotropical Wildlife Use and Conservation. University of Chicago Press, Chicago.

Mittermeier, R. A., J. L. Carr, I. R. Swingland, T. B. Werner, and R. B. Mast. 1992. Conservation of amphibians and reptiles. Pages 59–80 *in* K. Adler (ed.). Herpetology: Current Research on the Biology of Amphibians and Reptiles. Proceedings of the First World Congress of Herpetology. Society for the Study of Amphibians and Reptiles, Athens, Ohio.

Mohanty-Hejmadi, P., and G. Sahoo. 1994. Biology of the olive ridleys of Gahirmatha, Orissa, India. Pages 90–93 *in* K. A. Bjorndal, A. B. Bolten, D. A. Johnson, and P. J. Eliazar (compilers). Proceedings of the Fourteenth Annual Symposium on Sea Turtle Biology and Conservation. NOAA Technical Memorandum NMFS-SEFSC-351.

Moler, P. (ed.). 1992. Rare and Endangered Biota of Florida. Vol. 3, Amphibians and Reptiles. University Press of Florida, Gainesville.

Moll, D. 1976. Food and feeding strategies of the Ouachita map turtle *(Graptemys pseudogeographica ouachitensis)*. American Midland Naturalist 96:478–482.

———. 1977. Ecological investigations of turtles in a polluted ecosystem: The central Illinois River and adjacent flood plain lakes. Doctoral dissertation, Illinois State University, Normal.

———. 1979. Subterranean feeding by the Illinois mud turtle, *Kinosternon flavescens spooneri*. Journal of Herpetology 13:371–373.

———. 1980. Dirty river turtles. Natural History 5:42–49.

———. 1985. The trophic ecology of aquatic turtles: Investigations of the relationship of prey availability with dietary overlap and specialization. A.S.R.A. (Association for the Study of Reptilia and Amphibia) Journal 2 (4): 1–22.

———. 1986. The distribution, status, and level of exploitation of the freshwater turtle *Dermatemys mawei* in Belize, Central America. Biological Conservation 35:87–96.

———. 1989. Food and feeding behavior of the turtle, *Dermatemys mawei,* in Belize. Journal of Herpetology 23:445–447.

———. 1990. Population sizes and foraging ecology in a tropical freshwater stream turtle community. Journal of Herpetology 24:48–53.

———. 1994. The ecology of sea beach nesting in slider turtles *(Trachemys scripta venusta)* from Caribbean Costa Rica. Chelonian Conservation and Biology 1:107–116.

Moll, D., and K. P. Jansen. 1995. Evidence for a role in seed dispersal by two tropical herbivorous turtles. Biotropica 27:121–127.

Moll, D., and M. W. Klemens. 1996. Ecological characteristics of the pancake tortoise, *Malacochersus tornieri*, in Tanzania. Chelonian Conservation and Biology 2:26–35.

Moll, D., and E. O. Moll. 1990. The slider turtle in the Neotropics: Adaptation of a temperate species to a tropical environment. Pages 152–161 *in* J. W. Gibbons (ed.). Life History and Ecology of the Slider Turtle. Smithsonian Institution Press, Washington, D.C.

Moll, E. O. 1976. West Malaysian turtles: Utilization and conservation. Herpetological Review 7:163–166.

———. 1978a. Drumming along the Perak. Natural History 87:36–43.

———. 1978b. Report of research on the distribution, ecology, and management of coastal nesting turtles in Trengganu, West Malaysia (May–August 1978). Report to the New York Zoological Society, Bronx, N.Y.

———. 1979. Reproductive cycles and adaptations. Pages 305–331 *in* M. Harless and H. Morlock (eds.). Turtles: Perspectives and Research. Wiley, New York.

———. 1980a. Natural history of the river terrapin, *Batagur baska* (Gray), in Malaysia (Testudines: Emydidae). Malaysian Journal of Science 6 (A): 23–62.

———. 1980b. Tuntong laut: The river turtle that goes to sea. Nature Malaysiana 5:16–21.

———. 1982. Freshwater turtles: The drug trade. Hamadryad 7 (3): 21–22.

———. 1984. River terrapin recovery plan for Malaysia. Journal of Wildlife and Parks (Malaysia) 3:37–47.

———. 1985a. Estuarine turtles of tropical Asia: Status and management. Pages 214–226 *in* Proceedings of the Symposium on Endangered Marine Animals and Marine Parks. Central Marine Fisheries Research Institute, Cochin, India.

———. 1985b. Freshwater turtles. Sanctuary 5:49–59, 66.

———. 1986. Survey of the freshwater turtles of India. Pt. I. The genus *Kachuga*. Journal of the Bombay Natural History Society 83:538–552.

———. 1989a. Malaysia's efforts in conservation of the river terrapin. Pages 173–176 *in* Proceedings of the International Conference of National Parks and Protected Areas, Kuala Lumpur, Malaysia, 13–15 November. Department of Wildlife and National Parks, Kuala Lumpur, Malaysia.

———. 1989b. *Indotestudo forstenii*, Travancore tortoise. Page 118 *in* I. R. Swingland and M. W. Klemens (eds.). The Conservation Biology of Tortoises. Occasional Papers of the IUCN Species Survival Commission, no. 5. Gland, Switzerland.

———. 1990a. India's freshwater turtle resource with recommendations for management. Pages 501–515 *in* J. C. Daniel and J. S. Serrao (eds.). Conservation in Developing Countries: Problems and Prospects. Bombay Natural History Society and Oxford University Press, Bombay, India.

———. 1990b. Status and management of the river terrapin *(Batagur baska)* in tropical Asia. World Wide Fund for Nature-Asia, project no. 3901. Gland, Switzerland.

———. 1997. Effects of habitat alteration on river turtles of tropical Asia with emphasis on sand mining and dams. Pages 37–41 *in* J. Van Abbema (ed.). Proceedings: Conservation, Restoration, and Management of Tortoises and Turtles—an International Conference, July 1993, State University of New York at Purchase. New York Turtle and Tortoise Society, New York.

Moll, E. O., B. Groombridge, and J. Vijaya. 1986. Redescription of the cane turtle with notes on its natural history and classification. Journal of the Bombay Natural History Society 83 (supplement): 112–126.

Moll, E. O., and M. K. M. Khan. 1990. Turtles of Taman Negara. Journal of Wildlife and Parks 10:135–138.

Moll, E. O., and J. M. Legler. 1971. The life history of a Neotropical slider turtle, *Pseudemys scripta* (Schoepff), in Panama. Bulletin of the Los Angeles Museum of Natural History, Science 11:1–102.

Moll, E. O., K. E. Matson, and E. B. Krehbiel. 1981. Sexual and seasonal dichromatism in the Asian river turtle *Callagur borneoensis*. Herpetologica 37:181–194.

Moll, E. O., and J. Vijaya. 1986. Distributional records for some Indian turtles. Journal of the Bombay Natural History Society 83:57–62.

Moodie, K. B., and T. R. Van Devender. 1979. Extinction and extirpation in the herpetofauna of the Southern High Plains with emphasis on *Geochelone wilsonii* (Testudinae). Herpetologica 35:198–206.

Mora, J. M., and A. N. Ugalde. 1991. A note on the status and exploitation of *Pseudemys scripta emolli* (Reptilia: Emydidae) in northern Costa Rica. Bulletin of the Chicago Herpetological Society 26:111.

Morafka, D. J. 1982. The status and distribution of the Bolson tortoise *(Gopherus flavomarginatus)*. Pages 71–94 *in* R. B. Bury (ed.). North American Tortoises: Conservation and Ecology. U.S. Fish and Wildlife Service, Wildlife Research Report 12.

Morafka, D. J., G. Aguirre, and G. A. Adest. 1989. *Gopherus flavomarginatus*, Bolson tortoise. Pages 10–13 *in* I. R. Swingland and M. W. Klemens (eds.). The Conservation Biology of Tortoises. Occasional Papers of the IUCN Species Survival Commission, no. 5. Gland, Switzerland.

Morreale, S. J., and V. J. Burke. 1997. Conservation and biology of sea turtles in the northeastern United States. Pages 41–46 *in* T. Tyning (ed.). Status and Conservation of Turtles of the Northeastern United States. Serpent's Tale, Lanesboro, Minn.

Morreale, S. J., J. W. Gibbons, and J. D. Congdon. 1984. Significance of activity and movement in the yellow-bellied slider turtle *(Pseudemys scripta)*. Canadian Journal of Zoology 62:1038–1042.

Mortimer, J. A. 1982. Factors influencing beach selection by nesting sea turtles. Pages 45–51 *in* K. A. Bjorndal (ed.). Biology and Conservation of Sea Turtles. Smithsonian Institution Press, Washington, D.C.

———. 1984. Marine Turtles in the Republic of the Seychelles: Status and Management. International Union for Conservation of Nature and Natural Resources and World Wide Fund for Nature, project no. 1809. Gland, Switzerland.

———. 1985. Recovery of green turtles on Aldabra. Oryx 19:146–150.

———. 1987. Conservation of the population of *Podocnemis expansa* nesting at the Rio Trombetas. Interim report to Muse Paraense Emilio Goeldi, Belém, Pará, Brazil.

———. 1988a. Green turtle nesting at Aldabra Atoll—population estimates and trends. Biological Society of Washington 8:116–128.

———. 1988b. The pilot project to promote sea turtle conservation in southern Thailand with recommendations for a draft marine turtle conservation strategy for Thailand. Report to Wildlife Fund Thailand and World Wildlife Fund-USA.

———. 1988c. Management options for sea turtles: Re-evaluating priorities. Florida Defenders of the Environment Bulletin 25:1–4.

———. 1990a. Marine turtle conservation in Malaysia. Pages 21–24 *in* T. H. Richardson, J. I. Richardson, and M. Donnelly (compilers). Proceedings of the Tenth Annual Workshop on Sea Turtle Biology and Conservation. NOAA Technical Memorandum NMFS-SEFSC-278.

———. 1990b. The hawksbill turtle in the Republic of Seychelles: Its status and management. Paper presented at the Nagasaki International Symposium on the Resource Management of the Hawksbill Turtle, Nagasaki, Japan, 19–22 November.

———. 1991. Marine turtle populations of Pulau Redang: Their status and recommendations for their management. Report to World Wildlife Fund-Malaysia.

———. 1995a. Teaching critical concepts for the conservation of sea turtles. Marine Turtle Newsletter 71:1–2.

———. 1995b. Headstarting as a management tool. Pages 613–615 in K. Bjorndal (ed.). Biology and Conservation of Sea Turtles. Rev. edn. Smithsonian Institution Press, Washington, D.C.

Mortimer, J. A., J. U. Moreira dos Santos, C. da Silva Rosario, P. Sa, L. T. Silveira, O. C. Nascimento, S. S. Almeida, and A. Garcia. 1986. Biology and conservation of turtles in the region of the Rio Trombetas and the proposed construction of the hydroelectric dam at Cachoeira Porteira. Final Report to Museu Paraense Emilio Goeldi, Belém, Pará, Brazil.

Mount, R. H. 1976. Amphibians and reptiles. Pages 66–79 in H. Boschung (ed.). Endangered and Threatened Plants and Animals of Alabama. Bulletin of the Alabama Museum of Natural History 2.

Mrosovsky, N. 1981. Editorial. Marine Turtle Newsletter 19:1–2.

———. 1982. Sex ratio bias in hatchling sea turtles from artificially incubated eggs. Biological Conservation 23:309–314.

Mrosovsky, N., and M. H. Godfrey. 1995. Manipulating sex ratios: Turtle speed ahead! Chelonian Conservation and Biology 1:238–240.

Mrosovsky, N., S. R. Hopkins-Murphy, and J. I. Richardson. 1984. Sex ratio in sea turtles: Seasonal changes. Science (Washington, D.C.) 225:739–741.

Mrosovsky, N., and C. L. Yntema. 1980. Temperature dependence of sexual differentiation in sea turtles: Implications for conservation practices. Biological Conservation 18:271–280.

Myers, N. 1994. Playing God with nature: Do we have any other choice? Page 185 in D. D. Chiras. Environmental Science: Action for a Sustainable Future. Benjamin and Cummings Publishing, Redwood City, Calif.

Nair, P. N. R., and M. Badrudeen. 1975. On the occurrence of the soft-shelled turtle, Pelochelys bibroni (Owen), in marine environment. Indian Journal of Fisheries 22 (1/2): 270–274.

National Research Council. 1990. Decline of the Sea Turtles: Causes and Prevention. National Academy Press, Washington, D.C.

Nelson, E. W. 1921. Lower California and its natural resources. National Academy of Science Memoirs 16.

Nelson, J. 1989. Agriculture, wetlands, and endangered species: The Food Security Act of 1985. Endangered Species Technical Bulletin 14 (5): 1, 6–8.

Netting, M. G. 1936. Hibernation and migration of the spotted turtle, Clemmys guttata (Schneider). Copeia 1936:112.

Newbery, R. 1984. The American red-eared terrapin in South Africa. African Wildlife 38:186–189.

Ng, P. K. L., L. M. Chou, and T. J. Lam. 1993. The status and impact of introduced freshwater animals in Singapore. Biological Conservation 64:19–24.

Nicholls, R. E. 1977. The Running Press Book of Turtles. Running Press, Philadelphia.

Nicholson, L. 1978. The effects of roads on desert tortoise populations. Pages 127–129 *in* Desert Tortoise Council: Proceedings of the 1978 Symposium. Desert Tortoise Council, San Diego, Calif.

Nietschmann, B. 1973. Between Land and Water: The Subsistence Ecology of the Miskito Indians, Eastern Nicaragua. Seminar Press, New York.

———. 1979a. Caribbean Edge: The Coming of Modern Times to Isolated People and Wildlife. Bobbs-Merrill, New York.

———. 1979b. Ecological change, inflation, and migration in the far western Caribbean. Geographical Review 69:1–24.

———. 1982. The cultural context of sea turtle subsistence hunting in the Caribbean and problems caused by commercial exploitation. Pages 439–445 *in* K. A. Bjorndal (ed.). Biology and Conservation of Sea Turtles. Smithsonian Institution Press, Washington, D.C.

NMFS (National Marine Fisheries Service) and USFWS (U.S. Fish and Wildlife Service). 1991a. Recovery plan for U.S. population of loggerhead turtle. National Marine Fisheries Service, Washington, D.C.

———. 1991b. Recovery plan for U.S. population of the Atlantic green turtle *Chelonia mydas*. National Marine Fisheries Service, Washington, D.C.

———. 1992a. Recovery plan for leatherback turtles in the U.S. Caribbean, Atlantic and Gulf of Mexico. National Marine Fisheries Service, Washington, D.C.

———. 1992b. Recovery plan for hawksbill turtles in the U.S. Caribbean, Atlantic, and Gulf of Mexico. National Marine Fisheries Service, St. Petersburg, Fla.

———. 1995. Status reviews for sea turtles listed under the Endangered Species Act of 1973. National Marine Fisheries Service, Silver Spring, Md.

Noss, R. F., and A. R. Cooperrider. 1994. Saving Nature's Legacy: Protecting and Restoring Biodiversity. Island Press, Washington, D.C.

Noss, R. F., and L. D. Harris. 1986. Nodes, networks, and MUMs: Preserving diversity at all scales. Environmental Management 10:299–309.

Noss, R. F., E. T. LaRoe III, and J. M. Scott. 1995. Endangered ecosystems of the United States: A preliminary assessment of loss and degradation. National Biological Survey, Biological Report 28.

Obbard, M. E., and R. J. Brooks. 1981. Fate of overwintered clutches of the common snapping turtle *(Chelydra serpentina)* in Algonquin Park, Ontario. Canadian Field Naturalist 95:350–352.

Obendorf, D. L., J. Carson, and T. J. McManus. 1987. *Vibrio damsela* infection in a stranded leatherback turtle *(Dermochelys coriacea)*. Journal of Wildlife Diseases 23 (4): 666–668.

Obst, F. J. 1986. Turtles, Tortoises and Terrapins. Druckerei Fortschritt Erfurt, Edn. Leipzig, German Democratic Republic.

Odum, H. T. 1957. Trophic structure and productivity of Silver Springs, Florida. Ecological Monographs 27:55–112.

Ogren, L. 1989. Memorandum to Edward Klima, 17 November 1989. National Marine Fisheries Service F/Sec5/PRP.

Ogren, L., F. Berry, K. Bjorndal, H. Kumpf, R. Mast, G. Medina, H. Reichart, and R. Witham (eds.). 1989. Proceedings of the Second Western Atlantic Turtle Symposium. NOAA Technical Memorandum NMFS-SEFSC-226.

Ojasti, J. 1973. La problemática del tortuga arrau. Ministerio de Agricultura y Cria, Dirección de Recursos Naturales Renovables, Caracas.

————. 1995. Uso y conservación de la fauna silvestre en la Amazonia. Tratado de Cooperación Amazonica, Secretaria Pro-Tempore, Lima.

Oldemeyer, J. L. 1994. Livestock grazing and the desert tortoise in the Mojave desert. Pages 95–103 in R. B. Bury and D. J. Germano (eds.). Biology of North American Tortoises. National Biological Survey, Washington, D.C.

Olla, B. L., M. W. Davis, and C. H. Ryer. 1994. Behavioural deficits in hatchery-reared fish: Potential effects on survival following release. Aquaculture and Fisheries Management 25 (supplement 1): 19–34.

Ordoñez, G., M. Araúz Almengor, C. M. Somarriba Anria, and J. C. Castro. 1994. Ostional: A community which lives together with the olive ridley marine turtle, *Lepidochelys olivacea*. Pages 129–131 in B. A. Schroeder and B. E. Witherington (compilers). Proceedings of the Thirteenth Annual Workshop on Sea Turtle Biology and Conservation. NOAA Technical Memorandum NMFS-SEFSC-341.

Ordoñez, G., and J. Ballestero. 1994. Sea turtle conservation and management: Ostional development association work during 1993 in the Ostional Wildlife Refuge, Guanacaste, Costa Rica. Pages 268–269 in K. A. Bjorndal, A. B. Bolten, D. A. Johnson, and P. J. Eliazar (compilers). Proceedings of the Fourteenth Annual Symposium on Sea Turtle Biology and Conservation. NOAA Technical Memorandum NMFS-SEFSC-351.

Orr, D. W. 1990. The question of management. Conservation Biology 4:8–9.

Ostrom, E. 1990. Governing the Commons. The Evolution of Institutions for Collective Action. Cambridge University Press, New York.

Packard, G. C., and M. J. Packard. 1988. The physiological ecology of reptilian eggs and embryos. Pages 523–605 in C. Gans (ed.). Biology of the Reptilia. Vol. 16B, Defense and Life History. Academic Press, New York.

Packard, G. C., M. J. Packard, and T. J. Boardman. 1984. Influence of hydration of the environment on the pattern of nitrogen excretion by embryonic snapping turtles *(Chelydra serpentina)*. Journal of Experimental Biology 108:195–204.

Packard, G. C., M. J. Packard, T. J. Boardman, and M. D. Ashen. 1981. Possible adaptive value of water exchanges in flexible-shelled eggs of turtles. Science (Washington, D.C.) 213:471–473.

Packard, G. C., M. J. Packard, and W. H. N. Gutzke. 1985. Influence of hydration of the environment on eggs and embryos of the terrestrial turtle *Terrapene ornata*. Physiological Zoology 58 (5): 564–575.

Packard, G. C., M. J. Packard, K. Miller, and T. J. Boardman. 1988. Effects of temperature and moisture during incubation on carcass composition of hatchling snapping turtles *(Chelydra serpentina)*. Journal of Comparative Physiology B 158:117–125.

Packard, M. J., and G. C. Packard. 1986. Effect of water balance on growth and calcium mobilization of embryonic painted turtles *(Chrysemys picta)*. Physiological Zoology 59 (4): 398–405.

Padua, L. F. M., and C. J. R. Alho. 1984. Avaliacao do comportamento de nidificacao em *Podocnemis expansa* (Testudinata, Pelomedusidae) durante cinco anos em area de protecao. Brasil Florestal 59:59–61.

Paez, V., and B. Bock. 1993. The yellow-spotted Amazon river turtle: A summary of Project Teracay. New York Turtle and Tortoise Society NewsNotes 4 (2): 21.

Pappas, M. J., and B. J. Brecke. 1992. Habitat selection of juvenile Blanding's turtles, *Emydoidea blandingii*. Journal of Herpetology 26:233–234.

Parker, P. G., and H. H. Whiteman. 1993. Genetic diversity in fragmented populations of *Clemmys guttata* and *Chrysemys picta marginata* as shown by DNA fingerprinting. Copeia 1993:841–846.

Parmalee, P. W. 1989. Muskrat predation on softshell turtles. Journal of the Tennessee Academy of Science 64:225–227.

Parmenter, R. R. 1980. Effects of food availability and water temperature on the feeding ecology of pond sliders *(Chrysemys scripta)*. Copeia 1980:503–514.

Parmenter, R. R., and H. W. Avery. 1990. The feeding ecology of the slider turtle. Pages 257–266 *in* J. W. Gibbons (ed.). Life History and Ecology of the Slider Turtle. Smithsonian Institution Press, Washington, D.C.

Parsons, J. J. 1962. The Green Turtle and Man. University of Florida Press, Gainesville.

———. 1972. The hawksbill turtle and the tortoise shell trade. Pages 45–60 *in* Études de Géographie Tropicale Offertes à Pierre Gourou. Mouton, Paris.

Paukstis, F. L., and F. J. Janzen. 1990. Sex determination in reptiles: Summary of effects of constant temperatures of incubation on sex ratios of offspring. Smithsonian Herpetological Information Service 83:1–28.

Pennisi, E. 1996. A new look at maternal guidance. Science (Washington, D.C.) 273:1334–1336.

Perlin, J. 1989. A Forest Journey: The Role of Wood in the Development of Civilization. W. W. Norton, New York.

Petokas, P. J., and M. M. Alexander. 1980. The nesting of *Chelydra serpentina* in northern New York. Journal of Herpetology 14:239–244.

Pettan-Brewer, K. C. B., M. L. Drew, E. Ramsay, F. C. Mohr, and L. J. Lowenstine. 1996. Herpesvirus particles associated with oral and respiratory lesions in a California desert tortoise *(Gopherus agassizii)*. Journal of Wildlife Diseases 32 (3): 521–526.

Phillips, C. A., W. W. Dimmick, and J. L. Carr. 1996. Conservation genetics of the common snapping turtle *(Chelydra serpentina)*. Conservation Biology 10:397–405.

Platt, S. G., and L. W. Fontenot. 1992. The red-eared slider, *Trachemys scripta* (Weid), in South Korea. Bulletin of the Chicago Herpetological Society 27:113–114.

Plotkin, P. T., R. A. Byles, D. C. Rostal, and D. W. Owens. 1995. Independent versus socially facilitated oceanic migrations of the olive ridley, *Lepidochelys olivacea*. Marine Biology 122:137–143.

Plummer, M. V. 1976. Some aspects of nesting success in the turtle, *Trionyx muticus*. Herpetologica 32:353–359.

Polisar, J. 1992. Reproductive biology and exploitation of the Central American river turtle *Dermatemys mawii* in Belize. Master's thesis, University of Florida, Gainesville.

———. 1995. River turtle reproductive demography and exploitation patterns in Belize: Implications for management. Vida Silvestre Neotropical 4:10–19.

Polisar, J., and R. Horwich. 1994. Conservation of the large economically important river turtle *Dermatemys mawii* in Belize. Conservation Biology 8:338–342.

Polunin, N. V. C. 1975. Sea turtles: Reports on Thailand, West Malaysia and Indonesia, with a synopsis of data on the conservation status of sea turtles in the Indo-West Pacific Region. International Union for Conservation of Nature and Natural Resources, Morges, Switzerland. Mimeographed.

Polunin, N. V. C., and N. Sumertha Nuitja. 1982. Sea turtle populations of Indonesia and Thailand. Pages 353–362 *in* K. A. Bjorndal (ed.). Biology and Conservation of Sea Turtles. Smithsonian Institution Press, Washington, D.C.

Postel, S., and J. C. Ryan. 1991. Reforming forestry. Pages 74–92 *in* L. R. Brown (ed.).

State of the World, 1991: A Worldwatch Institute on Progress toward a Sustainable Society. W. W. Norton, New York.

Pough, F. H. 1980. The advantages of ectothermy for tetrapods. American Naturalist 115:92–112.

Primack, R. B. 1993. Essentials of Conservation Biology. Sinauer, Sunderland, Mass.

Pritchard, P. C. H. 1978. Comment on Tim Cahill's article "The Shame of Escobilla." Marine Turtle Newsletter 7:2–4.

———. 1979. Encyclopedia of Turtles. T. F. H. Publications, Neptune, N.J.

———. 1980. Record size turtles from Florida and South America. Chelonologica 1:113–123.

———. 1984. Piscivory in turtles and evolution of the long-necked Chelidae. Symposium of the Zoological Society London 52:87–110.

———. 1989. The Alligator Snapping Turtle: Biology and Conservation. Milwaukee Public Museum, Milwaukee, Wisc.

———. 1993. A ranching project for freshwater turtles in Costa Rica. Chelonian Conservation and Biology 1:48.

———. 1996. The Galápagos Tortoises: Nomenclatural and Survival Status. Chelonian Research Monographs, no. 1. Chelonian Research Foundation, Lunenburg, Mass.

Pritchard, P. C. H., and R. Márquez M. 1973. Kemp's Ridley Turtle or Atlantic Ridley, *Lepidochelys kempii*. International Union for Conservation of Nature and Natural Resources, Monograph no. 2. Morges, Switzerland.

Pritchard, P. C. H., and P. Trebbau. 1984. The Turtles of Venezuela. Contributions to Herpetology, no. 2. Society for the Study of Amphibians and Reptiles, Athens, Ohio.

Ramirez, J. P. 1986. Water development projects in the Rio Grande and their relationships to the Santa Ana and Rio Grande Valley National Wildlife Refuges. Report by U.S. Fish and Wildlife Service, Corpus Christi Field Office, for Santa Ana and Rio Grande Valley National Wildlife Refuges, Alamo, Texas.

Ramirez-de Veyra, R. T. D. 1994. Status of marine turtles in the Philippines. Pages 123–125 *in* K. A. Bjorndal, A. B. Bolten, D. A. Johnson, and P. J. Eliazar (compilers). Proceedings of the Fourteenth Annual Symposium on Sea Turtle Biology and Conservation. NOAA Technical Memorandum NMFS-SEFSC-351.

RANA International Foundation. 1994. RANA News, no. 1. Tervuren, Belgium.

Rao, R. J. 1986. Freshwater turtle conservation in National Chambal Sanctuary. Tigerpaper 13 (3): 28–29.

———. 1991. Conservation management of freshwater turtles in the National Chambal Sanctuary. Journal of the Ecological Society 4:43–53.

Raphael, B., M. W. Klemens, P. Moehlman, E. Dierenfeld, and W. B. Karesh. 1994. Blood values in free-ranging pancake tortoises *(Malacochersus tornieri)*. Journal of Zoo and Wildlife Medicine 25 (1): 63–67.

Ratnaswamy, M. J. 1995. Raccoon depredation of sea turtle nests at Canaveral National Seashore, Florida: Implications for species management and conservation. Doctoral dissertation, University of Georgia, Athens.

Raymond, P. W. 1984. Sea turtle hatchling disorientation and artificial beachfront lighting. Report to the Center for Environmental Education, Sea Turtle Rescue Fund. Center for Environmental Education, Washington, D.C.

Real, L. A. 1996. Sustainability and the ecology of infectious disease. BioScience 46:88–97.

Rebel, T. P. 1974. Sea Turtles and the Turtle Industry of the West Indies, Florida, and the Gulf of Mexico. Rev. edn. University of Miami Press, Miami.

Reese, D. A., and H. H. Welsh. 1997. Use of terrestrial habitat by western pond turtles, *Clemmys marmorata:* Implications for management. Pages 352–357 *in* J. Van Abbema (ed.). Proceedings: Conservation, Restoration, and Management of Tortoises and Turtles—an International Conference, July 1993, State University of New York at Purchase. New York Turtle and Tortoise Society, New York.

Regional Plan Association. 1991. Great Swamp Conservation Plan. Regional Plan Association, New York.

Reichart, H. A. 1993. Synopsis of biological data on the olive ridley sea turtle *Lepidochelys olivacea* (Eschscholtz, 1829) in the Western Atlantic. NOAA Technical Memorandum NMFS-SEFSC-336.

Reinert, H. K. 1991. Translocation as a conservation strategy for amphibians and reptiles: Some comments, concerns, and observations. Herpetologica 47:357–363.

Rhodin, A. G. J., F. Medem, and R. A. Mittermeier. 1981. The occurrence of neustophagia among podocnemine turtles. British Journal of Herpetology 6:175–176.

Rhodin, A. G. J., R. A. Mittermeier, and P. M. Hall. 1993. Distribution, osteology, and natural history of the Asian giant softshell turtle, *Pelochelys bibroni*, in Papua New Guinea. Chelonian Conservation and Biology 1:19–30.

Richard, J. D., and D. A. Hughes. 1972. Some observations of sea turtle nesting activity in Costa Rica. Marine Biology 16:297–309.

Rideout, B. A., R. J. Montali, L. G. Phillips, and C. H. Gardiner. 1987. Mortality of captive tortoises due to viviparous nematodes of the genus *Proatractis* (Family Atractidae). Journal of Wildlife Diseases 23 (1): 103–108.

Robinson, C., and J. R. Bider. 1988. Nesting synchrony—a strategy to decrease predation of snapping turtle *(Chelydra serpentina)* nests. Journal of Herpetology 22:470–473.

Robinson, J. G., and K. H. Redford. 1994. Community-based approaches to wildlife conservation in Neotropical forests. Pages 300–319 *in* D. Western and R. M. Wright (eds.). Natural Connections: Perspectives in Community-Based Conservation. Island Press, Washington, D.C.

Rodríguez, J. P., and F. Rojas-Suárez. 1995. Libro Rojo de la Fauna Venezolana. Provita, Caracas.

Roosenburg, W. M. 1990. The diamondback terrapin: Population dynamics, habitat requirements, and opportunities for conservation. Pages 227–234 *in* New Perspectives in the Chesapeake System: A Research and Management Partnership. Chesapeake Research Consortium, publication no. 137. Baltimore, Md.

———. 1996. Maternal condition and nest site choice: An alternative for the maintenance of environmental sex determination? American Zoologist 36 (2): 157–168.

Roosenburg, W. M., W. Cresko, M. Modesitte, and M. B. Robbins. 1997. Diamondback terrapin *(Malaclemys terrapin)* mortality in crab pots. Conservation Biology 11:1166–1172.

Rose, D. A. 1993. The politics of Mexican wildlife: Conservation, development, and the international system. Doctoral dissertation, University of Florida, Gainesville.

Rose, F. L., and F. W. Judd. 1982. Biology and status of Berlandier's tortoise *(Gopherus berlandieri)*. Pages 57–70 *in* R. B. Bury (ed.). North American Tortoises: Conservation and Ecology. U.S. Fish and Wildlife Service, Wildlife Research Report 12.

———. 1989. *Gopherus berlandieri*, Berlandier's tortoise. Pages 8–9 *in* I. R. Swingland and

M. W. Klemens (eds.). The Conservation Biology of Tortoises. Occasional Papers of the IUCN Species Survival Commission, no. 5. Gland, Switzerland.

Ross, D. A., and R. K. Anderson. 1990. Habitat use, movements, and nesting of *Emydoidea blandingii* in central Wisconsin. Journal of Herpetology 24:6–12.

Ross, J. P. 1982. Historical review of the decline of loggerhead, ridley and leatherback sea turtles. Pages 189–195 *in* K. A. Bjorndal (ed.). Biology and Conservation of Sea Turtles. Smithsonian Institution Press, Washington, D.C.

———. 1993. CITES criteria for sea turtle ranching. Marine Turtle Newsletter 61:23–24.

———. 1999. Ranching and captive breeding sea turtles: Evaluation as a conservation strategy. *In* K. L. Eckert, K. A. Bjorndal, F. A. Abreu-Grobois, and M. Donnelly (eds.). Research and Management Techniques for the Conservation of Sea Turtles. International Union for Conservation of Nature and Natural Resources, Species Survival Commission, Marine Turtle Specialist Group, publication no. 4. Washington, D.C.

Ross, J. P., and M. A. Barwani. 1982. Review of sea turtles in the Arabian area. Pages 373–383 *in* K. A. Bjorndal (ed.). Biology and Conservation of Sea Turtles. Smithsonian Institution Press, Washington, D.C.

Ross, J. P., S. Beavers, D. Mundell, and M. Airth-Kindree. 1989. The status of Kemp's ridley. Center for Marine Conservation, Washington, D.C.

Rowe, A. 1993. Today terrapins, tomorrow the world. BBC Wildlife 11 (4): 15.

Rust, R. W., and R. R. Roth. 1981. Seed production and seedling establishment in the mayapple, *Podophyllum peltatum* L. American Midland Naturalist 105:51–60.

Salmon, M., J. Wyneken, E. Fritz, and M. Lucas. 1992. Seafinding by hatchling sea turtles: Role of brightness, silhouette and beach slope as orientation cues. Behaviour 122:56–77.

Sarker, S. D., and L. Hossain. 1997. Population and habitat status of freshwater turtles and tortoises of Bangladesh and their conservation aspects. Pages 290–294 *in* J. Van Abbema (ed.). Proceedings: Conservation, Restoration, and Management of Tortoises and Turtles—an International Conference, July 1993, State University of New York at Purchase. New York Turtle and Tortoise Society, New York.

Sarto, L., S. Eckert, N. Garcia, and A. Barragan. 1996. Decline of the world's largest nesting assemblage of leatherback turtles. Marine Turtle Newsletter 74:2–5.

Saunders, D. A., R. J. Hobbs, and C. R. Margules. 1991. Biological consequences of ecosystem fragmentation: A review. Conservation Biology 5:18–32.

Schmidt, K. P. 1919. Contributions to the herpetology of the Belgium Congo based on the collection of the American Museum Congo Expedition 1909–1915. Pt. I. Turtles, crocodiles, lizards, and chameleons. Bulletin of the American Museum of Natural History 39:385–624.

Schneider, J. S., and G. D. Everson. 1989. The desert tortoise *(Xerobates agassizii)* in the prehistory of the southwestern Great Basin and adjacent areas. Journal of California and Great Basin Anthropology 11:175–202.

Schulman, A., S. Milton, and P. Lutz. 1994. Aragonite sand as a substrate and its effect on *Caretta caretta* nests. Page 134 *in* K. A. Bjorndal, A. B. Bolten, D. A. Johnson, and P. J. Eliazar (compilers). Proceedings of the Fourteenth Annual Symposium on Sea Turtle Biology and Conservation. NOAA Technical Memorandum NMFS-SEFSC-351.

Schulz, J. 1984. Turtle conservation strategy in Indonesia. International Union for Conservation of Nature and Natural Resources and World Wide Fund for Nature Report. Gland, Switzerland.

Schwartz, A., and R. Henderson. 1991. Amphibians and Reptiles of the West Indies: Descriptions, Distributions and Natural History. University of Florida Press, Gainesville.

Schwartz, E. R., C. W. Schwartz, and A. R. Kiester. 1984. The three-toed box turtle in central Missouri. Pt. II. A nineteen year study of home range, movements and population. Missouri Department of Conservation, Terrestrial Series no. 12. Jefferson City.

Scott, N. J., and R. A. Seigel. 1992. The management of reptile and amphibian populations: Species priorities and methodological and theoretical constraints. Pages 343–368 in D. R. McCullough and R. H. Barrett (eds.). Wildlife 2001: Populations. Elsevier Applied Science, London.

Scribner, K. T., J. E. Evans, S. J. Morreale, M. H. Smith, and J. W. Gibbons. 1986. Genetic divergence among populations of the yellow-bellied slider turtle (Pseudemys scripta) separated by aquatic and terrestrial habitats. Copeia 1986:691–700.

Seabrook, W. 1989. Feral cats (Felis catus) as predators of hatchling green turtles (Chelonia mydas). Journal of Zoology, London 219:83–88.

Seidel, M. E. 1978. Kinosternon flavescens (Agassiz). Catalog of American Amphibians and Reptiles 216.1–216.4. Society for the Study of Amphibians and Reptiles, Athens, Ohio.

———. 1994. Morphometric analysis and taxonomy of cooter and red-bellied turtles in the North American genus Pseudemys (Emydidae). Chelonian Conservation and Biology 1:117–130.

Seigel, R. A. 1993. Apparent long-term decline in diamondback terrapin populations at the Kennedy Space Center, Florida. Herpetological Review 24:102–103.

Seigel, R. A., and J. W. Gibbons. 1995. Workshop on the ecology, status, and management of the diamondback terrapin (Malaclemys terrapin), Savannah River Ecology Laboratory, 2 August 1994: Final results and recommendations. Chelonian Conservation and Biology 1:240–243.

Semlitsch, R. D., and J. W. Gibbons. 1989. Lack of largemouth bass predation on hatchling turtles (Trachemys scripta). Copeia 1989:1030–1031.

Settle, S. 1995. Status of nesting populations of sea turtles in Thailand and their conservation. Marine Turtle Newsletter 68:8–13.

Shaffer, H. B., P. Meylan, and M. L. McKnight. 1997. Tests of turtle phylogeny: Molecular, morphological, and paleontological approaches. Systematic Biology 46:235–268.

Shaffer, M. L. 1981. Minimum population sizes for species conservation. BioScience 31:131–134.

———. 1990. Nature Reserves, Island Theory and Conservation Practice. Smithsonian Institution Press, Washington, D.C.

———. 1994. Population viability analysis: Determining nature's share. Pages 195–196 in G. K. Meffe and C. R. Carroll (eds.). Principles of Conservation Biology. Sinauer, Sunderland, Mass.

Shaver, D. J. 1991. Feeding ecology of wild and head-started Kemp's ridley sea turtles in south Texas waters. Journal of Herpetology 25:327–334.

———. 1996. Head-started Kemp's ridley turtles nest in Texas. Marine Turtle Newsletter 74:5–7.

Shaver, D. J., D. Owens, A. H. Chaney, C. W. Caillouet, Jr., P. Burchfield, and R. Márquez M. 1988. Styrofoam box and beach temperatures in relation to incubation and sex ratios of Kemp's ridleys. Pages 103–108 in B. A. Schroeder (compiler). Proceedings of the Eighth Annual Workshop on Sea Turtle Conservation and Biology. NOAA Technical Memorandum NMFS-SEFSC-214.

Shealy, R. M. 1976. The natural history of the Alabama map turtle, *Graptemys pulchra* Baur, in Alabama. Bulletin of the Florida State Museum of Biological Sciences 21:47–111.

Shibata, Y. 1975. The zoological origin of the imported crude drug "gui-ban" from Hong Kong (Reptilia: Testudinata). Bulletin of the Osaka Museum of Natural History 29:73–80.

Shrestha, T. K. 1997. Status, biology, conservation, and management of tortoises and turtles in the Himalayan foothills of Nepal. Pages 278–286 in J. Van Abbema (ed.). Proceedings: Conservation, Restoration, and Management of Tortoises and Turtles—an International Conference, July 1993, State University of New York at Purchase. New York Turtle and Tortoise Society, New York.

Silas, E. G., and M. Rajagopalan. 1984. Recovery programme for olive ridley, *Lepidochelys olivacea* (Eschscholtz, 1829), along Madras coast. Pages 9–21 in Sea Turtle Research and Conservation. Central Marine Fisheries Research Institute, Bulletin 35. Cochin, India.

Siow, K. T., and E. O. Moll. 1982. Status and conservation of estuarine and sea turtles in west Malaysian waters. Pages 339–347 in K. A. Bjorndal (ed.). Biology and Conservation of Sea Turtles. Smithsonian Institution Press, Washington, D.C.

Sloan, K. N., K. A. Buhlmann, and J. E. Lovich. 1996. Stomach contents of commercially harvested adult alligator snapping turtles, *Macroclemys temminckii*. Chelonian Conservation and Biology 2:96–99.

Sloan, K. N., and J. E. Lovich. 1995. Exploitation of the alligator snapping turtle, *Macroclemys temminckii*, in Louisiana: A case study. Chelonian Conservation and Biology 1:221–222.

Smart, A. C., and I. G. Bride. 1993. The UK Trade in Live Reptiles and Amphibians. A Report to the RSPCA on the Nature and Status of the Reptile and Amphibian Pet Trade between 1980 and 1992. Durrell Institute of Conservation and Ecology, University of Kent at Canterbury, United Kingdom.

Smedley, M. A. 1932. Notes on the herpetological collections in the Selangor Museum. Bulletin of the Raffles Museum 7:9–17.

Smith, G. M., and C. W. Coates. 1938. Fibroepithelial growths of the skin in large marine turtles, *Chelonia mydas* (Linnaeus). Zoologica 23:93–98.

Smith, K. R., J. A. Hurley, and R. A. Seigel. 1997. Reproductive biology and demography of gopher tortoises *(Gopherus polyphemus)* from the western portion of the range. Chelonian Conservation and Biology 2:596–600.

Smith, L. L. 1997. Survivorship of hatchling gopher tortoises in north-central Florida. Pages 100–103 in J. Van Abbema (ed.). Proceedings: Conservation, Restoration, and Management of Tortoises and Turtles—an International Conference, July 1993, State University of New York at Purchase. New York Turtle and Tortoise Society, New York.

Smith, M. A. 1931. The Fauna of British India, Including Ceylon and Burma. Reptilia and Amphibia. Vol. 1, Loricata and Testudines. Taylor and Francis, London.

Smith, N. J. H. 1975. Destructive exploitation of the South American river turtle. Chelonia 2:1–9.

———. 1979. Aquatic turtles of Amazonia: An endangered resource. Biological Conservation 16:165–176.

Smith, P. W. 1951. A new frog and a new turtle from the western Illinois sand prairies. Bulletin of the Chicago Academy of Science 9:189–199.

Snipes, K. P., and E. L. Biberstein. 1982. *Pasteurella testudinis* sp. nov.: A parasite of desert tortoises. International Journal of Systematic Bacteriology 32:201–210.

Snipes, K. P., R. W. Kasten, J. M. Calagoan, and J. T. Boothby. 1995. Molecular character-
ization of *Pasteurella testudinis* isolated from desert tortoises *(Gopherus agassizii)* with
and without upper respiratory tract disease. Journal of Wildlife Diseases 31 (1): 22–29.

Snow, J. E. 1982. Predation on painted turtle nests: Nest survival as a function of nest
age. Canadian Journal of Zoology 60:3290–3292.

Snyder, N. F. R., S. R. Derrickson, S. R. Beissinger, J. W. Wiley, T. B. Smith, W. D. Toone,
and B. Miller. 1996. Limitations of captive breeding in endangered species recovery.
Conservation Biology 10:338–348.

Soulé, M. E. 1991. Conservation: Tactics for a constant crisis. Science (Washington, D.C.)
253:774–750.

South Pacific Commission. 1980. Joint SPC–NMFS Workshop on Marine Turtles in the
Tropical Pacific Islands, 11–14 December 1979. South Pacific Commission, Noumea,
New Caledonia.

Sowerby, J. de C., and E. Lear. 1872. Tortoises, Terrapins and Turtles. Henry Sotheran,
London. Reprint, Society for the Study of Amphibians and Reptiles, Athens, Ohio,
1972.

Spotila, J. R., A. E. Dunham, A. J. Leslie, A. Steyermark, P. T. Plotkin, and F. V. Paladino.
1996. Worldwide population decline of *Dermochelys coriacea:* Are leatherback turtles
going extinct? Chelonian Conservation and Biology 2:209–222.

Spring, C. S. 1982a. Subsistence hunting of marine turtles in Papua New Guinea. Pages
291–295 *in* K. A. Bjorndal (ed.). Biology and Conservation of Sea Turtles. Smithsonian
Institution Press, Washington, D.C.

————. 1982b. Status of marine turtle populations in Papua New Guinea. Pages 281–289
in K. A. Bjorndal (ed.). Biology and Conservation of Sea Turtles. Smithsonian Institution Press, Washington, D.C.

Stackhouse, J. 1992. 25,000 omnivorous turtles live on carrion, clean river. Anchorage
Daily News, Sunday, 27 September, section A, page 13.

Stancyk, S. E. 1982. Non-human predators of sea turtles and their control. Pages 139–152
in K. A. Bjorndal (ed.). Biology and Conservation of Sea Turtles. Smithsonian Institution Press, Washington, D.C.

Stancyk, S. E., O. R. Talbert, Jr., and J. M. Dean. 1980. Nesting activity of the loggerhead
turtle *Caretta caretta* in South Carolina. II. Protection of nests from raccoon predation
by transplantation. Biological Conservation 18:289–298.

Standora, E. A., and J. R. Spotila. 1985. Temperature dependent sex determination in sea
turtles. Copeia 1985:711–722.

Stanley, T. R., Jr. 1995. Ecosystem management and the arrogance of humanism. Conservation Biology 9:255–262.

Stebbins, R. C. 1985. A Field Guide to Western Reptiles and Amphibians. Houghton
Mifflin, Boston.

Stewart, G. R. 1993. Movements and survival of desert tortoises *(Gopherus agassizii)*
following relocation from the Luz Solar Electric Plant at Kramer Junction. Pages
234–261 *in* Desert Tortoise Council: Proceedings of the 1992 Symposium. Desert
Tortoise Council, San Diego, Calif.

Stoddart, D. R. 1984. Impact of man in the Seychelles. Pages 641–654 *in* D. R. Stoddart
(ed.). Biogeography and Ecology of the Seychelles Islands. Dr. W. Junk, The Hague,
Netherlands.

Stoddart, D. R., and J. F. Peake. 1979. Historical records of Indian Ocean giant tortoise populations. Philosophical Transactions of the Royal Society of London, Series B, Biological Sciences 286:147–161.

Stone, W. B., E. Kiviat, and S. A. Butkas. 1980. Toxicants in snapping turtles. New York Fish and Game Journal 27:39–50.

Storm, G. L., and W. L. Palmer. 1995. White-tailed deer in the Northeast. Pages 112–115 in E. T. LaRoe, G. S. Farris, C. E. Puckett, P. D. Doran, and M. J. Mac (eds.). Our Living Resources: A Report to the Nation on the Distribution, Abundance, and Health of U.S. Plants, Animals, and Ecosystems. National Biological Survey, Washington, D.C.

Stubbs, D. 1989a. Testudo hermanni, Hermann's tortoise. Pages 34–36 in I. R. Swingland and M. W. Klemens (eds.). The Conservation Biology of Tortoises. Occasional Papers of the IUCN Species Survival Commission, no. 5. Gland, Switzerland.

———. 1989b. Testudo marginata, marginated tortoise. Pages 41–42 in I. R. Swingland and M. W. Klemens (eds.). The Conservation Biology of Tortoises. Occasional Papers of the IUCN Species Survival Commission, no. 5. Gland, Switzerland.

———. 1995. Testudo hermanni in France. Pages 94–102 in D. Ballasina (ed.). Red Data Book on Mediterranean Chelonians. Edagricole-Edzioni Agricole, Bologna, Italy.

Stubbs, D., I. R. Swingland, A. Hailey, and E. Pulford. 1985. The ecology of the Mediterranean tortoise Testudo hermanni in northern Greece (the effects of a catastrophe on population structure and density). Biological Conservation 31:125–152.

Suwelo, I. S. 1990. Indonesian hawksbill turtle ranching: A pilot project. Marine Turtle Newsletter 49:16.

Swingland, I. R. 1989a. Geochelone elephantopus, Galápagos giant tortoise. Pages 24–28 in I. R. Swingland and M. W. Klemens (eds.). The Conservation Biology of Tortoises. Occasional Papers of the IUCN Species Survival Commission, no. 5. Gland, Switzerland.

———. 1989b. Geochelone gigantea, Aldabran giant tortoise. Pages 105–110 in I. R. Swingland and M. W. Klemens (eds.). The Conservation Biology of Tortoises. Occasional Papers of the IUCN Species Survival Commission, no. 5. Gland, Switzerland.

———. 1994. International conservation and captive management of tortoises. Pages 99–107 in J. B. Murphy, K. Adler, and J. T. Collins (eds.). Captive Management and Conservation of Amphibians and Reptiles. SSAR (Society for the Study of Amphibians and Reptiles) Contributions to Herpetology, vol. 11. Athens, Ohio.

Swingland, I. R., and M. W. Klemens. 1989. The Conservation Biology of Tortoises. Occasional Papers of the IUCN Species Survival Commission, no. 5. Gland, Switzerland.

Talbert, O. R., Jr., S. E. Stancyk, J. M. Dean, and J. M. Will. 1980. Nesting activity of the loggerhead turtle Caretta caretta in South Carolina. I. A rookery in transition. Copeia 1980:709–719.

Taskavak, E., and M. K. Atatür. 1995. Threats to survival of Euphrates soft-shelled turtle, (Rafetus euphraticus Daudin, 1802) in southeastern Anatolia. Pages 228–231 in Proceedings International Congress of Chelonian Conservation, July 1995, Gonfaron, France. Editions SOPTOM (Station d'observation et de protectiòn des tortues des maures), Gonfaron, France.

Taubes, G. 1992. A dubious battle to save the Kemp's ridley sea turtle. Science (Washington, D.C.) 256:614–616.

Taylor, E. H. 1970. The turtles and crocodiles of Thailand and adjacent waters; with a synoptic herpetological bibliography. University of Kansas Science Bulletin 49 (3): 87–179.

Taylor, R. W., Jr. 1982. Human predation on the gopher tortoise (Gopherus polyphemus) in north-central Florida. Bulletin of the Florida State Museum, Biological Science 28:79–102.

Temple, S. A. 1987. Predation on turtle nests increases near ecological edges. Copeia 1987:250–252.

Templeton, A. R. 1994. Coadaptation, local adaptation, and outbreeding depression. Pages 152–153 in G. K. Meffe and R. K. Carroll (eds.). Principles of Conservation Biology. Sinauer, Sunderland, Mass.

Theobald, W. 1868. Catalogue of reptiles in the Museum of the Asiatic Society of Bengal. Journal of the Asiatic Society Bengal. Extra number, 1–88.

Thirakhupt, K., and P. P. van Dijk. 1994. Species diversity and conservation of turtles in western Thailand. Natural History Bulletin of the Siam Society 42 (2): 207–258.

———. 1997. The turtles of western Thailand—pushed to the edge by progress. Pages 272–277 in J. Van Abbema (ed.). Proceedings: Conservation, Restoration, and Management of Tortoises and Turtles—an International Conference, July 1993, State University of New York at Purchase. New York Turtle and Tortoise Society, New York.

Thompson, F. G. 1953. Further evidence of the occurrence of the wood turtle, *Clemmys insculpta*, in northeastern Ohio. Herpetologica 9:74.

Thompson, M. B. 1983. Populations of the Murray River tortoise, *Emydura* (Chelodina): The effect of egg predation by the red fox, *Vulpes vulpes*. Australian Wildlife Research 11:491–499.

———. 1993. Hypothetical considerations of the biomass of chelid tortoises in the River Murray and the possible influences of predation by introduced foxes. Pages 219–224 in D. Lunney and D. Ayers (eds.). Herpetology in Australia—a Diverse Discipline. Transactions of the Royal Zoological Society of New South Wales, Mosman.

Thorbjarnarson, J. B., N. Pérez, and T. Escalona. 1997. Biology and conservation of aquatic turtles in the Cinaruco-Capanaparo National Park, Venezuela. Pages 109–112 in J. Van Abbema (ed.). Proceedings: Conservation, Restoration, and Management of Tortoises and Turtles—an International Conference, July 1993, State University of New York at Purchase. New York Turtle and Tortoise Society, New York.

Thornhill, G. M. 1982. Comparative reproduction of the turtle, *Chrysemys scripta elegans*, in heated and natural lakes. Journal of Herpetology 16:347–353.

Thrushfield, M. 1995. The ecology of disease. In Veterinary Epidemiology. 2nd edn. Blackwell Scientific Publications, Cambridge, Mass.

Tinkle, D. W., J. D. Congdon, and P. C. Rosen. 1981. Nesting frequency and success: Implications for the demography of painted turtles. Ecology 62:1426–1432.

Torok, L. S. 1994. The impacts of storm water discharges on an emergent bog community featuring a population of the bog turtles *(Clemmys muhlenbergii)* in Gloucester County, New Jersey. Bulletin of the Maryland Herpetological Society 30:51–61.

Townsend, C. H. 1902. Statistics of the fisheries of the Mississippi River and tributaries. U.S. Commission of Fish and Fisheries, Commissioner's Report for 1901: 659–740.

———. 1925. The Galápagos tortoises in their relation to the whaling industry. Zoologica 4 (3): 55–135.

Tryon, B. W. 1990. Bog turtles in the south: A question of survival. Bulletin of the Chicago Herpetological Society 25:57–66.

Tryon, B. W., and D. W. Herman. 1990. Status, conservation, and management of the bog turtle, *Clemmys muhlenbergii*, in the southeastern United States. Pages 36–53 in K. R. Beaman, F. Caporaso, S. McKeown, and M. D. Graff (eds.). Proceedings of the

First International Symposium on Turtles and Tortoises: Conservation and Captive Husbandry. California Turtle and Tortoise Club, Los Angeles, Calif.

Turner, F. B., P. A. Medica, and R. B. Bury. 1987. Age–size relationships of desert tortoises *(Gopherus agassizii)* in southern Nevada. Copeia 1987:974–979.

USFWS (U.S. Fish and Wildlife Service). 1989. Emergency action taken to protect the desert tortoise. Endangered Species Technical Bulletin 14:1, 5–6.

———. 1990a. Flattened Musk Turtle Recovery Plan. U.S. Fish and Wildlife Service, Jackson, Mich.

———. 1990b. Endangered and threatened wildlife and plants: Determination of threatened status for the Mojave population of the desert tortoise. Federal Register 55, no. 63: 12178–12191.

———. 1992a. Transfer of *Clemmys muhlenbergii* from Appendix II to Appendix I. Conference of the Parties 8. CITES Secretariat, Châtelaine-Genève, Switzerland.

———. 1992b. Inclusion of *Clemmys insculpta* on Appendix II. Conference of the Parties 8. CITES Secretariat, Châtelaine-Genève, Switzerland.

———. 1993a. Yellow-Blotched Map Turtle *(Graptemys flavimaculata)* Recovery Plan. U.S. Fish and Wildlife Service, Jackson, Mich.

———. 1993b. Draft recovery plan for the desert tortoise (Mojave population). U.S. Fish and Wildlife Service, Portland, Oreg.

———. 1994a. Federal Register 59, no. 234 (7 December): 63101–63105.

———. 1994b. Inclusion of all of the species in the genus *Terrapene* in Appendix II, retaining *Terrapene coahuila* in Appendix I. Conference of the Parties 9. CITES Secretariat, Châtelaine-Genève, Switzerland.

———. 1995a. Federal Register 60, no. 97 (19 May): 26897–26899.

———. 1995b. Changes in the list of species in appendices to the Convention on International Trade in Endangered Species of Wild Fauna and Flora. Federal Register 60, no. 189 (29 September): 50477–50503.

———. 1996a. Proposal to amend Appendices I and II of the Convention. Inclusion of all the species in the genus *Apalone* in Appendix II, in accordance with Article II 2(a). Conference of the Parties 10. CITES Secretariat, Châtelaine-Genève, Switzerland.

———. 1996b. Proposal to amend Appendices I and II of the Convention. Inclusion of *Macroclemys temminckii* in Appendix II, in accordance with Article II 2(a). Conference of the Parties 10. CITES Secretariat, Châtelaine-Genève, Switzerland.

———. 1996c. Federal Register 61, no. 133 (10 July): 36388–36389.

———. 1996d. Federal Register 61, no. 23 (2 February): 3894–3898.

———. 1996e. Federal Register 61, no. 15 (23 January): 1780–1783.

———. 1997. Endangered and threatened wildlife and plants; final rule to list the northern population of the bog turtle as threatened and the southern population as threatened due to similarity of appearance. Federal Register 62, no. 213: 59605–59623.

USFWS (U.S. Fish and Wildlife Service) and NMFS (National Marine Fisheries Service). 1992. Recovery Plan for the Kemp's Ridley Sea Turtle *(Lepidochelys kempii)*. National Marine Fisheries Service, St. Petersburg, Fla.

Valverde, R. A., and C. E. Gates. 1999. Population surveys on mass nesting beaches. *In* K. L. Eckert, K. A. Bjorndal, F. A. Abreu-Grobois, and M. Donnelly (eds.). Research and Management Techniques for the Conservation of Sea Turtles. International Union for Conservation of Nature and Natural Resources, Species Survival Commission, Marine Turtle Specialist Group, publication no. 4. Washington, D.C.

Van Abbema, J. (ed.). 1997. Proceedings: Conservation, Restoration, and Management of Tortoises and Turtles—an International Conference, July 1993, State University of New York at Purchase. New York Turtle and Tortoise Society, New York.

Van Denburgh, J. 1914. Expedition of the California Academy of Sciences to the Galápagos Islands 1905–1906. X. The gigantic land tortoises of the Galápagos Archipelago. Proceedings of the California Academy of Sciences, 4th ser., 2 (1): 203–374.

Van Dijk, P. P., and K. Thirakhupt. 1995. Southeast Asian *Chitra*. From distinction to extinction in 15 years? Pages 62–63 *in* Proceedings International Congress of Chelonian Conservation, July 1995, Gonfaron, France. Editions SOPTOM (Station d'observation et de protectiòn des tortues des maures), Gonfaron, France.

Vargas, P., P. Tello, and C. Aranda. 1994. Sea turtle conservation in Peru: The present situation and a strategy for immediate action. Pages 159–162 *in* K. A. Bjorndal, A. B. Bolten, D. A. Johnson, and P. J. Eliazar (compilers). Proceedings of the Fourteenth Annual Symposium on Sea Turtle Biology and Conservation. NOAA Technical Memorandum NMFS-SEFSC-351.

Varghese, G., and G. T. Tonapi. 1986. Observations on the identity of some Indian freshwater turtles and their feeding habits. Biological Conservation 37:87–92.

Verheijen, F. J. 1985. Photopollution: Artificial light optic spatial control systems fail to cope with. Incidents, causations, remedies. Experimental Biology 44:1–18.

Vickers, W. T. 1991. Hunting yields and game composition over ten years in an Amazon Indian territory. Pages 53–81 *in* J. Robinson and K. Redford (eds.). Neotropical Wildlife Use and Conservation. University of Chicago Press, Chicago.

Vinson, S. B., and L. Greenberg. 1986. The biology, physiology, and ecology of imported fire ants. Pages 193–226 *in* S. B. Vinson (ed.). Economic Impact and Control of Social Insects. Praeger Press, New York.

Vogt, R. C. 1980. Natural history of the map turtles *Graptemys pseudogeographica* and *G. ouachitensis* in Wisconsin. Tulane Studies in Zoology and Botany 22:17–48.

———. 1981a. Natural History of Amphibians and Reptiles of Wisconsin. Milwaukee Public Museum, Milwaukee, Wisc.

———. 1981b. Food partitioning in three sympatric species of map turtle, genus *Graptemys* (Testudinata, Emydidae). American Midland Naturalist 105:102–111.

———. 1994. Temperature controlled sex determination as a tool for turtle conservation. Chelonian Conservation and Biology 1:159–162.

———. 1995. Brazilian freshwater turtles, to eat or not to eat? Save them by eating them? Pages 279–280 *in* Proceedings International Congress of Chelonian Conservation, July 1995, Gonfaron, France. Editions SOPTOM (Station d'observation et de protectiòn des tortues des maures), Gonfaron, France.

Vogt, R. C., and J. J. Bull. 1982. Genetic sex determination in the spiny softshell *Trionyx spiniferus* (Testudines: Trionychidae). Copeia 1982:699–700.

———. 1984. Ecology of hatchling sex ratio in map turtles. Ecology 65:582–587.

Vogt, R. C., and O. Flores Villela. 1986. Determinacion del sexo en tortugas por la temperatura de incubacion de los huevos. Ciencia 37:21–32.

Vogt, R. C., and J. L. B. Villareal. 1993. Species abundance and biomass distribution in freshwater turtles. Page 51 *in* J. Van Abbema (ed.). Proceedings: Conservation, Restoration, and Management of Tortoises and Turtles—an International Conference, July 1993, State University of New York at Purchase. New York York Turtle and Tortoise Society, New York.

Walker, D., V. J. Burke, I. Barak, and J. C. Avise. 1995. A comparison of mtDNA restriction sites vs. control region sequences in phylogenetic assessment of the musk turtle (*Sternotherus minor*). Molecular Ecology 4:365–373.

Walker, P. 1989a. *Geochelone chilensis*, Chaco tortoise. Pages 20–21 *in* I. R. Swingland and M. W. Klemens (eds.). The Conservation Biology of Tortoises. Occasional Papers of the IUCN Species Survival Commission, no. 5. Gland, Switzerland.

———. 1989b. *Geochelone denticulata*, yellow-footed tortoise, forest tortoise. Pages 22–23 *in* I. R. Swingland and M. W. Klemens (eds.). The Conservation Biology of Tortoises. Occasional Papers of the IUCN Species Survival Commission, no. 5. Gland, Switzerland.

———. 1989c. *Geochelone carbonaria*, red-footed tortoise. Pages 17–19 *in* I. R. Swingland and M. W. Klemens (eds.). The Conservation Biology of Tortoises. Occasional Papers of the IUCN Species Survival Commission, no. 5. Gland, Switzerland.

Waller, T. 1997. Exploitation and trade of *Geochelone chilensis*. Pages 118–124 *in* J. Van Abbema (ed.). Proceedings: Conservation, Restoration, and Management of Tortoises and Turtles—an International Conference, July 1993, State University of New York at Purchase. New York Turtles and Tortoise Society, New York.

Waller, T., and P. A. Micucci. 1997. Land use and grazing in relation to the genus *Geochelone* in Argentina. Pages 2–9 *in* J. Van Abbema (ed.). Proceedings: Conservation, Restoration, and Management of Tortoises and Turtles—an International Conference, July 1993, State University of New York at Purchase. New York Turtle and Tortoise Society, New York.

Wamukoya, G., and R. D. Haller. 1995. Sea turtle conservation in Kenya: Community participation approach. Pages 121–122 *in* Proceedings International Congress of Chelonian Conservation, July 1995, Gonfaron, France. Editions SOPTOM (Station d'observation et de protectiòn des tortues des maures), Gonfaron, France.

Ward, F. P., C. J. Hohmann, J. F. Ulrich, and S. E. Hill. 1976. Seasonal microhabitat selections of spotted turtles (*Clemmys guttata*) in Maryland elucidated by radioisotope tracking. Herpetologica 32:60–64.

Warwick, C. 1985a. Terrapin farming in the United States. RSPCA (Royal Society for the Prevention of Cruelty to Animals) Today 49:24–25.

———. 1985b. The trade in red-eared terrapins. Animals International 16:8–9.

———. 1986. Red-eared terrapin farms and conservation. Oryx 20:237–240.

Warwick, C., and C. Steedman. 1988. Report on the use of red-eared turtles (*Trachemys scripta elegans*) as a food source utilized by man. Report to the People's Trust for Endangered Species, Surrey, United Kingdom.

Warwick, C., C. Steedman, and T. Holford. 1990. Ecological implications of the red-eared turtle trade. Texas Journal of Science 42:419–422.

WATS (Western Atlantic Turtle Symposium). 1983. Sea Turtle Manual of Research and Conservation Techniques. WATS, San José, Costa Rica.

Weaver, J. 1973. Profits, politics, and *Podocnemis*. International Turtle and Tortoise Society Journal 7:10–15.

Webb, R. G. 1961. Observations on the life histories of turtles (genus *Pseudemys* and *Graptemys*) in Lake Texoma, Oklahoma. American Midland Naturalist 65:193–214.

Webber, H. H., and P. F. Riordan. 1976. Criteria for candidate species for aquaculture. Aquaculture 7:107–123.

Werner, D. 1978. Trekking in the Amazon forest. Natural History 87:42–55.

Westhouse, R. A., E. R. Jacobson, R. K. Harris, K. R. Winter, and B. L. Homer. 1996. Respiratory and pharyngo-esophageal iridovirus infection in a gopher tortoise (*Gopherus polyphemus*). Journal of Wildlife Diseases 32 (4): 682–686.

Westman, W. E. 1990. Park management of exotic plant species: Problems and issues. Conservation Biology 4:251–260.

Wetherall, J. A., G. H. Balazs, R. A. Tokunaga, and M. Y. Y. Yong. 1993. Bycatch of marine turtles in north Pacific high-seas driftnet fisheries and impacts on the stocks. Bulletin of the North Pacific Commission 53 (3): 519–538.

Whitaker, R. 1997. Turtle rearing in village ponds. Pages 106–108 in J. Van Abbema (ed.). Proceedings: Conservation, Restoration, and Management of Tortoises and Turtles— an International Conference, July 1993, State University of New York at Purchase. New York Turtle and Tortoise Society, New York.

White, D., Jr., and D. Moll. 1992. Restricted diet of the common map turtle *Graptemys geographica* in a Missouri stream. Southwest Naturalist 37:317–318.

Whitney, G. G. 1994. From Coastal Wilderness to Fruited Plain: A History of Environmental Change in Temperate North America, 1500 to the Present. Cambridge University Press, New York.

Wibbels, T., J. J. Bull, and D. Crews. 1991b. Chronology and morphology of temperature-dependent sex determination. Journal of Experimental Zoology 260:371–381.

———. 1991c. Synergism between temperature and estradiol: A common pathway in turtle sex determination? Journal of Experimental Zoology 260:130–134.

Wibbels, T., N. Frazer, M. Grassman, J. Hendrickson, and P. Pritchard. 1989. Blue Ribbon Panel Review of the National Marine Fisheries Service Kemp's Ridley Headstart Program. National Marine Fisheries Service, Southeast Regional Office, St. Petersburg, Fla.

Wibbels, T., F. C. Killebrew, and D. Crews. 1991a. Sex determination in Cagle's map turtle: Implications for evolution, development, and conservation. Canadian Journal of Zoology 69:2693–2696.

Wilbur, H. M., and P. J. Morin. 1988. Life history evolution in turtles. Pages 387–439 in C. Gans and R. B. Huey (eds.). The Biology of the Reptilia. Vol. 16B, Defense and Life History. Alan R. Liss, New York.

Wilcove, D. S., C. H. McLellan, and A. P. Dobson. 1986. Habitat fragmentation in the temperate zone. Pages 237–256 in M. E. Soulé (ed.). Conservation Biology: The Science of Scarcity and Diversity. Sinauer, Sunderland, Mass.

Wilcox, B. A. 1980. Insular ecology and conservation. Pages 95–117 in M. E. Soulé and B. A. Wilcox (eds.). Conservation Biology: An Evolutionary–Ecological Perspective. Sinauer, Sunderland, Mass.

Wilcox, B. A., and D. D. Murphy. 1985. Conservation strategy: The effects of fragmentation on extinction. American Midland Naturalist 125:879–887.

Wilhoft, D. C., M. G. Del Baglivo, and M. D. Del Baglivo. 1979. Observations on mammalian predation of snapping turtle nests (Reptilia, Testudines, Chelydridae). Journal of Herpetology 13:435–438.

Wilkinson, C. R. 1993. Coral reefs of the world are facing widespread devastation: Can we prevent this through sustainable management practices? Pages 11–21 in R. Richmond (ed.). Proceedings of the Seventh International Coral Reef Symposium. University of Guam Press, Mangilao.

Willemsen, R. E. 1995. Status of *Testudo marginata* in Greece. Pages 103–109 *in* D. Ballasina (ed.). Red Data Book on Mediterranean Chelonians. Edagricole-Edzioni Agricole, Bologna, Italy.

Williams, E. C., and W. S. Packer. 1987. A long-term study of a box turtle *(Terrapene carolina)* population of Allee Memorial Woods, Indiana, with emphasis on survivorship. Herpetologica 43:328–335.

Williams, E. H., Jr., L. Bunkley-Williams, E. C. Peters, B. Pinto-Rodriguez, R. Matos-Morales, A. A. Mignucci-Giannoni, K. V. Hall, J. V. Rueda-Almonadid, J. Sybesma, I. Bonnelly de Calventi, and R. H. Boulon. 1994. An epizootic of cutaneous fibropapillomas in green turtles *Chelonia mydas* of the Caribbean: Part of a panzootic? Journal of Aquatic Animal Health 6:70–78.

Williams, P. 1993. NMFS to concentrate on measuring survivorship, fecundity of head-started Kemp's ridleys in the wild. Marine Turtle Newsletter 63:3–4.

Wilson, E. O. 1985. The biological diversity crisis. BioScience 35:700–706.

———. 1992. The Diversity of Life. Harvard University Press, Cambridge.

Wirot, N. 1979. The Turtles of Thailand. Siam Farm Zoological Garden, Bangkok.

Witham, R. 1973. Focal necrosis of the skin in tank-reared sea turtles. Journal of the American Veterinary Medical Association 163:656.

———. 1982. Disruption of sea turtle habitat with emphasis on human influence. Pages 519–522 *in* K. A. Bjorndal (ed.). Biology and Conservation of Sea Turtles. Smithsonian Institution Press, Washington, D.C.

Witham, R., and C. R. Futch. 1977. Early growth and oceanic survival of pen-reared sea turtles. Herpetologica 33 (4): 404–409.

Witherington, B. E. 1994a. Flotsam, jetsam, post-hatchling loggerheads, and the advecting surface smorgasbord. Pages 166–167 *in* B. A. Schroeder and B. E. Witherington (compilers). Proceedings of the Thirteenth Annual Workshop on Sea Turtle Biology and Conservation. NOAA Technical Memorandum NMFS-SEFSC-341.

———. 1994b. Some "lost-year" turtles found. Pages 194–197 *in* B. A. Schroeder and B. E. Witherington (compilers). Proceedings of the Thirteenth Annual Workshop on Sea Turtle Biology and Conservation. NOAA Technical Memorandum NMFS-SEFSC-341.

———. 1995. Hatchling orientation. Pages 577–578 *in* K. A. Bjorndal (ed.). Biology and Conservation of Sea Turtles. Rev. edn. Smithsonian Institution Press, Washington, D.C.

Witherington, B. E., and R. E. Martin. 1996. Understanding, assessing, and resolving light-pollution problems on sea turtle nesting beaches. Florida Marine Research Institute, Technical Report TR-2. St. Petersburg.

Witherington, B. E., and M. Salmon. 1992. Predation on loggerhead turtle hatchlings after entering the sea. Journal of Herpetology 26:226–228.

Wolff, P. L., and U. S. Seal. 1992. Disease and conservation of threatened species. *In* Briefing Book, International Conference on the Implications of Infectious Diseases on Captive Propagation and Reintroduction Programs of Threatened Species. International Union for Conservation of Nature and Natural Resources, Species Survival Commission, Gland, Switzerland.

———. 1993. Implications of infectious disease for captive propagation and reintroduction of threatened species. Journal of Zoo and Wildlife Medicine 24 (3): 229–230.

Wood, F. 1994. Cayman Turtle Farm. Cayman Turtle Farm Ltd., Cayman Islands, British West Indies.

————. 1991. It's time to stop headstarting Kemp's ridley. Marine Turtle Newsletter 55:7–8.

Wood, F., and J. Wood. 1993. Release and recapture of captive-reared green sea turtles, *Chelonia mydas*, in the waters surrounding the Cayman Islands. Herpetological Journal 3:84–89.

Wood, J. 1993. Cayman Turtle Farm C.I.T.E.S. exports—the facts. Marine Turtle Newsletter 60:18.

Wood, R. C., and R. Herlands. 1995. Terrapins, tires and traps: Conservation of the northern diamondback terrapin *(Malaclemys terrapin terrapin)* on the Cape May Peninsula, New Jersey, USA. Pages 254–256 *in* Proceedings International Congress of Chelonian Conservation, July 1995, Gonfaron, France. Editions SOPTOM (Station d'observation et de protection des tortues des maures), Gonfaron, France.

Woodbury, A. M., and R. Hardy. 1948. Studies of the desert tortoise, *Gopherus agassizii*. Ecological Monographs 18:145–200.

Woody, J. B. 1990. Is headstarting a reasonable conservation measure? On the surface, yes; in reality, no. Marine Turtle Newsletter 50:8–11.

————. 1991. It's time to stop headstarting Kemp's ridley. Marine Turtle Newsletter 55:7–8.

Wu, H. W. 1943. Notes on the plastron of *Testudo emys* from the ruins of the Shang Dynasty of Anyang. Sinensia, Hanking 14 (1–6): 107–109.

Yawetz, A., I. Sidis, and A. Gasith. 1983. Metabolism of parathion and brain cholinesterase inhibition in aroclor 1254-treated and untreated Caspan terrapin *(Mauremys caspica rivulata,* Emydidae, Chelonia) in comparison with two species of wild birds. Comparative Biochemistry and Physiology 75C:377–382.

Zhao, E., and K. Adler. 1993. Herpetology of China. Contributions to Herpetology, no. 10. Society for the Study of Amphibians and Reptiles, Athens, Ohio.

Zug, G. R. 1966. The penial morphology and the relationships of cryptodiran turtles. Occasional Papers of the Museum of Zoology, University of Michigan 647:1–24.

————. 1971. Buoyancy, locomotion, morphology of the pelvic girdle and hindlimb, and systematics of cryptodiran turtles. Miscellaneous Publications of the Museum of Zoology, University of Michigan 142:1–98.

Zweifel, R. G. 1989. Long-term ecological studies on a population of painted turtles, *Chrysemys picta*, on Long Island, NY. American Museum Novitates 2952:1–55.

INDEX